The Global Resurgence of Democracy

The Global Resurgence of Democracy

Second Edition

Edited by Larry Diamond
and Marc F. Plattner

The Johns Hopkins University Press
Baltimore and London

Printed in the United States of America on acid-free paper
9 8 7 6 5 4 3 2

The Johns Hopkins University Press
2715 North Charles Street
Baltimore, Maryland 21218-4363
www.press.jhu.edu

Chapters 1–5, 8–16, and 19 appeared in the first edition; the remaining chapters appeared in the following editions of *Journal of Democracy:* chapter 6 in vol. 5, no. 2 (1994); chapter 7 in vol. 5, no. 1 (1994); chapter 17 in vol. 4, no. 1 (1993); chapter 18 in vol. 5, no. 2 (1994); chapter 20 in vol. 3, no. 2 (1992); chapters 21–23 in vol. 5, no. 3 (1994); and chapters 24–32 in vol. 6, no. 2 (1995).

Library of Congress Cataloging-in-Publication Data

The global resurgence of democracy / edited by Larry Diamond and Marc F. Plattner. — 2nd ed.
p. cm.
Includes bibliographical references and index.
ISBN 0-8018-5304-4 (hc : alk. paper). —ISBN 0-8018-5305-2 (pbk. : alk. paper)
1. Democracy. 2. World politics—1989– I. Diamond, Larry Jay.
II. Plattner, Marc F., 1945–
JC421.G58 1996
321.8—dc20

96–16415
CIP

A catalog record for this book is available from the British Library.

CONTENTS

PREFACE AND ACKNOWLEDGMENTS

This second edition of *The Global Resurgence of Democracy* is a considerably revised and updated version of a volume that first appeared in 1993. Like its predecessor, it is composed entirely of a selection of essays originally published in the *Journal of Democracy*. A quarterly publication launched in January 1990, the *Journal* seeks to examine all aspects of the struggle to achieve and maintain democracy around the world. It is read by scholars and practitioners of democracy in every region of the world, and articles from its pages have been translated into more than 15 languages.

For this second edition we have once again chosen essays that address broad issues relating to the establishment and consolidation of democracy. Only 14 of the 29 essays included in the first edition have been retained in this volume, and 18 more recent essays have been added. This second edition is also divided into four sections: (I) The Democratic Moment; (II) Institutional Choices and Designs; (III) Civil Society and Democracy; and (IV) The Global Democratic Prospect.

Readers who compare the two editions will note that while the first two sections of the present volume have been only modestly transformed and expanded, the latter two are entirely new. The inclusion of a whole new section here on civil society reflects the intense interest shown in this subject in recent years not only by the *Journal* and its contributors but by scholars and democratic activists worldwide. We regret that to make room for this new material on civil society we were compelled to drop a very useful set of essays on the problem of political corruption. As for the concluding section, with its emphasis on prognostication, there was a special need for updating, and we have drawn principally upon a symposium on "Democracy's Future" that appeared in the Fifth Anniversary issue of the *Journal* in January 1995.

We have omitted some of the *Journal*'s most noteworthy articles only because these have already been reprinted in separate collections devoted to particular topics. Three such collections, all published by the Johns Hopkins University Press, have appeared to date: *Capitalism, Socialism, and Democracy Revisited* (1993); *Nationalism, Ethnic Conflict, and Democracy* (1994); and *Economic Reform and Democracy* (1995).

The *Journal* is published under the sponsorship of the National Endowment for Democracy, a private, nonprofit corporation that receives an annual appropriation from the United States Congress for a grant-making program to strengthen democratic institutions abroad. The *Journal* is now part of the International Forum for Democratic Studies, which was created in 1994 as the research and information arm of the Endowment. Both the *Journal* and the Forum are funded predominantly from private sources. Since 1991 the *Journal* has been published on behalf of the Endowment by the Johns Hopkins University Press.

As we have learned from our experience as coeditors, publishing a journal requires a great deal of effort and assistance. We are very pleased to have another opportunity to acknowledge the support of those institutions and individuals whose contributions have been indispensable to our work. First, we wish to thank the Board of Directors of the National Endowment for Democracy and especially the Endowment's president, our good friend Carl Gershman. Carl helped to conceive the idea of the *Journal* and has continued to give it his unflagging support, while scrupulously respecting its editorial integrity.

We are equally grateful to the members of our editorial board, who have generously volunteered their time to provide us both with overall editorial guidance and with evaluations of particular manuscripts. No less essential has been the financial assistance provided by a number of private foundations, especially the continuing support of the Lynde and Harry Bradley Foundation. Other important contributors have been the Smith Richardson, William H. Donner, John M. Olin, and Joyce Foundations, the Carnegie Corporation, and Pfizer Inc.

The *Journal* has always been blessed with a first-rate staff. The fine editorial hand of our senior editor Phil Costopoulos, who has been with us since the beginning, is in evidence throughout this volume. Other editors whose contributions are reflected here include Annette Theuring, Debra Liang, Patricia Loo, and Miriam Kramer, as well as a remarkable series of interns: Gary Rosen, Juliet Johnson, Kathy Vitz, Kurt Oeler, Susan M. Brown, Erin Logan, and Zerxes Spencer. We are also grateful for all the help and encouragement provided by our colleagues at both the book and journal divisions of the Johns Hopkins University Press.

Whatever merit this volume possesses is, of course, ultimately due to the arguments and insights of the authors whose essays are collected here. We are enormously grateful to them for their willingness to contribute to our pages. Finally, we wish to take note of the extraordinary efforts to secure and strengthen democracy made by men and women from every region of the globe. It is due to their courage and dedication that the international study of democracy has become so rich a field of inquiry and reflection.

INTRODUCTION

Larry Diamond and Marc F. Plattner

When historians look back on the twentieth century, they may well judge its last quarter as the greatest period of democratic ferment in the history of modern civilization. As Samuel P. Huntington observes in the essay that opens this volume, some 30 countries made transitions to democracy between 1974 and 1990. In the subsequent five years, some three dozen more countries—primarily in Central and Eastern Europe, the former Soviet Union, and Africa—inaugurated democracy, at least in their formal constitutional structures. By January 1996, Freedom House judged that 117 of the world's 191 countries were formally democratic—the most ever in history. Proportionally as well, the change was dramatic: at the dawn of 1996, 61 percent of the world's countries had constitutionally democratic systems with competitive, multiparty elections, compared with only 41 percent a decade previously.[1]

As Marc F. Plattner observes in his contribution to this collection, this global democratic resurgence has also occurred on the plane of ideology, with the utter "self-discrediting" of communist systems and of such other dictatorial regimes as "African socialism" and "bureaucratic authoritarianism." As a result, antidemocratic forces (especially on the left) have been weakened throughout the world, democracy has been left "with no serious geopolitical or ideological rivals," and democrats have regained their self-confidence. In fact, Plattner argues, liberal democracies today are widely regarded as "the only truly and fully modern societies."

In a formulation that has greatly influenced contemporary analyses, Huntington maintains that this current period of democratic growth—dating from the breakdowns of authoritarianism in Portugal, Spain, and Greece in 1974–75—represents a "third wave" of global democratic expansion. Both the first "long" wave from the 1820s to 1926 and the second wave from 1945 to 1962 gave way to "reverse waves" that significantly reduced both the number of democracies in the world and the sense of hope about the global prospects for democracy. As Plattner notes, prominent democratic intellectuals were led, in the depths of the second reverse wave in the early 1970s, to lament that "liberal democracy . . . has simply no relevance to the future. It is where the world was, not where it is going."[2]

The question that preoccupies Huntington is also the central issue of this book: Can democracy's third wave be sustained indefinitely, or will it ebb into a third reverse wave of democratic breakdowns at some point in the coming years?

There is no sign yet of a reverse wave of democratic breakdowns. Indeed, the continued growth in the number of countries with civilian governments chosen through multiparty, competitive elections, testifies to the persistent ideological hegemony of democracy in the world during the 1990s and to the consequences of what Huntington calls "snowballing," in which earlier democratic transitions stimulate and provide models for later ones. These "demonstration effects," so powerful in bringing about the downfall of military regimes in Latin American and communist regimes in Central and Eastern Europe, have reverberated powerfully in sub-Saharan Africa as well, where most countries have experienced some pressure for political transition and 18 countries (the most ever) were formally democratic at the start of 1996.

Still, the 1990s have also witnessed a less widely observed but disturbing countertrend: stagnation in the levels of actual freedom in the world. Since the early 1990s, the overall levels of political rights and civil liberties, as measured annually by Freedom House, have not significantly improved. Between 1992 and 1996, the number of "free" states—which may be taken as a more substantive indicator of liberal democracy—has barely changed, increasing from 75 to 76. While some countries have been added to this group, others have left it. More generally, during the first half of the 1990s gains in freedom in some countries were offset by losses in others. In Latin America and South Asia, for example, the overall trends in actual levels of freedom have been downward, and some postcommunist countries have slipped back as well from initial hopes for democracy. Moreover, between 1993 and 1996 the number of very repressive countries, rated "not free," increased significantly from 38 to 53.

Among the most striking trends in the early 1990s has been the declining proportion (from 85 percent in 1991 to 65 percent in 1996) of formal democracies which, in their actual behavior, are rated as "free." This growing gap between constitutional form and political reality raises the essential question of what democracy is and is not, the issue addressed by Philippe Schmitter and Terry Lynn Karl in chapter 4. Schmitter and Karl stress that there is no one form of democracy, and that Americans should be careful not to identify the concept of democracy too closely with their own institutions. Democracies can differ greatly in the degree to which they encourage consensus versus competition, shared power versus majoritarian rule, and public authority versus private action. Democratic regimes may be parliamentary or presidential, and federal or unitary. Contemporary democracies also vary widely in their levels of citizen participation, citizen access to power, checks and balances, governmental responsiveness, party strength, and political pluralism. These variations, particularly in constitutional design and electoral systems, may have far-reaching implications for the quality and stability of democracy (as Juan J. Linz and his critics and Arend Lijphart and his critics debate later in this volume) but, provided certain minimum criteria are met, they do not bear on whether or not democracy exists.

For Schmitter and Karl, "modern political democracy is a system of governance in which rulers are held accountable for their actions in the public realm by citizens, acting indirectly through the competition and cooperation of their elected representatives." This implies criteria very similar to Robert A. Dahl's conception of polyarchy[3]—extensive competition for power through regular, free, and fair elections; highly inclusive citizenship conferring rights of participation on virtually all adults; and, implicitly, extensive civil and political liberties to allow for pluralism of information and organization. But to this now conventional understanding Schmitter and Karl add some important qualifications. Between elections, citizens must be able to influence public policy through various nonelectoral means, like interest-group associations and social movements, which inevitably involve cooperation as well as competition among citizens. Popularly elected governments must be able to exercise their powers without obstruction or control by unelected officials (e.g., the military). And the polity must be self-governing.

The autonomous power of the military to dictate or obstruct policy, and the lack of accountability and effective citizen access are some of the serious problems that confront the new democracies of the third wave, and in a number of instances, may even provide grounds to question their classification as democracies at all. In addition, serious economic and cultural obstacles to the expansion of democracy may also be identified. A huge amount of theory and evidence suggests that democracy is more likely to take hold in more economically developed countries, and by 1990 most of the upper- and upper-middle-income countries had already become democratic.[4] Less developed countries are more prone to economic crises, intense social conflicts, and political violence and disorder, and as Huntington notes, democratic breakdowns in previous reverse waves owed much to poor regime performance in these dimensions. Most countries that remain in the upper reaches of Huntington's "political zone of transition" (as indicated by per capita GNP) are states whose predominant cultural orientations—Confucian or Islamic—are often regarded as inhospitable toward democracy. With the completion of Taiwan's democratic transition in its highly competitive direct elections during 1994, 1995, and 1996, it is increasingly difficult to maintain that Confucian culture is inconsistent with democracy; indeed, Taiwan's president, Lee Teng-hui, has eloquently argued just the opposite.[5] The progress toward democratic consolidation in South Korea, and the vitality of democracy in the Philippines and Thailand as well, belie the notion of a cultural obstacle to democracy in East Asia. Still, it is difficult to deny that culture plays some role in accounting for the stunning weakness of democracy in the Islamic world, and especially among the Arab states of the Middle East. Of the 43 countries with majority Muslim populations, only one (Mali) is rated "free" by Freedom House, and only seven have the formal structures of democracy. No Arab country is democratic, and 12 of the 16 Arab states are rated "not free." While levels of freedom have improved in some predominantly Muslim states, the growth of Islamist movements throughout Asia and the Middle East in recent years has pressured democratic regimes and constricted political rights and civil liberties, especially for women.[6]

While remaining skeptical about the universal viability of liberal democracy, Huntington cautions against cultural or economic determinism. Cultural legacies can gradually soften and change with time, and most great cultural traditions are "highly complex bodies of ideas . . . and beliefs," some of which may be compatible with democracy and some not. A more likely prospect than authoritarianism in much of rapidly developing East Asia, he suspects, is a "distinctly East Asian" form of democracy, akin to the Japanese dominant-party system, offering "competition for power but not alternation in power." More generally, he argues, the two most important factors determining the likelihood of democracy will be economic development and political leadership.

A different view of global political trends and prospects is offered in chapter 2 by Ken Jowitt in a prescient essay written shortly after the collapse of communist regimes in Central and Eastern Europe. Jowitt was among the first to recognize that the end of the Cold War and "the mass extinction of Leninist regimes" would open vast possibilities not only for democracy but for virulent nationalism and intense conflicts over borders and identities. Indeed, he anticipated the disintegration of both the Soviet Union and Yugoslavia, which occurred shortly after his essay was first published in January 1991. Criticizing Francis Fukuyama's thesis of the "end of history," Jowitt predicts here a period of acute "territorial, ideological, and political confusion." Rather than a new world order of peace and democracy, he warns of a "new world disorder" in which "leaders will matter more than institutions" and "new ways of life" may emerge, offering new ideologies that militantly reject existing institutions and beliefs, including liberal democracy. The prospects for democratic consolidation in the post-Leninist states are clouded by the Leninist legacy of pervasive distrust of the state and fellow citizens and by lack of experience with the values and habits of democratic politics. More generally, liberal capitalist democracy will remain vulnerable to challenge from movements and ideologies that scorn its "inordinate emphasis on individualism, materialism, technical achievement, and rationality." Rather than a continued global resurgence of democracy, Jowitt foresees an unstable and conflict-ridden world in which the progress of democracy will be, at best, slow and painful.

Writing at roughly the same time, Marc Plattner depicts a more hopeful picture in chapter 3. Authoritarian regimes seem doomed both by economic failure and economic success, and in a rapidly integrating, increasingly information-intensive world economy, "only democracy seems compatible with economic success in the advanced nations." Inevitably, Plattner concedes, some of the new democracies of recent years will "sink back into authoritarianism." Both he and Huntington expect that the current wave of democratic expansion will probably pause or come to an end at some point in the coming years, but for Plattner this does not necessarily portend another "reverse wave" or a serious challenge to the overall strength of democracy in the world: "Democracy's preeminence can be seriously challenged only by an ideology with universalist aspirations that proves capable of coming to power in an economically advanced or militarily powerful nation." For this reason, Russia and China may be the most important countries for democrats to watch in the coming years, along with the possibility of a successful and attractive nondemocratic model emerging in East Asia.

As Claude Ake makes clear in chapter 5, the quest for a democratic alternative to authoritarian misrule has become increasingly widespread in Africa in recent years. To some extent, this responds to international pressures, which have been growing as the end of the Cold War and the marginalization of Africa have "given the West more latitude to conduct its relations with Africa in a principled way." Ake applauds this democratic concern (however belated), and welcomes economic sanctions against antidemocratic regimes. He believes, however, that it is primarily indigenous democratic forces that have put democracy on the agenda in Africa, and that these forces must be strengthened if the democracy movement is to succeed. Arguing passionately that Africa needs democracy in order to develop, Ake refutes a number of myths: that democracy contradicts traditional African cultures; that it would cause ethnic rivalries to erupt into conflict; and that it must take second place to the needs of development. Ake shows that many traditional African polities "were infused with democratic values," that ethnic conflict has intensified with 30 years of authoritarian rule, and that the notion of a choice between democracy and development is both morally and empirically false. Postponing democracy has not promoted development in Africa; indeed, there is a growing consensus in Africa that the absence of democracy is the chief cause of the continent's developmental crisis. "The primary issue," Ake argues, "is not *whether* it is more important to eat well than to vote, but *who* is entitled to decide which is more important."

Section I concludes with two essays that ponder what Philippe C. Schmitter calls the "dangers and dilemmas" confronting the new democracies of the third wave. Democracy, Schmitter warns in chapter 6, is by no means fated to succeed, and although few third-wave democracies have so far "failed outright," there are two other very plausible alternatives to democratic consolidation: hybrid regimes that combine elements of autocracy and democracy, and democracies that "stumble on" indefinitely "without consolidating an acceptable and predictable set of rules for political competition and cooperation." Only by achieving such a broad, enduring procedural consensus can democracies ensure their stability, and this requires making "some arduous choices" with respect to five "extrinsic dilemmas" that they face. Many new democracies still need to define a consensus on the boundaries and identity of the nation-state. Virtually all of them need not only to achieve a vigorous capitalist economy (often through painful economic reform) but also to manage its excesses and moderate its inherent inequalities. New democracies must maintain governability in an era when political parties have ceded a considerable portion of the institutional terrain for political participation and communication to interest groups and social movements, which tend to flood the state with demands. They must establish political legitimacy in an era of professionalized politics, which generates large needs for party financing and political remuneration, and opportunities for corruption that breed public cynicism. And finally, they must find ways to reconcile the democratic imperative of civilian control over the military and police with a search for new and effective roles for these institutions, and with the often urgent need to rein in rising crime and disorder after the transition.

For Guillermo O'Donnell, in chapter 7, many of the new democracies in Latin America and elsewhere confront a distinctive set of problems that derive from their "delegative" character. In well-institutionalized or "representative" democracies, elected officials are held accountable not only "vertically," to voters at the ballot box, but also "horizontally," to other autonomous institutions within the government that can monitor their conduct and punish wrongdoing. In delegative democracies, by contrast, horizontal accountability "is extremely weak or nonexistent," and elected presidents rule in highly personalistic, paternalistic, and majoritarian fashion, with few effective constraints on their exercise of constitutional authority. Formal political institutions (especially legislatures and courts) are weak, and governance rests "on the premise that whoever wins election to the presidency is thereby entitled to govern as he or she sees fit," constrained only by the practical realities of power and the term of office. Delegative democracies may well be enduring, but they are not consolidated in the sense of having formal political institutions (other than elections) to which all major political actors are consensually committed. As a result, delegative democracies are prone to high levels of corruption and clientelism. They also tend to be less effective at overcoming protracted economic and social problems; although they facilitate swift and decisive executive action, in doing so they free executives of the need to consult opposing interests and build a consensus that would help to avoid gross mistakes and to make policy choices stable. The lack of dialogue and bargaining, the tendency to rule by decree and surprise, and the resulting polarization among parties, interests, and branches of government, only tend to heighten social conflict and diminish public regard for parties and politicians. This further weakens democracy and its formal institutions, while reinforcing the delegative nature of the system.

Institutional Choices and Designs

During the past decade, issues of constitutional design and institutional performance have resumed a central place in the debate over what facilitates and obstructs stable democracy. What types of political institutions are most likely to enable democracy to function effectively, and under what types of circumstances? What are the characteristic problems of democratic performance that institutional designers most need to gird the system against? These are the issues that occupy our contributors in Section II.

The central dilemma for constitution makers, Larry Diamond suggests in chapter 8, is that democratic performance is affected by a number of factors that pull in contradicatory directions. Institutional designs may maximize the capacity of the system to deal with one type of problem only to leave it defenseless against another. Diamond analyzes in particular three contradictions or "paradoxes" intrinsic to all democracies and particularly troubling for new ones. The first is the tension between conflict and consensus. By its very nature, democracy is a system of institutionalized competition for power, but if competition becomes too intense, the system can break down entirely. Democracies must therefore find mechanisms to mitigate conflict and cleavage with consensus. This may happen in the long run through the emergence of a civic culture. Along the way, democracies must take the initiative to reduce socioeconomic inequality through an incremental process of reform, and to institute appropriate structures and agreements, such as federalism and power-sharing "pacts," to manage ethnic and party cleavage. A second tension sets representativeness against governability. The former involves dispersing power and holding it accountable, while the latter requires "sufficient concentration and autonomy of power to choose and implement policies with energy and dispatch." Parliamentary rule with proportional representation (PR) may be admired for ensuring broad representation from a variety of social groups and interests, but it may also foster such a proliferation of political parties as to make it very difficult to form and maintain governments. In such cases, reducing representativeness (e.g., by modifying pure PR) may strengthen democracy. Finally, there is a contradiction between consent and effectiveness, in that electorates tend to judge government performance on short-run criteria while countries may only truly be able to improve their economic performance with structural reforms that can take many years to bear fruit. Getting public consent for these structural, market-oriented reforms, Diamond suggests, may require both short-term external aid and the negotiation of a broad agreement or pact among contending parties and social forces on the overall outlines of economic policy.

In chapter 9, Juan J. Linz argues that a key problem with democracy in Latin America and other developing regions has been a misguided choice of presidential rather than parliamentary government. In this widely cited essay, which has occasioned extensive debate among political thinkers and practitioners worldwide, Linz identifies a number of "perils of presidentialism." Because of their direct election by the people, presidents tend to make strong claims to democratic legitimacy that can assume a "plebiscitarian" and undemocratic character. When a president is elected with much less than a majority of the vote, as Salvador Allende was in Chile in 1970, the result can be a dramatic conflict between the president and a legislature opposed to his policies, each claiming legitimacy based on the expression of the popular will. The potential for deadlock is exacerbated by the president's relatively fixed term of office, which leaves "no room for the continuous readjustments that events may demand." A related problem is the greater difficulty of selecting a legitimate and effective successor in presidential systems. In general, Linz argues, "while parliamentarism imparts flexibility to the political process," permitting a change of leaders or reorganization of government in midterm, "presidentialism makes it rather rigid."

Another dimension of this rigidity is the absence of a constitutional monarch or ceremonial president who can act as a "moderating power" and provide "moral ballast" in times of crisis. In addition, presidentialism is poorly suited to the kind of coalition government that may be necessary to govern effectively in multiparty systems. Indeed, because of the "winner-take-all" character of presidential elections, presidentialism is much more likely to produce political polarization both during and after the election. The fact that "losers must wait at least four or five years without any access to executive power and patronage" further heightens the zero-sum character of presidential systems. This is a particularly dangerous feature for deeply divided societies, especially those with grave social and economic problems and significant extremist parties, because it raises even higher the electoral stakes and the potential for confrontation and polarization, For these and other reasons, Linz suggests that presidentialism is especially poorly suited for new and unconsolidated democracies, such as those emerging in Latin America, Asia, Eastern Europe, and Africa.

In the debate that follows in chapters 10 and 11, Donald L. Horowitz and Seymour Martin Lipset challenge Linz's broad conclusion about the advantages of parliamentary over presidential government. Horowitz, a leading scholar of ethnic conflict, observes that the Westminster version of parliamentary democracy also has winner-take-all features, and that postcolonial Africa and Asia (in contrast to Latin America) witnessed the breakdown primarily of parliamentary, not presidential, democracies. Coalition governments and power-sharing can occur under presidentialism, Horowitz maintains, noting not only the semi-consociational systems in Colombia and Venezuela that Linz acknowledges as "exceptions," but also the presidential system in Nigeria's Second Republic. Horowitz argues that most of Linz's complaints about presidentialism derive from the assumption that the president will be elected on a plurality or majority-runoff basis. However, different electoral rules—like the Nigerian requirement for a broad ethnic distribution of the vote for any presidential winner, or the Sri Lankan alternative-vote system—can avoid narrowly based outcomes and induce major presidential contenders to build broad ethnic coalitions. Linz's real quarrel, Horowitz suggests, "is not with the presidency, but with two features that epitomize the Westminster version of democracy: first, plurality elections that produce a majority of seats by shutting out third-party competitors; and second, adversary democracy, with its sharp divide between winners and losers, government and opposition."

Lipset takes an even more skeptical stance, questioning the importance of institutional choices altogether. The chief reason for the relative instability of democracy in Latin America, he suggests, is not presidentialism but economic and cultural factors that historically have rendered Latin, Catholic, and poorer countries more prone to authoritarianism. He claims that the same holds true today for Islamic countries, no matter what political institutions they adopt. The fact that the British colonial legacy is one of the most powerful correlates of democracy in the world today points up the salience of the cultural variable.

In his response, Linz acknowledges Horowitz's point about the importance of the way the constitutional system (parliamentary or presidential) interacts with the electoral system, as well as Lipset's point that a majoritarian parliamentary system like Britain's can give a prime minister more effective power than the typical president in a presidential system. Linz underscores, however, the plebiscitarian style and inflated expectations that tend more often to be associated with presidentialism, as well as the potential for conflict and even contested legitimacy between executive and legislature. Further, he questions the degree to which Horowitz's cases of Nigeria and Sri Lanka can be considered examples of successful presidentialism, and calls attention to another peril of presidential government: the weakening of political parties that comes with the ability of a president, as in Brazil, to constitute a government without systematically involving the parties that back him (including his own). Even the U.S. example of "successful presidentialism," Linz suggests, is increasingly dubious given the costs and problems of divided government in recent years. "The American system works or has worked in spite of, rather than because of, the presidential constitution," he maintains. Conceding the importance of culture, he emphasizes Lipset's own observation that political institutions are the only variables open to relatively rapid and deliberate manipulation. This makes "the search for those political institutions that will best suit the circumstances in this or that particular country . . . a modest quest, but a worthy one."

This quest also occupies Arend Lijphart in his analysis in chapter 13 of "constitutional choices for new democracies." Endorsing Linz's arguments in favor of parliamentary government, he suggests that the type of electoral system is a no less important institutional choice, and he points to the advantages of PR, especially for new democracies and deeply divided societies. Drawing upon and extending his previous work, Lijphart rejects majoritarian democracy in favor of the consensus model, which "tries to limit, divide, separate, and share power," and features multiple parties, coalition governments, and more equal executive-legislative power relations. By promoting a multiparty system, PR (combined with parliamentarism) is a key device for structuring democracy in this consensual way. But in addition to ensuring minority representation and so better managing ethnic conflict, PR, Lijphart argues, is preferable because it is intrinsically more democratic. Moreover, his data from the Western democracies suggest that parliamentary-PR systems have a higher quality of democracy, including higher rates of voter turnout, without the diminished governability and economic performance that many critics allege to be the "cost" of PR systems. Moderate PR systems, like those in Germany and Sweden, which give rise to a moderate number of parliamentary parties, seem to offer the best combination of power sharing and governability for new democracies.

In the debate in chapters 14 and 15, Guy Lardeyret and Quentin L. Quade argue strongly for the advantages of majoritarian democracy, Indeed, Lardeyret favors the most majoritarian system possible, which (as Lijphart indicates) is not presidentialism but rather parliamentary government combined with the single-member-district plurality method of election—i.e., the Westminster system. Because such plurality elections for the legislature tend to give rise to a two-party or two-party–dominant system, they create strong parliamentary governments, free of the need for coalitions, that fuse executive and legislative power. Lardeyret believes that the greatest danger lies in the fragmentation associated with parliamentary-PR systems, such as the Fourth Republic that faltered in his native France. Quentin L. Quade also cites this example, as well as pre-Mussolini Italy and Weimar Germany, to show how PR can foster not conciliation and compromise but fragmentation, extremism, and governmental paralysis. Like most critics of the consensus model, Quade focuses attention on the inherently greater fragility of coalition government.

Precisely because it gives such wide scope to the representation of "minorities," and thereby encourages polarization and party fragmentation, Lardeyret maintains that PR "is dangerous for countries faced with ethnic or cultural divisions." By contrast, "parties in plurality systems tend to be moderate because most votes are to be gained among the undecided voters of the center." Ethnic moderation will be greatest when members of the same ethnic group must compete against one another in single-member districts along cross-cutting political and ideological lines of cleavage. Lardeyret not only prefers plurality electoral systems for the stronger, more stable, and more decisive governments they produce, but (like Quade) also believes that they are "more democratic as well as more efficient." Unlike PR, plurality systems lock out extremist parties, marginalize small parties, and give the choice of who will govern to the voters rather than to party elites negotiating in secret after the election, sometimes for weeks or even months. Quade writes that "plurality voting encourages the competing parties to adopt a majority-forming attitude . . . to be moderate, to seek conciliation . . . —in short, to do *before* the election, in the public view, the very tasks that Lijphart applauds PR systems for doing *after* the election."

The institutional choice between PR (with parliamentary government) and plurality elections (whether in a presidential or parliamentary system) involves more than the empirical and analytical debate joined in chapters 14 and 15. At play here as well is a tension between competing values, such as representativeness and governability. PR systems risk some sacrifices in decisive governance and clear alternation of majorities in order to maximize the breadth of social groups and political forces represented in parliament. Opponents of PR put a higher priority on governability than on directly representing the many elements in society in the legislature. To be fair, however, few prominent students of democracy would advocate the kind of extreme PR—with virtually no minimum threshold of the vote necessary for entry into parliament—that prevailed for decades in Italy and Israel. (Political reform movements have modified both of those systems in recent years, though only slightly in Israel, where the electoral threshold remains quite low and members are elected only from a single national list.) As Lijphart emphasizes, there are many types and degrees of PR, and moderate PR with thresholds like the 5 percent minimum in Germany tends to give rise to only a moderate number of parties. In responding to Lardeyret and Quade in chapter 16, Lijphart not only defends his comparative analysis of the performance of PR and majoritarian systems; he also reiterates the normative case for PR—namely, "that disproportional election results are inherently unfair and undemocratic"—and notes that none of Britain's postwar governing parties carried a majority of the vote (a fact that has held true for all of India's one-party governments as well).

The conditional nature of electoral-system choice is the key theme stressed by Ken Gladdish in chapter 17. There is in practice a wide range of electoral-system formulas. Each one, he stresses, has costs as well as advantages, and the type of system that will best serve democracy in a given country depends on the nature of its social cleavages and patterns of political mobilization. How a country resolves the tension between representativeness and governability is a value choice that must be informed by the country's own particular history and culture. PR not only facilitates legislative fragmentation, and thus difficulty in forming and maintaining governments, but also may produce bizarre coalitions of expedience that cannot govern coherently—or minority cabinets that cannot govern with any confidence. Further, it has ambiguous consequences for representation, since party-list systems with large multimember districts (or in the extreme, as in Israel and the Netherlands, no districts at all) sacrifice direct linkage between voters and representatives. This lack of accountability of MPs to specific geographical constituencies has become a major issue in the debate over a permanent electoral system for South Africa.[7] Yet, particularly when there are more than two significant parties, as in Britain and India, plurality systems typically give rise to severely disproportional results, and they also tend to breed voter apathy in districts (often the vast majority) where the contest for the seat is a foregone conclusion. Crafting an electoral system thus involves hard choices that cannot be made theoretically or in the abstract, but must be done on the basis "of practicality and aptness relative to national circumstance."

Varying national circumstances have figured prominently in the design of electoral and other democratic institutions in postcommunist Central and Eastern Europe, as Jan Zielonka shows in chapter 18. As a result of historical and political factors (such as interwar traditions and the insecurity of new elites whose political strength had not yet been tested in competitive elections), "what Eastern Europe's democratic crafters faced was a choice not between plurality elections and PR, but rather between 'strong' and 'weak' versions of the latter." The early postcommunist years showed no clear correlation between electoral-system choice and the degree of institutional stability or democratic progress. For example, Poland's initially extreme form of PR did lead to legislative fragmentation and "a rapid succession of cabinets," but this did not seem to damage democracy or economic reform in Poland during 1992 and 1993. Bulgaria's more moderate system of PR produced a three-party parliament, but this left a quarter of the electorate unrepresented and did not preclude political stalemate. Moderating PR—with small electoral districts and a minimum threshold for parliamentary representation of 4 or 5 percent—probably makes sense, Zielonka concludes, and did sharply reduce the number of parties elected to parliament in Poland in 1993, but it has costs and "is hardly a cure-all for shaky institutions."

His detailed review of new institutions in the old East bloc gives Zielonka a certain skepticism about all theoretical positions in the debate over electoral-system design and parliamentary vs. presidential government. As Linz and others would have predicted, the institution of the presidency did create a syndrome of "dual legitimacy" in these postcommunist systems "that time and again has produced political deadlock." Moreover, presidents "failed to provide the most applauded benefit of presidentialism: strong and effective government." However, the new postcommunist presidents were not linked to any single party, did little to foster aggregation of parties, and had their plebiscitarian impulses circumscribed by the practical need to negotiate with both government and opposition parties in parliament. More important than the specific institutional design (which will be constrained by politics and history) is the need to "adopt clear rules of the institutional game" that define the roles and powers of major institutional actors, and to do so quickly after the transition. Particularly important for Zielonka, in this regard, is the timely adoption of an interim constitution "that deals mainly with the machinery of government rather than the rights of individual citizens." An overriding lesson of early postcommunist experience is the need for a workable constitutional compromise that facilitates effective governance while institutionalizing some separation of powers and checks and balances. A crucial dimension of this is an autonomous constitutional court, which, in mediating institutional disputes, clarifying the political rules, and guaranteeing the rights of all political contenders, strengthens commitment to the new constitutional system. If the constitution is imperfect, it can be revised or amended later, but if, as in Russia and Ukraine following the demise of communism, there is institutional confusion, it will give rise to incessant conflict and debilitating stalemates that can gravely endanger democratic development.

Civil Society and Democracy

Since the inception of the third wave of global democratization, one of the most dramatic developments in both intellectual and policy circles has been the vast increase in attention to "civil society." The rediscovery of civil society can be traced back to the late 1970s in Poland, when the intellectual fathers of Solidarity applied the term to their efforts to organize people independently of the totalitarian state. The subsequent popularity of the term has been fueled by the pivotal contribution that autonomous organization and movements have made to democratic transitions around the world. In Southern Europe and Latin America, the "resurrection" and courageous mobilization of civil society generated strong pressures to push the political transition process beyond "mere liberalization" to full democratization.[8] In the Philippines and South Korea, intense mobilization by a wide variety of organizations and movements in civil society proved crucial in bringing about the demise of authoritarian regimes. Similarly, in Africa in the 1990s, pressures for political liberalization and democratization were heavily driven from below by the coalescence of student, professional, trade union, business, and church groups disgusted with the abuses of authoritarian rule. As we learn from this section of our book, civil society was much weaker in the communist states of Eastern Europe and the Soviet Union, but the generation of alternative sources of information and the political pursuit of truth and principle, including the brave and often lonely efforts of human rights dissidents, helped to undermine the ideological hegemony of communist states and to pave the way for their demise.

All of this would seem to be a positive legacy for democracy. Yet, as the essays in this section demonstrate, in most of the communist world civil society remained severely stunted in its development, and the intensely oppositional character of anti-authoritarian civil society movements and coalitions did not well suit the wider, more complex range of functions that civil society must perform after the transition if it is to foster the consolidation of democracy. Thus a vigorous dialogue is now underway about the appropriate role of civil society after transition—how it must adapt, how it should relate to a new democratic state, and whether there can conceivably be "too much of a good thing." Fundamental to this discussion is the question of how we conceptualize civil society.

The six contributors to this section of our book do not manifest a precise consensus on the boundaries of civil society. Yet by and large, they share the general conception of civil society, advanced by Larry Diamond in chapter 19, as the realm of autonomous voluntary organizations, acting in the public sphere as an intermediary between the state and private life. From this perspective, civil society should not be viewed as synonymous with "society" and does not include all organizations and movements. It is bound by a legal order or a set of shared rules; it does not seek to win formal control over the state (that being the realm of political society); it is pluralistic in its diversity and tolerance for alternative organizations; and it is limited in its objectives, rather than seeking to represent the whole of a person's or community's interests.

Civil society may contribute to the consolidation of democracy in a number of ways, the elucidation of which is the chief preoccupation of Diamond's chapter. Checking and limiting the power of the state, which follows naturally from the oppositional character of civil society under authoritarian rule, is an important democracy-building function for civil society, but only one. Civil society also contributes to the consolidation of democracy to the extent that it stimulates political participation, develops a democratic culture of tolerance and bargaining, creates additional channels for articulating and representing interests, generates cross-cutting cleavages, recruits and trains new political leaders, improves the functioning of democratic institutions (as through election and human rights monitoring), widens and enriches the flow of information to citizens, and produces supporting coalitions on behalf of economic reform. In performing these nine functions, Diamond argues, civil society does not simply limit and monitor the state but also strengthens it, by "enhancing the accountability, responsiveness, inclusiveness, effectiveness, and hence legitimacy of the political system." A strong civil society, however, is not inevitably an unmitigated good for democracy. It depends in part on how civil society is organized in relation to the state. Corporatist systems, with singular, hierarchical interest associations, can be democratic, but are less likely to be so in transitional or newly democratic regimes with a history of authoritarian state corporatism. In these situations in particular, the autonomy of civil society from the state is crucial. But such autonomy can go too far in overwhelming a weak, penetrated state with an impossible agenda of demands. Thus a strong civil society must be balanced by a state with sufficient autonomy and capacity to mediate among various interest groups and respond to their demands in the context of a larger national interest. Democratic consolidation is best served when civil society and the state are mutually respectful and selectively cooperative rather than implacably hostile. Finally, civil society cannot be a substitute for party politics. Democratic consolidation requires, most of all, "coherent political parties with broad and relatively enduring bases of political support."

As the subsequent three chapters make clear, the challenge of building civil society is especially profound in the former communist states, where totalitarian systems destroyed all autonomous structures and levelled the social terrain of contending classes and interests from which a vibrant civil society arises. As Richard Rose observes, "communist rule transformed public opinion into private opinion," and forced all organized political, social, economic, and intellectual life into the ambit of the party-state. No modern state structure came as close to eliminating civil society entirely as the Stalinist system. From such decimation, the term "resurrection" does not begin to convey the magnitude of the challenge, one far beyond what most noncommunist countries confronted during their periods of transition.

In chapter 20, Bronislaw Geremek, a historian and leading Solidarity activist in Poland, traces the (re)emergence of civil society in Central and Eastern Europe to the anticommunist dissidents who refused "to participate in falsehood." From these initial stirrings of mental and moral resistance emerged the independent Polish trade-union movement Solidarity, which grew to more than three times the size of the Communist Party and eventually forced it from power. "Under the oppressive conditions of the communist system," Geremek writes, "the *very idea* of a civil society had real liberating power." But the hopes it generated were partly illusory. The demise of communism did not automatically bring the birth of a true democratic order. That is a much longer and more laborious task, Geremek warns. Political institutions must be given time to develop through successive elections and changes of governments. A democratic political culture must gradually take root. In the meantime, as the euphoria of the transition passes, a "postcommunist letdown" ensues in which the broad anticommunist coalition fragments, and civic approaches to politics must contend with populism, demagoguery, and virulent nationalism. By responding to the need for community and recalling the oppression of national feelings under communism, nationalism becomes a natural contender for popular sentiment in the postcommunist letdown. Another danger is apathy, which follows from the widespread cynicism with party politics among postcommunist publics. In these circumstances, democratic consolidation will require a new type of civil society, based not on resistance to the state but on cooperation with it, and engaged primarily in building democratic institutions, encouraging citizen activism, and educating citizens in respect for the law.

Among the most powerful obstacles to realizing this civic vision of postcommunist society is the pervasive legacy of distrust left by communist regimes everywhere. The problem of trust forms the central concern of Richard Rose's analysis in chapter 21, which is based in part on extensive, ongoing survey research in more than a dozen postcommunist countries. Democracy requires parties and interest groups that mediate between individuals and the state, but under communism these "institutions repressed rather than expressed people's real views." As a result, most citizens were left with virtually no institutions that appeared worthy of their trust and confidence. To be sure, postcommunist publics in Russia and Eastern Europe feel themselves markedly freer now, and censorship has given way to a "booming marketplace of ideas." However, freedom alone cannot undo the legacy of distrust, and even freely competitive elections have failed to produce representative government, because the winners do not represent organizations or constituencies with any broad base of popular trust and support. Like Geremek, Rose regards freedom as a necessary but insufficient condition for the construction of a democratic civil society. Deeper economic and social change is also needed to "'deconstruct' the monolithic institutions of the former party-state." Economic reform is vital to create the basis for competitive private enterprise and free trade unions. And political parties—the most distrusted institution in postcommunist Russia—must build grassroots constituencies and organizations. Ultimately, Rose concludes, institutions are more likely to win social trust if they are constructed from the bottom up rather than the top down. This implies greater emphasis on economic, social, civic, and political initiatives at the local level, where they will tend to be less corrupt and more responsive to actual needs.

Building such a civil society in Russia, M. Steven Fish argues in chapter 22, constitutes nothing less than a "fourth transition," parallel in scope and importance to the political, economic, and national transitions with which the country has been struggling since the demise of the Soviet Union. Embracing the view that there is a significant symbiosis between a democratic state and civil society, Fish identifies the "enfeeblement and fragmentation of state institutions" as a major obstacle to the development of civil society. In the political and social vacuum left by communism, criminal syndicates and corrupt transactions between state officials and the newly rich have tended to predominate, while the plane of moral activity has been dominated by religious cults and particular-istic, inward-looking networks. Democratic political parties, interest groups, and trade unions have found it difficult to take root in this context of inchoate state structures and amorphous legal norms. Like Rose, Fish sees economic reform as pivotal to the prospects for civil society in Russia. Privatization, in particular, has great potential for generating the broad differentiation of classes and interests (and the independent resources) that provides much of the raw material for a vibrant civil society. Amidst the rather dismal political and social trends in postcommunist Russia, Fish sees cause for hope in the fact that privatization of state enterprises has now progressed to "the threshold of irreversibility," unleashing the dynamism of young entrepreneurs and beginning to create a "genuine middle class of small property holders" that could be the keystone of a modern civil society. Already, new producers' associations outside of the old *nomenklatura*-dominated economic networks are pressing their interests in the political process, and the spread of property ownership has greatly enlarged the pools of autonomous resources from which nascent civil society organizations can draw support. But civil society is by no means destined to become the principal mediating force between the individual and the state in Russia. It could be eclipsed by illiberal, particularistic, ethnically chauvinist forms of mobilization, or by a new form of more or less authoritarian state corporatism, unless democratic forces organize with the same skill and passion that has so far been exhibited by criminal bosses, religious zealots, nationalist demagogues, and postcommunist communists.

In the noncommunist world, the Arab states have suffered from the most authoritarian governments and the weakest civil societies. In chapter 23, Iliya Harik resists a simplistic attribution of this pattern to the predominance of Islam. "Islamic thought is vast and complex," he reminds us, and advances not only principles that may justify authoritarian state corporatism (such as integral membership in the community) but also principles (such as individual integrity and economic liberty) that may foster a more pluralist vision of civil society. To be sure, history and cultural traditions have left large empty spaces in society that were filled by the state. Even those groups that would seem to be the most natural building blocks of civil society—"modern" associations and networks of businessmen, professionals, and intellectuals—have been rendered, through decades of state patronage and dependence, passive and suspicious of democracy. For Harik, this has two major implications. First, the immediate building blocks of civil society are the very communal and traditional associations that modernists deride, because these groups "are best able to mediate between citizens and their government, and . . . to restrain the latter's power." Second, as in the postcommunist world, the emergence of a democratically active civil society in the Arab world requires reducing the size of government and the scope of its activities and interventions, and creating an independent and resourceful private sector (not only in the economy but in culture and social life as well). Until that happens, political liberalization and democratization will only occur at the pleasure of ruling elites, and will be easily interrupted by them whenever it threatens their hegemony. This, Harik notes, has been the fate so far of political openings in the Arab world.

Since Alexis de Tocqueville wrote his seminal survey of democracy in America in the early nineteenth century, the vigor and pluralism of civil society has been considered one of the foundations of democratic vitality in the United States. In a widely cited essay reprinted here as chapter 24, Robert D. Putnam presents what he believes "is striking evidence . . . that the vibrancy of American civil society has notably declined over the past several decades." Like Tocqueville, Putnam believes that dense networks of personal interaction in all manner of associations breed a culture of trust, reciprocity, and concern for the community, as well as habits of civic engagement "that facilitate coordination and cooperation for mutual benefit." Because of their manifold positive consequences for economic development, social order, and democracy, social scientists term these norms and behavioral patterns "social capital." Drawing upon a wide range of indicators of civic engagement, Putnam asserts that America's social capital is in sharp decline. Even though average educational levels have risen, Putnam's data show steady and often substantial drops in participation in community meetings, political rallies, and even church groups; in participation in parent-teacher organizations; in membership in trade unions and civic and fraternal organizations; and in community volunteer work. Even recreationally, Americans are "bowling alone" rather than in teams and leagues. While issue-oriented national organizations have grown rapidly, Putnam argues that they do not generate the same degree of personal engagement and interaction, and thus the social trust and reciprocity that keep democracy healthy. Indeed, trust in other people, as well as in government and most other institutions, has sharply eroded in the United States, and is strongly correlated with associational membership and other indicators of civic engagement. Putnam considers several economic, demographic, and technological changes that may help to account for America's declining civic engagement, but his key point is the need "to explore creatively" how public policies may have accelerated this decline, and how different policies might help to reverse them.

The Global Democratic Prospect

Our volume concludes as it begins, pondering the future of democracy as the third wave enters its third decade and this politically volatile century draws to a close. Based on his statistical analysis of trends in education and income, Henry S. Rowen foresees a powerful rising tide of democracy in the coming decades, whatever the fate of individual countries or the possible short-term setbacks for the third wave. Freedom levels (as measured annually by Freedom House) can be expected to increase significantly in the developing world, Rowen anticipates, because they are highly correlated with national levels of education and income, and these will rise significantly in the developing world over the next three decades. Substantial increases in average years of schooling (by as much as 50 to 100 percent) can be confidently predicted for the bulk of developing countries, and each additional year of schooling improves the freedom rating of a country by an average of more than 6 percentage points. The maturation of the better-educated younger segments of the population, combined with steadily increasing school enrollments, will add about three years to the average years of schooling of work forces in the developing world by 2020. This, together with average annual growth rates in per capita income of about 3 percent during this period, will lead, Rowen predicts, to substantially greater levels of freedom and more "free" countries.

The six chapters that follow were originally published as a symposium on democracy's future in the fifth anniversary issue (January 1995) of the *Journal of Democracy*. We asked each of the contributors to ponder the future of the third wave of global democratization, to predict what factors would sustain or obstruct it, and to identify and assess its principal ideological and political rivals, now and in the years to come. These contributions offer a varied, thoughtful, and in some ways sobering set of reflections on democracy's future. None of the authors are quite as optimistic as Rowen, who envisions an underlying tide of structural forces leading ineluctably to continued democratic expansion. Several authors worry about the health and vitality of the established Western democracies, suggesting, as Samuel Huntington has, that their capacity to provide an appealing and successful model will strongly affect the general strength and momentum of democracy in the world.

Repeatedly, these essays press us beyond the gross distinction between democracy and nondemocracy to consider the wide variations in the character and quality of putatively democratic regimes. Rather than outright breakdown by coup or implosion, the key danger facing most new democracies of the third wave is, as Philippe C. Schmitter sees it, reversion to a hybrid regime of soft dictatorship (*dictablanda*, typically with much hidden military control) or sharply constrained democracy (*democradura*); or, as Marcin Król frames it, the failure ever to get beyond a superficial, "debased and counterfeit" version of democracy; or in Guillermo O'Donnell's view, "slow death" through "the gradual erosion of freedoms, guarantees, and processes that are vital to democracy."

The new democracies of the third wave are, to varying degrees, hollow, fragile, and insecure. Most scholars, including those in our symposium, consider the long-term survival of these democracies to be in question unless they can achieve consolidation. Consolidation is the process by which democracy acquires deep and widespread legitimacy among all major elite groups and the citizenry at large. In the seminal formulation of Juan Linz and Alfred Stepan, it involves three interrelated levels at which democracy becomes "the only game in town":

• Behaviorally, no politically significant group makes any serious attempt to overthrow democracy or secede from the state.
• Attitudinally, the overwhelming majority of the people believe that democratic procedures and institutions are the most appropriate way to govern their society, and the only acceptable way to bring about change.
• Constitutionally, all political actors, both inside and outside government, internalize the rules and norms of the democratic game and wage their conflicts strictly within the boundaries of democratic procedures and institutions.[9]

These criteria are consistent with numerous other formulations that view consolidation as a process of normalization and routinization of democratic norms and methods. In most of the new democracies of the third wave, this process has not yet fully transpired, leaving the regimes in a state of suspension somewhere between partial, hybrid, or "delegative" democracy and consolidated liberal democracy. A key question is whether such nonconsolidated and often partial democracies can persist indefinitely, or will at some point fail in some way if they do not achieve consolidation. This in turn depends on whether democracy will continue to enjoy the ideological hegemony it had throughout the 1980s and early 1990s, or will confront a new competitor with potentially wide, if not global, appeal.

For Francis Fukuyama, in chapter 26, the most serious competitor to liberal democracy in the coming years will not be Islamic fundamentalism, ultranationalism, or a revival of fascism or communism, but some form of the paternalistic Asian authoritarianism (often encompassing, as in Singapore and Malaysia, formal electoral competition) that has achieved spectacular economic success while constraining individual liberty. Yet the core of the successful Asian model is cultural rather than institutional: "a deeply engrained moral code that is the basis for strong social structures and community life." And this cultural code is compatible with democratic regimes—such as those in Japan, South Korea, and now Taiwan—no less than with authoritarian ones. Thus Fukuyama sees it as a "self-serving distortion of Confucianism" for Singaporean leader Lee Kuan Yew to equate Confucianism's cultural and religious essence with the kind of paternalistic authoritarianism Lee has built in Singapore. (In fact, Taiwan's president, Lee Teng-hui, has gone further to identify significant democratic currents in original Confucian thought that were muted by the imperial system of later centuries.[10])

More than at the levels of ideology or formal institutions, Fukuyama sees the struggle for democratic consolidation occurring at the deeper levels of civil society and especially culture (which is the most profound influence, but the slowest to change). Thus he argues, "The prestige of democratic institutions in the future will depend on Asian perceptions not so much of the effectiveness of Western institutions as of the problems of Western society and culture." Marcin Król makes a similar case for Western influence on Central and Eastern Europe in chapter 31. "If the West lowers its own democratic standards" or fails to deal with its policy problems, liberal democracy will lose much of its luster in the postcommunist East, and authoritarian alternatives might become "more and more attractive."

Even more than Fukuyama or Król, Philippe C. Schmitter in chapter 27 sees democracy's future as likely to be shaped by developments in the established liberal democracies rather than in the "fledgling neo-democracies." The growing disaffection of citizenries in the industrialized democracies stems from sweeping economic, technological, and social changes that are increasing inequality, diminishing individual economic security, and eroding the governance capacities of strictly national institutions. Increasingly, these globalizing and destabilizing changes will threaten such established principles of liberal democracy as individualism, voluntarism, and the sovereignty of the nation-state. Schmitter foresees three possible avenues of adaptation in response. The first, more liberalism, would entail greater reliance on market forces, but he argues, it would only accelerate trends of civic disengagement by reducing further the public sphere and increasing the emphasis on the individual. The second, which he terms "preliberal democracy," advances a diffuse agenda that includes decentralization of state power, greater reliance on direct democracy (as through referenda), term limits, and more grassroots civic participation. It lacks a coherent focus, however, and makes demands on ordinary citizens "that are unrealistic given the pace of contemporary life." Thus Schmitter favors some kind of "postliberal" democracy that accepts the current parameters—individualism, inequality, political parties, organized interest mediation—but would implement a provocative and eclectic reform agenda, including citizens' juries, interactive polls, and reciprocal representation between countries.

The implications of radical economic liberalism also concern Guillermo O'Donnell in chapter 28. The appropriateness for any given country of specific institutional arrangements and economic reform programs depends on the political, social, and historical context, he maintains. Challenging overly formulaic approaches to democratic design or reform, O'Donnell criticizes in particular the hegemony of economists, whose liberalizing reforms "have had the effect of gutting much of the state, with predictably deleterious consequences for long-term economic development." Building on the issues raised in his "delegative democracy" essay, O'Donnell warns that the increasing tendency to insulate technocratic policymakers from politics comes at the price of neglecting essential political considerations, such as the impact of supposedly rational and "correct" economic policies on the legitimacy and prestige of democratic institutions and politicians. Liberalizing economic reforms have scored important successes, he concedes, but they have no clear idea of how to help the poor or even how to regenerate sustainable growth. Meanwhile, the triumph of technocracy over politics may produce "delegative democracy," which in turn "may degenerate into thinly veiled authoritarianism."

In chapter 29, Muthiah Alagappa sees a mixed but largely hopeful outlook for democracy in East and Southeast Asia. In Taiwan and South Korea, democratic principles appear firmly entrenched, civil societies have matured, and, despite particular political and external problems in each country, the two systems appear on the road to consolidation. Greater challenges confront the region's two other emergent democracies: Thailand must constrain the military and institutionalize its party system; the Philippines must reduce its massive problems of poverty and inequality; and both countries must rein in widespread political corruption. While democratization is not in sight in any of the region's autocratic regimes, economic reform, and the rapid economic growth it has unleashed, have given rise to new, more politically aware and assertive classes and civil society groups in China and more recently Vietnam. The same process may occur in Burma, where the ruling military suffers an even more severe legitimacy crisis, and will gradually force the more stable military regime in Indonesia to find a new legtimating formula. In general, Alagappa believes that "the authoritarian-pluralist model contains the seeds of its own destruction," and that as in South Korea and Taiwan, economic development (the mainstay of authoritarian legitimacy today) will fuel demands for political reform and ultimately democratization. Still, like Huntington, Alagappa is cautious in predicting when and where further democratization will occur, because this also depends on the choices, actions, and coalitions of political elites (military and civilian) in each country.

When the *Journal of Democracy* began publishing in 1990, Africa was overwhelmingly authoritarian. Since then, as Michael Chege observes in chapter 30, most of sub-Saharan Africa's 45 states have experienced pressures for democratic transition, and more than two dozen have held competitive, multiparty elections. According to Freedom House, only 9 African countries were free at the start of 1996, but a total of 18 were formally democratic. Chege shows the wide variation in Africa's democratic experience during the 1990s, from successful transitions with hope for consolidation in South Africa and Benin, to stalemated or aborted transitions in Nigeria, Kenya, Cameroon, Zaire, and Togo, to state collapse and violent conflict in Somalia, Liberia, and Rwanda. Chege suggests, as we have emphasized elsewhere, that the instruments of democracy—constitutionalism, federalism, negotiation, and power sharing—offer more reliable means for managing explosive ethnic divisions.[11] The problem, however—as many of our authors indicate—is that multiparty elections alone do not make for democracy. Many democratic transitions have been marred by deeply flawed elections and subsequent repression of the opposition. At the same time, opposition forces in Kenya, Cameroon, Ghana, Nigeria, Zaire, and elsewhere have hurt themselves with their own ethnic and personal divisions and willingness to sell out to dictators. Nascent civil societies in Africa offer some hope of generating more abiding democratic commitment, but they also suffer from ethnic divisions and underdevelopment.

As we have indicated, the gap between the form and substance of democracy in postcommunist states is a major concern of Marcin Król in chapter 31. Already, the shallow nature of the party system and the generally chaotic, vitriolic nature of politics have turned many citizens off from the electoral process. This, Król says, is particularly dangerous given the weak capacity of civil society to constrain political leaders and mediate between them and the citizenry. The primary danger in East Central Europe is not that there will be a resurgence of communism or blatant authoritarianism, but that formal democratic structures will "persist without a liberal spirit to animate them," leading to nationalist or paternalistic "sham democracies." This underscores, for Król, the importance of the moral dimension of democracy—reconciling the market with social justice, religion with the state, and liberalism with national and patriotic feeling.

In our concluding essay, chapter 32, Jacques Rupnik further explores the "post-totalitarian blues" that have descended upon the once euphoric publics of Central and Eastern Europe. Postcommunist regimes have had to struggle with difficult issues of how radically to pursue "decommunization" (purging and punishing the old ruling elite) and how to construct a new constitutional system. While the more successful postcommunist regimes have varied in their approaches, Rupnik indicates that the moral impulse to sweeping purges may not only impair economic efficiency and governability but perpetuate the moral myth of "an innocent society." For Rupnik, as for Zielonka in chapter 18, the overriding imperative for postcommunist democracies is to develop the structure and culture of constitutionalism. This requires the prompt adoption of a wholly new constitution (at a rather brief "founding moment" of unity in the new regime) or, as in Poland and Hungary, the progressive amendment of the existing one. In either case, respect for the democratic process is key. Specific institutional designs must then, as several of our other contributors stress, fit the particular national circumstances (such as the need to assure fair representation of ethnic minorities). A second prerequisite is the legitimation of the state in a territorial sense, with consensus on its proper boundaries, lest the pursuit of free elections lead to the disintegration and warfare witnessed in Yugoslavia or the instability evident in and around Russia. Like Król, Rupnik sees potential authoritarian and nationalist dangers on the horizon (particularly in Russia and the Balkans), but no chance of a communist comeback. If ex-communists are returning to power in some countries, "it is precisely because they no longer embody the threat of a return to totalitarianism." Moreover, in Central Europe and the Baltics, the economic and political conditions for democratic consolidation are gradually emerging.

We conclude, then, as we began, on a note of a qualified optimism. In the coming decade or two, the fate of the new democracies of the third wave is likely to be quite varied. Some, such as the Czech Republic, Poland, Hungary, Chile, Argentina, South Korea, and Taiwan, appear headed toward consolidation. Many others, we expect, will progress more slowly and fitfully in that direction. In a number of cases, democratic consolidation will require concerted efforts by elected officials, political parties, and civil society to overcome the obstacles to full political democracy: corruption, lawlessness, institutional disarray, and covert domination by the military, bureaucracy, or landed oligarchs.

For the near term, and perhaps for some time to come, democracy will benefit from the continued absence of any alternative regime form that could appeal across regions and cultures. But within some major regions of the world, rival regime forms may be gaining in legitimacy, and democracy "by default" is intrinsically unstable. Ultimately, if a third reverse wave is to be avoided, democracies—new and old—must demonstrate that they can adequately address the most pressing problems of their respective societies while fulfilling the liberal promise of protecting individual freedom.

NOTES

1. *Freedom Review*, January–February 1996, 1.

2. The specific quote, as Plattner indicates, was from a 1975 article by Daniel Patrick Moynihan, "The American Experience," in *The Public Interest* 41 (Fall 1975): 6.

3. Robert A. Dahl, *Polyarchy: Participation and Opposition* (New Haven: Yale University Press, 1971).

4. On the strong positive relationship between economic development and democracy, see Seymour Martin Lipset, *Political Man: The Social Bases of Politics* (Baltimore: Johns Hopkins University Press, 1981), 27–86; Larry Diamond, "Economic Development and Democracy Reconsidered," in Gary Marks and Larry Diamond eds., *Reexamining Democracy* (Newbury Park, Calif.: Sage, 1992), 93–139; and Adam Przeworski et al., "What Makes Democracies Endure," *Journal of Democracy* 7 (January 1996): 39–55.

5. Lee Teng-hui, "Chinese Culture and Political Renewal," *Journal of Democracy* 6 (October 1995): 1–8.

6. *Freedom Review*, January–February 1996, 5.

7. Vincent Maphai, "The New South Africa: A Season for Power-Sharing," *Journal of Democracy* 7 (January 1996): 67–81.

8. Guillermo O'Donnell and Philippe C. Schmitter, *Transitions from Authoritarian Rule: Tentative Conclusions about Uncertain Democracies* (Baltimore: Johns Hopkins University Press, 1986), 48–56.

9. Juan J. Linz and Alfred Stepan, *Problems of Democratic Transition and Consolidation: Southern Europe, South America and Postcommunist Europe* (Baltimore: Johns Hopkins University Press, 1996).

10. Lee Teng-hui, "Chinese Culture and Political Renewal." See also Fukuyama's own more extensive reflections on this relationship in "Confucianism and Democracy," *Journal of Democracy* 6 (April 1995): 20–33.

11. See our introduction to Larry Diamond and Marc F. Plattner, eds., *Nationalism, Ethnic Conflict, and Democracy* (Baltimore: Johns Hopkins University Press, 1994), xxii–xxix.

I.
The Democratic Moment

1.
DEMOCRACY'S THIRD WAVE

Samuel P. Huntington

Samuel P. Huntington *is Eaton Professor of the Science of Government and director of the John M. Olin Institute for Strategic Studies at Harvard University. This article is based upon the 1989 Julian J. Rothbaum Lectures at the Carl Albert Center of the University of Oklahoma, which were published as* The Third Wave: Democratization in the Late Twentieth Century. *Copyright © 1991 by Samuel P. Huntington. Published by the University of Oklahoma Press.*

Between 1974 and 1990, at least 30 countries made transitions to democracy, just about doubling the number of democratic governments in the world. Were these democratizations part of a continuing and ever-expanding "global democratic revolution" that will reach virtually every country in the world? Or did they represent a limited expansion of democracy, involving for the most part its reintroduction into countries that had experienced it in the past?

The current era of democratic transitions constitutes the third wave of democratization in the history of the modern world. The first "long" wave of democratization began in the 1820s, with the widening of the suffrage to a large proportion of the male population in the United States, and continued for almost a century until 1926, bringing into being some 29 democracies. In 1922, however, the coming to power of Mussolini in Italy marked the beginning of a first "reverse wave" that by 1942 had reduced the number of democratic states in the world to 12. The triumph of the Allies in World War II initiated a second wave of democratization that reached its zenith in 1962 with 36 countries governed democratically, only to be followed by a second reverse wave (1960-1975) that brought the number of democracies back down to 30.

At what stage are we within the third wave? Early in a long wave, or at or near the end of a short one? And if the third wave comes to a halt, will it be followed by a significant third reverse wave eliminating many of democracy's gains in the 1970s and 1980s? Social science cannot provide reliable answers to these questions, nor can any social scientist. It may be possible, however, to identify some of the factors that will affect the future expansion or contraction of democracy in the world and to pose the questions that seem most relevant for the future of democratization.

One way to begin is to inquire whether the causes that gave rise to the third wave are likely to continue operating, to gain in strength, to weaken, or to be supplemented or replaced by new forces promoting democratization. Five major factors have contributed significantly to the occurrence and the timing of the third-wave transitions to democracy:

1) The deepening legitimacy problems of authoritarian regimes in a world where democratic values were widely accepted, the consequent dependence of these regimes on successful performance, and their inability to maintain "performance legitimacy" due to economic (and sometimes military) failure.

2) The unprecedented global economic growth of the 1960s, which raised living standards, increased education, and greatly expanded the urban middle class in many countries.

3) A striking shift in the doctrine and activities of the Catholic Church, manifested in the Second Vatican Council of 1963-65 and the transformation of national Catholic churches from defenders of the status quo to opponents of authoritarianism.

4) Changes in the policies of external actors, most notably the European Community, the United States, and the Soviet Union.

5) "Snowballing," or the demonstration effect of transitions earlier in the third wave in stimulating and providing models for subsequent efforts at democratization.

I will begin by addressing the latter three factors, returning to the first two later in this article.

Historically, there has been a strong correlation between Western Christianity and democracy. By the early 1970s, most of the Protestant countries in the world had already become democratic. The third wave of the 1970s and 1980s was overwhelmingly a Catholic wave. Beginning in Portugal and Spain, it swept through six South American and three Central American countries, moved on to the Philippines, doubled back to Mexico and Chile, and then burst through in the two Catholic countries of Eastern Europe, Poland and Hungary. Roughly three-quarters of the countries that transited to democracy between 1974 and 1989 were predominantly Catholic.

By 1990, however, the Catholic impetus to democratization had largely exhausted itself. Most Catholic countries had already democratized or, as in the case of Mexico, liberalized. The ability of Catholicism to promote further expansion of democracy (without expanding its own ranks) is limited to Paraguay, Cuba, and a few

Francophone African countries. By 1990, sub-Saharan Africa was the only region of the world where substantial numbers of Catholics and Protestants lived under authoritarian regimes in a large number of countries.

The Role of External Forces

During the third wave, the European Community (EC) played a key role in consolidating democracy in southern Europe. In Greece, Spain, and Portugal, the establishment of democracy was seen as necessary to secure the economic benefits of EC membership, while Community membership was in turn seen as a guarantee of the stability of democracy. In 1981, Greece became a full member of the Community, and five years later Spain and Portugal did as well.

In April 1987, Turkey applied for full EC membership. One incentive was the desire of Turkish leaders to reinforce modernizing and democratic tendencies in Turkey and to contain and isolate the forces in Turkey supporting Islamic fundamentalism. Within the Community, however, the prospect of Turkish membership met with little enthusiasm and even some hostility (mostly from Greece). In 1990, the liberation of Eastern Europe also raised the possibility of membership for Hungary, Czechoslovakia, and Poland. The Community thus faced two issues. First, should it give priority to broadening its membership or to "deepening" the existing Community by moving toward further economic and political union? Second, if it did decide to expand its membership, should priority go to European Free Trade Association members like Austria, Norway, and Sweden, to the East Europeans, or to Turkey? Presumably the Community can only absorb a limited number of countries in a given period of time. The answers to these questions will have significant implications for the stability of democracy in Turkey and in the East European countries.

The withdrawal of Soviet power made possible democratization in Eastern Europe. If the Soviet Union were to end or drastically curtail its support for Castro's regime, movement toward democracy might occur in Cuba. Apart from that, there seems little more the Soviet Union can do or is likely to do to promote democracy outside its borders. The key issue is what will happen within the Soviet Union itself. If Soviet control loosens, it seems likely that democracy could be reestablished in the Baltic states. Movements toward democracy also exist in other republics. Most important, of course, is Russia itself. The inauguration and consolidation of democracy in the Russian republic, if it occurs, would be the single most dramatic gain for democracy since the immediate post-World War II years. Democratic development in most of the Soviet republics, however, is greatly complicated by their ethnic heterogeneity and the unwillingness of the dominant nationality to allow equal rights to ethnic minorities. As Sir Ivor Jennings remarked years ago, "the people cannot decide until somebody decides who are the people." It may take years if not decades to resolve the latter issue in much of the Soviet Union.

During the 1970s and 1980s the United States was a major promoter of democratization. Whether the United States continues to play this role depends on its will, its capability, and its attractiveness as a model to other countries. Before the mid-1970s the promotion of democracy had not always been a high priority of American foreign policy. It could again subside in importance. The end of the Cold War and of the ideological competition with the Soviet Union could remove one rationale for propping up anti-communist dictators, but it could also reduce the incentives for any substantial American involvement in the Third World.

American will to promote democracy may or may not be sustained. American ability to do so, on the other hand, is limited. The trade and budget deficits impose new limits on the resources that the United States can use to influence events in foreign countries. More important, the ability of the United States to promote democracy has in some measure run its course. The countries in Latin America, the Caribbean, Europe, and East Asia that were most susceptible to American influence have, with a few exceptions, already become democratic. The one major country where the United States can still exercise significant influence on behalf of democratization is Mexico. The undemocratic countries in Africa, the Middle East, and mainland Asia are less susceptible to American influence.

Apart from Central America and the Caribbean, the major area of the Third World where the United States has continued to have vitally important interests is the Persian Gulf. The Gulf War and the dispatch of 500,000 American troops to the region have stimulated demands for movement toward democracy in Kuwait and Saudi Arabia and delegitimized Saddam Hussein's regime in Iraq. A large American military deployment in the Gulf, if sustained over time, would provide an external impetus toward liberalization if not democratization, and a large American military deployment probably could not be sustained over time unless some movement toward democracy occurred.

The U.S. contribution to democratization in the 1980s involved more than the conscious and direct exercise of American power and influence. Democratic movements around the world have been inspired by and have borrowed from the American example. What might happen, however, if the American model ceases to embody strength and success, no longer seems to be the winning model? At the end of the 1980s, many were arguing that "American decline" was the true reality. If people around the world come to see the United States as a fading power beset by political stagnation, economic inefficiency, and social chaos, its perceived failures will inevitably be seen as the failures of democracy, and the worldwide appeal of democracy will diminish.

Snowballing

The impact of snowballing on democratization was clearly evident in 1990 in Bulgaria, Romania, Yugoslavia, Mongolia, Nepal, and Albania. It also affected movements toward liberalization in some Arab and African countries. In 1990, for instance, it was reported that the "upheaval in Eastern Europe" had "fueled demands for change in the Arab world" and prompted leaders in Egypt, Jordan, Tunisia, and Algeria to open up more political space for the expression of discontent.[1]

The East European example had its principal effect on the leaders of authoritarian regimes, not on the people they ruled. President Mobutu Sese Seko of Zaire, for instance reacted with shocked horror to televised pictures of the execution by firing squad of his friend, Romanian dictator Nicolae Ceauşescu. A few months later, commenting that "You know what's happening across the world," he announced that he would allow two parties besides his own to compete in elections in 1993. In Tanzania, Julius Nyerere observed that "If changes take place in Eastern Europe then other countries with one-party systems and which profess socialism will also be affected." His country, he added, could learn a "lesson or two" from Eastern Europe. In Nepal in April 1990, the government announced that King Birendra was lifting the ban on political parties as a result of "the international situation" and "the rising expectations of the people."[2]

If a country lacks favorable internal conditions, however, snowballing alone is unlikely to bring about democratization. The democratization of countries A and B is not a reason for democratization in country C, unless the conditions that favored it in the former also exist in the latter. Although the legitimacy of democratic government came to be accepted throughout the world in the 1980s, economic and social conditions favorable to democracy were not everywhere present. The "worldwide democratic revolution" may create an external environment conducive to democratization, but it cannot produce the conditions necessary for democratization within a particular country.

In Eastern Europe the major obstacle to democratization was Soviet control; once it was removed, the movement to democracy spread rapidly. There is no comparable external obstacle to democratization in the Middle East, Africa, and Asia. If rulers in these areas chose authoritarianism before December 1989, why can they not continue to choose it thereafter? The snowballing effect would be real only to the extent that it led them to believe in the desirability or necessity of democratization. The events of 1989 in Eastern Europe undoubtedly encouraged democratic opposition groups and frightened authoritarian leaders elsewhere. Yet given the previous weakness of the former and the long-term repression imposed by the latter, it seems doubtful that the East European example will actually produce significant progress toward democracy in most other authoritarian countries.

By 1990, many of the original causes of the third wave had become significantly weaker, even exhausted. Neither the White House, the Kremlin, the European Community, nor the Vatican was in a strong position to promote democracy in places where it did not already exist (primarily in Asia, Africa, and the Middle East). It remains possible, however, for new forces favoring democratization to emerge. After all, who in 1985 could have foreseen that Mikhail Gorbachev would facilitate democratization in Eastern Europe?

In the 1990s the International Monetary Fund (IMF) and the World Bank could conceivably become much more forceful than they have heretofore been in making political democratization as well as economic liberalization a precondition for economic assistance. France might become more active in promoting democracy among its former African colonies, where its influence remains substantial. The Orthodox churches could emerge as a powerful influence for democracy in southeastern Europe and the Soviet Union. A Chinese proponent of *glasnost* could come to power in Beijing, or a new Jeffersonian-style Nasser could spread a democratic version of Pan-Arabism in the Middle East. Japan could use its growing economic clout to encourage human rights and democracy in the poor countries to which it makes loans and grants. In 1990, none of these possibilities seemed very likely, but after the surprises of 1989 it would be rash to rule anything out.

A Third Reverse Wave?

By 1990 at least two third-wave democracies, Sudan and Nigeria, had reverted to authoritarian rule; the difficulties of consolidation could lead to further reversions in countries with unfavorable conditions for sustaining democracy. The first and second democratic waves, however, were followed not merely by some backsliding but by major reverse waves during which most regime changes throughout the world were from democracy to authoritarianism. If the third wave of democratization slows down or comes to a halt, what factors might produce a third reverse wave?

Among the factors contributing to transitions away from democracy during the first and second reverse waves were:

1) the weakness of democratic values among key elite groups and the general public;

2) severe economic setbacks, which intensified social conflict and enhanced the popularity of remedies that could be imposed only by authoritarian governments;

3) social and political polarization, often produced by leftist governments seeking the rapid introduction of major social and economic reforms;

4) the determination of conservative middle-class and upper-class groups to exclude populist and leftist movements and lower-class groups from political power;

5) the breakdown of law and order resulting from terrorism or insurgency;

6) intervention or conquest by a nondemocratic foreign power;

7) "reverse snowballing" triggered by the collapse or overthrow of democratic systems in other countries.

Transitions from democracy to authoritarianism, apart from those produced by foreign actors, have almost always been produced by those in power or close to power in the democratic system. With only one or two possible exceptions, democratic systems have not been ended by popular vote or popular revolt. In Germany and Italy in the first reverse wave, antidemocratic movements with considerable popular backing came to power and established fascist dictatorships. In Spain in the first reverse wave and in Lebanon in the second, democracy ended in civil war.

The overwhelming majority of transitions from democracy, however, took the form either of military coups that ousted democratically elected leaders, or executive coups in which democratically chosen chief executives effectively ended democracy by concentrating power in their own hands, usually by declaring a state of emergency or martial law. In the first reverse wave, military coups ended democratic systems in the new countries of Eastern Europe and in Greece, Portugal, Argentina, and Japan. In the second reverse wave, military coups occurred in Indonesia, Pakistan, Greece, Nigeria, Turkey, and many Latin American countries. Executive coups occurred in the second reverse wave in Korea, India, and the Philippines. In Uruguay, the civilian and military leadership cooperated to end democracy through a mixed executive-military coup.

In both the first and second reverse waves, democratic systems were replaced in many cases by historically new forms of authoritarian rule. Fascism was distinguished from earlier forms of authoritarianism by its mass base, ideology, party organization, and efforts to penetrate and control most of society. Bureaucratic authoritarianism differed from earlier forms of military rule in Latin America with respect to its institutional character, its presumption of indefinite duration, and its economic policies. Italy and Germany in the 1920s and 1930s and Brazil and Argentina in the 1960s and 1970s were the lead countries in introducing these new forms of nondemocratic rule and furnished the examples that antidemocratic groups in other countries sought to emulate. Both these new forms of authoritarianism were, in effect, responses to social and economic development: the expansion of social mobilization and political participation in Europe, and the exhaustion of the import-substitution phase of economic development in Latin America.

Although the causes and forms of the first two reverse waves cannot generate reliable predictions concerning the causes and forms of a possible third reverse wave, prior experiences do suggest some potential causes of a new reverse wave.

First, systemic failures of democratic regimes to operate effectively could undermine their legitimacy. In the late twentieth century, the major nondemocratic ideological sources of legitimacy, most notably Marxism-Leninism, were discredited. The general acceptance of democratic norms meant that democratic governments were even less dependent on performance legitimacy than they had been in the past. Yet sustained inability to provide welfare, prosperity, equity, justice, domestic order, or external security could over time undermine the legitimacy even of democratic governments. As the memories of authoritarian failures fade, irritation with democratic failures is likely to increase. More specifically, a general international economic collapse on the 1929-30 model could undermine the legitimacy of democracy in many countries. Most democracies did survive the Great Depression of the 1930s; yet some succumbed, and presumably some would be likely to succumb in response to a comparable economic disaster in the future.

Second, a shift to authoritarianism by any democratic or democratizing great power could trigger reverse snowballing. The reinvigoration of authoritarianism in Russia or the Soviet Union would have unsettling effects on democratization in other Soviet republics, Bulgaria, Romania, Yugoslavia, and Mongolia; and possibly in Poland, Hungary, and Czechoslovakia as well. It could send the message to would-be despots elsewhere: "You too can go back into business." Similarly, the establishment of an authoritarian regime in India could have a significant demonstration effect on other Third World countries. Moreover, even if a major country does not revert to authoritarianism, a shift to dictatorship by several smaller newly democratic countries that lack many of the usual preconditions for democracy could have ramifying effects even on other countries where those preconditions are strong.

If a nondemocratic state greatly increased its power and began to expand beyond its borders, this too could stimulate authoritarian movements in other countries. This stimulus would be particularly strong if the expanding authoritarian state militarily defeated one or more democratic countries. In the past, all major powers that have developed economically have also tended to expand territorially. If China develops economically under authoritarian rule in the coming decades and expands its influence and control in East Asia, democratic regimes in the region will be significantly weakened.

Finally, as in the 1920s and the 1960s, various old and new forms of authoritarianism that seem appropriate to the needs of the times could emerge. Authoritarian nationalism could take hold in some Third World countries and also in Eastern Europe. Religious fundamentalism, which has been most dramatically prevalent in Iran, could come to power in other countries, especially in the Islamic world. Oligarchic authoritarianism could develop in both wealthy and poorer countries as a reaction to the leveling tendencies of democracy. Populist dictatorships could emerge in the future, as they have in the past, in response to democracy's protection of various forms of economic privilege, particularly in those countries where land tenancy is still an issue. Finally, communal dictatorships could be imposed in democracies with two or more distinct ethnic, racial, or religious groups, with one group trying to establish control over the entire society.

All of these forms of authoritarianism have existed in the past. It is not beyond the wit of humans to devise new ones in the future. One possibility might be a technocratic "electronic dictatorship," in which authoritarian rule is made possible and legitimated by the regime's ability to manipulate information, the media, and sophisticated means of communication. None of these old or new forms of authoritarianism is highly probable, but it is also hard to say that any one of them is totally impossible.

Obstacles to Democratization

Another approach to assessing democracy's prospects is to examine the obstacles to and opportunities for democratization where it has not yet taken hold. As of 1990, more than one hundred countries lacked democratic regimes. Most of these countries fell into four sometimes overlapping geocultural categories:

1) Home-grown Marxist-Leninist regimes, including the Soviet Union, where major liberalization occurred in the 1980s and democratic movements existed in many republics;

2) Sub-Saharan African countries, which, with a few exceptions, remained personal dictatorships, military regimes, one-party systems, or some combination of these three;

3) Islamic countries stretching from Morocco to Indonesia, which except for Turkey and perhaps Pakistan had nondemocratic regimes;

4) East Asian countries, from Burma through Southeast Asia to China and North Korea, which included communist systems, military regimes, personal dictatorships, and two semidemocracies (Thailand and Malaysia).

The obstacles to democratization in these groups of countries are political, cultural, and economic. One potentially significant political obstacle to future democratization is the virtual absence of experience with democracy in most countries that remained authoritarian in 1990. Twenty-three of 30 countries that democratized between 1974 and 1990 had had some history of democracy, while only a few countries that were nondemocratic in 1990 could claim such experience. These included a few third-wave backsliders (Sudan, Nigeria, Suriname, and possibly Pakistan), four second-wave backsliders that had not redemocratized in the third wave (Lebanon, Sri Lanka, Burma, Fiji), and three first-wave democratizers that had been prevented by Soviet occupation from redemocratizing at the end of World War II (Estonia, Latvia, and Lithuania). Virtually all the 90 or more other nondemocratic countries in 1990 lacked significant past experience with democratic rule. This obviously is not a decisive impediment to democratization—if it were, no countries would now be democratic—but it does make it more difficult.

Another obstacle to democratization is likely to disappear in a number of countries in the 1990s. Leaders who found authoritarian regimes or rule them for a long period tend to become particularly staunch opponents of democratization. Hence some form of leadership change within the authoritarian system usually precedes movement toward democracy. Human mortality is likely to ensure such changes in the 1990s in some authoritarian regimes. In 1990, the long-term rulers in China, Côte d'Ivoire, and Malawi were in their eighties; those in Burma, Indonesia, North Korea, Lesotho, and Vietnam were in their seventies; and the leaders of Cuba, Morocco, Singapore, Somalia, Syria, Tanzania, Zaire, and Zambia were sixty or older. The death or departure from office of these leaders would remove one obstacle to democratization in their countries, but would not make it inevitable.

Between 1974 and 1990, democratization occurred in personal dictatorships, military regimes, and one-party systems. Full-scale democratization has not yet occurred, however, in communist one-party states that were the products of domestic revolution. Liberalization has taken place in the Soviet Union, which may or may not lead to full-scale democratization in Russia. In Yugoslavia, movements toward democracy are underway in Slovenia and Croatia. The Yugoslav communist revolution, however, was largely a Serbian revolution, and the prospects for democracy in Serbia appear dubious. In Cambodia, an extraordinarily brutal revolutionary communist regime was replaced by a less brutal communist regime imposed by outside force. In 1990, Albania appeared to be opening up, but in China, Vietnam, Laos, Cuba, and Ethiopia, Marxist-Leninist regimes produced by home-grown revolutions seemed determined to remain in power. The revolutions in these countries had been nationalist as well as communist, and hence nationalism reinforced communism in a way that obviously was not true of Soviet-occupied Eastern Europe.

One serious impediment to democratization is the absence or weakness of real commitment to democratic values among political leaders in Asia, Africa, and the Middle East. When they are out of power, political leaders have good reason to advocate democracy. The test of their democratic commitment comes once they are in office. In Latin America, democratic regimes have generally been overthrown by military coups d'état. This has happened in Asia and the Middle East as well, but in these regions elected leaders themselves have also been responsible for ending democracy: Syngman Rhee and Park Chung Hee in Korea, Adnan Menderes in Turkey, Ferdinand Marcos in the Philippines, Lee Kwan Yew in Singapore, Indira Gandhi in India, and Sukarno in Indonesia. Having won power through the electoral system, these leaders then proceeded to undermine that system. They had little commitment to democratic values and practices.

Even when Asian, African, and Middle Eastern leaders have more or less abided by the rules of democracy, they often seemed to do so grudgingly. Many European, North American, and Latin American political leaders in the last half of the twentieth century were ardent and articulate advocates of democracy. Asian and African countries, in contrast, did not produce many heads of government who were also apostles of democracy. Who were the Asian, Arab, or African equivalents of Rómulo Betancourt, Alberto Llera Camargo, José Figueres, Eduardo Frei, Fernando Belaúnde Terry, Juan Bosch, José Napoleón Duarte, and Raúl Alfonsín? Jawaharlal Nehru and Corazon Aquino were, and there may have been others, but they were few in number. No Arab leader comes to mind, and it is hard to identify any Islamic leader who made a reputation as an advocate and supporter of democracy while in office. Why is this? This question inevitably leads to the issue of culture.

Culture

It has been argued that the world's great historic cultural traditions vary significantly in the extent to which their attitudes, values, beliefs, and related behavior patterns are conducive to the development of democracy. A profoundly antidemocratic culture would impede the spread of democratic norms in the society, deny legitimacy to democratic institutions, and thus greatly complicate if not prevent the emergence and effective functioning of those institutions. The cultural thesis comes in two forms. The more restrictive version states that only Western culture provides a suitable base for the development of democratic institutions and, consequently, that democracy is largely inappropriate for non-

Western societies. In the early years of the third wave, this argument was explicitly set forth by George Kennan. Democracy, he said, was a form of government "which evolved in the eighteenth and nineteenth centuries in northwestern Europe, primarily among those countries that border on the English Channel and the North Sea (but with a certain extension into Central Europe), and which was then carried into other parts of the world, including North America, where peoples from that northwestern European area appeared as original settlers, or as colonialists, and laid down the prevailing patterns of civil government." Hence democracy has "a relatively narrow base both in time and in space; and the evidence has yet to be produced that it is the natural form of rule for peoples outside those narrow perimeters." The achievements of Mao, Salazar, and Castro demonstrated, according to Kennan, that authoritarian regimes "have been able to introduce reforms and to improve the lot of masses of people, where more diffuse forms of political authority had failed."[3] Democracy, in short, is appropriate only for northwestern and perhaps central European countries and their settler-colony offshoots.

The Western-culture thesis has immediate implications for democratization in the Balkans and the Soviet Union. Historically these areas were part of the Czarist and Ottoman empires; their prevailing religions were Orthodoxy and Islam, not Western Christianity. These areas did not have the same experiences as Western Europe with feudalism, the Renaissance, the Reformation, the Enlightenment, the French Revolution, and liberalism. As William Wallace has suggested, the end of the Cold War and the disappearance of the Iron Curtain may have shifted the critical political dividing line eastward to the centuries-old boundary between Eastern and Western Christendom. Beginning in the north, this line runs south roughly along the borders dividing Finland and the Baltic republics from Russia; through Byelorussia and the Ukraine, separating western Catholic Ukraine from eastern Orthodox Ukraine; south and then west in Romania, cutting off Transylvania from the rest of the country; and then through Yugoslavia roughly along the line separating Slovenia and Croatia from the other republics.[4] This line may now separate those areas where democracy will take root from those where it will not.

A less restrictive version of the cultural obstacle argument holds that certain non-Western cultures are peculiarly hostile to democracy. The two cultures most often cited in this regard are Confucianism and Islam. Three questions are relevant to determining whether these cultures now pose serious obstacles to democratization. First, to what extent are traditional Confucian and Islamic values and beliefs hostile to democracy? Second, if they are, to what extent have these cultures in fact hampered progress toward democracy? Third, if they have significantly retarded democratic progress in the past, to what extent are they likely to continue to do so in the future?

Confucianism

Almost no scholarly disagreement exists regarding the proposition that traditional Confucianism was either undemocratic or antidemocratic. The only mitigating factor was the extent to which the examination system in the classic Chinese polity opened careers to the talented without regard to social background. Even if this were the case, however, a merit system of promotion does not make a democracy. No one would describe a modern army as democratic because officers are promoted on the basis of their abilities. Classic Chinese Confucianism and its derivatives in Korea, Vietnam, Singapore, Taiwan, and (in diluted fashion) Japan emphasized the group over the individual, authority over liberty, and responsibilities over rights. Confucian societies lacked a tradition of rights against the state; to the extent that individual rights did exist, they were created by the state. Harmony and cooperation were preferred over disagreement and competition. The maintenance of order and respect for hierarchy were central values. The conflict of ideas, groups, and parties was viewed as dangerous and illegitimate. Most important, Confucianism merged society and the state and provided no legitimacy for autonomous social institutions at the national level.

In practice Confucian or Confucian-influenced societies have been inhospitable to democracy. In East Asia only two countries, Japan and the Philippines, had sustained experience with democratic government prior to 1990. In both cases, democracy was the product of an American presence. The Philippines, moreover, is overwhelmingly a Catholic country. In Japan, Confucian values were reinterpreted and merged with autochthonous cultural traditions.

Mainland China has had no experience with democratic government, and democracy of the Western variety has been supported over the years only by relatively small groups of radical dissidents. "Mainstream" democratic critics have not broken with the key elements of the Confucian tradition.[5] The modernizers of China have been (in Lucian Pye's phrase) the "Confucian Leninists" of the Nationalist and Communist parties. In the late 1980s, when rapid economic growth in China produced a new series of demands for political reform and democracy on the part of students, intellectuals, and urban middle-class groups, the Communist leadership responded in two ways. First, it articulated a theory of "new authoritarianism," based on the experience of Taiwan, Singapore, and Korea, which claimed that a country at China's stage of economic development needed authoritarian rule to achieve balanced economic growth and contain the unsettling consequences of development. Second, the leadership violently suppressed the democratic movement in Beijing and elsewhere in June of 1989.

In China, economics reinforced culture in holding back democracy. In Singapore, Taiwan, and Korea, on the other hand, spectacular growth created the economic basis for democracy by the late 1980s. In these countries, economics clashed with culture in shaping political development. In 1990, Singapore was the only non-oil-exporting "high-income" country (as defined by the World Bank) that did not have a democratic political system, and Singapore's leader was an articulate exponent of Confucian values as opposed to those of Western democracy. In the 1980s, Premier Lee Kwan Yew made the teaching and promulgation of Confucian values a high priority for his city-state and took vigorous measures to limit and suppress dissent and to prevent media criticism of the government and its policies. Singapore was thus an authoritarian Confucian anomaly among the wealthy countries of the world. The interesting question is whether it will remain so now that Lee, who created the state, appears to be partially withdrawing from the political scene.

In the late 1980s, both Taiwan and Korea moved in a democratic direction. Historically, Taiwan had always been a peripheral part of China. It was occupied by the Japanese for 50 years, and its inhabitants rebelled in 1947 against the imposition of Chinese control. The Nationalist government arrived in 1949 humiliated by its defeat by the Communists, a defeat that made it impossible "for most Nationalist leaders to uphold the posture of arrogance associated with traditional Confucian notions of authority." Rapid economic and social development further weakened the influence of traditional Confucianism. The emergence of a substantial entrepreneurial class, composed largely of native Taiwanese, created (in very un-Confucian fashion) a source of power and wealth independent of the mainlander-dominated state. This produced in Taiwan a "fundamental change in Chinese political culture, which has not occurred in China itself or in Korea or Vietnam—and never really existed in Japan."[6] Taiwan's spectacular economic development thus overwhelmed a relatively weak Confucian legacy, and in the late 1980s Chiang Ching-kuo and Lee Teng-hui responded to the pressures produced by economic and social change and gradually moved to open up politics in their society.

In Korea, the classical culture included elements of mobility and egalitarianism along with Confucian components uncongenial to democracy, including a tradition of authoritarianism and strongman rule. As one Korean scholar put it, "people did not think of themselves as citizens with rights to exercise and responsibilities to perform, but they tended to look up to the top for direction and for favors in order to survive."[7] In the late 1980s, urbanization, education, the development of a substantial middle class, and the impressive spread of Christianity all weakened Confucianism as an obstacle to democracy in Korea. Yet it remained unclear whether the struggle between the old culture and the new prosperity had been definitively resolved in favor of the latter.

The East Asian Model

The interaction of economic progress and Asian culture appears to have generated a distinctly East Asian variety of democratic institutions. As of 1990, no East Asian country except the Philippines (which is, in many respects, more Latin American than East Asian in culture) had experienced a turnover from a popularly elected government of one party to a popularly elected government of a different party. The prototype was Japan, unquestionably a democracy, but one in which the ruling party has never been voted out of power. The Japanese model of dominant-party democracy, as Pye has pointed out, has spread elsewhere in East Asia. In 1990, two of the three opposition parties in Korea merged with the government party to form a political bloc that would effectively exclude the remaining opposition party, led by Kim Dae Jung and based on the Cholla region, from ever gaining power. In the late 1980s, democratic development in Taiwan seemed to be moving toward an electoral system in which the Kuomintang (KMT) was likely to remain the dominant party, with the Democratic Progressive Party confined to a permanent opposition role. In Malaysia, the coalition of the three leading parties from the Malay, Chinese, and Indian communities (first in the Alliance Party and then in the National Front) has controlled power in unbroken fashion against all competitors from the 1950s through the 1980s. In the mid-1980s, Lee Kwan Yew's deputy and successor Goh Chok Tong endorsed a similar type of party system for Singapore:

> I think a stable system is one where there is a mainstream political party representing a broad range of the population. Then you can have a few other parties on the periphery, very serious-minded parties. They are unable to have wider views but they nevertheless represent sectional interests. And the mainstream is returned all the time. I think that's good. And I would not apologize if we ended up in that situation in Singapore.[8]

A primary criterion for democracy is equitable and open competition for votes between political parties without government harassment or restriction of opposition groups. Japan has clearly met this test for decades with its freedoms of speech, press, and assembly, and reasonably equitable conditions of electoral competition. In the other Asian dominant-party systems, the playing field has been tilted in favor of the government for many years. By the late 1980s, however, conditions were becoming more equal in some countries. In Korea, the government party was unable to win control of the legislature in 1989, and this failure presumably was a major factor in its subsequent merger with two of its opponents. In Taiwan, restrictions on the opposition were gradually lifted. It is thus conceivable that other East Asian countries could join Japan in providing a level playing field for a game that the government party always wins. In 1990 the East Asian dominant-party systems thus spanned a continuum between democracy and authoritarianism, with Japan at one extreme, Indonesia at the other, and Korea, Taiwan, Malaysia, and Singapore (more or less in that order) in between.

Such a system may meet the formal requisites of democracy, but it differs significantly from the democratic systems prevalent in the West, where it is assumed not only that political parties and coalitions will freely and equally compete for power but also that they are likely to *alternate* in power. By contrast, the East Asian dominant-party systems seem to involve competition for power but not alternation in power, and participation in elections for all, but participation in office only for those in the "mainstream" party. This type of political system offers democracy without turnover. It represents an adaptation of Western democratic practices to serve not Western values of competition and change, but Asian values of consensus and stability.

Western democratic systems are less dependent on performance legitimacy than authoritarian systems because failure is blamed on the incumbents instead of the system, and the ouster and replacement of the incumbents help to renew the system. The East Asian societies that have adopted or appear to be adopting the dominant-party model had unequalled records of economic success from the 1960s to the 1980s. What happens, however, if and when their 8-percent growth rates plummet; unemployment, inflation, and other forms of economic distress escalate; or social and economic conflicts intensify? In a Western democracy the response would be to turn the incumbents out. In a dominant-party democracy, however, that would represent a revolutionary change. If the structure of political competition does not allow that to happen, unhappiness with the government could well lead to demonstrations, protests, riots, and efforts to mobilize popular support to overthrow the government. The government then would be tempted to respond by suppressing dissent and imposing authoritarian controls. The key question, then, is to what extent the East Asian dominant-party system presupposes uninterrupted and substantial economic growth. Can this system survive prolonged economic downturn or stagnation?

Islam

"Confucian democracy" is clearly a contradiction in terms. It is unclear whether "Islamic democracy" also is. Egalitarianism and voluntarism are central themes in Islam. The "high culture form of Islam," Ernest Gellner has argued, is "endowed with a number of features—unitarianism, a rule-ethic, individualism, scripturalism, puritanism, an egalitarian aversion to mediation and hierarchy, a fairly small load of magic—that are congruent, presumably, with requirements of modernity or modernization." They are also generally congruent with the requirements of democracy. Islam, however, also rejects any distinction between the religious community and the political community. Hence there is no equipoise between Caesar and God, and political participation is linked to religious affiliation. Fundamentalist Islam demands that in a Muslim country the political rulers should be practicing Muslims, *shari'a* should be the basic law, and *ulema* should have a "decisive vote in articulating, or at least reviewing and ratifying, all governmental policy."[9] To the extent that governmental legitimacy and policy flow from religious doctrine and religious expertise, Islamic concepts of politics differ from and contradict the premises of democratic politics.

Islamic doctrine thus contains elements that may be both congenial and uncongenial to democracy. In practice, however, the only Islamic country that has sustained a fully democratic political system for any length of time is Turkey, where Mustafa Kemal Ataturk explicitly rejected Islamic concepts of society and politics and vigorously attempted to create a secular, modern, Western nation-state. And Turkey's experience with democracy has not been an unmitigated success. Elsewhere in the Islamic world, Pakistan has made three attempts at democracy, none of which lasted long. While Turkey has had democracy interrupted by occasional military interventions, Pakistan has had bureaucratic and military rule interrupted by occasional elections.

The only Arab country to sustain a form of democracy (albeit of the consociational variety) for a significant period of time was Lebanon. Its democracy, however, really amounted to consociational oligarchy, and 40 to 50 percent of its population was Christian. Once Muslims became a majority in Lebanon and began to assert themselves, Lebanese democracy collapsed. Between 1981 and 1990, only two of 37 countries in the world with Muslim majorities were ever rated "Free" by Freedom House in its annual surveys: the Gambia for two years and the Turkish Republic of Northern Cyprus for four. Whatever the compatibility of Islam and democracy in theory, in practice they have rarely gone together.

Opposition movements to authoritarian regimes in southern and eastern Europe, in Latin America, and in East Asia almost universally have espoused Western democratic values and proclaimed their desire to establish democracy. This does not mean that they invariably would introduce democratic institutions if they had the opportunity to do so, but at least they articulated the rhetoric of democracy. In authoritarian Islamic societies, by contrast, movements explicitly campaigning for democratic politics have been relatively weak, and the most powerful opposition has come from Islamic fundamentalists.

In the late 1980s, domestic economic problems combined with the snowballing effects of democratization elsewhere led the governments of several Islamic countries to relax their controls on the opposition and to attempt to renew their legitimacy through elections. The principal initial beneficiaries of these openings were Islamic fundamentalist groups. In Algeria, the Islamic Salvation Front swept the June 1990 local elections, the first free elections since the country became independent in 1962. In the 1989 Jordanian elections, Islamic fundamentalists won 36 of 80 seats in parliament. In Egypt, many candidates associated with the Muslim Brotherhood were elected to parliament in 1987. In several countries, Islamic fundamentalist groups were reportedly plotting insurrections. The strong electoral showings of the Islamic groups partly reflected the absence of other opposition parties, some because they were under government proscription, others because they were boycotting the elections. Nonetheless, fundamentalism seemed to be gaining strength in Middle Eastern countries, particularly among younger people. The strength of this tendency induced secular heads of government in Tunisia, Turkey, and elsewhere to adopt policies advocated by the fundamentalists and to make political gestures demonstrating their own commitment to Islam.

Liberalization in Islamic countries thus enhanced the power of important social and political movements whose commitment to democracy was uncertain. In some respects, the position of fundamentalist parties in Islamic societies in the early 1990s raised questions analogous to those posed by communist parties in Western Europe in the 1940s and again in the 1970s. Would the existing governments continue to open up their politics and hold elections in which Islamic groups could compete freely and equally? Would the Islamic groups gain majority support in those elections? If they did win the elections, would the military, which in many Islamic societies (e.g., Algeria, Turkey, Pakistan, and Indonesia) is strongly secular, allow them to form a government? If they did form a government, would it pursue radical Islamic policies that would undermine democracy and alienate the modern and Western-oriented elements in society?

The Limits of Cultural Obstacles

Strong cultural obstacles to democratization thus appear to exist in Confucian and Islamic societies. There are, nonetheless, reasons to doubt whether these must necessarily prevent democratic development. First, similar cultural arguments have not held up in the past. At one point many scholars argued that Catholicism was an obstacle to democracy. Others, in the Weberian tradition, contended that Catholic countries were unlikely to develop economically in the same manner as Protestant countries. Yet in the 1960s, 1970s, and 1980s Catholic countries became democratic and, on average, had higher rates of economic growth than Protestant countries. Similarly, at one point Weber and others argued that countries with Confucian cultures would not achieve successful capitalist development. By the 1980s, however, a new generation of scholars saw Confucianism as a major cause of the spectacular economic growth of East Asian societies. In the longer run, will the thesis that Confucianism prevents democratic development be any more viable than the thesis that Confucianism prevents economic development? Arguments that particular cultures are permanent obstacles to change should be viewed with a certain skepticism.

Second, great cultural traditions like Islam and Confucianism are highly complex bodies of ideas, beliefs, doctrines, assumptions, and behavior patterns. Any major culture, including Confucianism, has some elements that are compatible with democracy, just as both Protestantism and Catholicism have elements that are clearly undemocratic. Confucian democracy may be a contradiction in terms, but democracy in a Confucian society need not be. The real question is which elements in Islam and Confucianism are favorable to democracy, and how and under what circumstances these can supersede the undemocratic aspects of those cultural traditions.

Third, cultures historically are dynamic, not stagnant. The dominant beliefs and attitudes in a society change. While maintaining elements of continuity, the prevailing culture of a society in one generation may differ significantly from what it was one or two generations earlier. In the 1950s, Spanish culture was typically described as traditional, authoritarian, hierarchical, deeply religious, and honor-and-status oriented. By the 1970s and 1980s, these words had little place in a description of Spanish attitudes and values. Cultures evolve and, as in Spain, the most important force bringing about cultural changes is often economic development itself.

Economics

Few relationships between social, economic, and political phenomena are stronger than that between the level of economic development and the existence of democratic politics. Most wealthy countries are democratic, and most democratic countries—India is the most dramatic exception—are wealthy. The correlation between wealth and democracy implies that transitions to democracy should occur primarily in countries at the mid-level of economic development. In poor countries democratization is unlikely; in rich countries it usually has already occurred. In between there is a "political transition zone": countries in this middle economic stratum are those most likely to transit to democracy, and most countries that transit to democracy will be in this stratum. As countries develop economically and move into the transition zone, they become good prospects for democratization.

In fact, shifts from authoritarianism to democracy during the third wave were heavily concentrated in this transition zone, especially at its upper reaches. The conclusion seems clear. Poverty is a principal—probably *the* principal—obstacle to democratic development. The future of democracy depends on the future of economic development. Obstacles to economic development are obstacles to the expansion of democracy.

The third wave of democratization was propelled forward by the extraordinary global economic growth of the 1950s and 1960s. That era of growth came to an end with the oil price increases of 1973-74. Between 1974 and 1990, democratization accelerated around the world, but global economic growth slowed down. There were, however, substantial differences in growth rates among regions. East Asian rates remained high throughout the 1970s and 1980s, and overall rates of growth in South Asia increased. On the other hand, growth rates in the Middle East, North Africa, Latin America, and the Caribbean declined sharply from the 1970s to the 1980s. Those in sub-Saharan Africa plummeted. Per capita GNP in Africa was stagnant during the late 1970s and declined at an annual rate of 2.2 percent during the 1980s. The economic obstacles to democratization in Africa thus clearly grew during the 1980s. The prospects for the 1990s are not encouraging. Even if economic reforms, debt relief, and economic assistance materialize, the World Bank has predicted an average annual rate of growth in per capita GDP for Africa of only 0.5 percent for the remainder of the century.[10] If this prediction is accurate, the economic obstacles to democratization in sub-Saharan Africa will remain overwhelming well into the twenty-first century.

The World Bank was more optimistic in its predictions of economic growth for China and the nondemocratic countries of South Asia. The current low levels of wealth in those countries, however, generally mean that even with annual per capita growth rates of 3 to 5 percent, the economic conditions favorable to democratization would still be long in coming.

In the 1990s, the majority of countries where the economic conditions for democratization are already present or rapidly emerging are in the Middle East and North Africa (see Table 1). The economies of many of these countries (United Arab Emirates, Kuwait, Saudi Arabia, Iraq, Iran,

Table 1 — Upper and Middle Income Nondemocratic Countries - GNP Per Capita (1988)

INCOME LEVEL	ARAB-MIDDLE EAST	SOUTHEAST ASIA	AFRICA	OTHER
Upper Income (>$6,000)	(UAE) (Kuwait) (Saudi Arabia)	Singapore		
Upper Middle Income ($2,000-5,500)	(Iraq) (Iran) (Libya) (Oman)* Algeria*		(Gabon)	Yugoslavia
Lower Middle Income ($500-2,200)	Syria Jordan* Tunisia*	Malaysia* Thailand*	Cameroon*	Paraguay
$1,000------				
	Morocco* Egypt* Yemen* Lebanon*		Congo* Côte d'Ivoire Zimbabwe Senegal* Angola	

Note: ( ) = major oil exporter
* = average annual GDP growth rate 1980-1988 > 3.0%

Source: World Bank, *World Bank Development Report 1990* (New York: Oxford University Press, 1990), 178-181.

Libya, Oman) depend heavily on oil exports, which enhances the control of the state bureaucracy. This does not, however, make democratization impossible. The state bureaucracies of Eastern Europe had far more power than do those of the oil exporters. Thus at some point that power could collapse among the latter as dramatically as it did among the former.

In 1988 among the other states of the Middle East and North Africa, Algeria had already reached a level conducive to democratization; Syria was approaching it; and Jordan, Tunisia, Morocco, Egypt, and North Yemen were well below the transition zone, but had grown rapidly during the 1980s. Middle Eastern economies and societies are approaching the point where they will become too wealthy and too complex for their various traditional, military, and one-party systems of authoritarian rule to sustain themselves. The wave of democratization that swept the world in the 1970s and 1980s could become a dominant feature of Middle Eastern and North African politics in the 1990s. The issue of economics versus culture would then be joined: What forms of politics might emerge in these countries when economic prosperity begins to interact with Islamic values and traditions?

In China, the obstacles to democratization are political, economic, and cultural; in Africa they are overwhelmingly economic; and in the rapidly developing countries of East Asia and in many Islamic countries, they are primarily cultural.

Economic Development and Political Leadership

History has proved both optimists and pessimists wrong about democracy. Future events will probably do the same. Formidable obstacles to the expansion of democracy exist in many societies. The third wave, the "global democratic revolution" of the late twentieth century, will not last forever. It may be followed by a new surge of authoritarianism sustained enough to constitute a third reverse wave. That, however, would not preclude a fourth wave of democratization developing some time in the twenty-first century. Judging by the record of the past, the two most decisive factors affecting the future consolidation and expansion of democracy will be economic development and political leadership.

Most poor societies will remain undemocratic so long as they remain poor. Poverty, however, is not inevitable. In the past, nations such as South Korea, which were assumed to be mired in economic backwardness, have astonished the world by rapidly attaining prosperity. In the 1980s, a new consensus emerged among developmental economists on the ways to promote economic growth. The consensus of the 1980s may or may not prove more lasting and productive than the very different consensus among economists that prevailed in the 1950s and 1960s. The new orthodoxy of neo-orthodoxy, however, already seems to have produced significant results in many countries.

Yet there are two reasons to temper our hopes with caution. First, economic development for the late, late, late developing countries—meaning largely Africa—may well be more difficult than it was for earlier developers because the advantages of backwardness come to be outweighed by the widening and historically unprecedented gap between rich and poor countries. Second, new forms of authoritarianism could emerge in wealthy, information-dominated, technology-based societies. If unhappy possibilities such as these do not materialize, economic development should create the conditions for the progressive replacement of authoritarian political systems by democratic ones. Time is on the side of democracy.

Economic development makes democracy possible; political leadership makes it real. For democracies to come into being, future political elites will have to believe, at a minimum, that democracy is the least bad form of government for their societies and for themselves. They will also need the skills to bring about the transition to democracy while facing both radical oppositionists and authoritarian hard-liners who inevitably will attempt to undermine their efforts. Democracy will spread to the extent that those who exercise power in the world and in individual countries want it to spread. For a century and a half after Tocqueville observed the emergence of modern democracy in America, successive waves of democratization have washed over the shore of dictatorship. Buoyed by a rising tide of economic progress, each wave advanced further—and receded less—than its predecessor. History, to shift the metaphor, does not sail ahead in a straight line, but when skilled and determined leaders are at the helm, it does move forward.

NOTES

1. *New York Times*, 28 December 1989, A13; *International Herald Tribune*, 12-13 May 1990, 6.

2. *The Times* (London), 27 May 1990; *Time*, 21 May 1990, 34-35; *Daily Telegraph*, 29 March 1990, 13; *New York Times*, 27 February 1990, A10, and 9 April 1990, A6.

3. George F. Kennan, *The Cloud of Danger* (Boston: Little, Brown, 1977), 41-43.

4. See William Wallace, *The Transformation of Western Europe* (London: Royal Institute of International Affairs-Pinter, 1990), 16-19.

5. See Daniel Kelliher, "The Political Consequences of China's Reform," *Comparative Politics* 18 (July 1986): 488-490; and Andrew J. Nathan, *Chinese Democracy* (New York: Alfred A. Knopf, 1985).

6. Lucian W. Pye with Mary W. Pye, *Asian Power and Politics: The Cultural Dimensions of Authority* (Cambridge: Harvard University Press, 1985), 232-236.

7. *New York Times*, 15 December 1987, A14.

8. Goh Chok Tong, quoted in *New York Times*, 14 August 1985, A13.

9. Ernest Gellner, "Up from Imperialism," *The New Republic*, 22 May 1989, 35-36; R. Stephen Humphreys, "Islam and Political Values in Saudi Arabia, Egypt, and Syria," *Middle East Journal* 33 (Winter 1979): 6-7.

10. World Bank, *World Development Report 1990* (New York: Oxford University Press, 1990), 8-11, 16, 160; and *Sub-Saharan Africa: From Crisis to Sustainable Growth* (Washington: World Bank, 1990).

2. THE NEW WORLD DISORDER

Ken Jowitt

Ken Jowitt *is Robson Professor of Political Science at the University of California at Berkeley. This article was adapted from two papers that were published in* The Crisis of Leninism and the Decline of the Left: The Revolutions of 1989, *edited by Daniel Chirot (1991), and* Global Transformations and the Third World, *edited by Robert Slater, Barry Schultz, and Steven R. Dorr (1992).*

For nearly half a century, international and national boundaries and identities have been shaped by the existence of a world of Leninist regimes led in varying ways and to different degrees by the Soviet Union. For half a century we have thought in terms of East and West; now, with the mass extinction of Leninist regimes, the East as such has vanished, taking the primary axis of international politics along with it. Thermonuclear Russia still exists, but the imperial construct called the Soviet bloc is gone, and the Soviet Union proper (itself an empire) may soon follow. The "Leninist extinction" has radically altered the geopolitical frame of reference that countries throughout the world have long used to bound and define themselves.

The Third World, for instance, has bounded and defined itself since its beginning at the Bandung Conference of 1955 by distinguishing itself from the West on the one hand and the Leninist world on the other. Whatever shared political identity the "nonaligned" states of Africa, Asia, and the Middle East have had has been largely negative: they were neither liberal nor Leninist. The Third World's ideological identity, its geographical borders, and its capacity to secure development assistance have all hinged upon the conflict between the other two worlds, one led by the United States, the other by the Soviet Union. Yet now the bipolar alignment with reference to which the nonaligned states of the Third World defined themselves has disappeared.

Boundaries are an essential component of a recognizable and coherent identity. Whether the borders in question are territorial, ideological, religious, economic, social, cultural, or amalgams thereof, their erosion or dissolution is likely to be traumatic. This is all the more so when boundaries have been organized and understood in highly categoric terms, as they were during the period of the Cold War.

We cannot expect the "clearing away" effect of Leninism's extinction to be self-contained, a political storm with an impact conveniently limited to the confines of what used to be the Leninist world. On the contrary, the Leninist extinction of 1989 has hurled the entire world into a situation not altogether unlike the one described in the Book of Genesis. Central points of reference and firm, even rigid, boundaries have given way to territorial, ideological, and political confusion and uncertainty. We now inhabit a world which, while not "without form and void" like the primordial chaos in Genesis, is nonetheless a great deal more fluid than it was just a very short while ago. The major imperatives of this world, moreover, will be the same as those facing Yahweh in Genesis: "naming and bounding."

We must respond to a world that will be increasingly unfamiliar, perplexing, and threatening. Many kinds of existing boundaries will come under assault; many will change. The task will be to establish new national and international boundaries and to identify—"name" and "bound"—the new entities that result.

In his much discussed essay on "The End of History," Francis Fukuyama has taken the view that "the triumph of the West, of the Western idea, is evident first of all in the total exhaustion of viable systematic alternatives to Western liberalism."[1] His allowance for the "sudden appearance of new ideologies or previously unrecognized contradictions in liberal societies" is a throwaway. For him, Hitler, the Nazi revolution, and World War II were a "diseased bypath in the general course of European development." Similarly, his allowance that the "fascist alternative may not have been played out yet in the Soviet Union," is a liberal Goliath's view of a possible fascist David. "Exceptions" on the order of the Nazi and Bolshevik regimes do not prove the liberal "rule"—the former almost destroyed liberalism, and the latter had the nuclear weapons to do so.

Fukuyama is correct to observe that liberal capitalism is now the only politically global civilization, and to suggest that "the present world seems to confirm that the fundamental principles of sociopolitical organization have not advanced terribly far since 1806." But neither of these propositions can justify his Idealist, ahistorical assertion that liberal capitalist civilization is the absolute end of history, the definitively final civilization. Indeed, there are enduring reasons why liberal capitalist democracy will always evoke external and internal challenges, as I will later attempt to show.

Fukuyama's vision of history's culmination and my Genesis image are both exaggerations, of course. But if a theorist's only choice is what type of error to make, I offer mine as likely to prove more accurate in assigning meaning and more helpful in attempting to influence the world that we are about to enter. The global transformation of boundaries and identities that the Leninist extinction has set in motion is more apt to resemble the world outlined in Genesis than the stingy and static picture of things to come that Fukuyama presents.

Shifting Boundaries

The cataclysm that befell the Leninist world in 1989 can be understood as a kind of mass extinction. In paleontology, a mass extinction is defined as the abrupt and accelerated termination of a species that is distributed globally or nearly so. What separates it from other forms of extinction is its rapid and comprehensive character. Leninism has suffered the sudden destruction of its "genetic" or identity-defining features—those that provided each Leninist regime, and the Leninist "regime-world" as a whole, with a continuously recognizable identity across time and space. The concept of class war, the correct ideological line, the vanguard party as the exclusive locus of leadership, and the Soviet Union as the incarnation of revolutionary socialism have all been rejected in the Soviet Union itself, and Soviet support was withdrawn from the Leninist replica regimes of Eastern Europe. The momentous result has been the collapse of these regimes and the emergence of successor governments aspiring to democracy and capitalism but faced with a distinct and unfavorable Leninist legacy.

That legacy includes a ghetto political culture that views the state with deep-seated suspicion; a distrustful society where people habitually hoard information, goods, and goodwill, and share them with only a few intimates; a widespread penchant for rumormongering that undercuts sober public discourse; and an untried, often apolitical leadership, barely familiar with and often disdainful of the politician's vocation. Moreover, the Soviet-enforced isolation of the nations of Eastern Europe from one another has sadly reinforced these countries' long-held tendencies toward mutual ignorance, distrust, and disdain. All in all, this is not a promising foundation for liberal capitalist democracy.

The first to change among those boundaries and identities that for half a century have determined the world's political, economic, and military complexion will probably be territorial borders. The most immediate and obvious border problems involve the Soviet Union and parts of Eastern Europe. Demands for sovereignty in Georgia, Azerbaijan, Ukraine, the Baltic states, Moldavia, and Russia itself have created turbulence and tension in one of the world's two thermonuclear superpowers. The recent strains between Czechs and Slovaks show how widespread the potential is for shifts in borders and political identities within the old Leninist imperium. In fact, it may turn out that it was a great deal easier to contain a well-bounded and identified Soviet bloc than to prevent the current crises of boundaries and identities in the same area from spilling over into adjacent areas.

The potential disintegration of Yugoslavia could remake the map of southeastern Europe. The Macedonian question is not settled, and could entangle Serbia, Bulgaria, and possibly Turkey. In fact, given the current crises in the Persian Gulf, Soviet Central Asia, Bulgaria, and Yugoslavia, Turkey may emerge as a pivotal nation in a radically reshaped political region comprising parts of the Middle East, the Balkans, and Central Asia.

The Soviet Union's Central Asian republics, home to many of the USSR's more than 50 million Muslims, are demanding sovereignty. In a recent *New York Times* report, Barbara Crossette observed: "Central Asia is an old idea taking on new life not only in Pakistan but also in the Muslim world beyond the Middle East—as far east as China's Xinjiang region. . . . [A] process, however tenuous and exploratory, of rediscovering old cultural, historical, religious, and commercial bonds is underway, perhaps most of all in Pakistan, the nation in the middle."[2] This has stirred concern in India, which fears that it may one day find itself facing an Islamic bloc stretching from the Pakistani frontier to the edges of Europe.

The Leninist world of East Asia, too, may undergo border and political-identity changes. Leninist rule in China rests on the continued presence of its founding cadres, leaders who have the one thing that Eastern Europe's Leninist rulers lacked in 1989: confidence in their own political and ideological purpose. But neither the Chinese, the North Korean, nor the Vietnamese regime can any longer define that purpose in practical terms. All are drifting toward extinction. In North Korea, the death of Kim Il Sung will immediately raise the threatening issue of unification with the South. In China, the inevitable dying off of the communist gerontocrats will raise the threat of centrifugal regionalism.

For decades, the compelling reality of the Soviet-American rivalry gave substance and stability to formal territorial boundaries in the Third World. The influence of Washington and Moscow on their respective Third World clients, given each superpower's fear that a change in boundaries might aid its rival, helped to stabilize international borders. The Leninist extinction and America's consequent declaration of the end of the Cold War have changed all that. Old historical issues and frames of reference have reasserted their claims on the attention of many Third World elites. President Hafez Assad of Syria has a mural in his office depicting the Battle of Hittin, where Saladin won a crucial victory over the Crusaders in 1187. Assad values it because Hittin was "where the Arabs defeated the West." His frame of reference is one that promises to become more salient and consequential in a world without Leninism.

In coming to grips with the Leninist extinction's global impact we must be ready for chaos in some places, opportunities in others, and for the slim but persistent possibility that new civilizations might emerge.

New Ways of Life

The emerging international environment's primary characteristic will be turbulence of an order not seen during the Cold War. In this new world, leaders will matter more than institutions, charisma more than political economy. It is precisely at such times—when existing boundaries and identities, international and national, institutional and psychological, are challenged—that charismatic leaders offer themselves as sources of certainty and promise. We can expect their appearance, for William James's observation that societies "at any given moment offer ambiguous potentialities of development . . . leaders give the form"[3] is particularly true of Genesis environments.

Even charismatic leaders, to the extent that they are constrained to act in the context of existing state institutions, will be of real but only limited consequence; they may affect the distribution of power in a larger or smaller area, but will be powerless to institute truly epochal changes. It is also possible, however, that in a turbulent, dislocating, traumatic Genesis environment the dissolution of existing boundaries and identities can generate a corresponding potential for the appearance of genuinely new *ways of life*.

A new way of life consists of a new ideology that militantly rejects existing social, economic, religious, administrative, political, and cultural institutions. It calls for the creation of new and better ones (this invidious element is essential); a new political language that "names" and delineates the new way of life; a new and potent institutional expression; the emergence of a social base from which members and leaders can be drawn; the assignment and acceptance of a great historical task demanding risk and sacrifice; and finally, a geographical or institutional core area able to furnish resources equal to the task of creating a new way of life.

Some historical examples should make the argument more evocative. Liberal ideology asserted a new social ontology in which the individual was the basis of social identity and responsibility. Capitalism and democracy (as Karl Polanyi so brilliantly grasped)[4] required a new way of life, not the mere redistribution of power. Nazism and Leninism made ideological demands of the same order (though not, of course, of the same content).

All new ways of life depend on a new political vocabulary; Leninism is unimaginable without its talk of "the dictatorship of the proletariat," "the vanguard party," "the correct line," and "democratic centralism." Similarly, every new way of life—social, economic, political, or cultural—must be embodied in a novel institution and partisan pattern of authoritative behavior. Absolutism had the royal court; liberalism, the market and Parliament; Leninism, the Party and the Plan. For each new way of life there must be a social base uprooted from its previous identity, available for a new one, and drawn to the new ideology. From this base a new elite can emerge: royalist officials, ascetic capitalist entrepreneurs, Bolshevik cadres, or SS men.

For a new way of life to assert itself, a determined minority must completely identify with a mission—establishing the supremacy of the king; of free trade and the market; of the race and the Fuhrer; or of the Party and the *kollectiv*—for a critical period during which new elites, practices, organizations, and beliefs can crystallize.

I am not claiming that a new way of life will inevitably appear in response to Leninism's extinction, merely that the historical "clearing away" and attendant trauma associated with this momentous event could occasion such a development. In the next decade and beyond, an unusual number of leaders and movements will appear to press for some new way of life or the restoration of some bygone glory. Saddam Hussein's current attempt to rouse the Arab Muslim peoples is only the first effort of this kind. Most or even all of the aspirants will fail. But they will be both signs and causes of growing national and international disorder. All this, in a sense, does mean the end of history—the history of the last 45 or even 200 years. But it does not mean the inexorable assimilation of the world to the current Western liberal way of life, nor even the continued adaptive strength of the liberal West.

Liberalism and Its Critics

The growth of disorder and turbulence, the appearance of charismatic leaders and movements, and the possible evolution of new ways of life will occur in a political universe that may now be running on inertia, but which is for the moment still well delineated nationally and internationally. The proliferation of Genesis environments does not mean that developments will be either apocalyptic or unintelligible. Precisely because Genesis environments develop out of and in opposition to more delineated and "named" environments, the theorist is well positioned to grasp the interconnections and meanings of events. After the extirpation of Fascism-Nazism and the extinction of Leninism, what next? What developments are most likely in a world dominated by the liberal capitalist democratic civilization? I confidently predict one general trend.

Liberal capitalist democracy has aroused a heterogeneous set of opponents: Romantic poets, Persian ayatollahs, aristocrats, the Roman Catholic Church, and fascists. For all the real and massive differences that separate these diverse oppositions, one can detect a shared critique. Liberal capitalist democracy is scorned for an inordinate emphasis on individualism, materialism, technical achievement, and rationality. While the Roman Catholic preference for the family over the individual as the basic unit of society and the Nazi preference for the "race" differ radically as positive alternatives, there is a common negative theme: liberal capitalism is indicted for undervaluing the essential collective dimension of human existence.

Similarly, liberal capitalism has regularly evoked passionate criticism of its tendency to ignore or marginalize the human need for security, and its repression of spontaneity and expressive human action. But nothing has been more central to liberal capitalism, or more capable of eliciting opposition over the last 200 years, than its elevation of rational impersonality as the organizing principle of social life. Liberal capitalist democracy rejects the ethos of heroic striving, awe, and mystery that throughout most of history has been seen as raising man above the level of the brutes and the realm of iron necessity. This rejection has evoked criticism from various sources within liberal societies; it has also helped to arouse countermovements as perverse as Nazism and Stalinism.

But no matter how impressive liberal capitalist democracy's triumphs over the Catholic Church, the Fascist and Nazi movements, and now Leninism may be, these remain *particular* victories. Precisely because liberal capitalist democracy has a partisan identity, it cannot be or do all things equally. As long as the West embodies this partisan identity, it will regularly witness the rise of both internal and external movements dedicated to destroying or reforming it—movements that in one form or another will stress ideals of group membership, expressive behavior, collective solidarity, and heroic action. A major locus for such movements will be the Third World.

Beginning with India's independence in 1947, many opponents of the liberal West have looked upon the Third World as a source of promise. But the promise has yet to be realized: with the possible exception of Islamic fundamentalism, no new way of life has emerged anywhere in the Third World. No new ideology has been embraced by leaders who go on to create a new political vocabulary for, and recruit a new leadership stratum from, a mobilized social base that can populate innovative institutions, pursue historically extraordinary tasks, and draw from a powerful and prestigious core area. No London, Moscow, Mecca, or Rome has arisen in the Third World. Instead, one generally sees depressingly familiar examples of tyranny, corruption, famine, and rage in prenational settings. Even so, it would be premature to dismiss the Third World as a potential source for a new way of life; most of the ex-colonial world, after all, has been independent for only a few decades.

Movements of Rage

Yet even if no new civilization emerges from the Third World, developments there do not augur well for the adoption of liberal capitalist democracy. I want to examine three such developments: the continuing obstacles to democratic consolidation; wars between Third World countries; and, above all, movements of rage.

It is amazing to contemplate the facility with which Latin Americanists who quite recently were gloomily speaking and writing about the "breakdown of democracy" have begun to enthuse about the "transition to democracy"—not only in Latin America but, by unwarranted extrapolation, in Eastern Europe and the Soviet Union as well. Economic and social development in a nation places the question of democracy on the agenda, but an irreversible transition to democracy requires much more in the way of sociocultural and institutional preconditions. The history of Argentina bears perpetual witness to this. Poorer countries like the Philippines, where democratic political institutions are facades that do not match the country's social and cultural "constitution" or the military's political culture, will find the transition to stable democracy even harder to achieve. Even India's circumscribed and faulty but still substantial democracy is beset by growing threats of regional, linguistic, and religious conflict as the Congress Party-based pan-Indian generation of bureaucrats, officers, and politicians passes from the scene.

The Leninist extinction favors an increase in the number of wars fought between Third World countries. Many such countries have been left (courtesy of colonialism) with arbitrary borders and fictive national identities; absent the old Soviet-American rivalry, Third World irredentisms will flare up more often and more intensely. Their significance will vary, ranging from sad but peripheral cases like Liberia, with its civil war and consequent invasion by several divided West African nations, to the Iraqi invasion of Kuwait with its massive international repercussions. Saddam Hussein's annexation of his oil-rich neighbor is a case of a Third World leader attempting to create favorable new boundaries and political identities in what he sees as a disrupted, and therefore both promising and threatening, environment.

In the near future the most extraordinary Third World trend may be the rise and triumph of what I call "movements of rage." Although not yet grouped together by theorists, some such movements have already emerged: the Mulele uprising in the Kwilu province of Zaire, the Tupamaros in Uruguay, the Khalq in Afghanistan, the Khmer Rouge in Kampuchea, and the Shining Path insurgency in Peru. All are revolutionary movements with a Leninist or Maoist vocabulary but an ethos akin to the thought of Frantz Fanon. Their motivating spirit is nihilistic rage against the legacy of Western colonialism. These movements typically originate in resentments held by provincial elites—men and women who seethe with loathing for the culture of the metropolis, and yet at the same time feel enraged at being excluded from it. Their murderous ire is aimed at those who have been "contaminated" by contact with Western culture: those who wear ties, speak European languages, or have Western educations.

Movements of rage are nihilistic backlashes against failure: the failure of the Third World to create productive economies, equitable societies, ethical elites, and sovereign nations. They are desperate responses to the fact that nothing seems to work. The hoped-for magical effect of adopted labels like "one-party democracy," "Leninism," or (as is now becoming fashionable) "market capitalist democracy" has been and will continue to be a disappointment for most Third World countries. Movements of rage are violent nativist responses to the resulting frustration and perplexity.

One can question whether I have proved the existence of a new type of revolutionary movement, a Third World variant of fascism. Very few of these movements have come to power, and when they do (as in Afghanistan and Kampuchea), they self-destruct. So did the Nazi regime—at the cost of 50 million lives.

In any case, the failure of many movements of rage to come to power so far tells us very little about their potential in a post-Leninist world, unless one believes that the Leninist extinction is a self-contained event. The burden of my entire argument has been to challenge that assumption. In the new, more turbulent Genesis environments emerging in Leninism's aftermath, one cannot gauge the potential for future movements of rage by generalizing from their earlier failures.

Instead, one must imagine a Third World increasingly neglected by the United States and the Soviet Union except when a very clear and pressing emergency occurs in a strategic location; a Third World where aggression occurs more and more frequently; where nuclear-weapons technology is more widely dispersed; where the few democracies that have any standing (such as India) may fail; and where checks on emigration to the West remove a vital escape valve. In this far from ideal world, movements of rage might indeed become a significantly disruptive international force, especially if one appears in a country like Mexico.

The Long March to Democracy

The Leninist extinction is not a surgical historical strike that will leave the liberal regimes of the West and their Third World allies unaffected. All horizons, including the West's, will be dramatically affected.

Yet does not the worldwide rush toward liberal capitalist democratic idioms, policies, and institutional facades refute this claim? And what of the shift by socialist parties to positions that differ insignificantly from their historic capitalist antagonists; the tentative moves toward a multiparty system in African socialist regimes; the belief by many East Europeans in the market's miraculous quality? These are not illusory phenomena; they are real. But how significant and persistent will they turn out to be? If one interprets these phenomena in developmental rather than static terms, then their significance also resides in the predictable surge of anger that will follow the equally predictable failure (in most cases) of the market and electoral democracy to produce sovereign, productive, equitable nations in the greater part of Eastern Europe, the former Soviet Union, and the Third World.

It would be more accurate to think of a "long march" rather than a simple transition to democracy. Not every route has to be a copy of a prior Western one; alternative courses will be possible, but exceptional. In the maelstrom of the Soviet Union and Eastern Europe, one must expect bishops, generals, and demagogues to be as prominent as entrepreneurs, intellectuals, and democrats. In a Third World ridden with failure and wracked with frustration, one must be prepared for rage. Finally, one must also take note of the emerging worldwide conflict between liberally oriented "civics" and insular "ethnics," a conflict that directly calls into question the value and status of liberal democratic individualism even in the West.

No amount of optimism about the twenty-first century should be allowed to obscure the significance of the nineteenth-century insight that political forms are integrally related to cultural and social patterns. It would be a shame if, with the defeat of the Leninist organizational weapon, Western intellectuals replaced it with a superficial notion of democratic institution building.

Democracy remains a possible outcome, though one that is historically rare and whose birth is usually painful. Those who wish democracy well should remember this, and make a patient effort to endure the "long march" that lies ahead.

NOTES

1. Francis Fukuyama, "The End of History?" *The National Interest* 16 (Summer 1989): 3-18.

2. Barbara Crossette, "Central Asia Rediscovers Its Identity," *New York Times*, 24 June 1990, E3.

3. William James, *The Will to Believe* (New York: Dover Publications, 1956), 227-8.

4. Karl Polanyi, *The Great Transformation: The Political and Economic Origins of Our Time* (Boston: Beacon Press, 1965). See especially chapters 3-10.

3.
THE DEMOCRATIC MOMENT

Marc F. Plattner

Marc F. Plattner *is coeditor of the* Journal of Democracy *and counselor at the National Endowment for Democracy. He is the author of* Rousseau's State of Nature *(1979), and the editor of* Human Rights in Our Time *(1984). His essay is an updated version of an April 1991 lecture at the John M. Olin Center for Inquiry into the Theory and Practice of Democracy at the University of Chicago.*

The dramatic events of August 1991 in Moscow should convince any remaining skeptics that the democratic revolutions of 1989 indeed marked a watershed in world history. The sudden downfall that year of long-entrenched Communist regimes throughout Eastern Europe dramatically transformed the face of world politics. Together with the remarkable changes that had already taken place in both the foreign and domestic policies of the Soviet Union, this development effectively brought to an end the period, beginning in 1945, that has generally been labeled the postwar or Cold War era. Yet despite the general consensus that we have now entered the post-Cold War era, there is sharp disagreement about what the nature and characteristics of this new period will be.

Before addressing this central question, it is worth briefly reviewing the Cold War era and the dynamics that brought it to a close. In the years following the Second World War, the militarily strongest and economically most advanced nations of the world became divided into two sharply opposed camps headed by two superpowers, the United States and the Soviet Union. The division of the world into East and West was marked by the "Iron Curtain" that ran through the middle of Germany and the heart of Central Europe. But the split between East and West was not only geopolitical; it was also a conflict between two fundamentally opposed ideologies—Leninist communism and liberal democracy. Many countries sought to maintain varying degrees of neutrality in this struggle, styling themselves as the Nonaligned Movement or the Third World, but they remained more an arena for superpower competition than a potent independent force in global politics. It is hard to quarrel with the characterization of the international system during the Cold War era as a bipolar world.

Although there was great immobility in this system from 1949 on, the changes that did take place generally seemed to strengthen the Soviet camp. It is now apparent to almost everyone that the communist regimes had long been disintegrating from within, but during most of the Cold War period communism seemed to be enjoying a slow but steady ascendancy. It gradually brought a number of additional non-European countries into its orbit; during the 1970s alone, new procommunist regimes emerged in some dozen nations. Even more significant was the seeming irreversibility of such gains. In fact, until the U.S. intervention in Grenada in 1983, not a single consolidated communist regime had ever been displaced.

Meanwhile, democracy, after receiving a brief ideological boost from the establishment of new democratic regimes during the wave of decolonization, seemed to be in deep trouble. The postcolonial democracies almost all soon failed, giving way to regimes that were authoritarian and generally "nonaligned," though with a strong admixture of hostility toward the West. The imposition of dictatorial rule in India by Indira Gandhi in 1975, seemingly bringing to an end the largest and most important democracy in the non-Western world, marked a low point for democratic fortunes. At that very moment, Daniel Patrick Moynihan, a staunch champion of liberal democracy, despairingly wrote:

> Liberal democracy on the American model increasingly tends to the condition of monarchy in the nineteenth century: a holdover form of government, one which persists in isolated or peculiar places here and there, and may even serve well enough for special circumstances, but which has simply no relevance to the future. It is where the world was, not where it is going.[1]

Although the late 1970s witnessed transitions to democracy in Spain and Portugal and its restoration in India, only in the 1980s did it become clear that Moynihan's pessimism was unfounded and that democracy was experiencing a true resurgence. The democratic tide swept through most of Latin America, reached such key Asian countries as the Philippines, Korea, Taiwan, and Pakistan, and by decade's end was beginning to make ripples in sub-Saharan Africa and even the Middle East. Moreover, the 1980s saw such Third World alternatives to democracy as African socialism and bureaucratic authoritarianism in Latin America revealed as political and economic failures.

Most dramatic, of course, was the growing crisis—and in some places the sudden collapse—of communism. Not only did the 1980s witness no new communist gains, but existing communist regimes were suddenly thrown on the defensive. Relatively new pro-Soviet regimes were challenged by U.S.-backed anticommunist insurgencies in Afghanistan, Angola, and Nicaragua. Yet while these armed resistance movements may have taken a physical, economic, and psychological toll on communist governments, it is noteworthy that so far they have nowhere come to power. Except for the cases of Romania and Ethiopia (where the victorious insurgent movements were Marxist in origin), East European and Third World communist regimes have ceded power largely through negotiations, elections, and other peaceful means.

This peaceful denouement was made possible, of course, by the internal crisis of communism at its very core in the Soviet Union. We are still very far from having an adequate understanding of how this once seemingly impregnable regime could crumble so quickly, or of the motives and strategies of the chief architect of its undoing, Mikhail Gorbachev. What does seem clear is that by the 1980s, Soviet communism faced a choice between continuing socioeconomic stagnation and reform. But modest reform proved incapable of overcoming stagnation, and more thoroughgoing reform proved impossible without decisively undermining the communist system. In the formulation of one of communism's most acute analysts, the Yugoslav dissident Milovan Djilas, the liberalization of communism turned out to be identical with the crisis of communism.

Even more damaging to communism than its economic failures and foreign policy reverses was its ideological self-discrediting. By attributing their system's shortcomings to its lack of economic markets and political democracy, the Soviet leaders effectively conceded the ideological struggle to the West, and dealt communism's worldwide appeal a mortal blow. Who wants to devote oneself to a cause that has been repudiated by its own most prominent spokesmen? Today's international political heroes are no longer leftist revolutionaries, but the peaceful protesters demanding democracy who were so brutally crushed in Tiananmen Square or who triumphed in Wenceslas Square (and, most recently, at the barricades surrounding the Russian Parliament). In this context, let us also note what may be viewed as a coda to the revolutions of 1989: the peaceful rejection of the Sandinistas at the polls by the people of Nicaragua, which ended the last pro-Soviet Third World regime still capable of eliciting passionate support in the West.

The Post-Cold War World

We thus find ourselves living in the new post-Cold War world—a world with one dominant principle of political legitimacy, democracy, and only one superpower, the United States. But how long can this, the democratic moment, last? Is democracy's unchallenged preeminence, with no serious geopolitical or ideological rivals, only transitory, a momentary worldwide "era of good feelings" that will soon give way to bitter new divisions? Or does it signal a lasting victory due either to democracy's own inherent strengths or to the shortcomings of antidemocratic regimes and ideologies?

The most forceful statement of the latter view, of course, is to be found in Francis Fukuyama's now famous article on "The End of History," where he asserts that we may be witnessing "the end point of man's ideological evolution and the universalization of Western liberal democracy as the final form of human government." While there is reason to be dubious about the metaphysical trappings and sweeping conclusions of Fukuyama's thesis, he was absolutely right with respect to what may be considered the essential premise of his essay—namely, "the total exhaustion of viable systematic alternatives to Western liberalism."[2]

The collapse of communism and the manifest failure of various authoritarian brands of Third Worldism have resulted in the absence of a single nondemocratic regime in the world with wide appeal. They have also led to a drastic weakening of openly antidemocratic forces within democratic regimes. Just as the defeat of fascism led to the virtual disappearance of the antidemocratic right in the West, so the downfall of communism seems to be causing the withering away of the antidemocratic left.

Moreover, it is not solely the extreme or antidemocratic left that has suffered from the crisis of "really existing socialism." For example, Miklós Haraszti, a former underground writer who is now a member of the Hungarian parliament, describes the current political spectrum in his country as follows:

> All in all what we have here is a quite classic European feature: a conservative and liberal side to modern society, where in conformity with the political reality of postcommunist democracy there is no left as such. . . . In postcommunist societies, you see, the left is dead. . . . So the structure we have now is an American kind of political split, and in that sense East European politics is closer to the U.S. rather than the West European model."[3]

Yet to some extent the development Haraszti describes in Eastern Europe can also be observed in Western Europe (and even Latin America), as socialist parties continue to move toward the center.[4] Without too much exaggeration, one might say that today there is no Left left. Everywhere in the more advanced countries, politics is tending to move closer to the U.S. model—not only in being influenced by American campaign and media techniques, but in the more important respect of being dominated by moderate center-left and center-right parties united in agreement on fundamental democratic principles and procedures, and increasingly on an acceptance of the market economy as well.

Even before the collapse of communism, the 1980s had witnessed a remarkable rehabilitation of free-market economics in the West. Not only had capitalism gained a new intellectual respectability, but the successful entrepreneur once again became an object of admiration. By contrast, state ownership of the means of production came to be identified not with economic progress but with stagnation. The eagerness of communist and especially postcommunist countries to transform themselves into market economies dramatically reinforced this trend.

The discrediting of traditional socialist economics contributed significantly to restoring the self-confidence of liberal democracy. It helped bring to an end a long-established tendency in the West to view modern democracy as moving "progressively" in the direction of an ever greater role for the state, and even to see socialism as the logical culmination of liberal democracy. From this perspective, no matter how retrograde communist states may have seemed with respect to their denial of civil and political liberties, they nonetheless had some claim to be more "modern," to represent the wave of the future. The evidence and testimony that have recently emerged from Eastern Europe and the Soviet Union have utterly undermined this way of thinking.

Rejoining World Civilization

Indeed, today it is the liberal democracies that are widely regarded as the only truly and fully modern societies. This sentiment is reflected in the often expressed desire on the part of Soviets and East Europeans to live in a "normal society." It is a sentiment that was shared not only by dissident intellectuals but also by many representatives of the ruling elites—especially by those who had traveled abroad—and it played a critical role in the demise of communist regimes.

These regimes founded their legitimacy on an ideology that claimed that its adherents constituted the vanguard of a new world. Yet the people living under these regimes came to realize that they were drifting into backwardness and stagnation, that the world was passing them by, that they were laboring under what Milan Šimečka called "the burden of wasted time."[15] In a speech to the Russian parliament, Boris Yeltsin blamed the socialist experiment for leaving the people of the Soviet Union "at the tail end of world civilization."[6]

When they speak of rejoining world civilization, Soviets and East Europeans mean that they want to return to "Europe"—to a market economy and to political democracy. Václav Klaus, the finance minister of Czechoslovakia and the elected leader of Civic Forum, recently stated in answer to a question about his country's economic policies: "We are absolutely not interested in a 'third way' solution. I believe that 'the third way' is the fastest way to the Third World."[7] Many others, both in the West and in the Third World itself, have now come to identify statist economies and nondemocratic polities with corruption and retrogression. Third World intellectuals whose greatest worry once was that their countries would be dominated by Western capital now voice the fear that Latin America or Africa will become "marginalized" from the world economy.

It is true, of course, that not all nondemocratic Third World regimes have been economic failures. In fact, some authoritarian regimes with relatively open, market-oriented economies—Taiwan, Korea, Chile—have achieved extraordinary economic success. Yet that very success, by fostering and augmenting the power of a self-reliant and outward-looking middle class, has raised popular demands for democratic government that have led to significant political transformations in all of these countries. Authoritarian rulers in developing countries seem to face a kind of Catch-22: they are undermined by both economic failure and economic success.

These economically successful Third World authoritarian regimes have held some attraction for certain communist reformers. This has led to the curious spectacle of Taiwan becoming a model in some quarters in Beijing and Pinochet becoming a hero in some quarters in Moscow. The arguments of many of those in both countries attracted by this "neoauthoritarian" model are similar: The premature introduction of political democracy, they assert, will allow popular opposition to forestall the painful measures necessary to introduce a market economy. A strong hand, à la Pinochet, is needed to implement the economic reforms, which will in turn lay the basis for the gradual transition to democracy. It is interesting to note that the strongest argument in favor of authoritarianism today is its alleged ability to dismantle a socialist economy. But even this neoauthoritarian doctrine seems to acknowledge the ultimate superiority of liberal democracy as the eventual goal toward which it aims.

While there may be room for debate about the relative capacity of democracies and market-oriented authoritarian regimes to achieve economic growth in developing countries, only democracy seems compatible with economic success in the advanced nations. Soviet-style command economies may have achieved substantial gains at an earlier phase of industrialization, but building more and bigger steel mills is no longer the measure of economic progress. In the era of computers and instant worldwide telecommunications, innovation, adaptability, and openness to the world economy are essential to maintaining economic competitiveness. And it is difficult for these characteristics to persist for long where political freedom is seriously curtailed.

Democracies also appear to enjoy a comparable advantage with respect to military power. Despite their generally pacific character, they are more capable of producing and operating the weapons that are essential to victory on the battlefield. As Adam Smith had already observed two centuries ago: "In modern war the great expense of firearms gives an evident advantage to the nation which can best afford that expense."[8] Today, as the war against Iraq has underlined, technological superiority is as essential as the ability to equip, deploy, and maintain a large force in the field. It would be rash, given the evidence of past Nazi and Soviet military achievements, to be overconfident about the inability of totalitarian powers to compete militarily with democracies. Yet it does seem that a growing sense of being unable to keep pace economically and technologically in their military competition with the United States was crucial in persuading the Soviet elite to embark on the path of reform.

Democracy seems, then, to enjoy superiority not merely in popular legitimacy and ideological appeal, but also in economic and military strength. And it is difficult to discern any powerful new nondemocratic ideological, economic, or military challengers on the horizon. All this would appear to suggest that, if we have not yet arrived at Fukuyama's "end of history," we may at least be entering a sustained period of peaceful democratic hegemony—a kind of "Pax Democratica."

A New Ideology?

Perhaps the most compelling counterargument to this view of democracy triumphant has been presented by Ken Jowitt.[9] Although writing in explicit opposition to Fukuyama, Jowitt agrees with him that the collapse of communism has resulted in a situation where "liberal capitalism is now the only politically global civilization." For Jowitt, however, this is only an initial and temporary effect of what he calls "the Leninist extinction." He argues that the sudden demise of one of the two camps long engaged in a comprehensive global struggle will lead not to the easy and unchallenged ascendancy of its rival but to a radical reshaping of all the previously fixed boundaries of international politics.

In the first place, this refers to the territorial borders that separate sovereign states. The Leninist extinction not only has fostered the breakup of the Soviet Union but is likely to unleash more open ethnic conflict and the redrawing of national borders among peoples who were previously restrained by Soviet imperial power. There is ample historical precedent for believing that the breakup of empires can lead to new eruptions of long-dormant conflicts between previously subject peoples. Brian Urquhart, who served for several decades as UN undersecretary general for special political affairs, has said that most of his professional life was spent dealing with the problems that the British Empire left in its wake—the Arab-Israeli conflict, the Indo-Pakistani conflict, the Nigerian civil war, the Cyprus dispute. (If Urquhart had stayed on the job a bit longer, he could have added the Iraq-Kuwait conflict to the list.) It would not be surprising if UN officials in the decades ahead were to find themselves similarly preoccupied with crises arising from conflicts between Armenians and Azeris, Hungarians and Romanians, or Croats and Serbs.

But Jowitt argues that the disorder spawned by the Leninist extinction will not be confined to the peoples who once lived under the Leninist yoke. During the Cold War, the superpowers' influence over their client states and their fear of a wider conflict helped to maintain the territorial status quo. Today superpower rivalry is much diminished as a source of Third World conflict, but by the same token it no longer serves to restrain the ambitions of local rulers. Saddam Hussein's invasion of Kuwait is a dramatic example of how the diminution of Soviet power might lead to new regional instability. To be sure, Saddam's expulsion from Kuwait has sent a most salutary message to Third World dictators contemplating territorial aggression. Yet there is reason to doubt that the West would respond so resolutely to aggression in a strategically less critical area of the world.

Jowitt's argument goes beyond asserting that the Leninist extinction will lead to an increase in local wars and a redrawing of territorial boundaries. For he asserts that the vacuum left behind by the "clearing away" of communism may well be filled by the emergence of new ideologies. Liberal democracy, he argues, cannot hold the field to itself because, in "its elevation of rational impersonality as the organizing principle of social life," it fails to satisfy certain basic human longings. Therefore, the West, in his words, "will regularly witness the rise of both internal and external movements dedicated to destroying or reforming it—movements that in one form or another will stress ideals of group membership, expressive behavior, collective solidarity, and heroic action."

Fukuyama might actually agree with a surprisingly large part of Jowitt's argument. For far from predicting the end of international conflict, Fukuyama envisages "a high and perhaps rising level of ethnic and nationalist violence," as well as the continuation of terrorism and wars of national liberation. Nor would he necessarily dispute Jowitt's prediction that we will see the emergence of what the latter calls "movements of rage" in the Third World—"nihilistic backlashes" against political and economic failure such as are embodied in groups like the Khmer Rouge or Peru's Sendero Luminoso. In a sense Fukuyama responds in advance to possible developments of this kind by stating: "Our task is not to answer exhaustively the challenges to liberalism promoted by every crackpot messiah around the world, but only those that are embodied in important social or political forces and movements, and which are therefore part of world history."

This finally brings us to the heart of the disagreement between these two authors. Fukuyama seems to contend that the liberal democratic idea has definitively triumphed among the advanced nations of the world, and thus that there will not again arise a major power animated by an antidemocratic ideology. Jowitt, by contrast, can envisage the emergence of a new ideology capable of generating a new "way of life"—an ideology whose power to move great nations would be comparable to that of Catholicism, liberal democracy, fascism, or Leninism.

Of course, one can only speculate about whether a potent and attractive new ideology will emerge to challenge democracy. Fukuyama persuasively points to the widespread appeal of liberal democracy, its ability to penetrate diverse cultures and win adherents around the world, and the absence of plausible contenders to dethrone it from its current hegemony. Much less convincing, however, is his suggestion that modern liberalism has resolved all the fundamental "contradictions" in human life. As Jowitt argues, liberalism will always leave many human beings unsatisfied and hence will generate powerful antiliberal movements. The real question is whether any such movement can succeed in attaining the economic success and broad appeal necessary to compete successfully with liberalism. The answer, which only the future can reveal, will be decisive for the fate of democracy.

Challenges and Competitors

Despite its broad popular appeal, democracy is not an easy form of government to maintain, especially in poorer countries that lack an educated populace, a substantial middle class, and a democratic culture. The events of the past decade and a half may have exploded the view that democracy can be sustained only in rich Western countries, but they should not give rise to an unwarranted optimism that expects democracy to be quickly achieved and uninterruptedly preserved throughout the world.

It is remarkable how few breakdowns of democracy there have been in the past few years, even under conditions as adverse as those in Peru or the Philippines. Some of the countries that have more recently installed freely elected governments—Nicaragua, Haiti, and Benin, for example—face still more daunting challenges in trying to create stable democratic institutions. Even the formerly communist countries, despite their European heritage and relatively higher levels of economic development, confront an enormously difficult task in seeking simultaneously to introduce market economies and to consolidate democratic political systems. All these experiments currently benefit both from the extraordinary worldwide momentum and prestige of democracy, and from still vivid memories of the tyrannical and unsuccessful regimes that they supplanted. Yet as these memories fade and the new democracies encounter the inevitable difficulties that lie ahead, it is only to be expected that some of them will sink back into authoritarianism.

Such backsliding would undoubtedly be a great misfortune for the people of these countries, and it could very easily create some serious economic and foreign policy problems for the established democracies. Yet its impact on the overall fortunes of democracy in the world would not be all that great, so long as no weighty new ideological rival to democracy appears on the scene. If the majority of the new democracies fail and revert to various local brands of authoritarianism, the view might once again become current that democracy is an unworkable or inappropriate system for developing countries, but the presumption would remain that it is the only form of government suitable for advanced and economically successful nations.

We would then have a kind of two-tier world, with the top tier consisting of a global democratic civilization and an integrated world economy, and the bottom tier occupied by backward, failed, or otherwise marginalized nations. In many ways this would be an ugly world to live in, and the plight of the bottom tier would have ramifications that could not be wholly and neatly sealed off and kept beyond the confines of the democratic countries. There would be problems of access to raw materials, illegal immigration, refugee flows, famine, terrorism, drug trafficking, and a host of other difficulties to contend with—many of which we are already facing. The problems would become even more acute if major economic or political breakdowns were to afflict such strategically located countries as Algeria or Mexico. Yet none of this by itself would pose a mortal threat to democratic hegemony.

Democracy's preeminence can be seriously challenged only by an ideology with universalist aspirations that proves capable of coming to power in an economically advanced or militarily powerful nation. Though there are no convincing signs of the emergence of such an ideology at this time, it is worth taking a brief look at the major alternatives often cited as competitors to democracy.

The first of these is nationalism, which is clearly enjoying a resurgence in many parts of the world, even as its influence appears to be waning elsewhere. Nationalism, however, is not a universalist ideology, but a category that embraces a myriad of particularisms. Serbian nationalism and Croatian nationalism may share many formal similarities, but the former will have no appeal to Croats and the latter no appeal to Serbs. Moreover, nationalism as such does not mandate any particular kind of political order. One can find Russian nationalists, for example, who are Communists, fascists, monarchists—or democrats. Nationalist passions may indeed threaten democracy in many specific circumstances, and ethnic strife can be a serious problem for established as well as new democracies. But in principle nationalism is by no means incompatible with democracy. In fact, as the case of the Baltic peoples makes clear, nationalist movements are often strongly democratic.

Turning next to religious doctrines, it is clear that radical or fundamentalist Islam is by far the most formidable competitor to democracy. Indeed, it is probably the most vital alternative to democracy to be found anywhere today. Only among Islamic peoples does opposition to dictatorial regimes frequently express itself in nondemocratic forms; in fact, in some Islamic countries free elections might well bring Islamicist rather than democratic oppositions to power. Yet it is doubtful that fundamentalist Islam can pose a serious global challenge to democracy.

Although Islam holds the allegiance of more than 800 million people who dominate a wide area stretching from West Africa to Southeast Asia, it does not appear to be attracting many adherents outside the Islamic world. Moreover, it is highly questionable whether Islamic fundamentalism can become the basis for economically or militarily successful regimes. When it burst upon the scene a little over a decade ago, the Ayatollah Khomeini's Iran seemed to have tremendous revolutionary élan. Yet it proved incapable of winning a bitter war against a much smaller neighbor, of exporting the revolution to other Islamic countries, or of running a modern economy. It now appears to be following more moderate policies that may help to improve the economy and to stabilize the regime, but it no longer seems to represent even the Islamic wave of the future.

Countries to Watch

Another possible competitor to democracy would be a reinvigorated communism, but the events of August 1991 in the Soviet Union show how unlikely it is that the remaining communist regimes can regain their former vitality. Particularly telling was the fact that the coup plotters made no reference at all to communism in justifying their actions. Even in China, whose octogenarian rulers remain committed communists, knowledgeable observers say that hardly anyone under the age of 40 still believes in Marxism-Leninism. Especially for an ideology oriented toward the future, the failure to attract the young is an unmistakable sign of decay. Communism today appears to be doomed to the fate that Moynihan foresaw for democracy in 1975: it is "a holdover form of government . . . which has simply no relevance to the future. It is where the world was, not where it is going."

The nature and the fate of the successor regimes in the Soviet Union and China will be of decisive importance for the future of democracy—not just because of their size and power but also because of the influence they can exert over Eastern Europe and East Asia respectively. If both these countries were successfully to follow the democratic path, the world might indeed approach Fukuyama's vision of an enduringly triumphant liberal democracy. But if they do not, they offer the most likely seedbeds for the birth of a new antidemocratic ideology.

Democrats have just gained the ascendancy in the Soviet Union, and the passing of Deng Xiaoping may open the way for a revival of the Chinese democratic movement that was so harshly repressed in Tiananmen Square. Yet there are also other important political currents and forces in both countries, including powerful military establishments. The emergence of a military-backed neoauthoritarian regime, possibly after a period of chaos or even civil war, may be as likely an outcome as a stable democracy in both Russia and China. Though a regime of this type might initially claim to be a temporary stop on the road toward democracy, it could easily wind up evolving in unpredictable and antidemocratic directions. And if such a regime were economically or militarily successful, it could quickly become an attractive model for other countries in its region and in the world.

Another possible source for a future alternative to liberal democracy may be Japan and the other noncommunist countries of East Asia. These countries have achieved spectacular economic progress through a synthesis of elements drawn from Confucian and other traditional influences, market economics, and democratic politics. The stability of democracy in Japan and the recent democratic openings in Korea and Taiwan could be taken as evidence of the triumph of liberal democracy in the region. Yet the political systems of these countries operate rather differently from those in the West. As Samuel P. Huntington has pointed out, "the East Asian dominant-party systems seem to involve competition for power but not alternation in power, and participation in elections for all, but participation in office only for those in the 'mainstream' party."[10]

It is not a foregone conclusion that the future will bring East Asia toward a greater convergence with Western-style liberal democracy; it might instead lead to an increased emphasis on those features that distinguish East Asian societies from the West. In that case, East Asia might gradually evolve a new ideology, which, given the extraordinary economic and technological dynamism of the region, could become extremely attractive to other nations as well.

Let us return, then, to the question with which we began: How long will the democratic moment last? I venture to predict that it will endure at least for the remainder of this century. Some recently established democracies will almost certainly fail during the coming decade, but other countries that are now under authoritarian or communist rule are likely to move toward democracy. Though it would be hazardous to forecast beyond that, the three key countries to watch in assessing the longer-term prospects for democracy in the world are Russia, China, and Japan.

There is one other key country, however, that has not yet been mentioned—the United States. If in 1980 a political analyst had sought to predict the future of communism on the basis of a survey of the international scene, he almost certainly would have gotten things very wrong; for he would have missed the most important factor—the largely hidden internal decay of the Soviet Union. This is certainly not meant to imply that the United States today is in an analogous situation. Yet as observers on all points of the U.S. political spectrum seem to agree, there are many reasons to worry about the political, economic, and cultural health of American democracy. A serious social or economic crisis in the United States would not only be terrible for Americans, it would have a devastating effect on the fortunes of democracy worldwide. Thus the highest priority for Americans must be to repair the fabric of our own democratic order.

That is not to advocate, however, that America "come home" and turn its back on its international responsibilities as the world's leading democracy. It is true that the energies and resources of the United States are not unlimited, but if properly directed, they are sufficient for both its domestic and international needs. There is no real conflict between improving democracy at home and supporting its spread and consolidation abroad. Just as the model provided by a healthy United States enhances the aspiration for democracy elsewhere, so the progress of the struggle for democracy around the world can give Americans renewed appreciation of the principles on which our country was founded and on which its future success depends.

NOTES

1. Daniel P. Moynihan, "The American Experiment," *The Public Interest* 41 (Fall 1975), 6.

2. Francis Fukuyama, "The End of History," *The National Interest* 16 (Summer 1989), 3-18.

3. Miklós Haraszti, "A Choice Between Resolution and Emotion," *East European Reporter*, Spring-Summer 1990, 76.

4. See Seymour Martin Lipset, "The Death of the Third Way," *The National Interest* 20 (Summer 1990), 25-37.

5. Milan Šimečka, "The Restoration of Freedom," *Journal of Democracy* 1 (Summer 1990): 3-12.

6. *Washington Post*, 31 March 1991, A23.

7. Interview with Václav Klaus, *NFF Update*, Winter 1991, 2.

8. Adam Smith, *The Wealth of Nations*, 2 vols. (Chicago: University of Chicago Press, 1976), 2:230.

9. Ken Jowitt, "The New World Disorder," *Journal of Democracy* 2 (Winter 1991): 11-20.

10. Samuel P. Huntington, "Democracy's Third Wave," *Journal of Democracy* 2 (Spring 1991): 27.

4. WHAT DEMOCRACY IS . . . AND IS NOT

Philippe C. Schmitter & Terry Lynn Karl

***Phillippe C. Schmitter** is professor of political science and former director of the Center for European Studies at Stanford University. **Terry Lynn Karl** is associate professor of political science and director of the Center for Latin American Studies at the same institution.* *The original, longer version of this essay was written at the request of the United States Agency for International Development, which is not responsible for its content.*

For some time, the word democracy has been circulating as a debased currency in the political marketplace. Politicians with a wide range of convictions and practices strove to appropriate the label and attach it to their actions. Scholars, conversely, hesitated to use it—without adding qualifying adjectives—because of the ambiguity that surrounds it. The distinguished American political theorist Robert Dahl even tried to introduce a new term, "polyarchy," in its stead in the (vain) hope of gaining a greater measure of conceptual precision. But for better or worse, we are "stuck" with democracy as the catchword of contemporary political discourse. It is the word that resonates in people's minds and springs from their lips as they struggle for freedom and a better way of life; it is the word whose meaning we must discern if it is to be of any use in guiding political analysis and practice.

The wave of transitions away from autocratic rule that began with Portugal's "Revolution of the Carnations" in 1974 and seems to have crested with the collapse of communist regimes across Eastern Europe in 1989 has produced a welcome convergence towards a common definition of democracy.[1] Everywhere there has been a silent abandonment of dubious adjectives like "popular," "guided," "bourgeois," and "formal" to modify "democracy." At the same time, a remarkable consensus has emerged concerning the minimal conditions that polities must meet in order to merit the prestigious appellation of "democratic." Moreover, a number of international organizations now monitor how well these standards are met; indeed, some countries even consider them when formulating foreign policy.[2]

What Democracy Is

Let us begin by broadly defining democracy and the generic *concepts* that distinguish it as a unique system for organizing relations between rulers and the ruled. We will then briefly review *procedures*, the rules and arrangements that are needed if democracy is to endure. Finally, we will discuss two operative *principles* that make democracy work. They are not expressly included among the generic concepts or formal procedures, but the prospect for democracy is grim if their underlying conditioning effects are not present.

One of the major themes of this essay is that democracy does not consist of a single unique set of institutions. There are many types of democracy, and their diverse practices produce a similarly varied set of effects. The specific form democracy takes is contingent upon a country's socioeconomic conditions as well as its entrenched state structures and policy practices.

Modern political democracy is a system of governance in which rulers are held accountable for their actions in the public realm by citizens, acting indirectly through the competition and cooperation of their elected representatives.[3]

A *regime or system of governance* is an ensemble of patterns that determines the methods of access to the principal public offices; the characteristics of the actors admitted to or excluded from such access; the strategies that actors may use to gain access; and the rules that are followed in the making of publicly binding decisions. To work properly, the ensemble must be institutionalized—that is to say, the various patterns must be habitually known, practiced, and accepted by most, if not all, actors. Increasingly, the preferred mechanism of institutionalization is a written body of laws undergirded by a written constitution, though many enduring political norms can have an informal, prudential, or traditional basis.[4]

For the sake of economy and comparison, these forms, characteristics, and rules are usually bundled together and given a generic label. Democratic is one; others are autocratic, authoritarian, despotic, dictatorial, tyrannical, totalitarian, absolutist, traditional, monarchic, oligarchic, plutocratic, aristocratic, and sultanistic.[5] Each of these regime forms may in turn be broken down into subtypes.

Like all regimes, democracies depend upon the presence of *rulers*, persons who occupy specialized authority roles and can give legitimate commands to others. What distinguishes democratic rulers from nondemocratic ones are the norms that condition how the former come to power and the practices that hold them accountable for their actions.

The *public realm* encompasses the making of collective norms and choices that are binding on the society and backed by state coercion. Its content can vary a great deal across democracies, depending upon preexisting distinctions between the public and the private, state and society, legitimate coercion and voluntary exchange, and collective needs and individual preferences. The liberal conception of democracy advocates circumscribing the public realm as narrowly as possible, while the socialist or social-democratic approach would extend that realm through regulation, subsidization, and, in some cases, collective ownership of property. Neither is intrinsically more democratic than the other—just *differently* democratic. This implies that measures aimed at "developing the private sector" are no more democratic than those aimed at "developing the public sector." Both, if carried to extremes, could undermine the practice of democracy, the former by destroying the basis for satisfying collective needs and exercising legitimate authority; the latter by destroying the basis for satisfying individual preferences and controlling illegitimate government actions. Differences of opinion over the optimal mix of the two provide much of the substantive content of political conflict within established democracies.

Citizens are the most distinctive element in democracies. All regimes have rulers and a public realm, but only to the extent that they are democratic do they have citizens. Historically, severe restrictions on citizenship were imposed in most emerging or partial democracies according to criteria of age, gender, class, race, literacy, property ownership, tax-paying status, and so on. Only a small part of the total population was eligible to vote or run for office. Only restricted social categories were allowed to form, join, or support political associations. After protracted struggle—in some cases involving violent domestic upheaval or international war—most of these restrictions were lifted. Today, the criteria for inclusion are fairly standard. All native-born adults are eligible, although somewhat higher age limits may still be imposed upon candidates for certain offices. Unlike the early American and European democracies of the nineteenth century, none of the recent democracies in southern Europe, Latin America, Asia, or Eastern Europe has even attempted to impose formal restrictions on the franchise or eligibility to office. When it comes to informal restrictions on the effective exercise of citizenship rights, however, the story can be quite different. This explains the central importance (discussed below) of procedures.

Competition has not always been considered an essential defining condition of democracy. "Classic" democracies presumed decision making based on direct participation leading to consensus. The assembled citizenry was expected to agree on a common course of action after listening to the alternatives and weighing their respective merits and demerits. A tradition of hostility to "faction," and "particular interests" persists in democratic thought, but at least since *The Federalist Papers* it has become widely accepted that competition among factions is a necessary evil in democracies that operate on a more-than-local scale. Since, as James Madison argued, "the latent causes of faction are sown into the nature of man," and the possible remedies for "the mischief of faction" are worse than the disease, the best course is to recognize them and to attempt to control their effects.[6] Yet while democrats may agree on the inevitability of factions, they tend to disagree about the best forms and rules for governing factional competition. Indeed, differences over the preferred modes and boundaries of competition contribute most to distinguishing one subtype of democracy from another.

"However central to democracy, elections occur intermittently and only allow citizens to choose between the highly aggregated alternatives offered by political parties..."

The most popular definition of democracy equates it with regular *elections*, fairly conducted and honestly counted. Some even consider the mere fact of elections—even ones from which specific parties or candidates are excluded, or in which substantial portions of the population cannot freely participate—as a sufficient condition for the existence of democracy. This fallacy has been called "electoralism" or "the faith that merely holding elections will channel political action into peaceful contests among elites and accord public legitimacy to the winners"—no matter how they are conducted or what else constrains those who win them.[7] However central to democracy, elections occur intermittently and only allow citizens to choose between the highly aggregated alternatives offered by political parties, which can, especially in the early stages of a democratic transition, proliferate in a bewildering variety. During the intervals between elections, citizens can seek to influence public policy through a wide variety of other intermediaries: interest associations, social movements, locality groupings, clientelistic arrangements, and so forth. *Modern democracy, in other words, offers a variety of competitive processes and channels for the expression of interests and values—associational as well as partisan, functional as well as territorial, collective as well as individual. All are integral to its practice.*

Another commonly accepted image of democracy identifies it with *majority rule*. Any governing body that makes decisions by combining the votes of more than half of those eligible and present is said to be democratic, whether that majority emerges within an electorate, a parliament, a committee, a city council, or a party caucus. For exceptional purposes (e.g., amending the constitution or expelling a member), "qualified majorities" of more than 50 percent may be required, but few would deny that democracy must involve some means of aggregating the equal preferences of individuals.

A problem arises, however, when *numbers* meet *intensities*. What happens when a properly assembled majority (especially a stable, self-perpetuating one) regularly makes decisions that harm some minority (especially a threatened cultural or ethnic group)? In these circumstances, successful democracies tend to qualify the central principle of majority rule in order to protect minority rights. Such qualifications can take the form of constitutional provisions that place certain matters beyond the reach of majorities (bills of rights); requirements for concurrent majorities in several different constituencies (confederalism); guarantees securing the autonomy of local or regional governments against the demands of the central authority (federalism); grand coalition governments that incorporate all parties (consociationalism); or the negotiation of social pacts between major social groups like business and labor (neocorporatism). The most common and effective way of protecting minorities, however, lies in the everyday operation of interest associations and social movements. These reflect (some would say, amplify) the different intensities of preference that exist in the population and bring them to bear on democratically elected decision makers. Another way of putting this intrinsic tension between numbers and intensities would be to say that "in modern democracies, votes may be counted, but influences alone are weighted."

Cooperation has always been a central feature of democracy. Actors must voluntarily make collective decisions binding on the polity as a whole. They must cooperate in order to compete. They must be capable of acting collectively through parties, associations, and movements in order to select candidates, articulate preferences, petition authorities, and influence policies.

But democracy's freedoms should also encourage citizens to deliberate among themselves, to discover their common needs, and to resolve their differences without relying on some supreme central authority. Classical democracy emphasized these qualities, and they are by no means extinct, despite repeated efforts by contemporary theorists to stress the analogy with behavior in the economic marketplace and to reduce all of democracy's operations to competitive interest maximization. Alexis de Tocqueville best described the importance of independent groups for democracy in his *Democracy in America*, a work which remains a major source of inspiration for all those who persist in viewing democracy as something more than a struggle for election and re-election among competing candidates.[8]

In contemporary political discourse, this phenomenon of cooperation and deliberation via autonomous group activity goes under the rubric of "civil society." The diverse units of social identity and interest, by remaining independent of the state (and perhaps even of parties), not only can restrain the arbitrary actions of rulers, but can also contribute to forming better citizens who are more aware of the preferences of others, more self-confident in their actions, and more civic-minded in their willingness to sacrifice for the common good. At its best, civil society provides an intermediate layer of governance between the individual and the state that is capable of resolving conflicts and controlling the behavior of members without public coercion. Rather than overloading decision makers with increased demands and making the system ungovernable,[9] a viable civil society can mitigate conflicts and improve the quality of citizenship—without relying exclusively on the privatism of the marketplace.

Representatives—whether directly or indirectly elected—do most of the real work in modern democracies. Most are professional politicians who orient their careers around the desire to fill key offices. It is doubtful that any democracy could survive without such people. The central question, therefore, is not whether or not there will be a political elite or even a professional political class, but how these representatives are chosen and then held accountable for their actions.

As noted above, there are many channels of representation in modern democracy. The electoral one, based on territorial constituencies, is the most visible and public. It culminates in a parliament or a presidency that is periodically accountable to the citizenry as a whole. Yet the sheer growth of government (in large part as a byproduct of popular demand) has increased the number, variety, and power of agencies charged with making public decisions and not subject to elections. Around these agencies there has developed a vast apparatus of specialized representation based largely on functional interests, not territorial constituencies. These interest associations, and not political parties, have become the primary expression of civil society in most stable democracies, supplemented by the more sporadic interventions of social movements.

The new and fragile democracies that have sprung up since 1974 must live in "compressed time." They will not resemble the European democracies of the nineteenth and early twentieth centuries, and they cannot expect to acquire the multiple channels of representation in gradual historical progression as did most of their predecessors. A bewildering array of parties, interests, and movements will all simultaneously seek political influence in them, creating challenges to the polity that did not exist in earlier processes of democratization.

Procedures that Make Democracy Possible

The defining components of democracy are necessarily abstract, and may give rise to a considerable variety of institutions and subtypes of democracy. For democracy to thrive, however, specific procedural norms must be followed and civic rights must be respected. Any polity that fails to impose such restrictions upon itself, that fails to follow the "rule of law" with regard to its own procedures, should not be considered democratic. These procedures alone do not define democracy, but their presence is indispensable to its persistence. In essence, they are necessary but not sufficient conditions for its existence.

Robert Dahl has offered the most generally accepted listing of what he terms the "procedural minimal" conditions that must be present for modern political democracy (or as he puts it, "polyarchy") to exist:

> 1) Control over government decisions about policy is constitutionally vested in elected officials.
>
> 2) Elected officials are chosen in frequent and fairly conducted elections in which coercion is comparatively uncommon.
>
> 3) Practically all adults have the right to vote in the election of officials.
>
> 4) Practically all adults have the right to run for elective offices in the government. . . .
>
> 5) Citizens have a right to express themselves without the danger of severe punishment on political matters broadly defined. . . .
>
> 6) Citizens have a right to seek out alternative sources of information. Moreover, alternative sources of information exist and are protected by law.
>
> 7) . . . Citizens also have the right to form relatively independent associations or organizations, including independent political parties and interest groups.[10]

These seven conditions seem to capture the essence of procedural democracy for many theorists, but we propose to add two others. The first might be thought of as a further refinement of item (1), while the second might be called an implicit prior condition to all seven of the above.

8) Popularly elected officials must be able to exercise their constitutional powers without being subjected to overriding (albeit informal) opposition from unelected officials. Democracy is in jeopardy if military officers, entrenched civil servants, or state managers retain the capacity to act independently of elected civilians or even veto decisions made by the people's representatives. Without this additional caveat, the militarized polities of contemporary Central America, where civilian control over the military does not exist, might be classified by many scholars as democracies, just as they have been (with the exception of Sandinista Nicaragua) by U.S. policy makers. The caveat thus guards against what we earlier called "electoralism"—the tendency to focus on the holding of elections while ignoring other political realities.

9) The polity must be self-governing; it must be able to act independently of constraints imposed by some other overarching political system. Dahl and other contemporary democratic theorists probably took

this condition for granted since they referred to formally sovereign nation-states. However, with the development of blocs, alliances, spheres of influence, and a variety of "neocolonial" arrangements, the question of autonomy has been a salient one. Is a system really democratic if its elected officials are unable to make binding decisions without the approval of actors outside their territorial domain? This is significant even if the outsiders are themselves democratically constituted and if the insiders are relatively free to alter or even end the encompassing arrangement (as in Puerto Rico), but it becomes especially critical if neither condition obtains (as in the Baltic states).

Principles that Make Democracy Feasible

Lists of component processes and procedural norms help us to specify what democracy is, but they do not tell us much about how it actually functions. The simplest answer is "by the consent of the people"; the more complex one is "by the contingent consent of politicians acting under conditions of bounded uncertainty."

In a democracy, representatives must at least informally agree that those who win greater electoral support or influence over policy will not use their temporary superiority to bar the losers from taking office or exerting influence in the future, and that in exchange for this opportunity to keep competing for power and place, momentary losers will respect the winners' right to make binding decisions. Citizens are expected to obey the decisions ensuing from such a process of competition, provided its outcome remains contingent upon their collective preferences as expressed through fair and regular elections or open and repeated negotiations.

The challenge is not so much to find a set of goals that command widespread consensus as to find a set of rules that embody contingent consent. The precise shape of this "democratic bargain," to use Dahl's expression,[11] can vary a good deal from society to society. It depends on social cleavages and such subjective factors as mutual trust, the standard of fairness, and the willingness to compromise. It may even be compatible with a great deal of dissensus on substantive policy issues.

All democracies involve a degree of uncertainty about who will be elected and what policies they will pursue. Even in those polities where one party persists in winning elections or one policy is consistently implemented, the possibility of change through independent collective action still exists, as in Italy, Japan, and the Scandinavian social democracies. If it does not, the system is not democratic, as in Mexico, Senegal, or Indonesia.

But the uncertainty embedded in the core of all democracies is bounded. Not just any actor can get into the competition and raise any issue he or she pleases—there are previously established rules that must be respected. Not just any policy can be adopted—there are conditions that must be met. Democracy institutionalizes "normal," limited political uncertainty. These boundaries vary from country to country. Constitutional guarantees of property, privacy, expression, and other rights are a part of this, but the most effective boundaries are generated by competition among interest groups and cooperation within civil society. Whatever the rhetoric (and some polities appear to offer their citizens more dramatic alternatives than others), once the rules of contingent consent have been agreed upon, the actual variation is likely to stay within a predictable and generally accepted range.

This emphasis on operative guidelines contrasts with a highly persistent, but misleading theme in recent literature on democracy—namely, the emphasis upon "civic culture." The principles we have suggested here rest on rules of prudence, not on deeply ingrained habits of tolerance, moderation, mutual respect, fair play, readiness to compromise, or trust in public authorities. Waiting for such habits to sink deep and lasting roots implies a very slow process of regime consolidation—one that takes generations—and it would probably condemn most contemporary experiences *ex hypothesi* to failure. Our assertion is that contingent consent and bounded uncertainty can emerge from the interaction between antagonistic and mutually suspicious actors and that the far more benevolent and ingrained norms of a civic culture are better thought of as a *product* and not a producer of democracy.

How Democracies Differ

Several concepts have been deliberately excluded from our generic definition of democracy, despite the fact that they have been frequently associated with it in both everyday practice and scholarly work. They are, nevertheless, especially important when it comes to distinguishing subtypes of democracy. Since no single set of actual institutions, practices, or values embodies democracy, polities moving away from authoritarian rule can mix different components to produce different democracies. It is important to recognize that these do not define points along a single continuum of improving performance, but a matrix of potential combinations that are *differently* democratic.

1) *Consensus*: All citizens may not agree on the substantive goals of political action or on the role of the state (although if they did, it would certainly make governing democracies much easier).

2) *Participation*: All citizens may not take an active and equal part in politics, although it must be legally possible for them to do so.

3) *Access*: Rulers may not weigh equally the preferences of all who come before them, although citizenship implies that individuals and groups should have an equal opportunity to express their preferences if they choose to do so.

4) *Responsiveness*: Rulers may not always follow the course of action preferred by the citizenry. But when they deviate from such a policy, say on grounds of "reason of state" or "overriding national interest," they must ultimately be held accountable for their actions through regular and fair processes.

5) *Majority rule*: Positions may not be allocated or rules may not be decided solely on the basis of assembling the most votes, although deviations from this principle usually must be explicitly defended and previously approved.

6) *Parliamentary sovereignty*: The legislature may not be the only body that can make rules or even the one with final authority in deciding which laws are binding, although where executive, judicial, or other public bodies make that ultimate choice, they too must be accountable for their actions.

7) *Party government*: Rulers may not be nominated, promoted, and disciplined in their activities by well-organized and programmatically coherent political parties, although where they are not, it may prove more difficult to form an effective government.

8) *Pluralism*: The political process may not be based on a multiplicity of overlapping, voluntaristic, and autonomous private groups. However, where there are monopolies of representation, hierarchies of association, and obligatory memberships, it is likely that the interests involved will be more closely linked to the state and the separation between the public and private spheres of action will be much less distinct.

9) *Federalism*: The territorial division of authority may not involve multiple levels and local autonomies, least of all ones enshrined in a constitutional document, although some dispersal of power across territorial and/or functional units is characteristic of all democracies.

10) *Presidentialism*: The chief executive officer may not be a single person and he or she may not be directly elected by the citizenry as a whole, although some concentration of authority is present in all democracies, even if it is exercised collectively and only held indirectly accountable to the electorate.

11) *Checks and Balances*: It is not necessary that the different branches of government be systematically pitted against one another, although governments by assembly, by executive concentration, by judicial command, or even by dictatorial fiat (as in time of war) must be ultimately accountable to the citizenry as a whole.

While each of the above has been named as an essential component of democracy, they should instead be seen either as indicators of this or that type of democracy, or else as useful standards for evaluating the performance of particular regimes. To include them as part of the generic definition of democracy itself would be to mistake the American polity for the universal model of democratic governance. Indeed, the parliamentary, consociational, unitary, corporatist, and concentrated arrangements of continental Europe may have some unique virtues for guiding polities through the uncertain transition from autocratic to democratic rule.[12]

What Democracy Is Not

We have attempted to convey the general meaning of modern democracy without identifying it with some particular set of rules and institutions or restricting it to some specific culture or level of development. We have also argued that it cannot be reduced to the regular holding of elections or equated with a particular notion of the role of the state, but we have not said much more about what democracy is not or about what democracy may not be capable of producing.

There is an understandable temptation to load too many expectations on this concept and to imagine that by attaining democracy, a society will have resolved all of its political, social, economic, administrative, and cultural problems. Unfortunately, "all good things do not necessarily go together."

First, democracies are not necessarily more efficient economically than other forms of government. Their rates of aggregate growth, savings, and investment may be no better than those of nondemocracies. This is especially likely during the transition, when propertied groups and administrative elites may respond to real or imagined threats to the "rights" they enjoyed under authoritarian rule by initiating capital flight, disinvestment, or sabotage. In time, depending upon the type of democracy, benevolent long-term effects upon income distribution, aggregate demand, education, productivity, and creativity may eventually combine to improve economic and social performance, but it is certainly too much to expect that these improvements will occur immediately—much less that they will be defining characteristics of democratization.

Second, democracies are not necessarily more efficient administratively. Their capacity to make decisions may even be slower than that of the regimes they replace, if only because more actors must be consulted. The costs of getting things done may be higher, if only because "payoffs" have to be made to a wider and more resourceful set of clients (although one should never underestimate the degree of corruption to be found within autocracies). Popular satisfaction with the new democratic government's performance may not even seem greater, if only because necessary compromises often please no one completely, and because the losers are free to complain.

Third, democracies are not likely to appear more orderly, consensual, stable, or governable than the autocracies they replace. This is partly a byproduct of democratic freedom of expression, but it is also a reflection of the likelihood of continuing disagreement over new rules and institutions. These products of imposition or compromise are often initially quite ambiguous in nature and uncertain in effect until actors have learned how to use them. What is more, they come in the aftermath of serious struggles motivated by high ideals. Groups and individuals with recently acquired autonomy will test certain rules, protest against the actions of certain institutions, and insist on renegotiating their part of the bargain. Thus the presence of antisystem parties should be neither surprising nor seen as a failure of democratic consolidation. What counts is whether such parties are willing, however reluctantly, to play by the general rules of bounded uncertainty and contingent consent.

"...democracies will have more open societies and polities than the autocracies they replace, but not necessarily more open economies."

Governability is a challenge for all regimes, not just democratic ones. Given the political exhaustion and loss of legitimacy that have befallen autocracies from sultanistic Paraguay to totalitarian Albania, it may seem that only democracies can now be expected to govern effectively and legitimately. Experience has shown, however, that democracies too can lose the ability to govern. Mass publics can become disenchanted with their performance. Even more threatening is the temptation for leaders to fiddle with procedures and ultimately undermine the principles of contingent consent and bounded uncertainty. Perhaps the most critical moment comes once the politicians begin to settle into the more predictable roles and relations of a consolidated democracy. Many will find their expectations frustrated; some will discover that the new rules of competition put them at a disadvantage; a few may even feel that their vital interests are threatened by popular majorities.

Finally, democracies will have more open societies and polities than the autocracies they replace, but not necessarily more open economies. Many of today's most successful and well-established democracies have historically resorted to protectionism and closed borders, and have relied extensively upon public institutions to promote economic development. While the long-term compatibility between democracy and capitalism does not seem to be in doubt, despite their continuous tension, it is not clear whether the promotion of such liberal economic goals as the right of individuals to own property and retain profits, the clearing function of markets, the private settlement of disputes, the freedom to produce without government regulation, or the privatization of state-owned enterprises necessarily furthers the consolidation of democracy. After all, democracies do need to levy taxes and regulate certain transactions, especially where private monopolies and oligopolies exist. Citizens or their representatives may decide that it is desirable to protect the rights of collectivities from encroachment by individuals, especially propertied ones, and they may choose to set aside certain forms of property for public or cooperative ownership. In short, notions of economic liberty that are currently put forward in neoliberal economic models are not synonymous with political freedom—and may even impede it.

Democratization will not necessarily bring in its wake economic growth, social peace, administrative efficiency, political harmony, free markets, or "the end of ideology." Least of all will it bring about "the end of history." No doubt some of these qualities could make the consolidation of democracy easier, but they are neither prerequisites for it nor immediate products of it. Instead, what we should be hoping for is the emergence of political institutions that can peacefully compete to form governments and influence public policy, that can channel social and economic conflicts through regular procedures, and that have sufficient linkages to civil society to represent their constituencies and commit them to collective courses of action. Some types of democracies, especially in developing countries, have been unable to fulfill this promise, perhaps due to the circumstances of their transition from authoritarian rule.[13] The democratic wager is that such a regime, once established, will not only persist by reproducing itself within its initial confining conditions, but will eventually expand beyond them.[14] Unlike authoritarian regimes, democracies have the capacity to modify their rules and institutions consensually in response to changing circumstances. They may not immediately produce all the goods mentioned above, but they stand a better chance of eventually doing so than do autocracies.

NOTES

1. For a comparative analysis of the recent regime changes in southern Europe and Latin America, see Guillermo O'Donnell, Philippe C. Schmitter, and Laurence Whitehead, eds., *Transitions from Authoritarian Rule*, 4 vols. (Baltimore: Johns Hopkins University Press, 1986). For another compilation that adopts a more structural approach see Larry Diamond, Juan Linz, and Seymour Martin Lipset, eds., *Democracy in Developing Countries*, vols. 2, 3, and 4 (Boulder, Colo.: Lynne Rienner, 1989).

2. Numerous attempts have been made to codify and quantify the existence of democracy across political systems. The best known is probably Freedom House's *Freedom in the World: Political Rights and Civil Liberties*, published since 1973 by Greenwood Press and since 1988 by University Press of America. Also see Charles Humana, *World Human Rights Guide* (New York: Facts on File, 1986).

3. The definition most commonly used by American social scientists is that of Joseph Schumpeter: "that institutional arrangement for arriving at political decisions in which individuals acquire the power to decide by means of a competitive struggle for the people's vote." *Capitalism, Socialism and Democracy* (London: George Allen and Unwin, 1943), 269. We accept certain aspects of the classical procedural approach to modern democracy, but differ primarily in our emphasis on the accountability of rulers to citizens and the relevance of mechanisms of competition other than elections.

4. Not only do some countries practice a stable form of democracy without a formal constitution (e.g., Great Britain and Israel), but even more countries have constitutions and

legal codes that offer no guarantee of reliable practice. On paper, Stalin's 1936 constitution for the USSR was a virtual model of democratic rights and entitlements.

5. For the most valiant attempt to make some sense out of this thicket of distinctions, see Juan Linz, "Totalitarian and Authoritarian Regimes" in *Handbook of Political Science*, eds. Fred I. Greenstein and Nelson W. Polsby (Reading, Mass.: Addision Wesley, 1975), 175-411.

6. "Publius" (Alexander Hamilton, John Jay, and James Madison), *The Federalist Papers* (New York: Anchor Books, 1961). The quote is from Number 10.

7. See Terry Karl, "Imposing Consent? Electoralism versus Democratization in El Salvador," in *Elections and Democratization in Latin America, 1980-1985*, eds. Paul Drake and Eduardo Silva (San Diego: Center for Iberian and Latin American Studies, Center for US/Mexican Studies, University of California, San Diego, 1986), 9-36.

8. Alexis de Tocqueville, *Democracy in America*, 2 vols. (New York: Vintage Books, 1945).

9. This fear of overloaded government and the imminent collapse of democracy is well reflected in the work of Samuel P. Huntington during the 1970s. See especially Michel Crozier, Samuel P. Huntington, and Joji Watanuki, *The Crisis of Democracy* (New York: New York University Press, 1975). For Huntington's (revised) thoughts about the prospects for democracy, see his "Will More Countries Become Democratic?," *Political Science Quarterly* 99 (Summer 1984): 193-218.

10. Robert Dahl, *Dilemmas of Pluralist Democracy* (New Haven: Yale University Press, 1982), 11.

11. Robert Dahl, *After the Revolution: Authority in a Good Society* (New Haven: Yale University Press, 1970).

12. See Juan Linz, "The Perils of Presidentialism," *Journal of Democracy* 1 (Winter 1990): 51-69, and the ensuing discussion by Donald Horowitz, Seymour Martin Lipset, and Juan Linz in *Journal of Democracy* 1 (Fall 1990): 73-91.

13. Terry Lynn Karl, "Dilemmas of Democratization in Latin America," *Comparative Politics* 23 (October 1990): 1-23.

14. Otto Kirchheimer, "Confining Conditions and Revolutionary Breakthroughs," *American Political Science Review* 59 (1965): 964-974.

5.
RETHINKING AFRICAN DEMOCRACY

Claude Ake

***Claude Ake** is director of the Center for Advanced Social Science at the University of Port Harcourt, Nigeria. A former president of the Council for the Development of Economic and Social Research, the umbrella social science organization in Africa, he has recently been a fellow at the Brookings Institution and the Woodrow Wilson Center for Scholars. His books include* The New World Order: A View From the South *(1992),* Democratization of Disempowerment in Africa *(1994), and* Democracy and Development in Africa *(1995).*

Issues of democratization and human rights are increasingly dominating the world's interest in Africa, overcoming a legacy of indifference to the fate of democracy on the continent. This legacy has its roots in the colonial era, when political discourse excluded not only democracy but even the idea of good government, and politics was reduced to the clash of one exclusive claim to power against another.

This attitude persisted even after Africa gained political independence. By deciding to take over the colonial system instead of transforming it in accord with popular nationalist aspirations, most African leaders found themselves on a collision course with their people. Faced with this challenge to their newly won power, they opted for "development," using it largely as an ideological blind. Resisting pressures for structural transformation and redistribution, they claimed that the overriding priority for Africa must be to seek development—the cake had to be baked before it could be shared. To discourage opposition and perpetuate their power, they argued that the problems of development demanded complete unity of purpose, justifying on these grounds the criminalization of political dissent and the inexorable march to political monolithism.

The rest of the world heartily encouraged these political tendencies. Africa's former colonial masters, anxious for leverage with the new leaders, embraced the idea of partnership in development and gave these regimes their indulgent support. The great powers ignored human rights violations and sought clients wherever they could. All these factors helped crystallize a climate of opinion in the West hostile to democracy in Africa. From time to time (as during the Carter administration in the United States) human rights abuses in Africa became an issue, but never democracy. On the rare occasions when Western leaders did discuss democracy in Africa, it was mainly to raise doubts about its feasibility.

Why is the West now suddenly preoccupied with the prospect of democracy in Africa? The reforms in Eastern Europe have contributed to this change of heart by providing the West with a dramatic vindication of its own values and a sense of the historical inevitability of the triumph of democracy. The aggressive vacuity of the Cold War has been replaced by the mission of democratization, a mission which, it is widely believed, will firmly consolidate the hegemony of Western values all over the world. Thus the West has come to regard democracy as an important item on the African agenda. This change in attitude also reflects the fact that the long struggle for democracy in Africa is beginning to show results, results too impressive and too widespread to be ignored: the popular rejection of military rule in Nigeria; the demise of apartheid in South Africa; the downfall of Samuel Doe in Liberia and Kérékou in Benin; the gains for pluralism and multipartyism in Niger, Madagascar, Cameroon, Zambia, Algeria, Gabon, Côte d'Ivoire, Guinea, Zaire, Mozambique, Angola, the Congo, and São Tomé and Príncipe; and the growing pressures for democratization in Kenya, Somalia, Sudan, Togo, Ghana, Sierra Leone, Ethiopia, Cameroon, and Zimbabwe.

The West's changing attitude toward democracy in Africa draws additional impetus from Africa's economic marginalization. The world economy is now driven less by trade than by capital movements; there has been a massive shift from the production of goods to the provision of services, and from material-intensive to knowledge-intensive industries. At the same time, advances in science and technology have created an increasing number of synthetic products more flexible and more versatile than those that Africa has traditionally exported. These changes have made Africa's primary economies far less relevant to the current economic needs of the West. Now, with the winding down of the Cold War, Africa's strategic significance to the West has also greatly declined. As Europe draws closer to unification, even the former colonial powers—notably France—are finding it necessary to downgrade their special relationships with their former colonies, relations far less useful now than they have been in the past.

The marginalization of Africa has given the West more latitude to conduct its relations with Africa in a principled way. In the past, the West adopted a posture of indifference to issues of human rights and democracy in Africa in order to avoid jeopardizing its economic and strategic interests and to facilitate its obsessive search for allies against communism. Now that these concerns have diminished, the West finds itself free to bring its African policies into greater harmony with its democratic principles.

The Desirability of Democracy

It is a striking fact that democracy is now on the agenda in Africa. But should it be? To answer this question, we must examine the traditional arguments against establishing democracies in Africa.

Africa, it has been claimed, has its own unique history and traditions and the introduction of democracy, an alien concept, would violate the integrity of African culture. This argument, premised on the misconception that democracy is solely a Western creation, stems from a confusion between the principles of democracy and their institutional manifestations. The principles of democracy include widespread participation, consent of the governed, and public accountability of those in power. These principles may prevail in a wide variety of political arrangements and practices, which naturally vary according to historical conditions. Traditional African political systems were infused with democratic values. They were invariably patrimonial, and consciousness was communal; everything was everybody's business, engendering a strong emphasis on participation. Standards of accountability were even stricter than in Western societies. Chiefs were answerable not only for their own actions but for natural catastrophes such as famine, epidemics, floods, and drought. In the event of such disasters, chiefs could be required to go into exile or "asked to die."

Another argument against democracy in Africa revolves around the social pluralism of African societies, particularly ethnic differences. Some contend that because African societies are replete with ethnic conflict, they must be firmly governed; the liberties of democracy would inflame ethnic rivalries and pose the danger of political disintegration. This argument has acquired credibility because of the high incidence of ethnic conflicts in Africa, some of which have been markedly destructive, most notably in Uganda, Equatorial Guinea, Burundi, Nigeria, and Rwanda.

Nonetheless, the problem is not ethnicity but bad leadership. There is nothing inherently conflictual about ethnic differences. They lead to strife only when they are politicized, and it is the elites who politicize ethnicity in their quest for power and political support. Leaders also gain a second advantage from exploiting ethnicity. Having incited ethnic-based conflict, they then use the threat of such conflict to justify political authoritarianism.

Even now, after 30 years of self-government, some African leaders still enlist this spurious defense to rationalize one-party rule. President Daniel arap Moi of Kenya, under increasing pressure to democratize, has repeatedly made this claim. So has Zambian president Kenneth Kaunda, who warned that the adoption of a multiparty system would bring "chaos, bloodshed, and death." President Paul Biya of Cameroon has defended the power monopoly of his Cameroon People's Democratic Movement with similar language; he stresses the party's vanguard role in creating "a united Cameroon devoid of ethnic, linguistic, and religious cleavages." Somehow these leaders cannot see that repeating this argument after 30 years is precisely its refutation. A treatment applied for 30 years that continues to worsen the illness cannot be right.

A third argument ties the issue of democratization to economic development, asserting that the quest for democracy must be considered in the context of Africa's most pressing needs, especially emancipation from "ignorance, poverty, and disease." The pursuit of democracy will not, it is argued, feed the hungry or heal the sick. Nor will it give shelter to the homeless. People must be educated and fed before they can appreciate democracy, for there is no choice in ignorance and there are no possibilities for self-fulfillment in extreme poverty.

This claim is as seductive as it is misguided. Even if it were true that democracy is competitive with development, it does not follow that people must be more concerned with improving nutrition than casting votes, or more concerned with health than with political participation. The primary issue is not *whether* it is more important to eat well than to vote, but *who* is entitled to decide which is more important. Once this is understood, the argument that democracy must be sacrificed to development collapses into the arbitrary insistence that we ought to decide for the peasants of Botswana and Burkina Faso whether they should prefer better health or the right to vote.

In any case, Africa's failed development experience suggests that postponing democracy does not promote development; during the past decades of authoritarianism, Africa's standard of living has been falling steadily, and its share of world trade and industrial output has been declining. Poverty in both relative and absolute terms is worsening so rapidly that sub-Saharan Africa's share of the developing world's poor will have grown from 16 percent in 1985 to 30 percent by the end of the century. The average growth rate for the region between 1980 and 1989 was *minus* 2.2 percent.

Perhaps it is misleading to talk about the failure of development in Africa, for in a sense it has never really been tried. When African leaders chose to take over the colonial system instead of transforming it and thus became alienated from their own people, the genuine pursuit of development became all but impossible. Besieged by the hostile forces unleashed by their repression, they became totally absorbed in survival, and relegated everything else, including development, to a very low priority. What passed for development was usually a crudely fabricated plan that an embattled and distracted leadership put together for the sake of appearances, often with an eye to luring prospective donors.

Any chance that this externally driven development would contribute significantly to material progress was doomed by authoritarianism. Development strategies, reflecting both the scientific dogmatism of development experts and the isolation of African leaders, worked from the top down and were imbued with attitudes hostile to the poor majority. The common people were seen as a major obstacle to development: their expectations were too high, they consumed too much of their meager incomes, they lacked ambition and self-reliance, they were too lazy and too superstitious. In short, the common people were inherent enemies of progress, even their own progress. This became a justification for disregarding their interests and for brutalizing them in the name of development. As a result, most Africans tend to view the state and its development agents as hostile forces to be evaded, cheated, or thwarted as opportunities permit. They conform as they must and get on with their struggle for survival. They are simply not available to be mobilized for development.

Apparently the lesson has been learned. At the April 1990 Bretton Woods Committee meeting in Washington, World Bank president Barber Conable listed better governance as the primary requirement for economic recovery in Africa. The World Bank's new African blueprint, *Sub-Saharan Africa: From Crisis to Sustainable Growth*, highlights the need for accountability, participation, and consensus building in order to achieve successful development. The Bank's press clips on the report demonstrate that this view has won approval all over the world.

A conference of over 500 groups representing nongovernmental organizations, grassroots organizations, United Nations agencies, and governments, which convened in February 1990 in Arusha, Tanzania under the auspices of the United Nations Economic Commission for Africa, adopted an "African Charter for Popular Participation in Development and Transformation." Its major point is that the absence of democracy is the primary cause of the chronic crisis in Africa. A speech by U.N. secretary general Javier Pérez de Cuéllar at the Arusha meeting identified an inescapable link between economic recovery in Africa and popular participation. In addition, a declaration entitled "The Political and Socio-Economic Situation in Africa and the Fundamental Changes Taking Place in the World," adopted by the Organization of African Unity in Addis Ababa, 9-11 July 1990, acknowledges that a political environment guaranteeing human rights and the rule of law would be more conducive to governmental accountability and probity and that "popular-based political processes would ensure the involvement of all . . . in development efforts." But how do we proceed with democratization?

Some Misconceptions

Several disturbing misconceptions persist about the process of democratization in Africa. One is the tendency to see democratization as an offshoot of the survival strategies that the African crisis has engendered. Some Africanists emphasize that, although African states are tottering under a protracted fiscal crisis and national institutions are in danger of disintegrating under the stress of economic austerity, there is tremendous vitality at the grassroots. People are organizing themselves in order to limit their vulnerability to a predatory state, to improvise rudimentary social welfare networks through community efforts, and to improve their material well-being. We get a picture of a thriving associational life, of a turning away from the state, of ordinary people assuming greater control over their own destinies.

This is certainly happening. Its democratic potential is limited, however, as the case of Kenya illustrates. Kenya is one of the African countries in which rural grassroots organizations are the most advanced, and it has achieved immense success in grassroots economic development. For instance, grassroots self-help development projects ("Harambee" projects) account for about 70 percent of the 1,400 secondary schools in the country and for a substantial proportion of the rural water-supply facilities, clinics, cattle dips, and community centers. Yet Kenya is anything but democratic. These grassroots organizations do not appear to have brought about, as of now, any substantial decentralization of power, and they have not diminished the state's arbitrariness and coercion. Part of the problem is that they are isolated and are not usually aggregated at higher organizational levels where they could have some potential for influencing policy.

Except in a few countries, such as Senegal, grassroots organizations in Africa do not significantly contribute to democracy. In fact, in their political effects they are not markedly different from the local government systems that African regimes have been instituting in order to lower administrative costs and deflect participatory pressures. That is the kind of reform that President Rawlings is currently putting in place in Ghana under the pretext of democratization. People are given some local political space, not to integrate them into a democratic polity but to separate them from meaningful participation at the national level; the granting of local authority is not a liberty but a constraint. It underlines the confinement of local people and their disenfranchisement. Initiatives and directives flow from the central to the local government in a strictly one-way traffic.

Recently, yet another misconception about the process of democratization in Africa has begun to emerge—the view that democratization entails "destatization." This theory has been finding fertile ground in the West, particularly among international financial institutions (IFIs), because it meshes with the liberal commitment to the primacy of the market and the notion that democracy is associated with minimal government. Having agreed that authoritarianism presents a serious obstacle to development, the IFIs now recommend as a solution reducing the expenditures, powers, and controls of the state. It is critical, however, to distinguish between the size of the state and its strength. The public sector in many African countries has grown too bloated. Indeed, the bloated state has become a strategy for massive corruption, and it makes sense to try to trim the state by reducing the extent of state economic ownership and control. But it is a very different matter to claim that democracy can be promoted in Africa by *weakening* the state. The state in Africa needs to become both leaner *and* stronger in order to carry out successfully its essential development tasks.

The coercive monolithism of most African political systems readily gives the impression of strong states with immense penetrative capacity, states which are everywhere doing everything. Yet African states are actually very weak. In Nigeria, for instance, the state has little influence on the lives of the rural people. Much of the development that has taken place in rural communities has occurred not because of the state but in spite of it. To many rural dwellers, the state exists primarily as a nuisance to be avoided in their daily struggle for survival. In most other African countries, state influence is even weaker. In Zaire, President Mobutu does not effectively control more than 40 percent of the nation's territory. The state delivers so few services that it is all but irrelevant to its citizens except when they encounter it on the rampage.

Only the violent arbitrariness of states like Zaire makes them seem so powerful. By contrast, in Western countries like the United States, the state is very strong and penetrates far more deeply into the lives of its citizens. The West has created societies that are very homogeneous, interdependent, cohesive, and amenable to control. The refinement of bureaucratic organization backed by modern science and technology has given these states extraordinary powers of intervention, penetration, and control. But their citizens do not find these powerful states threatening. Instead, they perceive a benign aloofness, an impression fostered by the use of state power according to law and, more importantly, by the virtual automation of conformity and control. Democracy is not, and can never be, a matter of weakening the state.

The Role of the West

What role, if any, should the West play in the democratization of Africa? Like development, democratization is not something that one people does for another. People must do it for themselves or it does not happen. The question of the role of the West in the democratization of Africa has arisen only because Africans have become more committed to the quest for democracy and are struggling determinedly to attain it. But the extent to which they will succeed depends in part on the international environment, in which the West currently plays a decisive role.

In recent months, Western leaders have articulately proclaimed their support for democracy in Africa, and news about Africa in the Western media is now dominated by issues of democratization. But what can the West do beyond verbal exhortations to democratize? The answer to this question must focus on the leverage available to the West in its relations with Africa. This leverage can be exerted in two ways: through bilateral relations and through Western influence over the IFIs, especially the International Monetary Fund (IMF) and the World Bank.

In the realm of bilateral relations, the West has already agreed to use its leverage over development assistance, aid, and investment to encourage support for human rights and democracy. The U.S. Congress has indicated that its limited aid will be awarded to "newly forming democracies" and not be wasted on autocratic regimes. U.S. assistant secretary of state for African affairs Herman Cohen, speaking at the April 1990 Bretton Woods Committee meeting in Washington, announced that, in addition to previous requirements on economic policy reform and human rights, democratization would become a third condition for U.S. assistance. On 8 May 1990, the U.S. ambassador to Kenya stated that "there is a strong tide flowing in our Congress, which controls the purse strings, to concentrate our economic assistance on those of the world's nations that nourish democratic institutions, defend human rights, and practice multiparty politics." He went on to suggest that this would be a "fact of political life in other donor countries tomorrow." Speaking at a meeting of the Overseas Development Council on 6 June 1990, British foreign secretary Douglas Hurd said that Britain's assistance will favor "countries tending toward pluralism, public accountability, respect for the rule of law, human rights, and market principles." President François Mitterand, addressing a French-African conference at La Baule in June 1990, stated that in the future French aid would flow "more enthusiastically" to countries moving toward democracy.

The West has already started using economic pressures to induce political change, a concept now referred to as political conditionality. A debate is currently raging about whether political conditionality is necessary or desirable. It is an odd debate because political conditionality has always been present, not only in bilateral relations but even in the relations of multilateral agencies with the Third World. I say this not to justify political conditionality by the fact that it has always existed; it is as unnecessary to justify it as it is useless to dispute its legitimacy. The very nature of relations between nations demands that political conditionality underlie economic relations. What appears to have started this debate over the obvious is the explicitness of political conditionality and its extension beyond the issues of friendly relations and human rights to democratization.

Democracy cannot be obtained by trying to convert undemocratic regimes through bribery and coercion. Democracy is not simply bestowed upon a nation from above. It may prevail with minimal conflict in those rare instances in which the rulers, recognizing the inevitable, concede gracefully. More often than not, it is won amidst considerable turmoil against the determined opposition of those in power. There are no easy paths to democracy, and offering incentives to autocrats is not the way to democratize.

This is not to say that sanctions have no place in encouraging democratization in Africa. On the contrary, sanctions can play an important role. They can weaken an antidemocratic regime's capacity to oppress and block democratic forces. In Benin, for instance, sanctions weakened President Kérékou and emboldened the democratic forces, creating considerable room for a democratic transition. In Liberia, sanctions contributed to the overthrow of President Samuel Doe. They could have the same effect in Kenya, Cameroon, Sierra Leone, Zambia, Somalia, Malawi, Ghana, and other African nations.

The question is whether the West can muster the political will to apply sanctions. While preaching the new line on political conditionality, the West confines its actions to relatively harmless gestures. Aid continues to flow to President arap Moi of Kenya despite his repulsive efforts to crush members of the democracy movement "like rats," and despite calls for sanctions by leaders of the democratic movement such as human rights lawyer Gibson Kamau Kuria. In May 1990, a thousand French troops intervened to protect Omar Bongo's 23-year-long rule in Gabon. Britain's support of political conditionality has yet to go beyond lectures on democracy, despite pressures from its media. An editorial in the influential *Times* of London on 11 July 1990, entitled "An Ignominious Silence," angrily reprimanded the government for neither condemning nor taking action against President arap Moi: "The British Government has had not one word to say about President Moi's savagery. This is a disgrace."

Western rationalizations for not imposing sanctions echo the old uncritical paternalism that has been such a comfort to Africa's autocrats in the past. One concern repeatedly expressed is that there may be no apparent alternative to the existing ruler. But this merely reflects the age-old policy of tyrants—namely ensuring that they have no competitors. To accept the absence of visible alternatives as an excuse for doing nothing is to reward the techniques of tyranny. Another standard argument asserts that withholding aid will hurt the economy and the people. But how can aid given to violently repressive leaders—rather than channeled through nongovernmental organizations—possibly help "the people," as opposed to helping these leaders themselves to remain in power? The plea that aid must continue in order not to impede national development overlooks the fact that most African leaders have been "underdeveloping" the continent for years in spite of aid—indeed, probably because of it. Between 1980 and 1988, sub-Saharan Africa received a total aid flow of

$83 billion, yet during the same period the average annual growth rate was minus 2.2 percent. In Zaire, one of the largest aid recipients in Africa, the average annual income has fallen to a fraction of what it was when President Mobutu came to power 25 years ago.

Political conditionality can weaken antidemocratic forces, but any serious effort to promote democracy must go further and seek to identify and strengthen democratic forces. This will be a difficult, messy, and disagreeable task. It will entail working around the government and reaching into civil society to support those groups struggling for democracy. Dictatorial regimes will object to this approach, and if it is not abandoned, confrontations will ensue, raising awkward questions about circumventing another country's sovereignty. Faced with such difficulties, the will of Western governments to support democracy may well weaken.

The Politics of Structural Adjustment

The importance of the international financial institutions to the success of any policy of political conditionality is underscored by the fact that the World Bank alone controls $12 billion of the $15 billion in international aid to Africa. As for the IMF, its power far surpasses its lending capacity and the financial resources it directly controls, because Western governments take their cue from the IMF in their relations with Africa. Any African country that cannot obtain IMF certification of aid-worthiness will get no cooperation from the West. Professor Adebayo Adedeji, the executive secretary of the United Nations Economic Commission for Africa, may well be right in saying that the IMF and the World Bank are now more powerful in Africa than the former colonial masters. These agencies, notorious in the past for presenting development as apolitical, today acknowledge that political factors have been a major stumbling block to the development effort in Africa. They are now calling for participation, the rule of law, transparency, accountability, and consensus building.

Yet despite their new recognition that political factors constrain development efforts, the IFIs still appear to believe that they are not in the business of politics. They think that political variables can simply be treated as an engineering problem and "factored in" to improve the effectiveness of their structural adjustment programs, and thus that they can avoid changing their overall approach to development. They argue that this does not mean turning their backs on democratization, because the cause of democracy is best served by pressing on with adjustment programs that strengthen the market relative to the state. They point out that privatization will enhance pluralism and that a freer market will decentralize decision making, multiply the centers of power, and strengthen civil society. This view is widely held in Western government circles and among intellectuals. Writing in the *Washington Post* on 24 May 1990, Chester Crocker, former U.S. assistant secretary of state for African affairs, argued that structural adjustment programs "are vital to the liberation of market forces, which in turn, represent the building blocks of pluralist democracy."

This is a dangerous error. In African countries, structural adjustment entails draconian measures that are unpalatable and often disastrous. Unemployment and inflation rise steeply, yet at the same time subsidies are removed and wages frozen. The combined effect of these measures can cause real incomes to fall as much as 50 percent. Given that 40 percent of the people in these countries already live below absolute poverty levels, structural adjustment does not entail minor inconvenience. These programs cause deep despair, widespread malnutrition, and premature death; as UNICEF reports indicate, much of the burden falls upon children.

As should be expected, adjustment policies generate a great deal of political opposition even in countries like Gabon, which implemented a relatively moderate version. Adjustment in that country meant cutting government spending by 50 percent, removing subsidies, freezing wages, dismissing public employees, and selling government-owned enterprises. Yet that was only the first phase. When the government announced the second wave of austerity measures in January 1990, there were protests and strikes in every government agency, including the postal, bus, rail, air traffic, and telephone services; even the police and the army went on strike. In all cases, adjustment programs have been vigorously resisted by the public. To implement them, governments have been forced to resort to a large dose of coercion. For this reason, African regimes have become more, not less, authoritarian over the past decade.

The IFIs have collaborated enthusiastically in this political authoritarianism. In *Sub-Saharan Africa: From Crisis to Sustainable Growth*, the World Bank argued quite correctly that "programs of action can be sustained only if they arise out of consensus built on dialogue within each country." Yet not once has the Fund or the Bank encouraged discussion and consensus building before the introduction of structural adjustment programs. In every case, they were quite content to settle the issues with the president of the client country or his economics or finance minister. Having done so, they constantly urged the necessity of political will to carry out the program—a euphemism for its coercive imposition.

No Easy Road

The indications are that political conditionality will not be seriously pursued in Africa by Western governments or the IFIs. In the United States, although many key congressional leaders strongly support political conditionality, the Bush administration has been circumspect. It remains preoccupied with keeping its options open, causing no offense to friendly governments, and avoiding conflicts in the pursuit of seemingly intangible objectives. Thus, despite considerable public and congressional pressure, the administration moved very slowly and reluctantly to impose sanctions on South Africa, Zaire, and Liberia. More recently, Congressional calls for sanctions against President arap Moi of Kenya elicited a visit to that country from assistant secretary of state Herman Cohen, after which a delighted arap Moi declared that relations between Kenya and the United States were back to normal. In Britain and France, the governments have been more reluctant still.

It is now beginning to look as though the economic and strategic marginalization of Africa may not, as has been assumed, encourage political conditionality by leaving the West freer to act on its democratic principles. This marginalization may instead make the West too indifferent to Africa to care even about democratization. In any case, Africa's marginalization has translated into reduced economic relations, investment, and trade and development assistance. External bank loans and credits to sub-Saharan Africa fell from $4 billion in 1980 to $1 billion in 1986, and private investment dropped from $2.3 billion in 1982 to $500 million in 1986. Africa's trade with Western Europe dropped by more than 25 percent between 1980 and 1987. Export credits from France to sub-Saharan Africa have fallen dramatically—investment is running at only $50 million a year, down from $1 billion a year in the early 1980s. U.S. bilateral aid to sub-Saharan Africa, at $1 billion in 1990, is only half its 1985 level. Political conditionality presupposes economic leverage. If current economic trends continue, the question of political conditionality may become moot.

Even if economic leverage remains available, the IFIs are unlikely to support political conditionality in more than a nominal way. They have become so fixated on structural adjustment that they will accept and protect any regime that submits to it. Somalia is a case in point. It is virtually isolated because of President Siad Barre's brutal dictatorship; even Italy, traditionally considered Somalia's "mother" country, has severed its ties. After the July 9 massacres in Mogadishu, the Italian government announced that it was withdrawing its ambassador, its military advisers, and its professors at the National University of Somalia. Yet the World Bank is currently processing a new loan of $18.5 million to Somalia; it approved $26.1 million earlier this year and $70 million last year.

By such actions, the IFIs give African leaders the chance to substitute structural adjustment for democratization. That is the preferred alternative for both sides, and it ensures their peaceful coexistence. The IFIs fear anything that will bring them into conflict with most African regimes and prevent them from doing business. In order to keep relations cordial and funds flowing, they readily collude in circumventing the economic conditionality that they themselves impose. If they subvert their own economic rules to keep the peace, it is easy to imagine how they would deal with political conditionality.

Still, the IFIs may be contributing to democratization in spite of themselves. If one is a Leninist and believes that "the worse, the better," one may indeed welcome their tenacity in pursuit of adjustment, for the escalation of political repression associated with it has helped to spawn the democracy movement in Africa. However, seeking progress by the intensification of contradictions is both costly and risky. It will cause a great deal of suffering and may give rise to extremist ideologies and political forms that serve neither development nor democracy.

Africans who have been struggling to bring democracy to their societies are now finding themselves the beneficiaries of growing international sympathy and support. All too often, however, well-wishers of African democracy in the West have been led astray by insensitivity to local conditions and erroneous theories (like those underlying the imposition of structural adjustment programs). Misguided support, however sincere, is bound to prove counterproductive. The West must guard against this by recognizing that Africa's democrats know what they are doing, and that they should be helped to advance their own agenda.

6.
DANGERS AND DILEMMAS OF DEMOCRACY

Philippe C. Schmitter

Philippe C. Schmitter *is professor of political science at Stanford University. He has previously taught at the University of Chicago and the European University Institute in Florence.* *This is an abbreviated version of a longer essay written at the request and with the financial support of UNESCO. It is published here with the permission of UNESCO's Division on Human Rights and Peace.*

The celebrations that have accompanied shifts from autocracy to democracy since 1974 have tended to obscure some serious dangers and dilemmas. Together, these presage a political future that, instead of embodying "the end of history," promises to be tumultuous, uncertain, and very eventful. Far from being secure in its foundations and practices, modern democracy will have to face unprecedented challenges in the 1990s and beyond.

For the world's established liberal democracies, the very absence in the present context of a credible "systemic" alternative is bound to generate new strains. Defenders of these regimes have long argued—and their citizens have generally agreed—that whatever its faults, this mode of political rule was clearly preferable to any of several forms of autocracy. Now, these external models for comparison have (mostly) disappeared, or in any case are no longer supported by the propaganda and military might of a great power. All that remains are internal standards for evaluation enshrined in a vast body of normative democratic theory and in the expectations of millions of ordinary citizens. What will happen when well-entrenched elite practices in such countries are measured against these long-subordinated ideals of equality, participation, accountability, responsiveness, and self-realization?

Second, the widespread desire of fledgling neodemocracies to imitate the basic norms and institutions of established liberal democracies is by no means a guarantee of success. There is no proof that democracy is inevitable, irrevocable, or a historical necessity. It neither fills some indispensable functional requisite of capitalism, nor corresponds to some ineluctable ethical imperative in social evolution. There is every reason to believe that its consolidation demands an extraordinary and continuous effort—one that many countries are unlikely to be able to make.

My focus here will be limited to the dangers and dilemmas inherent in the difficult and uncertain task of consolidating democracy in the aftermath of the recent collapse, overthrow, or self-transformation of autocracy. I will set aside the many problems involved in reforming and relegitimating "real existing" liberal democracies, although I know that the two challenges are linked in the longer run. To the extent that citizens in established democracies, who have long been accustomed to limited participation and accountability, begin to question these practices and to express their disenchantment openly, they are bound to have some impact on their counterparts in new democracies, who are just aspiring to acquire these same practices. Conversely, the failure of many of these young regimes to consolidate themselves will certainly shake the confidence of liberal democrats in the West and increase pressures for more substantial institutional and policy reforms.

An Exploration of Dangers

"Democracy," in some form or another, may well be the only legitimate and stable form of government in the contemporary world—if one sets aside those entrenched autocracies where monarchs, dictators, technocrats, fundamentalists, or nativists have thus far been able to sell the notion that competitive elections, freedom of association, civil liberties, and executive accountability are merely instruments of Western imperialism or manifestations of cultural alienation. It is striking how few contemporary parties or movements openly advocate a nondemocratic mode of rule. Even the above-mentioned *régimes d'exception* sometimes hold (rigged) elections, tolerate (limited) contestation, and usually claim that their (authoritarian) tutelage will eventually lead to some culturally appropriate kind of democracy.

If democracy has become "the only game in town" in so many polities, why bother to explore its dangers? Is not the absence of a plausible alternative enough to ensure the success of its consolidation in most if not all neodemocracies? The answer is no, for two reasons:

1) Democracy's current ideological hegemony could well fade as disillusionment with the actual performance of neodemocracies mounts and as disaffected actors revive old authoritarian themes or invent new ones.

2) Even if autocracy fails to experience a revival, democracies may stumble on without satisfying the aspirations of their citizens and without consolidating an acceptable and predictable set of rules for political competition and cooperation.[1]

The first scenario implies a "sudden death," usually by coup d'état; the second involves a "lingering demise," whereby democracy gradually gives way to a different form of rule.[2]

So far, the first scenario has occurred with astonishing rarity. One of the most striking things about the more than 40 transitions that have transpired since the demise of the Salazar-Caetano regime in Portugal on 25 April 1974 is how few of these experiments have failed outright. Soon after each of the previous periods of widespread democratization (in 1848-52, 1914-20, and 1945-56, respectively), many, if not most, of the affected polities regressed to the *status quo ante* or worse. Recent neodemocracies, however, have so far avoided this most serious danger. Moreover, even the few apparent exceptions—Burma, Burundi, Haiti, Togo, Gabon, the Congo, Algeria, Suriname—suggest that the most vulnerable moment usually comes with the attempt to hold a "founding election." If the autocrats tolerate such a vote and allow the rise of a government accountable to parliament, then the odds against outright regression improve dramatically. Thailand and Nigeria seem to be rather special cases of persistent oscillation in regime type. The former has shown signs recently of swinging back toward greater democracy, whereas the latter has yet to break the cycle. Haiti is a particularly telling example. Its initial experiment with free and contested elections of uncertain outcome resulted in a reassertion of military power. The democratic trajectory resumed after a short interlude, but again met with a violent overthrow by the armed forces. The outcome has long hung in the balance. In mid-1993, it seemed to be moving toward an internationally mediated solution with President Jean-Bertrand Aristide resuming office, but this subsequently met with the intransigence of the Haitian military. As the recent case of Guatemala demonstrates, massive external intervention, when combined with internal fragmentation, can quickly turn back an authoritarian challenge and even leave the polity more democratic than before.

Which is not to say that, having survived the founding experience, these polities are surely on the road to consolidation. There is no simple choice between *regression* to autocracy and *progression* to democracy, for at least two other alternatives are available: 1) a hybrid regime that combines elements of autocracy and democracy; and 2) persistent but unconsolidated democracy.

Especially when the transition is initiated and imposed from above, the previous rulers attempt to protect their interests by "embedding" authoritarian practices within the emergent regime. Where they liberalize without democratizing (i.e., where they concede certain individual rights but do not render themselves accountable to the citizenry), the hybrid has been labeled *dictablanda*. For those cases where they appear to democratize but do not liberalize (i.e., where elections are held, but under conditions that guarantee the victory of the governing party, that exclude specific sociopolitical groups from participating, or that deprive those elected of the effective capacity to govern), the neologism *democradura* has been proposed. Neither outcome in itself deserves to be called democratic, although both could lead eventually to competitive and accountable rule. *Dictablandas* may not last long, since liberalization can lead to a resurgent civil society that winds up gaining more rights than the autocrats ever meant to concede. Elections in *democraduras* have a habit of producing unexpected winners who, in turn, may use the authority of civilian government to reduce the prerogatives of authoritarian enclaves like the military. But let us not exaggerate. These hybrid arrangements can also serve as facades for enduring autocracy. Once external pressures diminish or internal foes lose resolve, the rulers may quickly revert to the *status quo ante* or worse.

Dictablandas and *democraduras* have become increasingly common, especially in Central America and Africa, as authoritarian rulers seek to introduce democratic mechanisms into their polities in order to placate international forces demanding democratization. Guatemala was one such *democradura* in which elections have been held regularly since 1984-85, but where civilian officials have found their actions restricted by the military. El Salvador, where elections since 1982 have been accompanied by the systematic violation of political and human rights, is another such case, although it may cross the threshold to democracy if UN-negotiated peace accords manage to guarantee a different context for the 1994 elections. Kenya, Togo, Gabon, Zaire, Côte d'Ivoire, and many other African cases seem more like *dictablandas*—increased contestation and even multiparty activities are tolerated, but elections (if held at all) are manipulated to favor the governing clique. In neither region do hybrid regimes seem capable of providing a stable solution to the problems of transition. In Central America, one can hope that their likely demise will give rise to genuine experiments with democracy. In Africa, they may be more usefully viewed as improvisations by rulers who are buying time, waiting for the international climate to change so they can engineer a regression to autocracy.[3]

In South America, Eastern Europe, and Asia the specter haunting the transition is not hybridization but nonconsolidation. Many polities in these regions may fail to establish a form of stable self-governance that is appropriate to their respective social structures or accepted by their respective citizenries. Democracy in its most generic sense persists after the demise of autocracy, but never gels into a specific, reliable, and generally accepted set of rules. These countries are "doomed" to remain democratic almost by default. No serious alternative to democracy seems available. Elections are held; associations are tolerated; rights may be respected; arbitrary treatment by authorities may decline—in other words, the procedural minima are met with some degree of regularity—but regular, acceptable, and predictable democratic patterns never quite crystallize. "Democracy" is not replaced, it just persists by acting in *ad hoc* and *ad hominem* ways as successive problems arise. Under these circumstances, there is no underlying consensus defining relations among parties, organized interests, and ethnic or religious groups.

Argentina is often cited as an exemplar of persistently unconsolidated democracy punctuated by periodic returns to dictatorship. Virtually no two successive elections proceed by the same rules; each party fears the hegemonic pretensions of its opponents; voter preferences swing dramatically from one party to another; constitutional rules are no guarantee against intervention by the central government; executive power is concentrated and exercised in a personalistic fashion; and segments of the military remain involved in a permanent conspiracy against elected officials. Brazil, Peru, and the Philippines also seem more or less to fit this description.[4] It is a bit too early to tell, but "Argentinization" may be the most likely prospect for several new democracies in Eastern Europe and the successor republics of the former Soviet Union.

A Taxonomy of Dilemmas

One way in which analysts have tried to introduce greater precision into this discussion of the dangers of democratization is through the notion of "dilemmas."[5] All new democracies, if they are to consolidate a viable set of institutions, must make difficult choices. Unlike the decisions of the transition, which are usually made in a hurry and under the influence of an overriding agreement on the need to get rid of autocracy, the choices involved in consolidation usually require protracted and explicit negotiations among actors who not only have much greater information about one another's intentions and resources, but are fully aware that the outcome will have a lasting impact on how they cooperate and compete in the future. There are no illusions that everyone or nearly everyone can benefit equally, but only the unavoidable realization that preferences with regard to rules and institutions are incompatible and that any alternatives chosen will hurt some and help others. It is by resolving these dilemmas, by making disagreeable procedural choices, that a given polity chooses "its" type of democracy. If these choices somehow do not get made, then the danger of regression, hybridization, or nonconsolidation increases greatly.

Given the high initial expectations of the people at large, it may come as a shock to realize that the fall of tyrants fails to spell the rise of endless harmony and good feelings: that the popular uprising or the resurrection of civil society is powerless to produce an actionable "general will"; that "honest democrats" can bicker incessantly over seemingly minor details; that the mere advent of democracy does not also bring freedom and equality, growth and equity, security and opportunity, efficiency and responsiveness, autonomy and accountability, *la pluie et le beau temps*. Is it any wonder, then, that disenchantment sets in and that more and more people begin to question whether democracy is really worth so much anxiety and uncertainty?

What is needed is some generic idea of what these dilemmas are. Obviously, each new democracy will have perplexing and painful choices to make that are peculiar to its own history, geostrategic situation, and natural and human resources, but there will surely be common threads. If we could specify these shared dilemmas, we would be better able to assess the probable dangers—although to predict the outcome in any given case, we would still have to incorporate an understanding of all the relevant particulars.

Let us begin by distinguishing two overall categories of dilemmas: 1) those that are *intrinsic* to modern democracy, no matter where it exists or when it came into existence; and 2) those that are *extrinsic*, in the sense that they call into question the compatibility of emerging democratic rules and practices with existing social, cultural, and economic circumstances.

Intrinsic Dilemmas

It may come as another shock to discover that democracy, even if stable and well-entrenched, does not always work well. These intrinsic difficulties will occupy us only briefly in this essay, partly because scholars have already extensively treated them, and also because it is the extrinsic class of dilemmas that most preoccupies new democracies. Still, it seems likely that the intrinsic dilemmas that I am about to list will interact with the difficulties of coming up with rules and practices compatible with prevailing social, cultural, or economic institutions.

1) *Oligarchy*: Roberto Michels was the first to observe that even in the most democratic of institutions, professional leaders and staff tend to possess certain advantages of incumbency that insulate them from the threat of being deposed by challengers. His "Iron Law" implies that parties, associations, and movements—to say nothing of legislatures—all become increasingly oligarchic and therefore less accountable to their members or the public at large.[6]

2) "*Free-riding*": Mancur Olson may not have been the first, but he has been the most systematic in demonstrating that much of what sustains and is produced by democracy consists of public goods to which individuals have no rational incentive to contribute voluntarily. In the absence of private selective payoffs, citizens in a democracy should "learn" that it is not worth their while to vote, to join associations or movements, or even to participate in public affairs since their various discrete contributions will normally have little or no impact upon the outcome. Increasingly, they will leave most of this activity to

professional "political entrepreneurs" acting more or less independently of their followers, constituents, or clients.[7]

3) "*Policy-cycling*": All modern democracies have to make decisions involving the uneven distribution of costs and benefits among groups and individuals. Whenever this is done by majority vote, rather than by unanimity, the possibility arises of "cycling," i.e., of unstable majorities formed by shifting coalitions composed of groups with incompatible preferences on other issues. If choices are presented pairwise, no stable majority emerges, and there may ensue a vacillating series of policy measures that pass in sequence, but have the net effect of alienating everyone.[8]

4) *Functional autonomy*: All democracies must depend for their survival on specialized institutions that cannot themselves be democratic—the armed forces and the central bank are the most obvious examples. For these to perform their respective functions efficiently, they must be insulated from popular pressures and partisan competition. To the extent that the role of such institutions increases in a more turbulent, competitive, and (as we shall see below) internationally interdependent environment, the power of the experts who run these institutions will increase at the expense of congressional and executive leaders accountable to the citizenry.

5) *Interdependence*: All contemporary democracies, even the largest and most powerful of them, are entangled in complex webs of interdependence with other democracies and some autocracies. In principle, elected national leaders are sovereign (i.e., accountable to no authority higher than their own countries' constitutions). In practice, however, they are quite limited in their ability to control the decisions of transnational firms, the movement of ideas and persons across their borders, and the impact of their neighbors' policies. Their authority confined to nation-states, these leaders find themselves decreasingly capable of ensuring the welfare and security of their own citizens.

Extrinsic Dilemmas

Such are the major generic dilemmas that are plaguing established democracies. They will have to be faced eventually by fledgling democracies. But before the institutions of the latter can become oligarchic, before the diminishing enthusiasm of their citizens teaches them to free-ride, before policy-cycling can settle in, maybe even before their armed forces and central banks can establish their functional autonomy, and before they can come to terms with their de facto restricted national sovereignty, politicians in new democracies are going to have to settle on rules and practices for resolving even more pressing extrinsic dilemmas.

The core of the problem with regard to these extrinsic dilemmas is well captured by the Spanish verb *adecuar*, which means to come up with solutions that are at least adequate, if less than optimal. The trick is to make binding and collective choices (or, as we shall see, nonchoices) between alternative institutional arrangements that are compatible with existing socioeconomic structures and cultural identities. In the longer run, it may become possible for consolidated democracies to change these "confining conditions."[9] In the shorter run, those polities that have democratized and *simultaneously* sought to produce rapid changes in the rights of property owners, the distribution of wealth, the balance of public-private power, and so forth have usually failed and, in so doing, rendered the consolidation of democracy much more difficult. The Portuguese learned this the hard way in 1974-75. The Spaniards next door took the lesson to heart and resolved their major extrinsic dilemmas one after another. The Chileans, faced with more deliberately placed "confining conditions" than any other recently democratizing nation, have moved very carefully and gradually to remove them. Alas, in Eastern Europe and the successor republics of the old Soviet Union, the gradualist option is unavailable. These countries face a knotty tangle of dilemmas that simultaneously demand urgent attention and force crucial decisions affecting virtually all realms of political, social, economic, and cultural life.[10]

The response to these extrinsic dilemmas may involve varying degrees of "reflection and choice." The "classic" model (best exemplified by the Philadelphia Convention of 1787) is that of a constituent assembly, composed of delegates deliberating (perhaps secretly) about the country's rules and institutions. Spain is the best recent example of how that founding moment can be seized to great effect.[11] In some countries, by contrast, the key players have agreed on a "nonchoice" by simply reviving some previously employed institutional format, either because the ensuing authoritarian period was short and relatively inconsequential (as in Greece in the late 1970s), or because some ancient founding document was thought still to be adequate (as in Argentina and Lithuania more recently). In the Philippines, the metaprocedural choices were made not by deliberation among elected representatives or by resuscitation of the past, but by a committee of experts. Chile continues to operate under a document imposed on it by onetime dictator Augusto Pinochet. Brazil and some East European countries have taken a long time before formally attempting to "adequate" their institutions. Russia stands out as an extreme case of incapacity to choose any set of self-limiting institutions.

Few democratizing countries face their extrinsic dilemmas in a purely reflective and logical manner. Most have historical experience to draw upon, even if they may be compelled to modify their choices in the light of subsequent economic, demographic, generational, and cultural changes. Sentiment and habit also play a role. This does not always ensure an adequate institutional fit, much less an optimal one, but at least the comforts of familiarity are secured.

The last 20 years of democratization have included an unusual number of polities that either have had virtually no previous experience with democracy (Paraguay, Mongolia, Albania, Bulgaria, Ethiopia, Angola, all the Central Asian republics, Taiwan, and Russia), or whose previous experiences with it have been notoriously short and unsuccessful (Hungary, Poland, Romania, Estonia, Latvia, Lithuania, Mali, the Congo, Benin, Togo, Thailand, and South Korea). In principle, this should place them in a more favorable position to select adequate institutions; in practice, one suspects that most will end up relying extensively (if clandestinely) upon outside advisors and foreign models. As we shall see below, political science may have little to say about what are the most adequate institutions for resolving specific dilemmas.

It should also be kept in mind that those who make the metachoices governing long-term democratic consolidation must also pay attention to banal near-term considerations like staying in office. This is especially significant today, when most democratizers are career politicians. They may have no other vocation and source of income than politics and, therefore, are even less likely to put general interests ahead of their own immediate interests in pursuing their political careers.

The single most important influence on these choices—beyond that of habit and precedent—is the mode of transition.[12] Differences in the level of mass mobilization (as opposed to elite domination) and in the extent of violence (as opposed to negotiation) produce variations in constraints and opportunities. The most favorable context for an eventual consolidation is a "pacted transition" in which elites from the previous autocracy and its opposition reach a stalemate and find themselves compelled to respect each other's interests. The least favorable is a revolution, with mobilized masses using force to topple the *ancien régime*. Falling somewhere in between are: imposed transitions, in which elements of the autocracy dictate the conditions and pace of the changeover; and reform transitions, in which mass mobilization plays a vital role but incumbents are not violently removed from power.

As we briefly describe the major extrinsic dilemmas, let us remember that only by knowing the habits instilled by a given country's experience with democracy, and only by situating the actors within their respective modes of transition, does it become possible to estimate the most adequate institutional response.

1) *Boundaries and identities*: If there is one overriding political requisite for democracy, it is the prior existence of a legitimate political unit. Before actors can expect to settle into a routine of competition and cooperation, they must have some reliable idea of who the other players are and what will be the physical limits of their playing field. The predominant principle in establishing these boundaries and identities is that of "nationality." Unfortunately, it is not always clear what constitutes a nation—before, during, or even after democratization. Common ancestry, language, symbols, and historical memories may all play a role, but there always remain residual elements of opportunistic choice and collective enthusiasm. All one can say for sure is that the sentiment of national identity and boundaries is the outcome of arcane and complex historical processes that are, nevertheless, subject to manipulation. Democratization itself may encourage actors to attempt such manipulations in order to create constituencies favorable to their respective purposes, but it does not and cannot resolve the issue. *There is simply no democratic way of deciding what a nation and its corresponding political unit should be.* Slogans such as the self-determination of peoples and devices such as plebiscites or referenda simply beg the question of who is eligible to vote within which constituencies, and whether the winning majority can legitimately impose its will on eventual minorities.

2) ***Capitalist production, accumulation, and distribution***: All of the established democracies are located in countries in which economic production and accumulation are largely in the hands of privately owned firms and in which distribution is mainly effected through market mechanisms. In all of these polities, however, the outcome of these processes is affected—admittedly in different ways and to different degrees—by public intervention that has been decided by democratic governments and generally supported by most of the citizenry. The paradoxical conclusion is inescapable that 1) capitalism must be a necessary (though not sufficient) condition for democracy; and 2) that capitalism must be modified significantly to make it compatible with democracy.

The dilemma is not merely the static one of deciding on what mix of public-private ownership, income redistribution, monetary intervention, welfare expenditure, health-and-safety regulation, consumer protection, credit subsidization, industrial promotion, tariff protection, and so on will best satisfy citizens' expectations of justice or fairness without stifling economic growth (and impeding the incumbents' chances for reelection). It also involves a dynamic set of choices concerning the development of capitalism at different stages and in different locations within the world system. Playing "catch-up" seems to require greater reliance on state intervention by peripheral economies; overcoming critical thresholds in capital accumulation may even require recourse to authoritarian methods, if not to outright bureaucratic-authoritarian rule.[13]

In the best of circumstances, the preceding autocracy may have already concentrated profits, encouraged private accumulation, increased the state's fiscal capacity, developed the country's physical infrastructure, and improved its international competitiveness, thereby doing much to resolve this dilemma. New democracies that have inherited this sort of legacy—Spain, Chile, and to a much lesser extent Turkey, Greece, Uruguay, and Brazil—have found the task of consolidation easier.

In the worst of circumstances, the *ancien régime* leaves a legacy of corruption, protectionism, price distortions, foreign indebtedness, inefficient public enterprises, trade imbalances, and fiscal instability. The Argentinean and Peruvian cases demonstrate how costly it is to put off dealing with these issues. The experience of Bolivia and, in a different way, Portugal suggest that it may be possible to tackle such problems and still make progress toward consolidation. The countries of Eastern Europe and the former Soviet Union find themselves in a dramatically more difficult situation. Not only must many of the institutions of pricing, credit, monetary policy, collective bargaining, consumer protection, and the like, be created *ex nihilo*, but this must be done at the same time that key political arrangements are being chosen. The first project often implies an exaggerated dependence on foreign models and advice; the latter will likely involve serious unexpected coincidences and unforeseen interaction effects.

It is important to stress that the problematic relationship between capitalism and democracy—"necessary, but necessarily modified"—is structural. It stems from the root difference between a polity that distributes power and status relatively equally and an economy that distributes property and income relatively unequally. This poses a dilemma no matter how well the economic system is performing at a given moment.[14]

Not surprisingly, however, most observers assume that crises in growth, employment, foreign-exchange earnings, and debt repayment bode ill for the consolidation of democratic rule, and few would question the long-run value of growth for political stability. But austerity may have some perverse advantages, at least for initial survivability. In the context of the difficult economic conditions of the late 1980s and early 1990s, the exhaustion of utopian ideologies and even of rival policy prescriptions has become painfully evident. Neither the extreme right nor the extreme left has a plausible alternative to offer. Populism, driven by the disappointment of rising expectations and disenchantment with the travails of democracy, is always a possibility, but unlike in the past, it can deliver no immediate rewards to the masses.

To the extent that this situation diminishes the rewards expected from engaging in antisystem activity, the likelihood is enhanced that some form of democracy will persist. This suggests that the conditions for bargaining over rules and institutions may be as favorable in times of austerity as in times of plenty. Such conditions are likely to worsen, however, when the economy is fitful, going through stop-and-go cycles or experiencing sudden gluts or shortages.

3) ***Overload and ungovernability***: Democracies are not anarchies. They must be capable of governing, of using public authority to modify the behavior of individual citizens, and of regulating the performance of firms and markets. One of the enduring mysteries of established democracies is their source of political obligation. Why do citizens generally obey the law and pursue their demands through regular institutional channels, even when there might seem to be a greater payoff and little fear of punishment from doing otherwise? The usual answers of political scientists rest on such abstract notions as "tradition," "trust in institutions," "socialization" and, of course, "legitimacy." Unfortunately, they are rarely very explicit about where these things come from in the first place—often noting only the gradual accumulation of custom and the explicit inculcation of norms through the educational system. These lessons are not likely to give much comfort to those concerned with the consolidation of democracy in a relatively short period of time.

Moreover, there is growing evidence from the older democracies that traditional partisan identifications, habits of self-restraint, trust in institutions, and belief in the legitimacy of rulers have all been persistently and markedly declining, whether measured by attitudes in surveys or behavior in polling booths or in the streets. The reasons for such declines have been extensively (if inconclusively) discussed: greater physical mobility, higher levels of education, more leisure time, decline in the quality of public education, increasing intellectual disaffection, and so forth.[15]

The problem for so many new democracies is that their own respective populations are often subject to the same trends and are therefore more mobile, educated, disaffected and, certainly, skeptical than were the citizens of older democracies when those countries went through their early phases of political development. Most importantly, modern mass communications have made citizens vastly more aware of events taking place elsewhere in the world and of alternative means for pursuing their interests and passions. Hence the shift away from political parties as the exclusive intermediaries for citizens and the primary source of legitimacy for rulers. Interest associations (and more recently, various kinds of social movements) have moved into this space. They are particularly important in expressing the demands of classes, professions, generations, religions, ethnic groups, and other segments of the population whose numbers preclude them from creating or dominating parties, but whose interests and passions motivate them to participate with special intensity.[16]

New democracies thus need legitimacy in order to build institutions, and institutions in order to establish legitimacy. Success will depend on many factors, especially the mode of transition and prior experience with democracy. Even though most new democracies today contain relatively sophisticated, well-informed groups whose interests are diverse and whose organizational skills are formidable, political parties will probably still provide the principal linkage between citizens and government, and it is likely that the choice of rules and institutions will involve bargaining between party leaders. Hence the nature of the emerging party system will be a major determinant of governability. But it will not be the only one. Today's fledgling democracies will not repeat the trajectory of their older cousins. They will have to cope with (and govern with) the full range of associations and movements that have accumulated in the meantime—all the exotic flora and fauna of a media-saturated, urbanized, postindustrial society.

4) *Corruption and decay*: At first glance, especially given recent headlines in Western Europe and the United States, this would seem an intrinsic dilemma. All democracies, old as well as new, are subject to the abuse of power and the appropriation of public goods for private benefit—evils ultimately held in check by the periodic opportunity citizens have to go to the polls and "throw the rascals out." The criteria of malfeasance may shift a bit from one culture to another; the magnitude seems to vary inversely with the extent to which capitalism offers alternative sources of self-enrichment. Democracies as a group are still far behind autocracies when it comes to either corruption or decay.

The element which makes the dilemma extrinsic is the professionalization of politics. When democratic politicians were mostly well-to-do male amateurs, positions of representation were usually unremunerated. Upon losing them, officeholders would return to private life, often at a profit to their fortunes. This began to change with the rise of socialist parties in the early twentieth century, and has continued unabated. Today, not only do those who hold elected office expect to be well-paid for their services, but many have no other source of income. Add to this the spiralling costs of getting elected and servicing one's constituents, and the problem of extracting sufficient revenues to pay for democratic politics becomes even more acute.

How do the citizens pay for democracy? At what point does its peculiar "political economy" become a serious impediment to its legitimacy, even its perpetuation? Some more senior democracies—Japan, France, Italy, and Spain—are currently facing this issue; others have had to deal with recurrent scandals in the past. New democracies are usually born in a burst of civic enthusiasm and moral outrage against the corrupt decadence of the *ancien régime*, so that the dilemma only emerges later. When it does, the effect can be particularly devastating, for politicians have less secure alternative sources of income, while citizens are less convinced of the need to pay their representatives generously.

What tends to compound the problem in fledgling democracies is that regime transition is often accompanied by the simultaneous need to make major transformations in other socioeconomic domains: property rights, industrial subsidies, price controls, privatization, deregulation, licensing of services and media, and the like. Even where the thrust of change is toward "unleashing market forces," the process of accomplishing this offers very attractive opportunities for illicit enrichment on the part of the politicians who set the norms, sell off the enterprises, and award the contracts. Ironically, while the long-term intent is precisely to reduce the rent seeking intrinsic to public ownership and regulation, the short-term effect is to increase the potential payoffs to be had from the exploitation of public authority.

The crux of the matter is that modern democratic practice, especially given its professionalization and the expansion of its policy tasks, has never come to terms with its own political economy. Understandably, democratic citizens find the financing of parties, the remunerating of deputies, the extracting of fees-for-service, and the profiting from government contracts to be murky and often repugnant. It should therefore come as no surprise to discover that they are reluctant to pay—even for the type of regime that they manifestly prefer.

5) ***External security and internal insecurity*:** The advent of democracy does not guarantee national security. Depending on a country's size, resources, strategic location, and neighbors, it may even make the problem worse. Fledgling democracies can present an attractive "target of opportunity" to aggressors—as the case of Bosnia tragically testifies. They may also, however, be able to count upon greater regional and global solidarity—consider Macedonia, where 1,100 foreign troops are now stationed to guard its territorial integrity.

Furthermore, almost every country undergoing the changeover to democracy has suffered from greater domestic insecurity: higher crime rates, increases in political violence, and more frequent disruptions of basic services. In a few cases, dissidents have even resorted to terrorism in their efforts to redefine the identity of the political unit (e.g., the Basque-based ETA in Spain); to bring about a rupture with capitalism (e.g., Sendero Luminoso in Peru); or simply to return the country to autocracy (e.g., the *carapintada* officer clique in Argentina).

At the center of the security dilemma lies the very delicate issue of civil-military and civil-police relations—a dilemma made all the more acute if the previous regime was a military dictatorship. Not only will the transition have to face the issues of extricating the armed forces from power and meting out justice for crimes committed during their tenure, but the consolidation will have to give the soldiers a satisfactory and credible role under democratic auspices. In the past, this was not too difficult since the communist threat could provide reason (or rationale) enough for retaining an autonomous national defense capability. Communism's collapse, plus that of most domestic armed insurrections, has left a "functional vacuum" in several areas of the world. Membership in NATO was sufficient in the 1970s to provide a *raison d'être* (and substantial military assistance) to the armed forces of Southern Europe's neodemocracies. Two of these, Greece and Turkey, even had plausible enemies in each other! Elsewhere, especially in Latin America, it will take more imagination to find the armies a plausible role.

Moreover, civilian governments in new democracies that lack border conflicts or internal insurrections find themselves assailed with competing demands from myriad newly enfranchised groups. To the extent that these governments are simultaneously following neoliberal strictures to cut budget imbalances, implement austerity measures, and privatize public (and often military-run) enterprises, the military must seem like the most likely place for cuts. One can hardly blame citizens for thinking that military expenditures were swollen under the preceding dictatorship and should be slashed drastically—just when the shift to a new mission might temporarily require additional expenditures. And these potential new missions—such as combatting drug traffic, policing common crime, repressing social unrest, building infrastructure, providing health and relief services to stricken areas, and participating in UN and regional peacekeeping forces—all have their risks. Some virtually invite officers to intervene in policy making outside their traditional domain; others are profoundly repugnant to their usual sense of mission; none of them would provide a sufficient excuse for maintaining existing levels of expenditure and personnel for very long.

Establishing control over the police can also pose some delicate choices—especially where it has previously been under the control of the military or the intelligence services. On the one hand, there is the enhanced need for policing due to the likely increase in crime. On the other, there is the enhanced expectation that the police will respect due process of law and basic human rights. Few things can be more subversive of trust in institutions and the legitimacy of the government than the popular perception that "nothing has changed" at the level of face-to-face contacts between police authorities and the population. Here is an area where a modest but firm investment in civilian control can yield high symbolic benefits (as happened in Spain), and where its absence can undermine not only the regime's legitimacy but the authority of the state itself.

As with all of these extrinsic dilemmas, the long-run prospects are favorable—provided that the neodemocracies cope with the nearer-term consequences of the choices that they have made (or not made) during the transition. Eventually, civil-police relations will become institutionalized, and guarantees for human rights will be made to stick. Internal security should stabilize, if not increase, once consolidation is accomplished. The proliferation of popularly accountable governments within a given region or across the entire globe should be good for external security. One of the few "invariant laws" of international relations is that democracies do not go to war with other democracies. Autocracies have frequently fought each other as well as democracies, but a world or a region populated by democracies is definitely likely to be less insecure and less violent. Its member states will still have their quarrels but are much more likely to resort to negotiation, mediation, or adjudication to settle them. Barring the regression of any of its members to autocracy, such a democratized region should be able to organize itself into a "security community" wherein the resort to arms would be unimaginable.[17] This, in turn, should facilitate a firm assertion of civilian supremacy and perhaps even a gradual reduction in military expenditures and personnel.

Forbearance and Disenchantment

This essay has suggested that there are some good reasons to be less than triumphal about the longer-term prospects for contemporary democratization. Historically, very few countries have ever consolidated democracy on their first try. All previous waves of regime change eventually receded—and it may be too early to tell how many polities will be swept back to autocracy this time. Certainly, those that have not yet resolved the dilemma of defining their national identity and territorial boundaries are unlikely to make much progress in other domains. Moreover, with most neodemocracies facing declining economic performance, accelerating inflation, heavy loads of foreign debt, severe budgetary and fiscal imbalances, and the pressure of international competition and capital flight in the new global economy, resolving the fundamental structural dilemmas concerning capitalist institutions is not getting any easier.

What is most striking so far is that citizens have responded to these dilemmas of choice and strains of adjustment by focusing their discontent on governments rather than on democracy as such. They have frequently voted transitional leaders and parties out of office, but they have rarely demanded or supported a return to authoritarianism in any guise. Despite this rather remarkable display of forbearance, there are growing signs of what the Spaniards have called *desencanto* (disenchantment) with democracy itself. The perception is widespread that corruption has increased and that decay has set in even *before* consolidation has been assured. With astonishing regularity, one hears complaints that professional politicians have arranged disproportionate salaries and perquisites for themselves; that political parties are clandestinely enriching themselves; that privileged groups are evading the law; that entrenched powers such as the military have protected and even increased their share of the budget; that crime has increased; that violations of human rights by police forces persist; that taxes are unfairly distributed or collected; and that unsavory nationals or even foreigners are reaping too many of the benefits from privatization and deregulation. Complaints like these suggest that one or more extrinsic dilemmas are not being addressed.

But these problems of economic suffering and political disappointment pale when compared to those generated by cultural conflict. Autocracies commonly suppress or manipulate ethnolinguistic minorities; nascent democracies then inherit the resulting resentments while providing an environment in which they can be freely aired. In Southern Europe and Latin America, where national borders and identities have long been secure, the demands of subnational groups proved to be relatively easy to accommodate through policies of territorial devolution, although in the case of the Spanish Basques this was accomplished only after a lengthy and bloody armed struggle. In Eastern Europe and Africa, where historical resentments run much deeper and existing political frontiers often run through rather than around nations, ethnolinguistic divisions can become explosive and easily overwhelm the usual social cleavages—of class, status, profession, generation, and the like—that underlie stable party and interest-group systems.

The suggestion that the current wave of regime changes is likely to be followed by fewer regressions to autocracy than in the past may prove of scant comfort to those presently attempting to consolidate new democracies. They still must face some formidable dilemmas and make some arduous choices before settling into the routinized patterns of political cooperation and competition that will ensure the perpetuation of democratic rule.

NOTES

1. See Juan Linz, *The Breakdown of Democratic Regimes: Crisis, Breakdown and Reequilibration* (Baltimore: Johns Hopkins University Press, 1978). Linz observed that, on many occasions in the interwar period, the worst enemies of democracy were themselves genuine democrats who believed that by taking certain extraordinary measures they were protecting democracy. The breakdown came, not because the alternative was so popular or overwhelming, but because the existing regime had transformed itself into a quasi-autocracy.

2. Cf. Guillermo O'Donnell, "Transitions, Continuities and Paradoxes," in Scott Mainwaring et al., eds., *Issues in Democratic Consolidation: The New South American Democracies in Comparative Perspective* (Notre Dame: University of Notre Dame Press, 1992), 17-56.

3. For a detailed account of this tendency in Africa, with some references to Latin America, see Max Liniger-Goumaz, *La démocrature: Dictature camouflée; démocratie truquée* (Paris: Editions L'Harmattan, 1992).

4. Guillermo O'Donnell has drawn attention to other aspects of this subset of countries, which he calls "delegative democracies." See his "Delegative Democracy," *Journal of Democracy* 5 (January 1994): 55-69.

5. The first to have done so (to my knowledge) was Terry Karl in her "Dilemmas of Democratization in Latin America," *Comparative Politics* 23 (October 1990): 1-23. Much of my thinking on this subject has been influenced by this article and subsequent conversations with her.

6. Roberto Michels, *Political Parties: A Sociological Study of the Oligarchic Tendencies of Modern Europe* (New York and London: The Free Press, 1962).

7. Mancur Olson, *The Logic of Collective Action: Public Goals and the Theory of Groups* (Cambridge: Harvard University Press, 1965).

8. The classic statement of this problem is Kenneth J. Arrow, *Social Choice and Individual Values* (New York: John Wiley, 1951). For a more recent restatement, along with other logical dilemmas of collective choice, see Dennis C. Mueller, *Public Choice II* (Cambridge: Cambridge University Press, 1989), 63ff.

9. Cf. Otto Kirchheimer, "Confining Conditions and Revolutionary Breakthroughs," *American Political Science Review* 59 (1965): 964-74.

10. Several authors have stressed this issue of simultaneity: Claus Offe, "Capitalism by Democratic Design? Democratic Theory Facing the Triple Transition in East Central Europe," *Social Research* 58 (Winter 1991): 865-92; Jon Elster, "Constitution-Making in Eastern Europe," *Public Administration* (forthcoming, 1994); Philippe C. Schmitter and Terry Karl, "The Types of Democracy Emerging in Southern and Eastern Europe and South and Central America," in Peter Volten, ed., *Bound to Change: Consolidating Democracy in Central Europe* (New York: IEWSS, 1992), 42-68.

11. A. Bonimé-Blanc, *Spain's Transition to Democracy: The Politics of Constitution-Making* (Boulder and London: Westview Press, 1987). For general remarks on the desirability of seizing this moment early, see Bruce Ackerman, *The Future of Liberal Revolution* (New Haven: Yale University Press, 1992).

12. Terry Lynn Karl and Philippe C. Schmitter, "Modes of Transition in Latin America, Southern and Eastern Europe," *International Social Science Journal* 128 (1991): 269-84; also Donald Share, "Transitions to Democracy and Transition Through Transaction," *Comparative Political Studies* 19 (1987): 545.

13. See Alexander Gerschenkron, *Economic Backwardness in Historical Perspective* (Cambridge: Harvard University Press, 1962); and Guillermo O'Donnell, *Modernization and Bureaucratic Authoritarianism: Studies in South American Politics* (Berkeley: University of California, Institute of International Studies, 1973).

14. No one has pursued this theme more exhaustively than Adam Przeworski. For his latest exploration, see *Democracy and the Market* (New York: Cambridge University Press, 1992).

15. The *locus classicus* of this discussion is Michel Crozier, Samuel P. Huntington, and Joji Watanuki, *The Crisis of Democracy* (New York: New York University Press, 1975). For Huntington's revised thoughts on the prospects for democracy, see his "Will More Countries Become Democratic?" *Political Science Quarterly* 99 (Spring 1984): 193-218.

16. This theme is further developed in Philippe C. Schmitter, "The Consolidation of Democracy and Representation of Social Groups," *American Behavioral Scientist* 35 (March-June 1992): 422-49.

17. See Michael W. Doyle, "Liberalism and World Politics," *American Political Science Review* 80 (December 1986): 1151-70; and Bruce Russett, "Political and Alternative Security: Towards a More Democratic and Therefore More Peaceful World," in Burns H. Weston, ed., *Alternative Security: Living Without Nuclear Deterrence* (Boulder, Colo.: Westview Press, 1990). For a case study of the impact of democratization upon foreign relations in the Southern Cone of Latin America, see Philippe C. Schmitter, "Change in Regime Type and Progress in International Relations," in Emanuel Adler and Beverly Crawford, eds., *Progress in Postwar International Relations* (New York: Columbia University Press, 1991), 89-127.

7.
DELEGATIVE DEMOCRACY

Guillermo O'Donnell

***Guillermo O'Donnell,** an Argentine political scientist, is Helen Kellogg Professor of International Studies and Academic Director of the Kellogg Institute of International Studies at the University of Notre Dame. His books include* Modernization and Bureaucratic-Authoritarianism *(1979);* Bureaucratic-Authoritarianism: Argentina, 1966-1973, in Comparative Perspective *(1988); and, with Philippe Schmitter and Laurence Whitehead,* Transitions from Authoritarian Rule *(1986).*

Here I depict a "new species," a type of existing democracies that has yet to be theorized. As often happens, it has many similarities with other, already recognized species, with cases shading off between the former and some variety of the latter. Still, I believe that the differences are significant enough to warrant an attempt at such a depiction. The drawing of neater boundaries between these types of democracy depends on empirical research, as well as more refined analytical work that I am now undertaking. But if I really have found a new species (and not a member of an already recognized family, or a form too evanescent to merit conceptualization), it may be worth exploring its main features.

Scholars who have worked on democratic transitions and consolidation have repeatedly said that, since it would be wrong to assume that these processes all culminate in the same result, we need a typology of democracies. Some interesting efforts have been made, focused on the consequences, in terms of types of democracy and policy patterns, of various paths to democratization.[1] My own ongoing research suggests, however, that the more decisive factors for generating various kinds of democracy are not related to the characteristics of the preceding authoritarian regime or to the process of transition. Instead, I believe that we must focus upon various long-term historical factors, as well as the degree of severity of the socioeconomic problems that newly installed democratic governments inherit.

Let me briefly state the main points of my argument: 1) Existing theories and typologies of democracy refer to *representative* democracy as it exists, with all its variations and subtypes, in highly developed capitalist countries. 2) Some newly installed democracies (Argentina, Brazil, Peru, Ecuador, Bolivia, Philippines, Korea, and many postcommunist countries) *are* democracies, in the sense that they meet Robert Dahl's criteria for the definition of polyarchy.[2] 3) Yet these democracies are not—and do not seem to be on the path toward becoming—representative democracies; they present characteristics that prompt me to call them *delegative* democracies (DD). 4) DDs are not consolidated (i.e., institutionalized) democracies, but they may be *enduring*. In many cases, there is no sign either of any imminent threat of an authoritarian regression, or of advances toward representative democracy. 5) There is an important interaction effect: the deep social and economic crisis that most of these countries inherited from their authoritarian predecessors reinforces certain practices and conceptions about the proper exercise of political authority that lead in the direction of delegative, not representative democracy.

The following considerations underlie the argument presented above:[3]

A) The installation of a democratically elected government opens the way for a "second transition," often longer and more complex than the initial transition from authoritarian rule.

B) This second transition is supposed to be from a democratically elected *government* to an institutionalized, consolidated democratic *regime*.

C) Nothing guarantees, however, that this second transition will occur. New democracies may regress to authoritarian rule, or they may stall in a feeble, uncertain situation. This situation may endure without opening avenues for institutionalized forms of democracy.

D) The crucial element determining the success of the second transition is the building of a set of institutions that become important decisional points in the flow of political power.

E) For such a successful outcome to occur, governmental policies and the political strategies of various agents must embody the recognition of a paramount shared interest in democratic institution building. The successful cases have featured a decisive coalition of broadly supported political leaders who take great care in creating and strengthening democratic political institutions. These institutions, in turn, have made it easier to cope with the social and economic problems inherited from the authoritarian regime. This was the case in Spain, Portugal (although not immediately after democratic installation), Uruguay, and Chile.

F) In contrast, the cases of delegative democracy mentioned earlier have achieved neither institutional progress nor much governmental effectiveness in dealing with their respective social and economic crises.

Before elaborating these themes in greater detail, I must make a brief excursus to explain more precisely what I mean by institutions and institutionalization, thereby bringing into sharper focus the patterns that fail to develop under delegative democracy.

On Institutions

Institutions are regularized patterns of interaction that are known, practiced, and regularly accepted (if not necessarily normatively approved) by social agents who expect to continue interacting under the rules and norms formally or informally embodied in those patterns. Sometimes, but not necessarily, institutions become formal organizations: they materialize in buildings, seals, rituals, and persons in roles that authorize them to "speak for" the organization.

I am concerned here with a subset: *democratic* institutions. Their definition is elusive, so I will delimit the concept by way of some approximations. To begin with, democratic institutions are political institutions. They have a recognizable, direct relationship with the main themes of politics: the making of decisions that are mandatory within a given territory, the channels of access to decision-making roles, and the shaping of the interests and identities that claim such access. The boundaries between what is and is not a political institution are blurred, and vary across time and countries.

We need a second approximation. Some political institutions are formal organizations belonging to the constitutional network of a polyarchy: these include congress, the judiciary, and political parties. Others, such as fair elections, have an intermittent organizational embodiment but are no less indispensable. The main question about all these institutions is how they work: are they really important decisional points in the flow of influence, power, and policy? If they are not, what are the consequences for the overall political process?

Other factors indispensable for the workings of democracy in contemporary societies—those that pertain to the formation and representation of collective identities and interests—may or may not be institutionalized, or they may be operative only for a part of the potentially relevant sectors. In representative democracies, those patterns are highly institutionalized and organizationally embodied through pluralist or neocorporatist arrangements.

The characteristics of a functioning institutional setting include the following:

1) *Institutions both incorporate and exclude.* They determine which agents, on the basis of which resources, claims, and procedures, are accepted as valid participants in their decision-making and implementation processes. These criteria are necessarily selective: they fit (and favor) some agents; they may lead others to reshape themselves in order to meet them; and for various reasons, they may be impossible

to meet, or unacceptable, for still others. The scope of an institution is the degree to which it incorporates and excludes its set of potentially relevant agents.

2) *Institutions shape the probability distribution of outcomes.* As Adam Przeworski has noted, institutions "process" only certain actors and resources, and do so under certain rules.[4] This predetermines the range of feasible outcomes, and their likelihood within that range. Democratic institutions, for example, preclude the use or threat of force and the outcomes that this would generate. On the other hand, the subset of democratic institutions based on the universality of the vote, as Philippe Schmitter and Wolfgang Streeck have argued, is not good at processing the intensity of preferences.[5] Institutions of interest representation are better at processing the intensity of preferences, although at the expense of the universalism of voting and citizenship and, often, of the "democraticness" of their decision making.

3) *Institutions tend to aggregate, and to stabilize the aggregation of, the level of action and organization of agents interacting with them.* The rules established by institutions influence strategic decisions by agents as to the degree of aggregation that is more efficacious for them in terms of the likelihood of favorable outcomes. Institutions, or rather the persons who occupy decision-making roles within them, have limited information-processing capabilities and attention spans. Consequently, those persons prefer to interact with relatively few agents and issues at a time.[6] This tendency toward aggregation is another reason for the exclusionary side of every institution.

4) *Institutions induce patterns of representation.* For the same reasons, institutions favor the transformation of the many potential voices of their constituencies into a few that can claim to speak as their representatives. Representation involves, on the one hand, the acknowledged right to speak for some relevant others and, on the other, the ability to deliver the compliance of those others with what the representative decides. Insofar as this capability is demonstrated and the given rules of the game are respected, institutions and their various representatives develop an interest in their mutual coexistence as interacting agents.

5) *Institutions stabilize agents/representatives and their expectations.* Institutional leaders and representatives come to expect behaviors within a relatively narrow range of possibilities from a set of actors that they expect to meet again in the next round of interactions. Certain agents may not like the narrowing of expected behaviors, but they anticipate that deviations from such expectations are likely to be counterproductive. This is the point at which it may be said that an institution (which probably has become a formal organization) is strong. The institution is in equilibrium; it is in nobody's interest to change it, except in incremental and basically consensual ways.

6) *Institutions lengthen the time-horizons of actors.* The stabilization of agents and expectations entails a time dimension: institutionalized interactions are expected to continue into the future among the same (or a slowly and rather predictably changing) set of agents. This, together with a high level of aggregation of representation and of control of their constituencies, is the foundation for the "competitive cooperation" that characterizes institutionalized democracies: one-shot prisoner's dilemmas can be overcome,[7] bargaining (including logrolling) is facilitated, various trade-offs over time become feasible, and sequential attention to issues makes it possible to accommodate an otherwise unmanageable agenda. The establishment of these practices further strengthens the willingness of all relevant agents to recognize one another as valid interlocutors, and enhances the value that they attach to the institution that shapes their interrelationships. This virtuous circle is completed when most democratic institutions achieve not only reasonable scope and strength but also a high density of multiple and stabilized interrelationships. This makes these institutions important points of decision in the overall political process, and a consolidated, institutionalized democracy thus emerges.

A way to summarize what I have said is that, in the functioning of contemporary, complex societies, democratic political institutions provide a crucial level of mediation and aggregation between, on one side, structural factors and, on the other, not only individuals but also the diverse groupings under which society organizes its multiple interests and identities. This intermediate—i.e., institutional—level has an important impact on the patterns of organization of society, bestowing representation upon some participants in the political process and excluding others. Institutionalization undeniably entails heavy costs—not only exclusion but also the recurring, and all too real, nightmares of bureaucratization and boredom. The alternative, however, submerges social and political life in the hell of a colossal prisoner's dilemma.

This is, of course, an ideal typical description, but I find it useful for tracing, by way of contrast, the peculiarities of a situation where there is a dearth of democratic institutions. A noninstitutionalized democracy is characterized by the restricted scope, the weakness, and the low density of whatever political institutions exist. The place of well-functioning institutions is taken by other nonformalized but strongly operative practices—clientelism, patrimonialism, and corruption.

Characterizing Delegative Democracy

Delegative democracies rest on the premise that whoever wins election to the presidency is thereby entitled to govern as he or she sees fit, constrained only by the hard facts of existing power relations and by a constitutionally limited term of office. The president is taken to be the embodiment of the nation and the main custodian and definer of its interests. The policies of his government need bear no resemblance to the promises of his campaign—has not the president been authorized to govern as he (or she) thinks best? Since this paternal figure is supposed to take care of the whole nation, his political base must be a movement, the supposedly vibrant overcoming of the factionalism and conflicts associated with parties. Typically, winning presidential candidates in DDs present themselves as above both political parties and organized interests. How could it be otherwise for somebody who claims to embody the whole of the nation? In this view, other institutions—courts and legislatures, for instance—are nuisances that come attached to the domestic and international advantages of being a democratically elected president. Accountability to such institutions appears as a mere impediment to the full authority that the president has been delegated to exercise.

Delegative democracy is not alien to the democratic tradition. It is more democratic, but less liberal, than representative democracy. DD is strongly majoritarian. It consists in constituting, through clean elections, a majority that empowers someone to become, for a given number of years, the embodiment and interpreter of the high interests of the nation. Often, DDs use devices such as runoff elections if the first round of elections does not generate a clear-cut majority.[8] This majority must be created to support the myth of legitimate delegation. Furthermore, DD is strongly individualistic, but more in a Hobbesian than a Lockean way: voters are supposed to choose, irrespective of their identities and affiliations, the individual who is most fit to take responsibility for the destiny of the country. Elections in DDs are a very emotional and high-stakes event: candidates compete for a chance to rule virtually free of all constraints save those imposed by naked, noninstitutionalized power relations. After the election, voters/delegators are expected to become a passive but cheering audience of what the president does.

Extreme individualism in constituting executive power combines well with the organicism of the Leviathan. The nation and its "authentic" political expression, the leader and his "Movement," are postulated as living organisms.[9] The leader has to heal the nation by uniting its dispersed fragments into a harmonious whole. Since the body politic is in disarray, and since its existing voices only reproduce its fragmentation, delegation includes the right (and the duty) of administering the unpleasant medicines that will restore the health of the nation. For this view, it seems obvious that only the head really knows: the president and his most trusted advisors are the alpha and the omega of politics. Furthermore, some of the problems of the nation can only be solved by highly technical criteria. *Técnicos*, especially in economic policy, must be politically shielded by the president against the manifold resistance of society. In the meantime, it is "obvious" that resistance—be it from congress, political parties, interest groups, or crowds in the streets—has to be ignored. This organicistic discourse fits poorly with the dry arguments of the technocrats, and the myth of delegation is consummated: the president isolates himself from most political institutions and organized interests, and bears sole responsibility for the successes and failures of "his" policies.

This curious blend of organicistic and technocratic conceptions was present in recent bureaucratic-authoritarian regimes. Although the language (but not the organicistic metaphors) was different, those conceptions were also present in communist regimes. But there are important differences between these regimes and DDs. In DDs, parties, the congress, and the press are generally free to voice their criticisms. Sometimes the courts, citing what the executive typically dismisses as "legalistic, formalistic reasons," block unconstitutional policies. Workers' and capitalists' associations often complain loudly. The party (or coalition) that elected the president despairs about its loss of popularity, and refuses parliamentary support for the policies he has "foisted" on them. This increases the political isolation of the president, his difficulties in forming a stable legislative coalition, and his propensity to sidestep, ignore, or corrupt the congress and other institutions.

Here it is necessary to elaborate on what makes representative democracy different from its delegative cousin. Representation necessarily involves an element of delegation: through some procedure, a collectivity authorizes some individuals to speak for it, and eventually to commit the collectivity to what the representative decides. Consequently, representation and delegation are not polar opposites. It is not always easy to make a sharp distinction between the type of democracy which is organized around "representative delegation" and the type where the delegative element overshadows the representative one.

Representation entails accountability: somehow representatives are held responsible for their actions by those they claim to be entitled to speak for. In institutionalized democracies, accountability runs not only vertically, making elected officials answerable to the ballot box, but also horizontally, across a network of relatively autonomous powers (i.e., other institutions) that can call into question, and eventually punish, improper ways of discharging the responsibilities of a given official. Representation and accountability entail the republican dimension of democracy: the existence and enforcement of a careful distinction between the public and the private interests of office holders. Vertical accountability, along with the freedom to form parties and to try to influence public opinion, exists in both representative and delegative democracies. But the horizontal accountability characteristic of representative democracy is extremely weak or nonexistent in delegative democracies. Furthermore, since the institutions that make horizontal accountability effective are seen by delegative presidents as unnecessary encumbrances to their "mission," they make strenuous efforts to hamper the development of such institutions.

Notice that what matters is not only the values and beliefs of officials (whether elected or not) but also the fact that they are embedded in a network of institutionalized power relations. Since those relations may be mobilized to impose punishment, rational actors will calculate the likely costs when they consider undertaking improper behavior. Of course, the workings of this system of mutual responsibility leave much to be desired everywhere. Still, it seems clear that the rule-like force of certain codes of conduct shapes the behavior of relevant agents in representative democracies much more than in delegative democracies. Institutions do matter, particularly when the comparison is not among different sets of strong institutions but between strong institutions and extremely weak or nonexistent ones.

Because policies are carried out by a series of relatively autonomous powers, decision making in representative democracies tends to be slow and incremental and sometimes prone to gridlock. But, by this same token, those policies are usually vaccinated against gross mistakes, and they have a reasonably good chance of being implemented: moreover, responsibility for mistakes tends to be widely shared. As noted, DD implies weak institutionalization and, at best, is indifferent toward strengthening it. DD gives the president the apparent advantage of having practically no horizontal accountability. DD has the additional apparent advantage of allowing swift policy making, but at the expense of a higher likelihood of gross mistakes, of hazardous implementation, and of concentrating responsibility for the outcomes on the president. Not surprisingly, presidents in DDs tend to suffer wild swings in popularity: one day they are acclaimed as providential saviors, and the next they are cursed as only fallen gods can be.

Whether it is due to culture, tradition, or historically-structured learning, the plebiscitary tendencies of delegative democracy were detectable in most Latin American (and, for that matter, many post-communist, Asian, and African) countries long before the present social and economic crisis. This kind of rule has been analyzed as a chapter in the study of authoritarianism, under such names as caesarism, bonapartism, *caudillismo*, populism, and the like. But it should also be seen as a peculiar type of democracy that overlaps with and differs from those authoritarian forms in interesting ways. Even if DD belongs to the democratic genus, however, it could hardly be less congenial to the building and strengthening of democratic political institutions.

Comparisons with the Past

The great wave of democratization prior to the one we are now witnessing occurred after World War II, as an imposition by the Allied powers on defeated Germany, Italy, Japan, and to some extent Austria. The resulting conditions were remarkably different from the ones faced today by Latin America and the postcommunist countries: 1) In the wake of the destruction wrought by the war, the economic expectations of the people probably were very moderate. 2) There were massive injections of capital, principally but not exclusively (e.g., the forgiving of Germany's foreign debt) through the Marshall Plan. 3) As a consequence, and helped by an expanding world economy, the former Axis powers soon achieved rapid rates of economic growth. These were not the only factors at work, but they greatly aided in the consolidation of democracy in those countries. Furthermore, these same factors contributed to political stability and to stable public policy coalitions: it took about 20 years for a change of the governing party in Germany, and the dominant parties in Italy and Japan held sway for nearly half a century.

In contrast, in the transitions of the 1970s and 1980s, reflecting the much less congenial context in which they occurred, victory in the first election after the demise of the authoritarian regime guaranteed that the winning party would be defeated, if not virtually disappear, in the next election. This happened in Spain, Portugal, Greece, Argentina, Bolivia, Brazil, Ecuador, Peru, Uruguay, Korea, and the Philippines. But this pattern appears together with important variations in the social and economic performance of the new governments. Most of these countries inherited serious socioeconomic difficulties from the preceding authoritarian regimes, and were severely affected by the worldwide economic troubles of the 1970s and early 1980s. In all of them, the socioeconomic problems at some point reached crisis proportions and were seen to require decisive government action. Yet however serious the economic problems of the 1970s in Southern Europe may have been, they appear mild when compared to those besetting the newly democratized postcommunist and Latin American countries (with Chile as a partial exception). Very high inflation, economic stagnation, a severe financial crisis of the state, a huge foreign and domestic public debt, increased inequality, and a sharp deterioration of social policies and welfare provisions are all aspects of this crisis.

Again, however, important differences emerge among the Latin American countries. During its first democratic government under President Sanguinetti, the Uruguayan economy performed quite well: the annual rate of inflation dropped from three to two digits, while GNP, investment, and real wages registered gradual increases. The government pursued incremental economic policies, most of them negotiated with congress and various organized interests. Chile under President Aylwin has followed the same path. By contrast, Argentina, Brazil, and Peru opted for drastic and surprising economic stabilization "packages": the Austral Plan in Argentina, the Cruzado Plan in Brazil, and the Inti Plan in Peru. Bolivia, too, adopted this kind of stabilization package in the 1980s. Although this program—closer than the previously mentioned ones to the prescriptions of the international financial organizations—has been praised for its success in controlling inflation, GNP and investment growth remain anemic. Moreover, the brutality with which worker protests against the program were suppressed hardly qualifies as democratic.

These "packages" have been disastrous. They did not solve any of the inherited problems; rather, it is difficult to find a single one that they did not worsen. Disagreement lingers about whether these programs were intrinsically flawed, or suffered from corrigible defects, or were sound but undone by "exogenous" political factors. However that may be, it is clear that the experience of these failures reinforced the decision by the democratic leaders of Chile to avoid this ruinous road. This makes Uruguay—a country that inherited from the authoritarian regime a situation that was every bit as bad as Argentina's or Brazil's—a very interesting case. Why did the Uruguayan government not adopt its own stabilization package, especially during the euphoria that followed the first stages of the Austral and the Cruzado plans? Was it because President Sanguinetti and his collaborators were wiser or better informed than their Argentinean, Brazilian, and Peruvian counterparts? Probably not. The difference is that Uruguay is a case of *redemocratization*, where Congress went to work effectively as soon as democracy was restored. Facing a strongly institutionalized legislature and a series of constitutional restrictions and historically embedded practices, no Uruguayan president could have gotten away with decreeing a drastic stabilization package. In Uruguay, for the enactment of many of the policies typically contained in those packages, the president must go through Congress. Furthermore, going through Congress means having to negotiate not only with parties and legislators, but also with various organized interests. Consequently, against the presumed preferences of some of its top members, the economic policies of the Uruguayan government were "condemned" to be incremental and limited to quite modest goals—such as achieving the decent performance we have seen. Looking at Uruguay—and, more recently, Chile—one learns about the difference between having or not having a network of institutionalized powers that gives texture to the policy-making process. Or, in other words, about the difference between representative and delegative democracy.

The Cycle of Crisis

Now I will focus on some South American cases of delegative democracy—Argentina, Brazil, and Peru. There is no need to detail the depth of the crisis that these countries inherited from their respective authoritarian regimes. Such a crisis generates a strong sense of urgency and provides fertile terrain for unleashing the delegative propensities that may be present in a given country. Problems and demands mount up before inexperienced governments that must operate through a weak and disarticulated (if not disloyal) bureaucracy. Presidents get elected by promising that they—being strong, courageous, above parties and interests, *machos*—will save the country. Theirs is a "government of saviors" (*salvadores de la patria*). This leads to a "magical" style of policy making: the delegative "mandate" supposedly bestowed by the majority, strong political will, and technical knowledge should suffice to fulfill the savior's mission—the "packages" follow as a corollary.

The longer and deeper the crisis, and the less the confidence that the government will be able to solve it, the more rational it becomes for everyone to act: 1) in a highly disaggregated manner, especially in relation to state agencies that may help to alleviate the consequences of the crisis for a given group or sector (thus further weakening and corrupting the state apparatus); 2) with extremely short time-horizons; and 3) with the assumption that everyone else will do the same. In short, there is a general scramble for narrow, short-term advantage. This prisoner's dilemma is the exact opposite of the conditions that foster both strong democratic institutions and reasonably effective ways of dealing with pressing national problems.

Once the initial hopes are dashed and the first packages have failed, cynicism about politics, politicians, and government becomes the pervading mood. If such governments wish to retain some popular support, they must both control inflation and implement social policies which show that, even though they cannot rapidly solve most of the underlying problems, they do care about the fate of the poor and (politically more important) of the recently impoverished segments of the middle class. But minimal though it may be, this is a very tall order. These two goals are extremely difficult to harmonize, at least in the short run—and for such flimsy governments little other than the short run counts.

Governments like to enjoy sustained popular support, and politicians want to be reelected. Only if the predicaments described above were solvable within the brief compass of a presidential term would electoral success be a triumph instead of a curse. How does one win election and how, once elected, does one govern in this type of situation? Quite obviously—and most destructively in terms of the building of public trust that helps a democracy to consolidate—by saying one thing during the campaign and doing the contrary when in office. Of course, institutionalized democracies are not immune to this trick, but the consequences are more devastating when there are few and weak institutions and a deep socioeconomic crisis afflicts the country. Presidents have gained election in Argentina, Bolivia, Ecuador, and Peru by promising expansionist economic policies and many other good things to come with them, only to enact severe stabilization packages immediately or shortly after entering office. Whatever the merits of such policies for a given country at a given time, their surprise adoption does nothing to promote public trust, particularly if their immediate and most visible impact further depresses the already low standard of living of most of the population.

Moreover, the virtual exclusion of parties and congress from such momentous decisions has several malign consequences. First, when the executive finally, and inevitably, needs legislative support, he is bound to find a congress that is resentful and feels no responsibility for policies it had no hand in making. Second, the congress is further weakened by its own hostile and aloof attitude, combined with the executive's public condemnations of its slowness and "irresponsibility." Third, these squabbles promote a sharp decline in the prestige of *all* parties and politicians, as opinion polls from many Latin American and postcommunist countries abundantly show. Finally, the resulting institutional weakness makes it ever more difficult to achieve the other magical solution when the packages fail: the socioeconomic pact.

From Omnipotence to Impotence

If we consider that the logic of delegation also means that the executive does nothing to strengthen the judiciary, the resulting dearth of effective and autonomous institutions places immense responsibility on the president. Remember that the typical incumbent in a DD has won election by promising to save the country without much cost to anyone, yet soon gambles the fate of his government on policies that entail substantial costs for many parts of the population. This results in policy making under conditions of despair: the shift from wide popularity to general vilification can be as rapid as it is dramatic. The result is a curious mixture of governmental omnipotence and impotence. Omnipotence begins with the spectacular enactment of the first policy packages and continues with a flurry of decisions aimed at complementing those packages and, unavoidably, correcting their numerous unwanted consequences. This accentuates the anti-institutional bias of DDs and ratifies traditions of high personalization and concentration of power in the executive. The other side of the coin is extreme weakness in making those decisions into effective long-term regulations of societal life.

As noted above, institutionalized democracies are slow at making decisions. But once those decisions are made, they are relatively more likely to be implemented. In DDs, in contrast, we witness a decision-making frenzy, what in Latin America we call *decretismo*. Because such hasty, unilateral executive orders are likely to offend important and politically mobilized interests, they are unlikely to be implemented. In the midst of a severe crisis and increasing popular impatience, the upshot is usually new flurries of decisions which, because of the experience many sectors have had in resisting the previous ones, are even less likely to be implemented. Furthermore, because of the way those decisions are made, most political, social, and economic agents can disclaim responsibility. Power was delegated to the president, and he did what he deemed best. As failures accumulate, the country finds itself stuck with a widely reviled president whose goal is just to hang on until the end of his term. The resulting period of passivity and disarray of public policy does nothing to help the situation of the country.

Given this scenario, the "natural" outcome in Latin America in the past would have been a successful coup d'etat. Clearly, DDs, because of their institutional weaknesses and erratic patterns of policy making, are more prone to interruption and breakdown than representative democracies. At the moment, however—for reasons mostly linked to the international context, which I cannot discuss here—DDs exhibit a rather remarkable capacity for endurance. With the partial exception of Peru, where the constitutional breakdown was led by its delegative president, no successful coups d'etat have taken place.

The economic policy undertaken by DDs is not always condemned to be widely perceived as a failure, particularly in the aftermath of hyperinflation or long periods of extremely high inflation.[10] This is the case in Argentina today under President Menem, although it is not clear how sustainable the improved economic situation is. But such economic achievements, as well as the more short-lived ones of Collor (Brazil), Alfonsín (Argentina), and García (Peru) at the height of the apparent successes of their economic packages, can lead a president to give the ultimate proof of the existence of a delegative democracy. As long as their policies are recognized as successful by electorally weighty segments of the population, delegative presidents find it simply abhorrent that their terms should be constitutionally limited; how could these "formal limitations" preclude the continuation of their providential mission? Consequently, they promote—by means that further weaken whatever horizontal accountability still exists—constitutional reforms that would allow their reelection or, failing this, their continuation at the apex of government as prime ministers in a parliamentary regime. Oddly enough, successful delegative presidents, at least while they believe they are successful, may become proponents of some form of parliamentarism. In contrast, this kind of maneuver was out of the question in the cases of the quite successful President Sanguinetti of Uruguay and the very successful President Aylwin of Chile, however much they might have liked to continue in power. Again, we find a crucial difference between representative and delegative democracy.[11]

As noted, among the recently democratized countries of Latin America only Uruguay and Chile, as soon as they *re*democratized, revived earlier political institutions that the other Latin American countries (as well as most postcommunist ones) lack. This is the rub: effective institutions and congenial practices cannot be built in a day. As consolidated democracies show, the emergence, strengthening, and legitimation of these practices and institutions take time, during which a complex process of positive learning occurs. On the other hand, to deal effectively with the tremendous economic and social crisis faced by most newly democratized countries would require that such institutions already be in place. Yet the crisis itself severely hinders the arduous task of institutionalization.

This is the drama of countries bereft of a democratic tradition: like all emerging democracies, past and present, they must cope with the manifold negative legacies of their authoritarian past, while wrestling with the kind of extraordinarily severe social and economic problems that few if any of the older democracies faced at their inception.

Although this essay has been confined largely to a typological exercise, I believe that there is some value in identifying a new species, especially since in some crucial dimensions it does not behave as other types of democracy do. Elsewhere I have further elaborated on the relationship between DDs and socioeconomic crisis and on related theoretical issues,[12] and I intend to present more comprehensive views in the future. Here I can only add that an optimist viewing the cycles I have described would find that they possess a degree of predictability, thus supplying some ground on which longer-term perspectives could be built. Such a view, however, begs the question of how long the bulk of the population will be willing to play this sort of game. Another optimistic scenario would have a decisive segment of the political leadership recognizing the self-destructive quality of those cycles, and agreeing to change the terms on which they compete and govern. This seems to me practically the only way out of the problem, but the obstacles to such a roundabout but ultimately happy outcome are many.

NOTES

This essay is a revised and abridged version of a text of the same title published in Portuguese by *Novos Estudos CEBRAP* 31 (October 1991): 25-40, and as Kellogg Institute Working Paper No. 172 (March 1992). Some of the ideas in this essay originated in conversations I had in the 1980s with Luis Pásara concerning the emerging patterns of rule in several Latin American countries. For the preparation of the present version I was privileged to receive detailed comments and suggestions from David Collier.

1. Terry Lynn Karl and Philippe C. Schmitter, "Modes of Transition and Types of Democracy in Latin America, Southern and Eastern Europe," *International Social Science Journal* 128 (May 1991): 269-84.

2. See Robert A. Dahl, *Polyarchy: Participation and Opposition* (New Haven: Yale University Press, 1971); and idem., *Democracy and Its Critics* (New Haven: Yale

University Press, 1989). I draw further distinctions concerning various characteristics of polyarchies in a recent paper entitled "On the State, Democratization and Some Conceptual Problems (A Latin American View with Glances at Some Post-Communist Countries)," *World Development* 21 (1993): 1355-69 (also published as Kellogg Institute Working Paper No. 192 (April 1993).

3. For a more detailed discussion, see my essay "Transitions, Continuities and Paradoxes" in Scott Mainwaring, Guillermo O'Donnell, and J. Samuel Valenzuela, eds., *Issues in Democratic Consolidation: The New South American Democracies in Comparative Perspective* (Notre Dame, Indiana: University of Notre Dame Press, 1992), 17-56.

4. Adam Przeworski, "Democracy as a Contingent Outcome of Conflicts," in Jon Elster and Rume Slagstad, eds., *Constitutionalism and Democracy* (Cambridge: Cambridge University Press, 1988), 59-80.

5. Wolfgang Streeck and Philippe C. Schmitter, "Community, Market, State—and Associations? The Prospective Contribution of Interest Governance to Social Order," in Wolfgang Streeck and Philippe C. Schmitter, eds., *Private Interest Government: Beyond Market and State* (London: Sage Publications, 1985), 1-29.

6. See James March and Johan Olsen, *Rediscovering Institutions: The Organizational Basis of Politics* (New York: The Free Press, 1989).

7. A prisoner's dilemma exists when, even if all of the agents involved could make themselves better off by cooperating among themselves, it nonetheless proves rational for each of them, irrespective of what the others decide, not to cooperate. In this sense, institutions may be seen as social inventions that serve to make cooperation the rational preference.

8. Arturo Valenzuela, "Latin America: Presidentialism in Crisis," *Journal of Democracy* 4 (October 1993): 17, notes that "all of the countries (except for Paraguay) that drafted new constitutions in the 1980s and early 1990s (Guatemala, El Salvador, Colombia, Ecuador, Peru, Chile, and Brazil) instituted the French system of a *ballotage*, or second round, for presidential races." Of these countries, Guatemala and El Salvador did not qualify as polyarchies, Chile's constitution was a product of the Pinochet regime, and Ecuador, Peru, and Brazil are among the purest cases of DD.

9. Giorgio Alberti has insisted on the importance of *movimientismo* as a dominant feature of politics in many Latin American countries. See his "Democracy by Default, Economic Crisis, and Social Anomie in Latin America" (Paper presented to the Twenty-fifth World Congress of Political Science, Buenos Aires, 1991).

10. I discuss these themes in my essay "On the State, Democratization, and Some Conceptual Problems," cited in note 2 above.

11. I do not ignore the important discussions currently underway about various forms of presidentialism and parliamentarism, of which recent and interesting expressions are Scott Mainwaring and Matthew Shugart, "Juan Linz, Presidentialism, and Democracy: A Critical Appraisal," Kellogg Institute Working Paper No. 200 (July 1993); Alfred Stepan and Cindy Skach, "Constitutional Frameworks and Democratic Consolidation: Parliamentarism versus Presidentialism," *World Politics* 46 (October 1993): 1-22; and Arturo Valenzuela, "Latin America: Presidentialism in Crisis," cited in note 8 above. In the present text I discuss patterns that are independent of those institutional factors, although they may be convergent in their consequences. Clearly, presidentialism has more affinity with DD than parliamentarism. However, if delegative propensities are strong in a given country, the workings of a parliamentary system could be rather easily subverted or lead to impasses even worse than the ones discussed here.

12. I must refer again to my essay "On the State, Democratization, and Some Conceptual Problems," cited in note 2 above.

II.
Institutional Choices and Designs

8. THREE PARADOXES OF DEMOCRACY

Larry Diamond

***Larry Diamond** is coeditor of the* Journal of Democracy *and senior research fellow at the Hoover Institution. He is coeditor, with Juan Linz and Seymour Martin Lipset, of the multivolume series* Democracy in Developing Countries *(1988-89) and author of* Class, Ethnicity, and Democracy in Nigeria *(1988). He has written widely on problems of democracy and democratic transitions in Nigeria and the Third World.*

The world in 1990 is in the grip of a democratic revolution. Throughout the developing world, peoples are resisting and rebelling against communist and authoritarian rule. The ferment has spread to the world's most isolated, unlikely, and forgotten places: Burma, Mongolia, Nepal, Zaire, even Albania. From the postcommunist world of Eastern Europe to the post-bureaucratic-authoritarian nations of Latin America, from the poverty-stricken heart of tropical Africa to newly rich and industrializing East Asia, nations are on the march toward democracy. Never in human history have so many independent countries been demanding or installing or practicing democratic governance. Never in history has awareness of popular struggles for democracy spread so rapidly and widely across national borders. Never have democrats worldwide seemed to have so much cause for rejoicing.

But committed democrats would do well to restrain their impulse to celebrate. Democracy is the most widely admired type of political system but also perhaps the most difficult to maintain. Alone among all forms of government, democracy rests on a minimum of coercion and a maximum of consent. Democratic polities inevitably find themselves saddled with certain "built-in" paradoxes or contradictions. The tensions these cause are not easy to reconcile, and every country that would be democratic must find its own way of doing so.

This essay explores three contradictions that will bear very heavily on the struggles now underway around the world to develop and institutionalize democracy. My analysis will draw on evidence gleaned from a comparative study of experiences with democracy in 26 developing countries.[1]

Many of the problems that democracy has experienced in the developing world spring from three tensions or paradoxes that inhere in democracy's very nature. First is the tension between *conflict* and *consensus*. Democracy is, by its nature, a system of institutionalized competition for power. Without competition and conflict, there is no democracy. But any society that sanctions political conflict runs the risk of its becoming too intense, producing a society so conflict-ridden that civil peace and political stability are jeopardized. Hence the paradox: Democracy requires conflict—but not too much; competition there must be, but only within carefully defined and universally accepted boundaries. Cleavage must be tempered by consensus.[2]

A second tension or contradiction sets *representativeness* against *governability*. Democracy implies an unwillingness to concentrate power in the hands of a few, and so subjects leaders and policies to mechanisms of popular representation and accountability. But to be stable, democracy (or any system of government) must have what Alexander Hamilton called "energy"—it must always be able to act, and at times must do so quickly and decisively. Government must not only respond to interest-group demands; it must be able to resist them and mediate among them as well. This requires a party system that can produce a government stable and cohesive enough to represent and respond to competing groups and interests in society without being paralyzed or captured by them. Representativeness requires that parties speak to and for these conflicting interests; governability requires that parties have sufficient autonomy to rise above them.

This leads to the third contradiction, between *consent* and *effectiveness*. Democracy means, literally, "rule by the people," or at least rule with the consent of the governed. This is the message of people all over the world who are fed up with the repression and corruption of authoritarian or totalitarian ruling elites. As the articles in this publication attest, people across the globe are making it clear that they want the right to turn their rulers out of office, to be governed only with their consent.

But founding a democracy and preserving it are two different things. To be stable, democracy must be deemed legitimate by the people; they must view it as the best, the most appropriate form of government for their society. Indeed, *because* it rests on the consent of the governed, democracy depends on popular legitimacy much more than any other form of government. This legitimacy requires a profound moral commitment and emotional allegiance, but these develop only over time, and partly as a result of effective performance. Democracy will not be valued by the people unless it deals effectively with social and economic problems and achieves a modicum of order and justice.

If democracy does not work, people may prefer *not* to be governed through their own consent—they may choose not to put up with the pain of political choice any longer. Herein lies the paradox: Democracy requires consent. Consent requires legitimacy. Legitimacy requires effective performance. But effectiveness may be sacrificed to consent. Elected leaders will always be reluctant to pursue unpopular policies, no matter how wise or necessary they may be.

These three paradoxes have important implications for the development of democracy in those underdeveloped polities of Eastern Europe and what is commonly called "the Third World" that are struggling now, after so much repression and frustration, to build lasting democracies. Let us consider the implications of each of these paradoxes, beginning with the last.

Consent versus Effectiveness

Democracies—and especially new democracies—suffer from a special problem with regard to government performance: Popular assessments of how the government has done tend to take the short view. Democratic governments everywhere—in the industrialized world every bit as much as the developing one—are thus constantly tempted to trim their policies with an eye on the next election. This may make good political sense in the short run, but it does not make for good *economic* policy. And when we are talking about performance, it is primarily economic performance that counts.

Authoritarian regimes like Pinochet's Chile are not dependent on popular consent, and can therefore afford politically to make their populations suffer through long periods of economic austerity and structural adjustment for the sake of long-term payoffs. Chile's economy is booming now—but at what price in human suffering, poverty, unemployment, and political repression over the past 15 years?

East European and many Latin American countries need urgently to implement sweeping structural reforms to generate productive and internationally competitive economies. But how long and how hard will new democratic or democratizing governments push economic reform if the short-term pain proves devastating, while the gains, however great, will not become apparent until well after the next election?

In such circumstances, the consolidation of democracy—so intimately linked to structural economic reform—requires the negotiation of some kind of agreement or "pact" among competing political parties and social forces on: 1) the broad direction and principles of structural economic reform, which all parties will support, no matter which one(s) come to power; 2) a renunciation of certain political appeals and strategies—in particular an irresponsible but tempting politics of outbidding; 3) sacrifices that all social forces will share, including demands they will mutually postpone, during the critical and highly unstable period of economic adjustment and democratic installation; and 4) a method of ensuring that the burdens of adjustment are shared more or less fairly and eased by relief measures for the hardest-hit groups, such as workers rendered jobless by structural reforms.[3]

Such pacts may be as narrow as agreements on core principles of long-term economic policy, or may be far-reaching enough to produce broad coalitions capable of governing in the name of a firm policy consensus. One possible model in this regard may be the political and economic pacts negotiated by elites in Venezuela in 1958 that facilitated the successful and enduring restoration of democracy there. In addition to sharing power, these pacts set the broad outlines of the country's major economic policies, thus removing potentially contentious issues from partisan debate.[4]

The scale of the relief required to make economic reform politically palatable may lie well beyond what the bankrupt and debt-ravaged economies of Eastern Europe, Latin America, Africa, and other developing countries (such as the Philippines) can finance on their own. Successful adjustment through democracy would seem to require an international compact as well. The industrialized democracies and the international community could offer substantial new investment and aid and genuine debt reduction in exchange for reforms designed to break the economic stranglehold of statism and launch these countries into self-sustaining growth.

What reforms and principles might serve as the basic tenets of a new economic policy consensus for these troubled democracies?

The past four decades of Third World economic development have furnished invaluable lessons for distinguishing the policies that work from those that do not. Broadly speaking, market-oriented economies develop, while state-socialist economies fall behind. Internationally open and competitive economies work; closed (or at least rigidly and persistently closed) economies do not. Economies grow when they foster savings, investment, and innovation, and when they reward individual effort and initiative. Economies stagnate and regress when bloated, mercantilist, hyperinterventionist states build "a structure of inflexible favoritisms for different groups, curtailing change, experimentation, competition, innovation, and social mobility."[5]

Furthermore, economies that invest in the human capital of the poor by meeting their basic human needs develop a continuing momentum of growth. But those that effectively prevent half, two-thirds, or more of the population from gaining the skills and opportunities needed to partake in and benefit from development ultimately founder.

Democratic development, like democratic culture, requires a considerable measure of balance, moderation, and respect for all interests. Markets must be sufficiently open, flexible, and competitive to generate increases in savings, investment, and rates of return. This requires getting or keeping the state off the backs of producers. But the state must be sufficiently involved to ensure that there is adequate investment in human and physical capital, and that development is responsible to environmental and other community interests. Taxes must be substantial enough (and sufficiently fairly and efficiently collected) to provide revenue for these essential purposes, but must also be limited and designed so that they operate "in ways most neutral to the incentives to save, invest, and efficiently allocate resources."[6]

Around these general principles lies much variation, and also much complexity. Countries develop with differing types and mixes of state involvement in fostering indigenous enterprise (and even temporarily protecting it). But countries fall behind when the state becomes the *dominant* producer and employer, or an enduring protector of inefficient economic actors, whether capital or labor.

Perhaps the most important lesson from our comparative study of 26 countries is very simple, but very commonly neglected. Whatever the exact shape of a country's policy, it can only work if it is pursued consistently and pragmatically. Drastic shifts between radical populist redistributive policies and radical neoliberal austerity policies are bound to invite economic miseries and crises of the sort that now threaten the future of democracy in Argentina, Brazil, and Peru.

This is not the inevitable fate of electoral regimes in the developing world. Botswana, Colombia, and (more problematically) India, with very different development levels and natural resource endowments, have all achieved steady economic growth through stable, prudent policies. Entrepreneurs at all levels in these countries can save, invest, profit, and reinvest with some confidence in a predictable future. Most notably perhaps, Colombia's eclectic, pragmatic economic policies have produced constant growth with low inflation in the three decades since its democratic transition. Although India is often believed to be an economic basket case, it has in fact achieved significant socioeconomic development in the past three decades—and would have done much better had its population not doubled to 800 million. Since independence, India has achieved self-sufficiency in agriculture, significant industrialization, and quite tangible improvements in literacy, life expectancy, and infant mortality. It has done all this, moreover, while holding inflation and foreign borrowing to some of the lowest levels in the developing world.

If India can develop, why cannot Africa? With a population more than half again as large as Africa's—and no greater bounty of natural resources, plus a level of poverty as great as Africa's at independence—why has India been able to perform so much better economically?

The answers are in part political, for they involve policies and institutions. India had the political institutions—not only the bureaucracy but also a stable and institutionalized political party system—to pursue a consistent and pragmatic long-run strategy for economic development. By and large it worked, although there is still enough inefficiency, corruption, and waste—deriving from a misplaced socialist idealism and a suffocating statism—to threaten the economic progress that India has made so far.

This comparative evidence holds two important lessons. The first is that democracies do not, inherently, perform worse economically than dictatorships. Very probably, they do not *inherently* perform better, either. The policies chosen—and the skill with which they are implemented—are far more important. The second is that, since consistency, prudence, and pragmatism in policy are so important to economic development, struggling young democracies must give serious thought to how they can form and maintain a broad consensus on economic policy. This will require creative institution-building, public education, and elite accommodation. Above all, it will require political leadership with courage, vision, and determination.

This brings us back, then, to our second paradox—how to balance representativeness and accountability with the need for governability?

Representativeness versus Governability

Governability requires sufficient concentration and autonomy of power to choose and implement policies with energy and dispatch. This generally conflicts with the need to hold power accountable to popular scrutiny, representation, and control. In some respects, however, vigorous public accountability may strengthen the capacity to govern and the effectiveness of government. This is most clearly seen with regard to political corruption.

Widespread government corruption is poisonous to democracy. It impedes economic growth by misdirecting the flow of capital and resources, and by distorting investment decisions and economic competition generally. Although some have argued that corruption may enhance political legitimacy by dispersing material benefits, these are typically concentrated rather than "spread around." A narrow class of government officials and their business cronies is enriched at the expense of the bulk of the population—and of the legitimacy of the entire democratic system.

Moreover, where the prospect of ill-gotten gain is an important motive for the pursuit of office, the democratic process becomes a mere power struggle rather than a contest over policies. The premium on political power becomes so great that competing forces will do anything to win. This threatens the very essence of the democratic process—free, fair, and peaceful elections.

Statism exacerbates corruption by giving public officials numerous opportunities to collect rents from the state's regulatory activities. But opportunities for corruption are perennial features of public life everywhere. The only remedy is accountability, which requires a free press willing and able to expose corruption; an organized citizenry ready to monitor the political process and the conduct of public officials; and an assertive, independent legal system equipped to prosecute and punish official misconduct.

These are at least some of the ways in which accountability serves governability. They involve limiting the power of the state, and especially the executive, in order to prevent abuses. But there are trade-offs, for if power is too limited or too diffused, government may be hamstrung.

Each country must find its own way of resolving this universal tension. Juan Linz has argued that parliamentary systems may be preferable in most developing countries because, *inter alia*, they make the executive branch more accountable before the legislature, avoid the rigidity and winner-take-all features of presidentialism, and at the same time serve governability by preventing the potential deadlock that can arise in a presidential system when the presidency is controlled by one party and the legislature by others.[7]

But here, too, there are no pat formulas, and some countries may be better served by the more decisive character of presidential systems, by the greater stability of presidential cabinets, and by the possibility that presidentialism provides to elect a single, overarching national leader in ways (and with rules) that induce the recruitment of broad constituencies.[8]

A vigorous civil society enhances not only the accountability, but also the representativeness and vitality of democracy. Voluntary associations represent a crucial institutional supplement to democratic political parties. The persistence of democracy in India and Costa Rica for four decades, and in Venezuela since 1958, owes much to these countries' dense networks of autonomous voluntary associations and mass media. These not only check and scrutinize state power; they also enhance the legitimacy of democracy by providing new means to express political interests; increasing the political awareness, efficacy, and confidence of citizens; and training and recruiting new political leaders.

At the same time, however, democratic governments and parties must have some autonomy from group demands in order to make and implement tough decisions. If political parties are too weak or too penetrated by other social groups; if the bureaucracy is a captive of such parties or interests; if the elected government cannot stand above, reconcile, and at times resist interest-group pressures; then that government may be unable to formulate workable policies. Such weakness could produce a regime-threatening crisis of confidence.

The relationship among party systems, electoral systems, and constitutional structure introduces another profound tension between representativeness and governability. In principle, the purest way to represent diverse social groups and interests, especially in deeply divided societies, is through proportional representation (PR). In fact, where social cleavages are multiple, deep, and politically mobilized, to obstruct their representation through the party system by abandoning PR would be to risk political alienation, turmoil, and violence that could threaten democratic stability.[8] The purer the form of PR, and the lower the minimum percentage of the vote required for a party to enter the parliament, the more significant parties there will tend to be and the more parliament will tend to mirror in its political composition the balance of social, cultural, and ideological interests in society.[10] This may make the system more representative—but less governable and even less accountable, for three reasons.

First, if none of the parliamentarians is elected from (manageably sized) territorial districts, none of them is individually accountable to any clearly identifiable portion of the electorate, other than the party bosses or electors who put them on the party list of candidates. Second, with the fragmentation of the party system, voters may keep getting virtually the same coalition governments, with minor shifts in cabinet portfolios, no matter how the vote may change among parties. Thus, it becomes difficult truly to change policy, and to "throw the rascals out." This may enhance stability of policy, even as it leads to frequent changes in government (as in Italy), but at the cost of denying voters clear electoral choice. Third, in a situation of evenly balanced large parties and numerous small parties, the latter derive vastly inordinate bargaining leverage or "blackmail" potential in negotiations to form a government. This leads either to an undemocratic concession of power and resources to these fringe groups or to a "national unity" coalition government so divided that it cannot act. This conundrum has increasingly crippled democratic politics in Israel, where electoral reform has become the rallying cry of an outraged Israeli population.

In such circumstances, a political system may be made *more* stably democratic by making it somewhat *less* representative. Thus West Germany, reflecting on the polarization and instability of the Weimar Republic, set an electoral threshold of five percent of the vote for a party to enter the Bundestag, and got a stable system comprising two dominant parties plus one or two minor ones. Reflecting on the political fragmentation and polarization that in 1980 brought its democracy down for the second time in as many decades, Turkey in 1982 adopted a ten-percent threshold and other changes that have also produced a much more consolidated party system. In the past year, a bipartisan electoral-reform commission in Israel has produced a wisely balanced proposal that, while retaining PR, would set the threshold at 3.5 percent and elect, as in West Germany, half the members of parliament from territorial districts and half from national party lists.[11]

There are, of course, more drastic mechanisms for streamlining the party system, such as the election of legislators from single-member districts by plurality vote and the presidential system. Either one will tend strongly to reduce the number of parties; the two together are a natural recipe for a two-party system. But we have already mentioned the problems with presidentialism, and in a situation with more than two parties enjoying significant electoral support—such as Britain in the last parliamentary election or India since independence—the plurality method of election by district can magnify a party's national electoral plurality into a staggering parliamentary majority. This may produce not governability so much as a decidedly undemocratic imbalance and arrogance of power. Part of the riddle of democracy is that its paradoxes are not often resolved through recourse to blunt and simple alternatives.

Conflict versus Consensus

Perhaps the most basic tension in democracy is between conflict and consensus. Democracy implies dissent and division, but on a basis of consent and cohesion. It requires that the citizens assert themselves, but also that they accept the government's authority. It demands that the citizens care about politics, but not too much. This is why Gabriel Almond and Sidney Verba, in their classic book *The Civic Culture*, called the democratic political culture "mixed." It balances the citizen's role as participant (as agent of political competition and conflict) with his or her role as subject (obeyer of state authority), and as "parochial" member of family, social, and community networks outside politics.[12] The subject role serves governability while the parochial role tempers political conflict by limiting the politicization of social life.

Other closely related elements of democratic political culture include tolerance of opposition and dissent; trust in fellow political actors; a willingness to cooperate, accommodate, and compromise; and hence a certain flexibility, moderation, civility, and restraint in one's partisanship. It is well understood that sturdy habits of moderation and conciliation make it possible for democracies to balance conflict and consensus.[13] To honor these virtues in deed as well as in speech is often one of the most important challenges facing nascent and troubled democracies.

How do such democratic habits develop? Certainly they are fostered by education, which, as Almond and Verba showed, increases a host of "democratic" tendencies in the individual. Socioeconomic development can also enhance democratic values and practices to the extent that it improves the income, education, skills, and life chances of citizens. Again we see why investment in human capital is so important for the preservation of democracy.

Yet is there not considerable historical evidence to suggest that democratic culture is as much the product as the cause of effectively functioning democracy? Elites may "back into" democracy for a variety of strategic reasons—including, for example, the historic lack or exhaustion of other means for resolving conflict,[14] or the unavailability in today's Eastern Europe or Latin America of any other legitimate alternative. Subsequently, however, the successful practice of democracy demonstrates the value of participation, tolerance, and compromise—indeed the efficacy and intrinsic desirability of democracy itself. Over time, citizens of a democracy become habituated to its norms and values, gradually internalizing them.[15] The trick, then, is for democracies to survive long enough—and function well enough—for this process to occur.

But this returns us to the paradox. To survive and function well, democracy must moderate conflict. But the cultural mechanisms for doing so do not develop overnight. In the meantime, how can conflicts be contained so that political cleavage and competition do not rip society apart?

Cleavages tend to run along lines of class, ethnicity (including religion and region), and party. The problem of class cleavage presents a paradox within a paradox. For democracy to be stable, class cleavage must be moderate. For class cleavage to be moderate, economic inequality must be moderate too. Severe inequality tends eventually to generate intense, violent political polarization, as Peru and the Philippines are discovering. To avoid this, to achieve a moderate degree of inequality, socioeconomic reforms must be undertaken. At a minimum, these include prudent investments in education, health care, housing, and other social services. In some cases, more thoroughgoing reforms, including land reform, may be necessary. But this may ignite the bitter resistance of entrenched elites, especially large landowners and employers of cheap labor. And therein lies the rub: to moderate class conflict in the long run, a political system may need to risk aggravating it in the short run.

There is no obvious way out of this conundrum. Democracy often gains a purchase in tense and conflict-ridden situations only when certain especially contentious issues are ruled off the agenda. But the nettle must eventually be grasped, for democracy cannot endure if massive inequality and exclusion go unchallenged. By its very nature, democracy permits only incremental reform rather than revolutionary change. Opposing interests must somehow be reconciled. Land may need to be redistributed—but only after its owners are fairly compensated and given opportunities to reinvest their assets in other productive enterprises. Wages may need to be increased, but only at a pace that will not threaten severe damage to corporate profits and economic growth. For only in a context of economic growth can inequality be reduced in a way that brings an enduring reduction in poverty.

Getting reform on the agenda requires that disadvantaged and excluded economic groups organize and mobilize politically. But if reform is to be adopted without provoking a crisis that might destroy democracy, the costs to privileged economic interests of overturning democracy must be kept greater than the costs of the reforms themselves. This requires realism and incrementalism on the part of those groups pressing for reform. It also requires sufficient overall effectiveness, stability, and guarantees for capital on the part of the democratic regime so that privileged economic actors will have a lot to lose by turning against it.

Ethnic and Party Cleavages

The social sciences may have discerned few true laws, but one that can be confidently stated concerns ethnicity: Ethnic cleavages do not die. They cannot be extinguished through repression or assimilation; however, they can be managed so that they do not threaten civil peace, and people of different groups are able to coexist tranquilly while maintaining their ethnic identities.

There are four principal mechanisms for managing ethnicity politically within a democratic framework: federalism, proportionality in the distribution of resources and power, minority rights (to cultural integrity and protection against discrimination), and sharing or rotation of power, in particular through coalition arrangements at the center.[16]

As the experiences of India and Nigeria demonstrate, and as Donald Horowitz has noted, federal systems are particularly effective in managing ethnic tension because they utilize a variety of mechanisms for reducing conflict. First, they *disperse conflict* by transferring much of it to state and local levels. They also generate *intraethnic conflict*, pitting different factions of ethnic groups against one another in the struggle for control of state and local governments. Third, they may induce *interethnic cooperation* as states find the need to coalesce with one another in shifting ways depending on the issue at the center. Fourth, they may generate *crosscutting cleavages* if some ethnic groups are split into different states, with different interests, advantages, and needs. Fifth, they can *reduce disparities* by enabling backward and minority peoples to rise within their own state bureaucracies and educational systems.[17]

More generally, federal systems give all major territorially based ethnic groups some control over their own affairs, and some chance to gain power and control resources at multiple levels. This points to another virtual law: the impossibility of stable democracy in a society where ethnic cleavages are deep and power is heavily centralized. There are compelling independent reasons why decentralization of power and strong local and state government promote the vitality of democracy, but these are especially striking imperatives in divided societies.

Finally, party cleavage can represent, independent of class and ethnicity, a quite sufficient basis for violent and destructive conflict. Even in the absence of deep differences over ideology and program, political parties represent competing organizations for the conquest of state power, and the greater and more pervasive the power of the state, the more will parties want to get it and keep it at any price. This is another reason why statism is so toxic to democracy: not only because it breeds corruption and economic inefficiency, but also because it raises the premium on political power to a degree approaching a zero-sum game. When so much is at stake in the electoral contest, trust, tolerance, civility, and obedience to the rules become formidably difficult to maintain. A balanced political culture—in which people care about politics, but not too much—is possible only in structural circumstances where people can *afford* not to care too much, where wealth, income, status, and opportunities for upward mobility are not mere functions of political power.

In Eastern Europe and much of the developing world, restraining the partisan battle requires deflating the state and invigorating the private economy. But it requires more as well. Where parties are only beginning to take shape, where open political life is only just emerging after decades of repression and fear, the culture of tolerance, trust, accommodation, and cooperation is yet to be born. Passions are intense, memories bitter. People lack the basis of mutual trust and respect on which they might combine political efforts or at least pursue their own political interests prudently and flexibly.

In such circumstances, elite actions, choices, and postures can have a formative impact in shaping the way their followers approach political discourse and conflict. Opposing party leaders must take the lead in crafting understandings and working relationships that bridge historic differences, restrain expectations, and establish longer, more realistic time horizons for their agendas. Pacts or formal arrangements for sharing power represent only one dimension of this general imperative. At a minimum, competing party elites must set an accommodating and civil tone for political life. Above all, they must manifest a faith in the democratic process and a commitment to its rules that supersedes the pursuit of power or other substantive goals.

Building among political competitors such a system of "mutual security," as Robert Dahl calls it, of transcendent respect for the rules of the game, may demand not only faith but a leap of faith from political leaders. They must believe that whatever results from the democratic process will, in the long run, serve their interests better than an intransigence that risks the breakdown of democracy. Among the manifold uncertainties that attend the founding of all new regimes, probably nothing is more important to democracy than the presence of party leaders with the courage and vision to join hands in taking this leap.

NOTES

1. Larry Diamond, Juan J. Linz, and Seymour Martin Lipset, eds., *Democracy in Developing Countries: Vol. 2, Africa; Vol. 3, Asia; Vol. 4, Latin America* (Boulder, Colorado: Lynne Rienner Publishers, 1988 and 1989).

2. Gabriel A. Almond and Sidney Verba, *The Civic Culture: Political Attitudes and Democracy in Five Nations* (Boston: Little, Brown and Co., 1965), 356-360.

3. O'Donnell and Schmitter define a pact as "an explicit, but not always publicly explicated or justified, agreement among a select set of actors which seeks to define (or better, to redefine) rules governing the exercise of power on the basis of mutual guarantees for the 'vital interests' of those entering into it." I enlarge slightly on their usage to denote an agreement on the basis of guarantees for the overall *national* interest. Guillermo O'Donnell and Philippe C. Schmitter, *Transitions from Authoritarian Rule: Tentative Conclusions about Uncertain Democracies* (Baltimore: Johns Hopkins University Press, 1986), 37-38.

4. Terry Lynn Karl, "Petroleum and Political Pacts: The Transition to Democracy in Venezuela," in *Transitions from Authoritarian Rule: Latin America*, eds. Guillermo O'Donnell, Philippe Schmitter and Laurence Whitehead (Baltimore: Johns Hopkins University Press, 1986), 210-215.

5. Nicolas Ardito-Barletta, "Democracy and Development," *The Washington Quarterly* 13 (Summer 1990): 161-171.

6. Ibid., 163.

7. "The Perils of Presidentialism," *Journal of Democracy* 1 (Winter 1990): 51-69.

8. Such possibilities for presidentialism in multiethnic societies are considered by Donald Horowitz, *Ethnic Groups in Conflict* (Berkeley: University of California Press, 1985), 636-639.

9. G. Bingham Powell, Jr., *Contemporary Democracies: Participation, Stability, and Violence* (Cambridge: Harvard University Press, 1982), 123-132.

10. Arend Lijphart, *Democracies: Patterns of Majoritarian and Consensus Government in Twenty-One Countries* (New Haven: Yale University Press, 1984), 150-168.

11. Israel-Diaspora Institute, "Electoral Reform in Israel—An Abstract," Tel-Aviv, Israel, February 1990.

12. Almond and Verba, op. cit., 339-360.

13. Robert Dahl, *Polyarchy: Participation and Opposition* (New Haven: Yale University Press, 1971), 150-162.

14. Michael G. Burton and John Higley, "Elite Settlements," *American Sociological Review* 52 (June 1987): 295-307.

15. Dankwart Rustow, "Transitions to Democracy: Toward a Dynamic Model," *Comparative Politics* 2 (April 1970): 358-361.

16. A more specific and far-reaching arrangement of these principles is embodied in "consociational democracy," which consists of a "grand coalition" cabinet in a parliamentary system; a mutual veto to protect minority interests; proportionality in political representation, civil service appointments, and revenue allocation; and considerable autonomy for each ethnic group in its own affairs. Arend Lijphart, *Democracy in Plural Societies: A Comparative Exploration* (New Haven: Yale University Press, 1977).

17. Horowitz, op. cit., 597-613.

9.
THE PERILS OF PRESIDENTIALISM

Juan J. Linz

***Juan J. Linz**, Sterling Professor of Political and Social Science at Yale University, is widely known for his contributions to the study of authoritarianism and totalitarianism, political parties and elites, and democratic breakdowns and transitions to democracy. In 1987 he was awarded Spain's* Principe de Asturias *prize in the social sciences. The following essay is based on a paper he presented in May 1989 at a conference in Washington, D.C., organized by the Latin American Studies Program of Georgetown University, with support from the Ford Foundation. An annotated, revised, and expanded version of this essay (including a discussion of semipresidential systems) appeared under the title "Presidential or Parliamentary Democracy: Does It Make a Difference?" in* The Failure of Presidential Democracy *edited by the author and Professor Arturo Valenzuela of Georgetown University.*

As more of the world's nations turn to democracy, interest in alternative constitutional forms and arrangements has expanded well beyond academic circles. In countries as dissimilar as Chile, South Korea, Brazil, Turkey, and Argentina, policymakers and constitutional experts have vigorously debated the relative merits of different types of democratic regimes. Some countries, like Sri Lanka, have switched from parliamentary to presidential constitutions. On the other hand, Latin Americans in particular have found themselves greatly impressed by the successful transition from authoritarianism to democracy that occurred in the 1970s in Spain, a transition to which the parliamentary form of government chosen by that country greatly contributed.

Nor is the Spanish case the only one in which parliamentarism has given evidence of its worth. Indeed, the vast majority of the stable democracies in the world today are parliamentary regimes, where executive power is generated by legislative majorities and depends on such majorities for survival.

By contrast, the only presidential democracy with a long history of constitutional continuity is the United States. The constitutions of Finland and France are hybrids rather than true presidential systems, and in the case of the French Fifth Republic, the jury is still out. Aside from the United States, only Chile has managed a century and a half of relatively undisturbed constitutional continuity under presidential government—but Chilean democracy broke down in the 1970s.

Parliamentary regimes, of course, can also be unstable, especially under conditions of bitter ethnic conflict, as recent African history attests. Yet the experiences of India and of some English-speaking countries in the Caribbean show that even in greatly divided societies, periodic parliamentary crises need not turn into full-blown regime crises and that the ousting of a prime minister and cabinet need not spell the end of democracy itself.

The burden of this essay is that the superior historical performance of parliamentary democracies is no accident. A careful comparison of parliamentarism as such with presidentialism as such leads to the conclusion that, on balance, the former is more conducive to stable democracy than the latter. This conclusion applies especially to nations with deep political cleavages and numerous political parties; for such countries, parliamentarism generally offers a better hope of preserving democracy.

Parliamentary vs. Presidential Systems

A parliamentary regime in the strict sense is one in which the only democratically legitimate institution is parliament; in such a regime, the government's authority is completely dependent upon parliamentary confidence. Although the growing personalization of party leadership in some parliamentary regimes has made prime ministers seem more and more like presidents, it remains true that barring dissolution of parliament and a call for new elections, premiers cannot appeal directly to the people over the heads of their representatives. Parliamentary systems may include presidents who are elected by direct popular vote, but they usually lack the ability to compete seriously for power with the prime minister.

In presidential systems an executive with considerable constitutional powers—generally including full control of the composition of the cabinet and administration—is directly elected by the people for a fixed term and is independent of parliamentary votes of confidence. He is not only the holder of executive power but also the symbolic head of state and can be removed between elections only by the drastic step of impeachment. In practice, as the history of the United States shows, presidential systems may be more or less dependent on the cooperation of the legislature; the balance between executive and legislative power in such systems can thus vary considerably.

Two things about presidential government stand out. The first is the president's strong claim to democratic, even plebiscitarian, legitimacy; the second is his fixed term in office. Both of these statements stand in need of qualification. Some presidents gain office with a smaller proportion of the popular vote than many premiers who head minority cabinets, although voters may see the latter as more weakly legitimated. To mention just one example, Salvador Allende's election as president of Chile in 1970—he had a 36.2-percent plurality obtained by a heterogeneous coalition—certainly put him in a position very different from that in which Adolfo Suárez of Spain found himself in 1979 when he became prime minister after receiving 35.1 percent of the vote. As we will see, Allende received a six-year mandate for controlling the government even with much less than a majority of the popular vote, while Suárez, with a plurality of roughly the same size, found it necessary to work with other parties to sustain a minority government. Following British political thinker Walter Bagehot, we might say that a presidential system endows the incumbent with both the "ceremonial" functions of a head of state and the "effective" functions of a chief executive, thus creating an aura, a self-image, and a set of popular expectations which are all quite different from those associated with a prime minister, no matter how popular he may be.

But what is most striking is that in a presidential system, the legislators, especially when they represent cohesive, disciplined parties that offer clear ideological and political alternatives, can also claim democratic legitimacy. This claim is thrown into high relief when a majority of the legislature represents a political option opposed to the one the president represents. Under such circumstances, who has the stronger claim to speak on behalf of the people: the president or the legislative majority that opposes his policies? Since both derive their power from the votes of the people in a free competition among well-defined alternatives, a conflict is always possible and at times may erupt dramatically. There is no democratic principle on the basis of which it can be resolved, and the mechanisms the constitution might provide are likely to prove too complicated and aridly legalistic to be of much force in the eyes of the electorate. It is therefore no accident that in some such situations in the past, the armed forces were often tempted to intervene as a mediating power. One might argue that the United States has successfully rendered such conflicts "normal" and thus defused them. To explain how American political institutions and practices have achieved this result would exceed the scope of this essay, but it is worth noting that the uniquely diffuse character of American political parties—which, ironically, exasperates many American political scientists and leads them to call for responsible, ideologically disciplined parties—has something to do with it. Unfortunately, the American case seems to be an exception; the development of modern political parties, particularly in socially and ideologically polarized countries, generally exacerbates, rather than moderates, conflicts between the legislative and the executive.

The second outstanding feature of presidential systems—the president's relatively fixed term in office—is also not without drawbacks. It breaks the political process into discontinuous, rigidly demarcated periods, leaving no room for the continuous readjustments that events may demand. The duration of the president's mandate becomes a crucial factor in the calculations of all political actors, a fact which (as we shall see) is fraught with important consequences. Consider, for instance, the provisions for succession in case of the president's death or incapacity: in some cases, the automatic successor may have been elected separately and may represent a political orientation different from the president's; in other cases, he may have been imposed by the president as his running mate without any consideration of his ability to exercise executive power or maintain popular support. Brazilian history provides us with examples of the first situation, while Maria Estela Martínez de Perón's succession of her husband in Argentina illustrates the second. It is a paradox of presidential government that while it leads to the personalization of power, its legal mechanisms may also lead, in the event of a sudden midterm succession, to the rise of someone whom the ordinary electoral process would never have made the chief of state.

Paradoxes of Presidentialism

Presidential constitutions paradoxically incorporate contradictory principles and assumptions. On the one hand, such systems set out to create a strong, stable executive with enough plebiscitarian legitimation to stand fast against the array of particular interests represented in the legislature. In the Rousseauian conception of democracy implied by the idea of "the people," for whom the president is supposed to speak, these interests lack legitimacy; so does the Anglo-American notion that democracy naturally involves a jostle—or even sometimes a melee—of interests. Interest group conflict then bids fair to manifest itself in areas other than the strictly political. On the other hand, presidential constitutions also reflect profound suspicion of the personalization of power: memories and fears of kings and caudillos do not dissipate easily. Foremost among the constitutional bulwarks against potentially arbitrary power is the prohibition on reelection. Other provisions like legislative advice-and-consent powers over presidential appointments, impeachment mechanisms, judicial independence, and institutions such as the Contraloría of Chile also reflect this suspicion. Indeed, political intervention by the armed forces acting as a *poder moderador* may even be seen in certain political cultures as a useful check on overweening executives. One could explore in depth the contradictions between the constitutional texts and political practices of Latin American presidential regimes; any student of the region's history could cite many examples.

It would be useful to explore the way in which the fundamental contradiction between the desire for a strong and stable executive and the latent suspicion of that same presidential power affects political decision making, the style of leadership, the political practices, and the rhetoric of both presidents and their opponents in presidential systems. It introduces a dimension of conflict that cannot be explained wholly by socioeconomic, political, or ideological circumstances. Even if one were to accept the debatable notion that Hispanic societies are inherently prone to *personalismo*, there can be little doubt that in some cases this tendency receives reinforcement from institutional arrangements.

Perhaps the best way to summarize the basic differences between presidential and parliamentary systems is to say that while parliamentarism imparts flexibility to the political process, presidentialism makes it rather rigid. Proponents of presidentialism might reply that this rigidity is an advantage, for it guards against the uncertainty and instability so characteristic of parliamentary politics. Under parliamentary government, after all, myriad actors—parties, their leaders, even rank-and-file legislators—may at any time between elections adopt basic changes, cause realignments, and, above all, make or break prime ministers. But while the need for authority and predictability would seem to favor presidentialism, there are unexpected developments—ranging from the death of the incumbent to serious errors in judgment committed under the pressure of unruly circumstances—that make presidential rule less predictable and often weaker than that of a prime minister. The latter can always seek to shore up his legitimacy and authority, either through a vote of confidence or the dissolution of parliament and the ensuing new elections. Moreover, a prime minister can be changed without necessarily creating a regime crisis.

Considerations of this sort loom especially large during periods of regime transition and consolidation, when the rigidities of a presidential constitution must seem inauspicious indeed compared to the prospect of adaptability that parliamentarism offers.

Zero-sum Elections

The preceding discussion has focused principally on the institutional dimensions of the problem; the consideration of constitutional provisions—some written, some unwritten—has dominated the analysis. In addition, however, one must attend to the ways in which political competition is structured in systems of direct presidential elections; the styles of leadership in such systems; the relations between the president, the political elites, and society at large; and the ways in which power is exercised and conflicts are resolved. It is a fair assumption that institutional arrangements both directly and indirectly shape the entire political process, or "way of ruling." Once we have described the differences between parliamentary and presidential forms of government that result from their differing institutional arrangements, we shall be ready to ask which of the two forms offers the best prospect for creating, consolidating, and maintaining democracy.

Presidentialism is ineluctably problematic because it operates according to the rule of "winner-take-all"—an arrangement that tends to make democratic politics a zero-sum game, with all the potential for conflict such games portend. Although parliamentary elections can produce an absolute majority for a single party, they more often give representation to a number of parties. Power-sharing and coalition-forming are fairly common, and incumbents are accordingly attentive to the demands and interests of even the smaller parties. These parties in turn retain expectations of sharing in power and, therefore, of having a stake in the system as a whole. By contrast, the conviction that he possesses independent authority and a popular mandate is likely to imbue a president with a sense of power and mission, even if the plurality that elected him is a slender one. Given such assumptions about his standing and role, he will find the inevitable opposition to his policies far more irksome and demoralizing than would a prime minister, who knows himself to be but the spokesman for a temporary governing coalition rather than the voice of the nation or the tribune of the people.

Absent the support of an absolute and cohesive majority, a parliamentary system inevitably includes elements that become institutionalized in what has been called "consociational democracy." Presidential regimes may incorporate consociational elements as well, perhaps as part of the unwritten constitution. When democracy was reestablished under adverse circumstances in Venezuela and Colombia, for example, the written constitutions may have called for presidential government, but the leaders of the major parties quickly turned to consociational agreements to soften the harsh, winner-take-all implications of presidential elections.

The danger that zero-sum presidential elections pose is compounded by the rigidity of the president's fixed term in office. Winners and losers are sharply defined for the entire period of the presidential mandate. There is no hope for shifts in alliances, expansion of the government's base of support through national-unity or emergency grand coalitions, new elections in response to major new events, and so on. Instead, the losers must wait at least four or five years without any access to executive power and patronage. The zero-sum game in presidential regimes raises the stakes of presidential elections and inevitably exacerbates their attendant tension and polarization.

On the other hand, presidential elections do offer the indisputable advantage of allowing the people to choose their chief executive openly, directly, and for a predictable span rather than leaving that decision to the backstage maneuvering of the politicians. But this advantage can only be present if a clear mandate results. If there is no required minimum plurality and several candidates compete in a single round, the margin between the victor and the runner-up may be too thin to support any claim that a decisive plebiscite has taken place. To preclude this, electoral laws sometimes place a lower limit on the size of the winning plurality or create some mechanism for choosing among the candidates if none attains the minimum number of votes needed to win; such procedures need not necessarily award the office to the candidate with the most votes. More common are run-off provisions that set up a confrontation between the two major candidates, with possibilities for polarization that have already been mentioned. One of the possible consequences of two-candidate races in multiparty systems is that broad coalitions are likely to be formed (whether in run-offs or in preelection maneuvering) in which extremist parties gain undue influence. If significant numbers of voters identify strongly with such parties, one or more of them can plausibly claim to represent the decisive electoral bloc in a close contest and may make demands accordingly. Unless a strong candidate of the center rallies widespread support against the extremes, a presidential election can fragment and polarize the electorate.

"In a polarized society with a volatile electorate, no serious candidate in a single-round election can afford to ignore parties with which he would otherwise never collaborate."

In countries where the preponderance of voters is centrist, agrees on the exclusion of extremists, and expects both rightist and leftist candidates to differ only within a larger, moderate consensus, the divisiveness latent in presidential competition is not a serious problem. With an overwhelmingly moderate electorate, anyone who makes alliances or takes positions that seem to incline him to the extremes is unlikely to win, as both Barry Goldwater and George McGovern discovered to their chagrin. But societies beset by grave social and economic problems, divided about recent authoritarian regimes that once enjoyed significant popular support, and in which well-disciplined extremist parties have considerable electoral appeal, do not fit the model presented by the United States. In a polarized society with a volatile electorate, no serious candidate in a single-round election can afford to ignore parties with which he would otherwise never collaborate.

A two-round election can avoid some of these problems, for the preliminary round shows the extremist parties the limits of their strength and allows the two major candidates to reckon just which alliances they must make to win. This reduces the degree of uncertainty and promotes more rational decisions on the part of both voters and candidates. In effect, the presidential system may thus reproduce something like the negotiations that "form a government" in parliamentary regimes. But the potential for polarization remains, as does the difficulty of isolating extremist factions that a significant portion of the voters and elites intensely dislike.

The Spanish Example

For illustration of the foregoing analysis, consider the case of Spain in 1977, the year of the first free election after the death of Francisco Franco. The parliamentary elections held that year allowed transitional prime minister Adolfo Suárez to remain in office. His moderate Union del Centro Democratico (UCD) emerged as the leading party with 34.9 percent of the vote and 167 seats in the 350-seat legislature. The Socialist Party (PSOE), led by Felipe González, obtained 29.4 percent and 118 seats, followed by the Communist Party (PCE) with 9.3 percent and 20 seats, and the rightist Alianza Popular (AP), led by Manuel Fraga, with 8.4 percent and 16 seats.

These results clearly show that if instead of parliamentary elections, a *presidential* contest had been held, no party would have had more than a plurality. Candidates would have been forced to form coalitions to have a chance of winning in a first or second round. Prior to the election, however, there was no real record of the distribution of the electorate's preferences. In this uncertain atmosphere, forming coalitions would have proven difficult. Certainly the front-runners would have found themselves forced to build unnecessarily large winning coalitions.

Assuming that the democratic opposition to Franco would have united behind a single candidate like Felipe González (something that was far from certain at the time), and given both the expectations about the strength of the Communists and the ten percent of the electorate they actually represented, he would never have been able to run as independently as he did in his campaign for a seat in parliament. A popular-front mentality would have dominated the campaign and probably submerged the distinct identities that the different parties, from the extremists on the left to the Christian Democrats and the moderate regional parties in the center, were able to maintain in most districts. The problem would have been even more acute for the center-rightists who had supported reforms, especially the *reforma pactada* that effectively put an end to the authoritarian regime. It is by no means certain that Adolfo Suárez, despite the great popularity he gained during the transition process, could or would have united all those to the right of the Socialist Party. At that juncture many Christian Democrats, including those who would later run on the UCD ticket in 1979, would not have been willing to abandon the political allies they had made during the years of opposition to Franco; on the other hand, it would have been difficult for Suárez to appear with the support of the rightist AP, since it appeared to represent the "continuist" (i.e., Francoist) alternative. For its part, the AP would probably not have supported a candidate like Suárez who favored legalization of the Communist Party.

Excluding the possibility that the candidate of the right would have been Fraga (who later became the accepted leader of the opposition), Suárez would still have been hard-pressed to maintain throughout the campaign his distinctive position as an alternative to any thought of continuity with the Franco regime. Indeed, the UCD directed its 1977 campaign as much against the AP on the right as against the Socialists on the left. Moreover, given the uncertainty about the AP's strength and the fear and loathing it provoked on the left, much leftist campaigning also targeted Fraga. This had the effect of reducing polarization, especially between longtime democrats, on the one hand, and newcomers to democratic politics (who comprised important segments of both the UCD's leadership and its rank and file), on the other. Inevitably, the candidate of the right and center-right would have focused his attacks on the left-democratic candidate's "dangerous" supporters, especially the Communists and the parties representing Basque and Catalan nationalism. In replying to these attacks the candidate of the left and center-left would certainly have pointed to the continuity between his opponent's policies and those of Franco, the putative presence of unreconstructed Francoists in the rightist camp, and the scarcity of centrist democrats in the right-wing coalition.

"There can be no doubt that in the Spain of 1977, a presidential election would have been far more divisive than the parliamentary elections..."

There can be no doubt that in the Spain of 1977, a presidential election would have been far more divisive than the parliamentary elections that actually occurred. Had Suárez rejected an understanding with Fraga and his AP or had Fraga—misled by his own inflated expectations about the AP's chances of becoming the majority party in a two-party system—rejected any alliance with the Suaristas, the outcome most likely would have been a plurality for a candidate to the left of both Suárez and Fraga. A president with popular backing, even without a legislative majority on his side, would have felt himself justified in seeking both to draft a constitution and to push through political and social changes far more radical than those the Socialist Prime Minister Felipe González pursued after his victory in 1982. It is important to recall that González undertook his initiatives when Spain had already experienced five years of successful democratic rule, and only after both a party congress that saw the defeat of the PSOE's utopian left wing and a campaign aimed at winning over the centrist majority of Spanish voters. Spanish politics since Franco has clearly felt the moderating influence of parliamentarism; without it, the transition to popular government and the consolidation of democratic rule would probably have taken a far different—and much rougher—course.

Let me now add a moderating note of my own. I am *not* suggesting that the polarization which often springs from presidential elections is an inevitable concomitant of presidential government. If the public consensus hovers reliably around the middle of the political spectrum and if the limited weight of the fringe parties is in evidence, no candidate will have any incentive to coalesce with the extremists. They may run for office, but they will do so in isolation and largely as a rhetorical exercise. Under these conditions of moderation and preexisting consensus, presidential campaigns are unlikely to prove dangerously divisive. The problem is that in countries caught up in the arduous experience of establishing and consolidating democracy, such happy circumstances are seldom present. They certainly do not exist when there is a polarized multiparty system including extremist parties.

The Style of Presidential Politics

Since we have thus far focused mostly on the implications of presidentialism for the electoral process, one might reasonably observe that while the election is one thing, the victor's term in office is another: once he has won, can he not set himself to healing the wounds inflicted during the campaign and restoring the unity of the nation? Can he not offer to his defeated opponents—but not to the extremist elements of his own coalition—a role in his administration and thus make himself president of all the people? Such policies are of course possible, but must depend on the personality and political style of the new president and, to a lesser extent, his major antagonists. Before the election no one can be sure that the new incumbent will make conciliatory moves; certainly the process of political mobilization in a plebiscitarian campaign is not conducive to such a turn of events. The new president must consider whether gestures designed to conciliate his recent opponents might weaken him unduly, especially if he risks provoking his more extreme allies into abandoning him completely. There is also the possibility that the opposition could refuse to reciprocate his magnanimity, thus causing the whole strategy to backfire. The public rejection of an olive branch publicly proffered could harden positions on both sides and lead to more, rather than less, antagonism and polarization.

Some of presidentialism's most notable effects on the style of politics result from the characteristics of the presidential office itself. Among these characteristics are not only the great powers associated with the presidency but also the limits imposed on it—particularly those requiring cooperation with the legislative branch, a requirement that becomes especially salient when that branch is dominated by opponents of the president's party. Above all, however, there are the time constraints that a fixed term or number of possible terms imposes on the incumbent. The office of president is by nature two-dimensional and, in a sense, ambiguous: on the one hand, the president is the head of state and the representative of the entire nation; on the other hand, he stands for a clearly partisan political option. If he stands at the head of a multiparty coalition, he may even represent an option within an option as he deals with other members of the winning electoral alliance.

The president may find it difficult to combine his role as the head of what Bagehot called the "deferential" or symbolic aspect of the polity (a role that Bagehot thought the British monarch played perfectly and which, in republican parliamentary constitutions, has been successfully filled by presidents such as Sandro Pertini of Italy and Theodor Heuss of West Germany) with his role as an effective chief executive and partisan leader fighting to promote his party and its program. It is not always easy to be simultaneously the president, say, of all Chileans and of the workers; it is hard to be both the elegant and courtly master of La Moneda (the Chilean president's official residence) and the demagogic orator of the mass rallies at the soccer stadium. Many voters and key elites are likely to think that playing the second role means betraying the first—for should not the president as head of state stand at least somewhat above party in order to be a symbol of the nation and the stability of its government? A presidential system, as opposed to a constitutional monarchy or a republic with both a premier and a head of state, does not allow such a neat differentiation of roles.

Perhaps the most important consequences of the direct relationship that exists between a president and the electorate are the sense the president may have of being the only elected representative of the whole people and the accompanying risk that he will tend to conflate his supporters with "the people" as a whole. The plebiscitarian component implicit in the president's authority is likely to make the obstacles and opposition he encounters seem particularly annoying. In his frustration he may be tempted to define his policies as reflections of the popular will and those of his opponents as the selfish designs of narrow interests. This identification of leader with people fosters a certain populism that may be a source of strength. It may also, however, bring on a refusal to acknowledge the limits of the mandate that even a majority—to say nothing of a mere plurality—can claim as democratic justification for the enactment of its agenda. The doleful potential for displays of cold indifference, disrespect, or even downright hostility toward the opposition is not to be scanted.

Unlike the rather Olympian president, the prime minister is normally a member of parliament who, even as he sits on the government bench, remains part of the larger body. He must at some point meet his fellow legislators upon terms of rough equality, as the British prime minister regularly does during the traditional question time in the House of Commons. If he heads a coalition or minority government or if his party commands only a slim majority of seats, then he can afford precious little in the way of detachment from parliamentary opinion. A president, by contrast, heads an independent branch of government and meets with members of the legislature on his own terms. Especially uncertain in presidential regimes is the place of opposition leaders, who may not even hold public office and in any case have nothing like the quasi-official status that the leaders of the opposition enjoy in Britain, for example.

The absence in presidential regimes of a monarch or a "president of the republic" who can act symbolically as a moderating power deprives the system of flexibility and of a means of restraining power. A generally neutral figure can provide moral ballast in a crisis or act as a moderator between the premier and his opponents—who may include not only his parliamentary foes but military leaders as well. A parliamentary regime has a speaker or presiding member of parliament who can exert some restraining influence over the parliamentary antagonists, including the prime minister himself, who is after all a member of the chamber over which the speaker presides.

The Problem of Dual Legitimacy

Given his unavoidable institutional situation, a president bids fair to become the focus for whatever exaggerated expectations his supporters may harbor. They are prone to think that he has more power than he really has or should have and may sometimes be politically mobilized against any adversaries who bar his way. The interaction between a popular president and the crowd acclaiming him can generate fear among his opponents and a tense political climate. Something similar might be said about a president with a military background or close military ties—which are facilitated by the absence of the prominent defense minister one usually finds under cabinet government.

Ministers in parliamentary systems are situated quite differently from cabinet officers in presidential regimes. Especially in cases of coalition or minority governments, prime ministers are much closer to being on an equal footing with their fellow ministers than presidents will ever be with their cabinet appointees. (One must note, however, that there are certain trends which may lead to institutions like that of *Kanzlerdemokratie* in Germany, under which the premier is free to choose his cabinet without parliamentary approval of the individual ministers. Parliamentary systems with tightly disciplined parties and a prime minister who enjoys an absolute majority of legislative seats will tend to grow quite similar to presidential regimes. The tendency to personalize power in modern politics, thanks especially to the influence of television, has attenuated not only the independence of ministers but the degree of collegiality and collective responsibility in cabinet governments as well.)

A presidential cabinet is less likely than its parliamentary counterpart to contain strong and independent-minded members. The officers of a president's cabinet hold their posts purely at the sufferance of their chief; if dismissed, they are out of public life altogether. A premier's ministers, by contrast, are not his creatures but normally his parliamentary colleagues; they may go from the cabinet back to their seats in parliament and question the prime minister in party caucuses or during the ordinary course of parliamentary business just as freely as other members can. A president, moreover, can shield his cabinet members from criticism much more effectively than can a prime minister, whose cabinet members are regularly hauled before parliament to answer queries or even, in extreme cases, to face censure.

One need not delve into all the complexities of the relations between the executive and the legislature in various presidential regimes to see that all such systems are based on dual democratic legitimacy: no democratic principle exists to resolve disputes between the executive and the legislature about which of the two actually represents the will of the people. In practice, particularly in those developing countries where there are great regional inequalities in modernization, it is likely that the political and social outlook of the legislature will differ from that held by the president and his supporters. The territorial principle of representation, often reinforced by malapportionment or federal institutions like a nonproportional upper legislative chamber, tends to give greater legislative weight to small towns and rural areas. Circumstances like these can give the president grounds to question the democratic credentials of his legislative opponents. He may even charge that they represent nothing but local oligarchies and narrow, selfish clienteles. This may or may not be true, and it may or may not be worse to cast one's ballot under the tutelage of local notables, tribal chieftains, landowners, priests, or even bosses than under that of trade unions, neighborhood associations, or party machines. Whatever the case may be, modern urban elites will remain inclined to skepticism about the democratic bona fides of legislators from rural or provincial districts. In such a context, a president frustrated by legislative recalcitrance will be tempted to mobilize the people against the putative oligarchs and special interests, to claim for himself alone true democratic legitimacy as the tribune of the people, and to urge on his supporters in mass demonstrations against the opposition. It is also conceivable that in some countries the president might represent the more traditional or provincial electorates and could use their support against the more urban and modern sectors of society.

Even more ominously, in the absence of any principled method of distinguishing the true bearer of democratic legitimacy, the president may use ideological formulations to discredit his foes; institutional rivalry may thus assume the character of potentially explosive social and political strife. Institutional tensions that in some societies can be peacefully settled through negotiation or legal means may in other, less happy lands seek their resolution in the streets.

The Issue of Stability

Among the oft-cited advantages of presidentialism is its provision for the stability of the executive. This feature is said to furnish a welcome contrast to the tenuousness of many parliamentary governments, with their frequent cabinet crises and changes of prime minister, especially in the multiparty democracies of Western Europe. Certainly the spectacle of political instability presented by the Third and Fourth French Republics and, more recently, by Italy and Portugal has contributed to the low esteem in which many scholars—especially in Latin America—hold parliamentarism and their consequent preference for presidential government. But such invidious comparisons overlook the large degree of stability that actually characterizes parliamentary governments. The superficial volatility they sometimes exhibit obscures the continuity of parties in power, the enduring character of coalitions, and the way that party leaders and key ministers have of weathering cabinet crises without relinquishing their posts. In addition, the instability of presidential cabinets has been ignored by students of governmental stability. It is also insufficiently noted that parliamentary systems, precisely by virtue of their surface instability, often avoid deeper crises. A prime minister who becomes embroiled in scandal or loses the allegiance of his party or majority coalition and whose continuance in office might provoke grave turmoil can be much more easily removed than a corrupt or highly unpopular president. Unless partisan alignments make the formation of a democratically legitimate cabinet impossible, parliament should eventually be able to select a new prime minister who can form a new government. In some more serious cases, new elections may be called, although they often do not resolve the problem and can even, as in the case of Weimar Germany in the 1930s, compound it.

The government crises and ministerial changes of parliamentary regimes are of course excluded by the fixed term a president enjoys, but this great stability is bought at the price of similarly great rigidity. Flexibility in the face of constantly changing situations is not presidentialism's strong suit. Replacing a president who has lost the confidence of his party or the people is an extremely difficult proposition. Even when polarization has intensified to the point of violence and illegality, a stubborn incumbent may remain in office. By the time the cumbersome mechanisms provided to dislodge him in favor of a more able and conciliatory successor have done their work, it may be too late. Impeachment is a very uncertain and time-consuming process, especially compared with the simple parliamentary vote of no confidence. An embattled president can use his powers in such a way that his opponents might not be willing to wait until the end of his term to oust him, but there are no constitutional ways—save impeachment or resignation under pressure—to replace him. There are, moreover, risks attached even to these entirely legal methods; the incumbent's supporters may feel cheated by them and rally behind him, thus exacerbating the crisis. It is hard to imagine how the issue could be resolved purely by the political leaders, with no recourse or threat of recourse to the people or to nondemocratic institutions like the courts or—in the worst case—the military. The intense antagonisms underlying such crises cannot remain even partially concealed in the corridors and cloakrooms of the legislature. What in a parliamentary system would be a government crisis can become a full-blown regime crisis in a presidential system.

The same rigidity is apparent when an incumbent dies or suffers incapacitation while in office. In the latter case, there is a temptation to conceal the president's infirmity until the end of his term. In event of the president's death, resignation, impeachment, or incapacity, the presidential constitution very often assures an automatic and immediate succession with no interregnum or power vacuum. But the institution of vice-presidential succession, which has worked so well in the United States, may not function so smoothly elsewhere. Particularly at risk are countries whose constitutions, like the United States Constitution before the passage of the Twelfth Amendment in 1804, allow presidential tickets to be split so that the winning presidential candidate and the winning vice-presidential candidate may come from different parties. If the deceased or outgoing president and his legal successor are from different parties, those who supported the former incumbent might object that the successor does not represent their choice and lacks democratic legitimacy.

Today, of course, few constitutions would allow something like the United States' Jefferson-Burr election of 1800 to occur. Instead they require that presidential and vice-presidential candidates be nominated together, and forbid ticket-splitting in presidential balloting. But these formal measures can do nothing to control the criteria for nomination. There are undoubtedly cases where the vice-president has been nominated mainly to balance the ticket and therefore represents a discontinuity with the president. Instances where a weak vice-presidential candidate is deliberately picked by an incumbent jealous of his own power, or even where the incumbent chooses his own wife, are not unknown. Nothing about the presidential system guarantees that the country's voters or political leaders would have selected the vice-president to wield the powers they were willing to give to the former president. The continuity that the institution of automatic vice-presidential succession seems to ensure thus might prove more apparent than real. There remains the obvious possibility of a caretaker government that can fill in until new elections take place, preferably as soon as possible. Yet it hardly seems likely that the severe crisis which might have required the succession would also provide an auspicious moment for a new presidential election.

The Time Factor

Democracy is by definition a government pro tempore, a regime in which the electorate at regular intervals can hold its governors accountable and impose a change. The limited time that is allowed to elapse between elections is probably the greatest guarantee against overweening power and the last hope for those in the minority. Its drawback, however, is that it constrains a government's ability to make good on the promises it made in order to get elected. If these promises were far-reaching, including major programs of social change, the majority may feel cheated of their realization by the limited term in office imposed on their chosen leader. On the other hand, the power of a president is at once so concentrated and so extensive that it seems unsafe not to check it by limiting the number of times any one president can be reelected. Such provisions can be frustrating, especially if the incumbent is highly ambitious; attempts to change the rule in the name of continuity have often appeared attractive.

Even if a president entertains no inordinate ambitions, his awareness of the time limits facing him and the program to which his name is tied cannot help but affect his political style. Anxiety about policy discontinuities and the character of possible successors encourages what Albert Hirschman has called "the wish of *vouloir conclure*." This exaggerated sense of urgency on the part of the president may lead to ill-conceived policy initiatives, overly hasty stabs at implementation, unwarranted anger at the lawful opposition, and a host of other evils. A president who is desperate to build his Brasilia or implement his program of nationalization or land reform before he becomes ineligible for reelection is likely to spend money unwisely or risk polarizing the country for the sake of seeing his agenda become reality. A prime minister who can expect his party or governing coalition to win the next round of elections is relatively free from such pressures. Prime ministers have stayed in office over the course of several legislatures without rousing any fears of nascent dictatorship, for the possibility of changing the government without recourse to unconstitutional means always remained open.

The fixed term in office and the limit on reelection are institutions of unquestionable value in presidential constitutions, but they mean that the political system must produce a capable and popular leader every four years or so, and also that whatever "political capital" the outgoing president may have accumulated cannot endure beyond the end of his term.

All political leaders must worry about the ambitions of second-rank leaders, sometimes because of their jockeying for position in the order of succession and sometimes because of their intrigues. The fixed and definite date of succession that a presidential constitution sets can only exacerbate the incumbent's concerns on this score. Add to this the desire for continuity, and it requires no leap of logic to predict that the president will choose as his lieutenant and successor-apparent someone who is more likely to prove a yes-man than a leader in his own right.

The inevitable succession also creates a distinctive kind of tension between the ex-president and his successor. The new man may feel driven to assert his independence and distinguish himself from his predecessor, even though both might belong to the same party. The old president, for his part, having known the unique honor and sense of power that come with the office, will always find it hard to reconcile himself to being out of power for good, with no prospect of returning even if the new incumbent fails miserably. Parties and coalitions may publicly split because of such antagonisms and frustrations. They can also lead to intrigues, as when a still-prominent former president works behind the scenes to influence the next succession or to undercut the incumbent's policies or leadership of the party.

Of course similar problems can also emerge in parliamentary systems when a prominent leader finds himself out of office but eager to return. But parliamentary regimes can more easily mitigate such difficulties for a number of reasons. The acute need to preserve party unity, the deference accorded prominent party figures, and the new premier's keen awareness that he needs the help of his predecessor even if the latter does not sit on the government bench or the same side of the house—all these contribute to the maintenance of concord. Leaders of the same party may alternate as premiers; each knows that the other may be called upon to replace him at any time and that confrontations can be costly to both, so they share power. A similar logic applies to relations between leaders of competing parties or parliamentary coalitions.

The time constraints associated with presidentialism, combined with the zero-sum character of presidential elections, are likely to render such contests more dramatic and divisive than parliamentary elections. The political realignments that in a parliamentary system may take place between elections and within the halls of the legislature must occur publicly during election campaigns in presidential systems, where they are a necessary part of the process of building a winning coalition. Under presidentialism, time becomes an intensely important dimension of politics. The pace of politics is very different under a presidential, as opposed to a parliamentary, constitution. When presidential balloting is at hand, deals must be made not only publicly but decisively—for the winning side to renege on them before the next campaign would seem like a betrayal of the voters' trust. Compromises, however necessary, that might appear unprincipled, opportunistic, or ideologically unsound are much harder to make when they are to be scrutinized by the voters in an upcoming election. A presidential regime leaves much less room for tacit consensus-building, coalition-shifting, and the making of compromises which, though prudent, are hard to defend in public.

Consociational methods of compromise, negotiation, and power-sharing under presidential constitutions have played major roles in the return of democratic government to Colombia, Venezuela, and, more recently, Brazil. But these methods appeared as necessary antinomies—deviations from the rules of the system undertaken in order to limit the voters' choices to what has been termed, rather loosely and pejoratively, *democradura*. The restoration of democracy will no doubt continue to require consociational strategies such as the formation of grand coalitions and the making of many pacts; the drawback of presidentialism is that it rigidifies and formalizes them. They become binding for a fixed period, during which there is scant opportunity for revision or renegotiation. Moreover, as the Colombian case shows, such arrangements rob the electorate of some of its freedom of choice; parliamentary systems, like that of Spain with its *consenso*, make it much more likely that consociational agreements will be made only *after* the people have spoken.

Parliamentarism and Political Stability

This analysis of presidentialism's unpromising implications for democracy is not meant to imply that no presidential democracy can be stable; on the contrary, the world's most stable democracy—the United States of America—has a presidential constitution. Nevertheless, one cannot help tentatively concluding that in many other societies the odds that presidentialism will help preserve democracy are far less favorable.

While it is true that parliamentarism provides a more flexible and adaptable institutional context for the establishment and consolidation of democracy, it does not follow that just any sort of parliamentary regime will do. Indeed, to complete the analysis one would need to reflect upon the best type of parliamentary constitution and its specific institutional features. Among these would be a prime-ministerial office combining power with responsibility, which would in turn require strong, well-disciplined political parties. Such features—there are of course many others we lack the space to discuss—would help foster responsible decision making and stable governments and would encourage genuine party competition without causing undue political fragmentation. In addition, every country has unique aspects that one must take into account—traditions of federalism, ethnic or cultural heterogeneity, and so on. Finally, it almost goes without saying that our analysis establishes only probabilities and tendencies, not determinisms. No one can guarantee that parliamentary systems will never experience grave crisis or even breakdown.

In the final analysis, all regimes, however wisely designed, must depend for their preservation upon the support of society at large—its major forces, groups, and institutions. They rely, therefore, on a public consensus which recognizes as legitimate authority only that power which is acquired through lawful and democratic means. They depend also on the ability of their leaders to govern, to inspire trust, to respect the limits of their power, and to reach an adequate degree of consensus. Although these qualities are most needed in a presidential system, it is precisely there that they are most difficult to achieve. Heavy reliance on the personal qualities of a political leader—on the virtue of a statesman, if you will—is a risky course, for one never knows if such a man can be found to fill the presidential office. But while no presidential constitution can guarantee a Washington, a Juárez, or a Lincoln, no parliamentary regime can guarantee an Adenauer or a Churchill either. Given such unavoidable uncertainty, the aim of this essay has been merely to help recover a debate on the role of alternative democratic institutions in building stable democratic polities.

10. COMPARING DEMOCRATIC SYSTEMS

Donald L. Horowitz

Donald L. Horowitz, *James B. Duke Professor of Law and Political Science at Duke University, has done extensive studies of divided societies and of institutional design for democratizing countries. He is the author of numerous books including* Ethnic Groups in Conflict *(1985) and* A Democratic South Africa? Constitutional Engineering in a Divided Society *(1991).*

In "The Perils of Presidentialism" [*Journal of Democracy* 1 (Winter 1990): 51-69], Professor Juan Linz makes the claim that parliamentary systems are "more conducive to stable democracy" than are presidential systems. "This conclusion," he continues, "applies especially to nations with deep political cleavages and numerous political parties." This theme forms a *leitmotiv* in Professor Linz's recent works, has been picked up by other scholars, and runs the risk of becoming conventional wisdom before it receives searching scrutiny.

Linz argues that the presidential office introduces an undesirable element of winner-take-all politics into societies that need mechanisms of conciliation instead. A presidential candidate is either elected or not, whereas in parliamentary systems many shades of outcome are possible. Moreover, a directly elected president may think he has a popular "mandate," even if he has been elected with only a small plurality of the vote, perhaps even less than 40 percent. The potential for conflict is accordingly enhanced.

Conflict is promoted, in Linz's view, by the separation of powers that divides the legislature from the president. The fixed term of a separately elected president makes for rigidity between elections. By contrast, parliamentary systems are able to resolve crises at any time simply by changing leaders or governments. Separate presidential election also produces weak cabinets and fosters electoral contests in which extremists either have too much influence or the whole society becomes polarized.

This is a powerful indictment, supported by an abiding concern for the stability of precarious democratizing regimes. Linz's claims, however, are not sustainable. First, they are based on a regionally skewed and highly selective sample of comparative experience, principally from Latin America. Second, they rest on a mechanistic, even caricatured, view of the presidency. Third, they assume a particular system of electing the president, which is not necessarily the best system. Finally, by ignoring the functions that a separately elected president can perform for a divided society, they defeat Linz's own admirable purposes.

Presidentialism and Political Instability

As frequent references to Brazil, Colombia, Venezuela, and Chile attest, Linz believes that presidentialism has contributed to instability in Latin America. If, however, his focus had been on instability in postcolonial Asia and Africa, the institutional villain would surely have been parliamentary systems. Indeed, Sir Arthur Lewis argued 25 years ago in his lectures on *Politics in West Africa* that the inherited Westminster system of parliamentary democracy was responsible for much of the authoritarianism then emerging in English-speaking Africa. What Lewis emphasized was the winner-take-all features of the Westminster model, in which anyone with a parliamentary majority was able to seize the state.

Lewis's understanding conforms to that of many Africans seeking to restore democratic rule. The most impressive efforts at redemocratization, those of Nigeria in 1978-79 and again at the present time, involve adoption of a presidential system to mitigate societal divisions. Under the parliamentary system inherited at independence, a cluster of ethnic groups from the north had managed to secure a majority of seats and shut all other groups out of power. This game of total inclusion and exclusion characterized Nigerian politics after 1960, precipitating the military coups of 1966 and the war of Biafran secession from 1967 to 1970. By choosing a separation of powers, the Nigerians aimed to prevent any group from controlling the country by controlling parliament.

Now it is possible that parliamentary systems helped stifle democracy in Africa while presidential systems helped stifle it in Latin America, but there are grounds for doubt. Linz refers to the emergence of conciliatory practices in the presidential systems of Colombia, Venezuela, and Brazil, but he dismisses them as "deviations." Chile under Salvador Allende, on the other hand, is regarded as closer to the norm, with presidentialism exacerbating social conflict. Yet at least some research by Arturo Valenzuela suggests that, before Allende, many Chilean presidents actually bolstered centrist, moderating tendencies. The experience of the presidency in the United States, where the presidency was invented, is also explained away as "an exception." Consequently, Chile's exacerbated conflict is traced to its presidency, while the moderated conflict of the

United States is said to have other roots. Political success has, so to speak, many parents; political failure, only one: the presidency.

In a variety of ways, Linz characterizes the presidency as a rigid institution, conducive to zero-sum politics. But that is the straw presidency he has conjured, rather than the presidency in fact. He says, for example, that parliamentary systems, unlike presidential systems, do not dichotomize winners and losers. In parliamentary regimes, coalition governments may form; and government and opposition may cooperate in the legislative process.

These outcomes, however, are equally possible in presidential systems. The Nigerian Second Republic had both a president and a coalition in the legislature. In presidential systems, moreover, government and opposition frequently cooperate in the legislative process. The United States Congress is notorious for such cooperation. Linz ascribes this cooperation to the "uniquely diffuse" party system of the United States. That party system has its roots in federalism, which also underpins the way the president is elected. Does that not argue against condemnation of a single institution like the presidency without examining the total configuration of institutions proposed for a given country?

It is difficult to see how a presidential system could produce more absolute win-or-lose outcomes than a parliamentary system does. One of Linz's objections to presidentialism is that it sets up a needless conflict between the executive and the legislature, especially if the two are controlled by different parties. But if the two are controlled by different parties, the system has not produced a winner-take-all result. It is difficult to complain about interbranch checks and balances and winner-take-all politics at the same time.

The presidency, says Linz, is an office that encourages its occupant to think that he has more power than he actually does. Where several candidates have contested, a president elected with, say, one-third of the vote gains the full power of the office. (The example of Allende, elected with a 36.2-percent plurality, is cited.) The new president can make appointments, propose and veto legislation, and, given his fixed term of office, even survive fluctuations in the strength of party support. A crisis in government during a fixed presidential term becomes, according to Linz, a constitutional crisis, since there is generally no lawful way to bring down a failed president in the middle of his term. By contrast, a parliamentary government that has lost its majority in the legislature will fall, whether or not elections are due. So conflict is routinized and need not ripen into a crisis.

Before responding to these claims, it is necessary to underscore a central assumption of the Linz analysis: that the president will be elected under a plurality (first-past-the-post) system or a majority system, with a runoff election if necessary. From this assumption follow most of Linz's complaints. Consequently, it needs to be said clearly that presidents do not need to be elected on a plurality or majority-runoff basis. In divided societies, as I shall explain shortly, presidents should be elected by a different system, one that ensures broadly distributed support for the president. This greatly alleviates the problem of the narrowly elected president who labors under the illusion that he has a broader mandate. Winner-take-all is a function of electoral systems, not of institutions in the abstract.

Modes of Presidential Election

Electoral assumptions color all of Linz's analysis. He suggests that presidential candidates in plurality systems habitually cultivate the political extremes to facilitate election, thus giving the extremes influence denied them in a parliamentary system. But the supposed need to make concessions to extremists for the sake of building a plurality dissolves if presidents are not elected in this manner. By the same token, the influence of extremists in parliamentary systems is variable. One thing governing it, as the Israeli system shows, is the mode of election.

Electing the president by a majority attained in a runoff between the top two candidates poses a different problem, according to Linz. The runoff may facilitate alliances among moderates, but it also promotes a "confrontation" between the top two candidates, with a possibility that the society as a whole might become polarized.

Now, in fact, election of the president by straight plurality or majority vote is not a principle in favor with all those who have adopted presidential constitutions lately. Even the Electoral College system by which presidents of the United States are chosen is far more complex than a straight majority or runoff system. Presidential candidates in the United States are induced by the way electoral votes are distributed among the states to make discerning judgments about which interests are powerful in which states. The process cannot be captured in terms of extremism or polarization. But since Linz is especially keen to discourage presidentialism in societies with deep cleavages, it is preferable to focus on examples of presidential electoral systems in two such severely divided societies: Nigeria and Sri Lanka.

In the Nigerian Second Republic, which began in 1979, a presidential system was created. (The same presidency and electoral system will be used in the Third Republic, scheduled to begin in 1992.) To be elected, a president needed a plurality plus distribution. The successful candidate was required to have at least 25 percent of the vote in no fewer than two-thirds of the then-19 states. This double requirement was meant to ensure that the president had support from many ethnic groups. To put the point in Linz's terms, the aim was to shut out ethnic extremists and elect a moderate, centrist president. That is precisely the sort of president the Nigerians elected under the new system. The extremists, in fact, were elected to parliament, not the presidency. Nor was there any of the polarization that Linz associates with majority runoffs. Carefully devised presidential-election arrangements can bolster the center and knit together the rent fabric of a divided society. In choosing a presidential electoral system with incentives for widely distributed support, the Nigerians were rejecting winner-take-all politics. They aimed instead for a president bent on conciliation rather than on conflict. They succeeded.

In 1978, Sri Lanka also moved to a presidential system. Its principal purpose was to create a political executive with a fixed term that would permit the incumbent to make unpopular decisions, particularly those concerning the reduction of ethnic conflict. A majority requirement was instituted. Since most candidates were unlikely to gain a majority in Sri Lanka's multiparty system, a method of alternative voting was adopted. Each voter could vote for several candidates, ranking them in order of preference. If no candidate attained a majority of first preferences, the top two candidates would be put into what amounted to an instant runoff. The second preferences of voters for all other candidates would then be counted (and likewise for third preferences) until one of the top two gained a majority. It was expected that presidential candidates would build their majority on the second and third choices of voters whose preferred candidate was not among the top two. This would put ethnic minorities (especially the Sri Lankan Tamils) in a position to require compromise as the price for their second preferences. So, again, the presidential system would rule out extremists, provide incentives to moderation, and encourage compromise in a fragmented society.

The majority requirement originated in a fear that Linz shares. Like him, the Sri Lankans were concerned that a plurality election could result in the choice of a president who enjoyed the support of only 30 or 35 percent of the voters and perhaps had won election by a very narrow margin. Lest such a chief executive think himself in possession of a "mandate," the Sri Lankans insisted on aggregating second and subsequent preferences in order to produce the requisite majority. The ease of devising such a system entirely vitiates the objection.

Indeed, had the Sri Lankans and Nigerians adopted their presidential electoral systems earlier, there is every reason to think that their conflicts would have been moderated by those systems. Instead, their conflicts worsened because of the winner-take-all rules that governed their parliamentary systems and excluded minorities from power.

Insubstantial Differences

The remaining elements of the indictment—the rigidity of the fixed term, the weak cabinet, and the prospects for abuse of presidential power—are all said to be inherent drawbacks of presidentialism. All are insubstantial in practice.

It is true, of course, that presidents serve during a fixed term of years and cannot be removed on a vote of no confidence. Nevertheless, the fixed term of a directly elected president is not more likely than the more flexible term of a parliamentary government to cause a governmental crisis. When parliamentary regimes begin with secure majorities, they tend to serve their full terms. The exception occurs when a government calls an early election to take advantage of its transient popularity. In theory, it is easier to remove a parliamentary government in the middle of its term than it is to remove a president. In practice, however, the need seldom arises unless the government consists of an unstable coalition because the society is fragmented. In that event, there is a good case for shifting to a presidential system, supported by a mode of election that fosters conciliation and consensus building. That, in fact, would be a sound interpretation of what the French did when they created the presidency of the Fifth Republic in 1958.

In presidential systems, as Linz observes, cabinets are typically weaker than they are in parliamentary systems. The weakness of cabinet ministers in presidential systems is due in part to the separation of powers. Since cabinet ministers are not elected legislators, they owe their offices to the president. If the president is conciliatory, they too will be conciliatory—which is more important for the polities about which Linz is properly concerned than whether cabinet ministers are weak or strong.

In any case, the difference is exaggerated. Linz argues that the weakness of the cabinet is a function of the undue strength of the president. But there is another reason. In the United States, for example, cabinets are composed as they are because they represent special interests: agriculture, commerce, labor, and so on. What this means is that the president does *not* have a completely free hand in selecting them. Furthermore, strong prime ministers like Margaret Thatcher or Indira Gandhi have been able to dominate and reshuffle their parliamentary cabinets with impunity. This distinction between the two systems is breaking down.

Finally, abuse of power is hardly a presidential monopoly. Parliamentary regimes in Asia and Africa have produced more than their share of abuses of power. In Latin America and southern Europe, as well as Asia and Africa, abuse of power is made possible principally by the military coup or the growth of single-party hegemony. On this score, there is nothing to choose between presidential and parliamentary systems. Both have succumbed.

Choosing Among Democratic Institutions

Although the sharp distinction between presidential and parliamentary systems is unwarranted, Linz's disquiet is not. He has genuine cause for concern about the institutions adopted by democratizing states, particularly those with deep cleavages and numerous parties. He is right to worry about winner-take-all outcomes and their exclusionary consequences in such societies. Nevertheless, it is Westminster, the Mother of Parliaments, that produces such outcomes as often as any presidential system does.

As this suggests, Linz's quarrel is not with the presidency, but with two features that epitomize the Westminster version of democracy: first, plurality elections that produce a majority of seats by shutting out third-party competitors; and second, adversary democracy, with its sharp divide between winners and losers, government and opposition. Because these are Linz's underlying objections, it is not difficult to turn his arguments around against parliamentary systems, at least where they produce coherent majorities and minorities. Where no majority emerges and coalitions are necessary, sometimes—but only sometimes—more conciliatory processes and outcomes emerge. As a result, Linz's thesis boils down to an argument not against the presidency but against plurality election, not in favor of parliamentary *systems* but in favor of parliamentary *coalitions*.

These are indeed important arguments, because democratizing societies need to think, and think hard, about electoral systems that foster conciliation and governmental systems that include rather than exclude. Prominent among innovations they might consider are presidents chosen by an electoral formula that maximizes the accommodation of contending political forces. Democratic innovators can only be aided by Linz's emphasis on institutional design. But they can only be distracted by his construction of an unfounded dichotomy between two systems, divorced from the electoral and other governmental institutions in which they operate.

11. THE CENTRALITY OF POLITICAL CULTURE

Seymour Martin Lipset

Seymour Martin Lipset *is Hazel Professor of Public Policy at George Mason University and a senior fellow of the Hoover Institution at Stanford University. His many books include* Political Man, The First New Nation, Revolution and Counterrevolution, *and* Consensus and Conflict. *His most recent book is* American Exceptionalism: A Double-Edged Sword *(1996).*

Juan Linz and Donald Horowitz are to be commended for reviving the discussion of the relationship between constitutional systems—presidential or parliamentary—and the conditions that make for stable democracy. Linz, basing himself largely on the Latin American experience, notes that most presidential systems have repeatedly broken down. Horowitz, a student of Asia and Africa, emphasizes that most parliamentary systems, particularly those attempted in almost all African countries and some of the new nations of postwar Asia, have also failed. He could also have pointed to the interwar collapse of democratic parliamentarism in Spain, Portugal, Greece, Italy, Austria, Germany, and most of Eastern Europe. Conversely, in addition to the successful parliamentary regimes of northern Europe and the industrialized parts of the British Commonwealth, countries such as France under the Fifth Republic, pre-Allende Chile, Costa Rica, and Uruguay (for most of this century) offer examples of stable and democratic presidentialism.

Clearly, it is not obvious that constitutional variations in type of executive are closely linked to democratic or authoritarian outcomes. As Linz emphasizes, parliamentary government (especially where there are several parties but none with a clear majority) gives different constituencies more access to the decision-making process than they would enjoy in presidential systems, and presumably helps bind these constituencies to the polity. Under presidential government, those opposed to the president's party may regard themselves as marginalized, and thus may seek to undermine presidential legitimacy. Because presidential government entrusts authority and ultimate responsibility to a single person, some scholars regard it as inherently unstable; failures can lead to a rejection of the symbol of authority. Power seems more diversified in parliamentary regimes.

The reality is more complicated. Given the division of authority between presidents and legislatures, prime ministers and their cabinets are more powerful and may pay less attention to the importunings of specific groups. A prime minister with a majority of parliament behind him has much more authority than an American president. Basically, such parliaments vote to support the budgets, bills, and policies that the government presents. Government members must vote this way, or the cabinet falls and an election is called. Unlike members of a legislative branch, opposition parliamentarians, though free to debate, criticize, or vote against the policies set by the executive, rarely can affect them.

The situation is quite different in a presidential system. The terms of the president and cabinet are not affected by votes in the legislature. As a result, party discipline is much weaker in, say, the U.S. Congress than it is in the British Parliament. In the United States and other presidential systems, the representation of diverse interests and value groups in different parties leads to cross-party alliances on various issues. Local interests are better represented in Congress, since a representative will look for constituency support to get reelected and can vote against his president or party. An MP, however, must go with his prime minister and his party, even if doing so means alienating constituency support.

The fact that presidencies make for weak parties and weak executives, while parliaments tend to have the reverse effect, certainly affects the nature of and possibly the conditions for democracy. But much of the literature wrongly assumes the opposite: that a president is inherently stronger than a prime minister, and that power is more concentrated in the former. I should emphasize that a condition for a strong cabinet government is the need to call a new election when a cabinet loses a parliamentary vote. Where parliament continues and a new cabinet is formed from a coalition of parties, no one of which has a majority, parliamentary cabinets may be weak, as in the Weimar Republic, the Third and Fourth French Republics, or contemporary Israel and India.

In my recent book *Continental Divide*, which compares the institutions and values of the United States and Canada, I note that the difference between presidential and parliamentary systems in comparable continent-spanning, federal polities results in two weak parties in the United States and multiple strong ones in Canada. The U.S. system appears to be the more stable of the two; since 1921, Canada has seen the rise and fall of over half a dozen important "third parties." The U.S. system's emphasis on electing one person president or governor forces the "various groups . . . [to] identify with one or another of the two major electoral alliances on whatever basis of division is most salient to them. Each major alliance or coalition party contains different interest groups which fight it out in primaries."

I conclude with respect to Canada that its "electoral changes have clearly been the result not of great instability or tension," but rather of the political system. In effect, the need for disciplined parliamentary parties "encourages the transformation of political protest, of social movements, of discontent with the dominant party in one's region or other aspects of life, into third, fourth, or fifth parties." The loose parties inherent in the presidential system of the U.S. absorb protest more easily within traditional mechanisms than do the parliamentary parties of Canada.

The Cultural Factor

The question remains, why have most Latin American polities not functioned like the U.S. political system? The answer lies in economic and cultural factors. If we look at the comparative record, it still suggests, as I noted in 1960 in *Political Man*, that long-enduring democracies are disproportionately to be found among the wealthier and more Protestant nations. The "Fourth" or very undeveloped world apart, Catholic and poorer countries have been less stably democratic. The situation has of course changed somewhat in recent times. Non-Protestant southern European countries like Greece, Italy, Portugal, and Spain have created parliamentary democracies, while most Catholic Latin American countries have competitive electoral systems with presidential regimes.

I will not reiterate my past discussions of the diverse social conditions for democracy, other than to note that the correlations of democracy with Protestantism and a past British connection point up the importance of cultural factors. In this connection, it may be noted that in Canada the "Latin" (French-speaking and Catholic) province of Quebec seemingly lacked the conditions for a pluralistic party system and democratic rights until the 1960s, while the anglophone and Protestant part of the country has had a stable multiparty system with democratic guarantees for close to a century. In seeking to explain in 1958 why "French Canadians have not really believed in democracy for themselves," and did not have a functioning competitive party system, political scientist Pierre Trudeau, who would later serve as prime minister of Canada for 16 years, wrote, "French Canadians are Catholics; and Catholic nations have not always been ardent supporters of democracy. They are authoritarian in spiritual matters; and . . . they are often disinclined to seek solutions in temporal matters through the mere counting of heads."[1]

Trudeau mentioned other factors, of course, particularly those inherent in the minority and economically depressed situation of his linguistic compatriots, but basically, as he noted, Canada had two very different cultures and political systems within the same set of governmental and constitutional arrangements. Quebec, like most of South America, may be described as Latin and American, and its pre-1960 politics resembled that of other Latin societies more than it did any in the anglophone world, whether presidential or parliamentary. Quebec, of course, has changed greatly since the early 1960s, and now has a stable two-party system. But these political developments have occurred in tandem with major adjustments in the orientation and behavior of the Catholic Church, in the content of the educational system, and in economic development and mobility, particularly among the francophones. What has not changed is the formal political system.

Islamic countries may also be considered as a group. Almost all have been authoritarian, with monarchical or presidential systems of government. It would be hard to credit the weakness of democracy among them to their political institutions. Some writers claim that Islamic faith makes political democracy in a Western sense extremely difficult, since it recognizes no separation of the secular and religious realms. Such claims should not be categorical, since, as with Christianity, doctrines and practices can evolve over time.

This emphasis on culture is reinforced by Myron Wiener's observation that almost all of the postwar "new nations" that have become enduring democracies are former British colonies, as are various others, such as Nigeria and Pakistan, which maintained competitive electoral institutions for briefer periods. Almost none of the former Belgian, Dutch, French, Portuguese, or Spanish colonies have comparable records. In the comparative statistical analyses that I have been conducting of the factors associated with democracy among the Third World countries, past experience with British rule emerges as one of the most powerful correlates of democracy.

Cultural factors deriving from varying histories are extraordinarily difficult to manipulate. Political institutions—including electoral systems and constitutional arrangements—are more easily changed. Hence, those concerned with enhancing the possibilities for stable democratic government focus on them. Except for the case of the Fifth French Republic, and the barriers placed on small-party representation in West Germany, there is little evidence, however, that such efforts have had much effect, and the latter case is debatable.

NOTES

1. Pierre Elliot Trudeau, *Federalism and the French Canadians* (New York: St. Martin's Press, 1968), 108.

12. THE VIRTUES OF PARLIAMENTARISM

Juan J. Linz

***Juan J. Linz** is Sterling Professor of Political and Social Science at Yale University. His English-language publications include* Crisis, Breakdown and Reequilibrium*—volume one of the four-volume work,* The Breakdown of Democratic Regimes, *which he edited with Alfred Stepan. His article "The Perils of Presidentialism" appeared in the Winter 1990 issue of the* Journal of Democracy.

The critical comments that Professor Horowitz and Professor Lipset have offered on my essay provide stimulating contributions to the debate over the respective merits of various forms of democratic politics. This debate is most timely, as controversy seems to be subsiding about the merits of democracy versus other types of government. My essay, itself an abbreviated version of a much longer paper still in progress, was meant as a spur to further study of the problem.[1] By raising more questions than can be answered given the current state of our knowledge about how democracy works, Horowitz and Lipset confirm the need for more research and reflection.

To avoid any misunderstanding, I must stress that I did not argue that *any* parliamentary system is *ipso facto* more likely to ensure democratic stability than *any* presidential system. Nor was I suggesting that any parliamentary regime will make better policy decisions than any presidential government, which would be an even harder case to make. There are undoubtedly bad forms of both these types of government. My essay did not discuss possible new forms of presidentialism, confining itself instead to the existing democratic presidential systems and excluding detailed consideration of the United States, which I consider quite exceptional.[2] I do not think that I have constructed a "straw-man" version of presidentialism; my analysis is based on careful study of many prominent presidential systems, though I did not include the Nigerian and Sri Lankan versions of presidentialism that Professor Horowitz so skillfully discusses. Yet my article (like Horowitz's comments) also omits consideration of the many possible varieties of parliamentarism, and of the complex issues surrounding semipresidential or semiparliamentary systems with dual executives. These deserve separate analysis.

I agree with Professor Horowitz that the study of democratic regimes cannot be separated from the study of electoral systems, and acknowledge that my analysis does not cover all possible methods of presidential election. The Nigerian system represents a unique method of presidential election that might be applicable in federal states, particularly multiethnic ones, but I doubt very much that one could justify it in more homogeneous societies, even in the federal states of Latin America. My analysis concentrates on the two most common methods of election: the simple majority or plurality system, and the two-candidate runoff. The case where an electoral college may make a decision irrespective of the popular vote is left out, as is the very special case of Bolivia. The Bolivian Congress chooses among presidential candidates without regard to their popular vote totals, a practice that has certainly not contributed to either political stability or accountability in that country. I also refrained from mentioning the practice of directly electing a plural executive or a president and vice-president to represent two different constituencies (of Greek and Turkish Cypriots, for example). My argument concerns the *likelihood* of certain patterns of politics in the most common types of presidential systems, and does not attempt an exhaustive analysis of all types of directly elected executives. The patterns in question are likely to contribute to instability or difficulties in the performance of presidential executives. I use the word "likelihood" to stress that those consequences need not be present in each and every presidential system, or lead to the breakdown of democracy itself. On the contrary, recent experience shows that even rather inept democratic regimes stand a good chance of surviving simply because all relevant actors find the nondemocratic alternatives to be even less satisfactory.

Horowitz stresses that the majoritarian implications of presidentialism—the "winner-take-all" features that I have emphasized—may also be present in parliamentary systems with plurality elections in single-member districts, especially under the two-party systems that so often go together with Westminster-style parliamentary government. In societies that are polarized, or fragmented by multiple cleavages, a multiparty system with proportional representation may allow the formation of alternative coalitions (as in Belgium, for example), and thus forestall dangerous zero-sum outcomes.

As for parliamentary systems with plurality elections, Mrs. Thatcher is certainly a first above unequals, like a president, and probably has more power than an American chief executive. Certainly, parliamentary democracies in which a single disciplined party obtains the absolute majority of all seats find themselves in what is close to a "winner-take-all" situation. But this is not the most frequent pattern in parliamentary systems, particularly when there is proportional representation. Indeed, Horowitz implies that I should probably extend some of my concerns about the style of politics in presidentialism to take in the case of such majoritarian prime ministers, and that I might have a slight bias in favor of stable coalition government. I must once again note that I am dealing with ideal types that cannot subsume all of the possible varieties of political systems; indeed, I deal only with the more frequent tendencies in those ideal types. Nevertheless, while the actual situation of a powerful prime minister like Mrs. Thatcher might be comparable to that of a president with a legislative majority, the de jure difference is still significant. If Mrs. Thatcher were to falter or otherwise make herself a liability, for instance, the Conservative majority in the House of Commons could unseat her without creating a constitutional crisis. There would be no need to let her linger ineffectually in office like former presidents Raúl Alfonsín of Argentina or Alan García of Peru. Parliamentary elections may be called not only to benefit from popularity, but also when governing becomes difficult because of a lack of cohesion among the parliamentary majority. That was what happened in Spain in 1982, when Prime Minister Leopoldo Calvo Sotelo's dissolution of the Cortes allowed Felipe González to assume power at the head of a Socialist majority. Moreover, in cases where the parliamentary majority remains intact but the prime minister becomes discredited or exhausted (like Spanish premier Adolfo Suárez in 1981), he can resign without having to wait for the end of his term or a coup to remove him from office.

The "winner-take-all" character of the presidential election and the "unipersonal" executive (to use Arend Lijphart's term) does not rule out either weak presidents in particular or a weak presidency in general, Horowitz's suggestion to the contrary notwithstanding. The "all" that the winner takes may not include much effective power, especially if congressional support is not forthcoming. This is doubly so if popular support ebbs as the next election approaches. Presidents, especially those who come to power after a plebiscitarian or populist campaign, often find that the power they possess is hopelessly insufficient to meet the expectations they have generated. Constant presidential efforts to obtain new powers or invoke emergency authority are reflections of this fact.

Horowitz fails to address the basic problem of the competing claims to legitimacy of presidents and congresses, and the resulting potential for conflict between the two branches. Presidents occasionally win such conflicts, no doubt, but my argument is about institutions, not about how particular persons will fare in this or that set of circumstances. Horowitz might respond that conflicts between the legislature and the executive are not inevitable in a presidential democracy. That may be, but they are certainly likely. Although they have not caused democracy to break down in the United States, it should be recalled that for most of U.S. history, the party that controlled the presidency also controlled both houses of Congress. More recently, divided control has led to a politics of stalemate and mutual recrimination. Moreover, as a deeply institutionalized democracy, the United States is much better able to survive these difficulties of presidentialism than are many new or weak democracies in the developing world.

Horowitz tends to overstate my position by ignoring the necessarily qualified nature of my analysis. I was merely trying to evaluate the existing evidence and offer an estimate of probabilities; I would never place myself in the absurd position of claiming certitude about matters that remain only partly understood.

Varieties of Presidentialism

Horowitz further claims that my sample is skewed and highly selective, drawing as it does mostly on Latin American cases. I did not do a quantitative analysis, but the presidential systems of Latin America, together with those of the Philippines and South Korea (which I also had in mind), comprise almost all of the world's pure presidential regimes; the only exceptions are the systems of the United States, Nigeria, and Sri Lanka. Horowitz bases much of his argument on these last two countries.[3] I did not limit my generalizations to Latin America, since I think them largely valid for South Korea and the Philippines as well. The South Korean presidential election of 1987, for instance, saw Roh Tae Woo of the Democratic Justice Party (DJP) win office with 36.6 percent of the vote—almost the same percentage of the vote (34.7) as Adolfo Suárez's UCD garnered in Spain in 1977. Roh's victory frustrated opposition leaders Kim Young Sam and Kim Dae Jung, who had insisted on a direct presidential election and then split 55 percent of the vote between them.

As for Africa, close attention to the postcolonial history of that continent does not sustain Horowitz's claim that "the institutional villain would surely have been parliamentary systems." It was not simply parliamentarism, but rather democratic institutions as a whole—alien and weakly rooted as they were—that failed in Africa. The British Westminster model has winner-take-all features, to be sure, but these were even more prominent in presidential systems. Indeed, the emergence of authoritarian regimes in countries like Ghana, Uganda, and Senegal coincided with and was consolidated by "constitutional change from a parliamentary to a presidential system, with extreme concentration of power in the presidency and marked diminution of legislative authority."[4]

Horowitz criticizes me for holding a mechanistic and even caricatured view of the presidency. Certainly my main effort was to analyze the mechanics of presidential systems, but I think that my remarks on the style of politics in presidential countries, the responses of voters to presidential elections, the patterns of interaction among political leaders in presidential systems, and so on, raised my essay far above the level of the merely mechanical. I might be guilty of caricature, but many observers of the Latin American scene find my characterizations to be fairly accurate descriptions of events in those countries.

Horowitz's third claim—that I did not deal with each and every possible system for electing a president—is accurate enough, though I did cover the predominant ones (with the exceptions he presents). As for his fourth point, concerning the functions that a separately elected president can perform in a divided society, I concede that under certain very special circumstances (like those of Nigeria and perhaps Sri Lanka), a president *might* be able to help build political consensus. Still, there are counterexamples like Cyprus and Lebanon (to mention two other presidential systems) which show that presidentialism cannot overcome certain types of cleavages. Moreover, in view of the failure of Nigeria's Second Republic and the transition from military rule to a presidential Third Republic that is now underway, the jury is still out on the Nigerian presidency. The same might be said about Sri Lanka, where ethnic violence continues to rage and the deterioration of democratic institutions and liberties has yet to be reversed. The political problems of multiethnic societies under whatever system of rule (democratic or authoritarian, for that matter) present complexities that I could not address within the confines of a short essay.

Horowitz insists that a presidential electoral system with incentives for seeking widely distributed support (as in Nigeria) can obviate the winner-take-all politics that prevail in most presidential systems, particularly those with a weak separation of powers, no true federalism, and no strong judiciary. I have no doubt that requiring each candidate to gain, say, at least 25 percent of the vote in no fewer than two-thirds of the states will tend to produce a president with broad support across ethnic-cum-territorial divisions, thereby reducing ethnic polarization. But in any event, none of this did much to mitigate the winner-take-all aspect of Nigeria's presidential system. That system twice gave a minority party the exclusive right to constitute the executive branch, and helped to undermine democracy by spurring the massive rigging of the 1983 presidential election. Such a system can also backfire by leading to the election of a weak compromise candidate. Perhaps I overgeneralized from the cases included in my analysis, but to make contrary generalizations on the basis of highly unusual arrangements seems to me even less satisfactory. I still wonder how easy it is for Sri Lanka's president to make the sorts of unpopular decisions of which he is supposed to be capable (thanks to a method of election that aggregates second and subsequent preferences) in the face of a hostile legislative majority.

Much more research is needed concerning the composition and stability of cabinets in presidential systems. The president's secure tenure in office for the whole of a fixed term does not mean that his cabinet is immune to remodeling. In parliamentary systems, even those with unstable governments, cabinet members tend to accumulate considerable experience. The premiers generally have served in government before, and the system benefits from the accumulated political and administrative experience of the executive ministers. In most presidential systems, that experience is likely to be lost with a change of presidents, since each chief executive is likely to select those persons in whom he has personal confidence. In addition, since the president and his cabinet do not absolutely require the confidence of congress or the parties represented there, he can choose advisors and ministers from outside the political class and, as Brazilian presidents seem to have done, from parties besides his own—even from those that opposed his election. This might seem admirable and occasionally might work well, but it weakens parties by encouraging factionalism and clientelism. Just as a president who cannot be reelected is hard to hold accountable for his performance, a president who forms a cabinet without systematically involving the parties that back him makes it difficult for the voters to hold parties accountable in the next election. My analysis focuses on multiparty rather than two-party systems, but even in a two-party system it is not clear whom the voters will blame: the president's party, or the party with the majority in congress that obstructed his otherwise presumably successful performance.

The Problem of Divided Government

Giovanni Sartori has used the U.S. experience to argue that once the pattern of undivided consonant majorities (the coincidence of presidential and legislative majorities) and consociational practices (especially bipartisan concurrence in foreign affairs) is broken, there emerges an antagonistically divided government whose two main elements perceive that their respective electoral interests are best served by the failure of the other institution. For a Democrat-controlled Congress to cooperate with a Republican administration is to aid the election of future Republican presidents. Conversely, a president whose party is the minority in Congress will seek to restore undivided government by running against Congress. In short, he will play the "blame game." Thus the answer to the question of whether presidentialism provides for effective government is, with reference to its most acclaimed incarnation, a resounding no. The American system works or has worked in spite of, rather than because of, the presidential constitution of the United States. To the extent that it can still perform, it needs three things that tend to unblock it: flexibility or lack of ideological rigidity; weak, undisciplined parties; and pork-barrel and locality-oriented politics.[5]

These considerations weigh against the notion that since the United

States is both a successful democracy and a presidential regime, other presidential systems should also stand a good chance of being similarly successful. I cannot go into greater detail here, but recommend Fred Riggs's excellent study of the uniqueness of the U.S. political system, a system of which the presidency forms but a single part.[6]

At stake here are two separate issues: the stability of the democratic system, and the quality of its performance. Not all presidential regimes are unstable, nor are all of them weak in spite of their apparent strength. Many, however, have proven unstable and quite weak, though I would never exclude the possibility of a stable and strong presidential system if the president has the support of both an electoral and a legislative majority. Yet such a combination is rare in actual presidential systems, and might not be a good thing anyway: a popular president with a disciplined party behind him might defeat the constitutional scheme of checks and balances, thus obviating a key advantage of presidentialism. Even so, as Michael Coppedge's excellent study of the Venezuelan presidential system shows, a ban on presidential reelection hurts the president's ability to govern in the latter part of his term.[7]

I am grateful to Professor Horowitz for his comments, especially regarding the unusual systems of Nigeria and Sri Lanka. As I said at the outset, we need more systematic comparisons and more research on particular examples of presidential government (a largely neglected subject) before we can reach final conclusions. None of the existing research challenges my basic claim, which is that certain structural problems inherent in presidentialism make it likely that many presidential systems will run into serious difficulties of a sort that some parliamentary systems have successfully overcome. After all necessary qualifications have been made, my conclusion might be reformulated as follows: certain parliamentary systems are more likely than most of their presidential counterparts to solve certain knotty problems of multiparty politics. Even as I make qualifications, however, I am anxious that we avoid the error of forsaking comparative analysis for mere assessment of particular political systems, considered in isolation. Comparative analysis has to settle for probabilities rather than certainties, and therefore will always be open to question. The need for such analysis, however, is beyond question.

The Importance of Institutions

Professor Lipset's comments rightly stress the effect of economic, social, historical, and cultural factors on the fate of democracy in many countries past, present, and future. These factors operate more or less independently of political institutions. Culture, as Lipset notes, is difficult if not impossible to change. Historical legacies do not fully disappear, and socioeconomic transformation cannot be achieved by fiat, so we are left with the search for those political institutions that will best suit the circumstances in this or that particular country. This is a modest quest, but a worthy one. Presidentialism, parliamentarism, or some hybrid of the two; centralism or federalism; one-round or two-round elections—in every case the question is the same: what mix of laws and institutions will direct the contending interests of a given society into peaceful and democratic channels? Here is where I seek to make a contribution.

Lipset's able comparison between the United States and Canada confirms that even when societies are relatively similar, the type of democratic government each one has does make a difference. His observation that prime ministers who command a solid majority (not necessarily from one party) may have more power than presidents indirectly contributes to my argument. Also intriguing are Lipset's assertions about the greater weight of interest groups and local interests in presidential systems; if proven, they would be grist for the mill of those who complain about the invidious clientelism that pervades presidential countries like the Philippines and Brazil. He notes too the weakness both of parties and of presidents who depend on them for support. Will more research confirm my hypothesis that presidentialism helps to make parties weaker and less responsible? Would parliamentarism oblige parties to behave differently?

NOTES

1. See Oscar Godoy Arcaya, ed., *Hacia una democracia moderna: La opción parlamentaria* (Santiago: Ediciones Universidad Catolica de Chile, 1990), for a Spanish version of my extended paper, as well as those by Arend Lijphart and Arturo Valenzuela. I expect to publish it as an introductory essay in a book I will edit jointly with Arturo Valenzuela which will include country studies by many authors and theoretical contributions by Lijphart and Giovanni Sartori that in part support my argument, but also disagree with some of the points I make.

2. Fred W. Riggs, "The Survival of Presidentialism in America: Para-Constitutional Practices," *International Political Science Review* 9 (October 1988): 247-78.

3. Horowitz also refers to Colombia as a more successful case of presidentialism, but that country's transition to and early maintenance of presidential democracy was made possible only by the *Concordancia* of 1958, an arrangement under which the two major parties agreed to suspend their electoral competition for the presidency and accept alternating terms in power instead. While this helped to stabilize the country after a period of civil war and dictatorship, it can hardly be considered a model of democratic politics, or a method for making government accountable to the voters. To call it a deviation may be too mild.

4. Larry Diamond, "Introduction: Roots of Failure, Seeds of Hope," in *Democracy in Developing Countries*, vol. 2, *Africa*, eds. Larry Diamond, Juan J. Linz, and Seymour Martin Lipset (Boulder, Colo.: Lynne Rienner, 1988), 3.

5. Giovanni Sartori, "Neither Presidentialism nor Parliamentarism," (unpublished paper given at Georgetown University, May 1989).

6. Riggs, op. cit.

7. Michael Coppedge, "Venezuela: Democratic Despite Presidentialism," (unpublished paper given at Georgetown University, May 1989).

13.
CONSTITUTIONAL CHOICES FOR NEW DEMOCRACIES

Arend Lijphart

***Arend Lijphart**, professor of political science at the University of California at San Diego, is a specialist in comparative politics whose current research involves the comparative study of democratic regimes and electoral systems. His recent books include* Electoral Laws and Their Political Consequences *(1986), coedited with Bernard Grofman;* Electoral Systems and Party Systems: A Study of Twenty-Seven Democracies, 1945-1990 *(1994) in collaboration with Don Aitkin; and* Post-Communist Transformation in Eastern Europe *(1995), coedited with Beverly Crawford. This essay is a revised version of a paper first presented to the Philippine Council for Foreign Relations.*

Two fundamental choices that confront architects of new democratic constitutions are those between plurality elections and proportional representation (PR) and between parliamentary and presidential forms of government. The merits of presidentialism and parliamentarism were extensively debated by Juan J. Linz, Seymour Martin Lipset, and Donald L. Horowitz in the Fall 1990 issue of the *Journal of Democracy*.[1] I strongly concur with Horowitz's contention that the electoral system is an equally vital element in democratic constitutional design, and therefore that it is of crucial importance to evaluate these two sets of choices in relation with each other. Such an analysis, as I will try to show, indicates that the combination of parliamentarism with proportional representation should be an especially attractive one to newly democratic and democratizing countries.

The comparative study of democracies has shown that the type of electoral system is significantly related to the development of a country's party system, its type of executive (one-party vs. coalition cabinets), and the relationship between its executive and legislature. Countries that use the plurality method of election (almost always applied, at the national level, in single-member districts) are likely to have two-party systems, one-party governments, and executives that are dominant in relation to their legislatures. These are the main characteristics of the Westminster or *majoritarian* model of democracy, in which power is concentrated in the hands of the majority party. Conversely, PR is likely to be associated with multiparty systems, coalition governments (including, in many cases, broad and inclusive coalitions), and more equal executive-legislative power relations. These latter characteristics typify the *consensus* model of democracy, which, instead of relying on pure and concentrated majority rule, tries to limit, divide, separate, and share power in a variety of ways.[2]

Three further points should be made about these two sets of related traits. First, the relationships are mutual. For instance, plurality elections favor the maintenance of a two-party system; but an existing two-party system also favors the maintenance of plurality, which gives the two principal parties great advantages that they are unlikely to abandon. Second, if democratic political engineers desire to promote either the majoritarian cluster of characteristics (plurality, a two-party system, and a dominant, one-party cabinet) or the consensus cluster (PR, multipartism, coalition government, and a stronger legislature), the most practical way to do so is by choosing the appropriate electoral system. Giovanni Sartori has aptly called electoral systems "the most specific manipulative instrument of politics."[3] Third, important variations exist among PR systems. Without going into all the technical details, a useful distinction can be made between *extreme* PR, which poses few barriers to small parties, and *moderate* PR. The latter limits the influence of minor parties through such means as applying PR in small districts instead of large districts or nationwide balloting, and requiring parties to receive a minimum percentage of the vote in order to gain representation, such as the 5-percent threshold in Germany. The Dutch, Israeli, and Italian systems exemplify extreme PR and the German and Swedish systems, moderate PR.

The second basic constitutional choice, between parliamentary and presidential forms of government, also affects the majoritarian or consensus character of the political system. Presidentialism yields majoritarian effects on the party system and on the type of executive, but a consensus effect on executive-legislative relations. By formally separating the executive and legislative powers, presidential systems generally promote a rough executive-legislative balance of power. On the other hand, presidentialism tends to foster a two-party system, as the presidency is the biggest political prize to be won, and only the largest parties have a chance to win it. This advantage for the big parties often carries over into legislative elections as well (especially if presidential and legislative elections are held simultaneously), even if the legislative elections are conducted under PR rules. Presidentialism usually produces cabinets composed solely of members of the governing party. In fact, presidential systems concentrate executive power to an even greater degree than does a one-party parliamentary cabinet—not just in a single *party* but in a single *person.*

Explaining Past Choices

My aim is not simply to describe alternative democratic systems and their majoritarian or consensus characteristics, but also to make some practical recommendations for democratic constitutional engineers. What are the main advantages and disadvantages of plurality and PR and of presidentialism and parliamentarism? One way to approach this question is to investigate why contemporary democracies made the constitutional choices they did.

Figure 1 illustrates the four combinations of basic characteristics and the countries and regions where they prevail. The purest examples of the combination of presidentialism and plurality are the United States and democracies heavily influenced by the United States, such as the Philippines and Puerto Rico. Latin American countries have overwhelmingly opted for presidential-PR systems. Parliamentary-plurality systems exist in the United Kingdom and many former British colonies, including India, Malaysia, Jamaica, and the countries of the so-called Old Commonwealth (Canada, Australia, and New Zealand). Finally, parliamentary-PR systems are concentrated in Western Europe. Clearly, the overall pattern is to a large extent determined by geographic, cultural, and colonial factors—a point to which I shall return shortly.

Figure 1 — Four Basic Types of Democracy

	Presidential	Parliamentary
Plurality Elections	United States Philippines	United Kingdom Old Commonwealth India Malaysia Jamaica
Proportional Representation	Latin America	Western Europe

Very few contemporary democracies cannot be accommodated by this classification. The major exceptions are democracies that fall in between the pure presidential and pure parliamentary types (France and Switzerland), and those that use electoral methods other than pure PR or plurality (Ireland, Japan, and, again, France).[4]

Two important factors influenced the adoption of PR in continental Europe. One was the problem of ethnic and religious minorities; PR was designed to provide minority representation and thereby to counteract potential threats to national unity and political stability. "It was no accident," Stein Rokkan writes, "that the earliest moves toward proportional representation (PR) came in the ethnically most heterogeneous countries." The second factor was the dynamic of the democratization process. PR was adopted "through a convergence of pressures from below and from above. The rising working class wanted to lower the thresholds of representation in order to gain access to the legislatures, and the most threatened of the old-established parties demanded PR to protect their position against the new waves of mobilized voters created by universal suffrage."[5] Both factors are relevant for contemporary constitution making, especially for the many countries where there are deep ethnic cleavages or where new democratic forces need to be reconciled with the old antidemocratic groups.

The process of democratization also originally determined whether parliamentary or presidential institutions were adopted. As Douglas V. Verney has pointed out, there were two basic ways in which monarchical power could be democratized: by taking away most of the monarch's personal political prerogatives and making his cabinet responsible to the popularly elected legislature, thus creating a parliamentary system; or by removing the hereditary monarch and substituting a new, democratically elected "monarch," thus creating a presidential system.[6]

Other historical causes have been voluntary imitations of successful democracies and the dominant influence of colonial powers. As Figure 1 shows very clearly, Britain's influence as an imperial power has been enormously important. The U.S. presidential model was widely imitated in Latin America in the nineteenth century. And early in the twentieth century, PR spread quickly in continental Europe and Latin America, not only for reasons of partisan accommodation and minority protection, but also because it was widely perceived to be the most democratic method of election and hence the "wave of the democratic future."

This sentiment in favor of PR raises the controversial question of the *quality* of democracy achieved in the four alternative systems. The term "quality" refers to the degree to which a system meets such democratic norms as representativeness, accountability, equality, and participation.  The claims and counterclaims are too well-known to require lengthy treatment here, but it is worth emphasizing that the differences between the opposing camps are not as great as is often supposed. First of all,

PR and plurality advocates disagree not so much about the respective effects of the two electoral methods as about the weight to be attached to these effects. Both sides agree that PR yields greater proportionality and minority representation and that plurality promotes two-party systems and one-party executives. Partisans disagree on which of these results is preferable, with the plurality side claiming that only in two-party systems can clear accountability for government policy be achieved.

In addition, both sides argue about the *effectiveness* of the two systems. Proportionalists value minority representation not just for its democratic quality but also for its ability to maintain unity and peace in divided societies. Similarly, proponents of plurality favor one-party cabinets not just because of their democratic accountability but also because of the firm leadership and effective policy making that they allegedly provide. There also appears to be a slight difference in the relative emphasis that the two sides place on quality and effectiveness. Proportionalists tend to attach greater importance to the *representativeness* of government, while plurality advocates view the *capacity to govern* as the more vital consideration.

Finally, while the debate between presidentialists and parliamentarists has not been as fierce, it clearly parallels the debate over electoral systems. Once again, the claims and counterclaims revolve around both quality and effectiveness. Presidentialists regard the direct popular election of the chief executive as a democratic asset, while parliamentarists think of the concentration of executive power in the hands of a single official as less than optimally democratic. But here the question of effectiveness has been the more seriously debated issue, with the president's strong and effective leadership role being emphasized by one side and the danger of executive-legislative conflict and stalemate by the other.

Evaluating Democratic Performance

How can the actual performance of the different types of democracies be evaluated? It is extremely difficult to find quantifiable measures of democratic performance, and therefore political scientists have rarely attempted a systematic assessment. The major exception is G. Bingham Powell's pioneering study evaluating the capacity of various democracies to maintain public order (as measured by the incidence of riots and deaths from political violence) and their levels of citizen participation (as measured by electoral turnout).[7] Following Powell's example, I will examine these and other aspects of democratic performance, including democratic representation and responsiveness, economic equality, and macroeconomic management.

Due to the difficulty of finding reliable data outside the OECD countries to measure such aspects of performance, I have limited the analysis to the advanced industrial democracies. In any event, the Latin American democracies, given their lower levels of economic development, cannot be considered comparable cases. This means that one of the four basic alternatives—the presidential-PR form of democracy prevalent only in Latin America—must be omitted from our analysis.

Although this limitation is unfortunate, few observers would seriously argue that a strong case can be made for this particular type of democracy. With the clear exception of Costa Rica and the partial exceptions of Venezuela and Colombia, the political stability and economic performance of Latin American democracies have been far from satisfactory. As Juan Linz has argued, Latin American presidential systems have been particularly prone to executive-legislative deadlock and ineffective leadership.[8] Moreover, Scott Mainwaring has shown persuasively that this problem becomes especially serious when presidents do not have majority support in their legislatures.[9] Thus the Latin American model of presidentialism combined with PR legislative elections remains a particularly unattractive option.

The other three alternatives—presidential-plurality, parliamentary-plurality, and parliamentary-PR systems—are all represented among the firmly established Western democracies. I focus on the 14 cases that unambiguously fit these three categories. The United States is the one example of presidentialism combined with plurality. There are four cases of parliamentarism-plurality (Australia, Canada, New Zealand, and the United Kingdom), and nine democracies of the parliamentary-PR type (Austria, Belgium, Denmark, Finland, Germany, Italy, the Netherlands, Norway, and Sweden). Seven long-term, stable democracies are excluded from the analysis either because they do not fit comfortably into any one of the three categories (France, Ireland, Japan, and Switzerland), or because they are too vulnerable to external factors (Israel, Iceland, and Luxembourg).

Since a major purpose of PR is to facilitate minority representation, one would expect the PR systems to outperform plurality systems in this respect. There is little doubt that this is indeed the case. For instance, where ethnic minorities have formed ethnic political parties, as in Belgium and Finland, PR has enabled them to gain virtually perfect proportional representation. Because there are so many different kinds of ethnic and religious minorities in the democracies under analysis, it is difficult to measure systematically the *degree* to which PR succeeds in providing more representatives for minorities than does plurality. It is possible, however, to compare the representation of women—a minority in political rather than strictly numerical terms—systematically across countries. The first column of Table 1 shows the percentages of female members in the lower (or only) houses of the national legislatures in these 14 democracies during the early 1980s. The 16.4-percent average for the parliamentary-PR systems is about four times higher than the 4.1

Table 1 — Women's Legislative Representation, Innovative Family Policy, Voting Turnout, Income Inequality, and the Dahl Rating of Democratic Quality

	Women's Repr. 1980-82	Family Policy 1976-80	Voting Turnout 1971-80	Income Top 20% 1985	Dahl Rating 1969
Pres.-Plurality (N=1)	4.1	3.00	54.2%	39.9%	3.0
Parl.-Plurality (N=4)	4.0	2.50	75.3	42.9	4.8
Parl.-PR (N=9)	16.4	7.89	84.5	39.0	2.2

Note: The one presidential-plurality democracy is the United States; the four parliamentary-plurality democracies are Australia, Canada, New Zealand, and the United Kingdom; and the nine parliamentary-PR democracies are Austria, Belgium, Denmark, Finland, Germany, Italy, the Netherlands, Norway, and Sweden.

Sources: Based on Wilma Rule, "Electoral Systems, Contextual Factors and Women's Opportunity for Election to Parliament in Twenty-Three Democracies," *Western Political Quarterly* 40 (September 1987): 483; Harold L. Wilensky, "Common Problems, Divergent Policies: An 18-Nation Study of Family Policy," *Pubiic Affairs Report* 31 (May 1990): 2; personal communication by Harold L. Wilensky to the author, dated 18 October 1990; Robert W. Jackman, "Political Institutions and Voter Turnout in the Industrial Democracies," *American Political Science Review* 81 (June 1987): 420; World Bank, *World Development Report 1989* (New York: Oxford University Press, 1989), 223; Robert A. Dahl, *Polyarchy: Participation and Opposition* (New Haven: Yale University Press, 1971), 232.

percent for the United States or the 4.0-percent average for the parliamentary-plurality countries. To be sure, the higher social standing of women in the four Nordic countries accounts for part of the difference, but the average of 9.4 percent in the five other parliamentary-PR countries remains more than twice as high as in the plurality countries.

Does higher representation of women result in the advancement of their interests? Harold L. Wilensky's careful rating of democracies with regard to the innovativeness and expansiveness of their family policies—a matter of special concern to women—indicates that it does.[10] On a 13-point scale (from a maximum of 12 to a minimum of 0), the scores of these countries range from 11 to 1. The differences among the three groups (as shown in the second column of Table 1) are striking: the PR countries have an average score of 7.89, whereas the parliamentary-plurality countries have an average of just 2.50, and the U.S. only a slightly higher score of 3.00. Here again, the Nordic countries have the highest scores, but the 6.80 average of the non-Nordic PR countries is still well above that of the plurality countries.

The last three columns of Table 1 show indicators of democratic quality. The third column lists the most reliable figures on electoral participation (in the 1970s); countries with compulsory voting (Australia,

Belgium, and Italy) are not included in the averages. Compared with the extremely low voter turnout of 54.2 percent in the United States, the parliamentary-plurality systems perform a great deal better (about 75 percent). But the average in the parliamentary-PR systems is still higher, at slightly above 84 percent. Since the maximum turnout that is realistically attainable is around 90 percent (as indicated by the turnouts in countries with compulsory voting), the difference between 75 and 84 percent is particularly striking.

Another democratic goal is political equality, which is more likely to prevail in the absence of great economic inequalities. The fourth column of Table 1 presents the World Bank's percentages of total income earned by the top 20 percent of households in the mid-1980s.[11] They show a slightly less unequal distribution of income in the parliamentary-PR than in the parliamentary-plurality systems, with the United States in an intermediate position.

Finally, the fifth column reports Robert A. Dahl's ranking of democracies according to ten indicators of democratic quality, such as freedom of the press, freedom of association, competitive party systems, strong parties and interest groups, and effective legislatures.[12] The stable democracies range from a highest rating of 1 to a low of 6. There is a slight pro-PR bias in Dahl's ranking (he includes a number-of-parties variable that rates multiparty systems somewhat higher than two-party systems), but even when we discount this bias we find striking differences between the parliamentary-PR and parliamentary-plurality countries: six of the former are given the highest score, whereas most of the latter receive the next to lowest score of 5.

No such clear differences are apparent when we examine the effect of the type of democracy on the maintenance of public order and peace. Parliamentary-plurality systems had the lowest incidence of riots during the period 1948-77, but the highest incidence of political deaths; the latter figure, however, derives almost entirely from the high number of political deaths in the United Kingdom, principally as a result of the Northern Ireland problem. A more elaborate statistical analysis shows that societal division is a much more important factor than type of democracy in explaining variation in the incidence of political riots and deaths in the 13 parliamentary countries.[13]

A major argument in favor of plurality systems has been that they favor "strong" one-party governments that can pursue "effective" public policies. One key area of government activity in which this pattern should manifest itself is the management of the economy. Thus advocates of plurality systems received a rude shock in 1987 when the average per capita GDP in Italy (a PR and multiparty democracy with notoriously uncohesive and unstable governments) surpassed that of the United Kingdom, typically regarded as the very model of strong and effective government. If Italy had discovered large amounts of oil in the

Mediterranean, we would undoubtedly explain its superior economic performance in terms of this fortuitous factor. But it was not Italy but Britain that discovered the oil!

Economic success is obviously not solely determined by government policy. When we examine economic performance over a long period of time, however, the effects of external influences are minimized, especially if we focus on countries with similar levels of economic development. Table 2 presents OECD figures from the 1960s through the 1980s for the three most important aspects of macroeconomic performance—average annual economic growth, inflation, and unemployment rates.

Table 2 — Economic Growth, Inflation, and Unemployment (in percent)

	Economic Growth 1961-88	Inflation 1961-88	Unemployment 1965-88
Pres.-Plurality (N=1)	3.3	5.1	6.1
Parl.-Plurality (N=4)	3.4	7.5	6.1
Parl.-PR (N=9)	3.5	6.3	4.4

Sources: *OECD Economic Outlook*, No. 26 (December 1979), 131; No. 30 (December 1981), 131, 140, 142; No. 46 (December 1989), 166, 176, 182.

Although Italy's economic growth has indeed been better than that of Britain, the parliamentary-plurality and parliamentary-PR countries as groups do not differ much from each other or from the United States. The slightly higher growth rates in the parliamentary-PR systems cannot be considered significant. With regard to inflation, the United States has the best record, followed by the parliamentary-PR systems. The most sizable differences appear in unemployment levels; here the parliamentary-PR countries perform significantly better than the plurality countries.[14] Comparing the parliamentary-plurality and parliamentary-PR countries on all three indicators, we find that the performance of the latter is uniformly better.

Lessons for Developing Countries

Political scientists tend to think that plurality systems such as the United Kingdom and the United States are superior with regard to democratic quality and governmental effectiveness—a tendency best explained by the fact that political science has always been an Anglo-American-oriented discipline. This prevailing opinion is largely contradicted, however, by the empirical evidence presented above. Wherever significant differences appear, the parliamentary-PR systems almost invariably post the best records, particularly with respect to representation, protection of minority interests, voter participation, and control of unemployment.

This finding contains an important lesson for democratic constitutional engineers: the parliamentary-PR option is one that should be given serious consideration. Yet a word of caution is also in order, since parliamentary-PR democracies differ greatly among themselves. Moderate PR and moderate multipartism, as in Germany and Sweden, offer more attractive models than the extreme PR and multiparty systems of Italy and the Netherlands. As previously noted, though, even Italy has a respectable record of democratic performance.

But are these conclusions relevant to newly democratic and democratizing countries in Asia, Africa, Latin America, and Eastern Europe, which are trying to make democracy work in the face of economic underdevelopment and ethnic divisions? Do not these difficult conditions require strong executive leadership in the form of a powerful president or a Westminster-style, dominant one-party cabinet?

With regard to the problem of deep ethnic cleavages, these doubts can be easily laid to rest. Divided societies, both in the West and elsewhere, need peaceful coexistence among the contending ethnic groups. This requires conciliation and compromise, goals that in turn require the greatest possible inclusion of representatives of these groups in the decision-making process. Such power sharing can be arranged much more easily in parliamentary and PR systems than in presidential and plurality systems. A president almost inevitably belongs to one ethnic group, and hence presidential systems are particularly inimical to ethnic power sharing. And while Westminster-style parliamentary systems feature collegial cabinets, these tend not to be ethnically inclusive, particularly when there is a majority ethnic group. It is significant that the British government, in spite of its strong majoritarian traditions, recognized the need for consensus and power sharing in religiously and ethnically divided Northern Ireland. Since 1973, British policy has been to try to solve the Northern Ireland problem by means of PR elections and an inclusive coalition government.

As Horowitz has pointed out, it may be possible to alleviate the problems of presidentialism by requiring that a president be elected with a stated minimum of support from different groups, as in Nigeria.[15] But this is a palliative that cannot compare with the advantages of a truly collective and inclusive executive. Similarly, the example of Malaysia shows that a parliamentary system can have a broad multiparty and multiethnic coalition cabinet in spite of plurality elections, but this requires elaborate preelection pacts among the parties. These exceptions prove the rule: the ethnic power sharing that has been attainable in Nigeria and Malaysia only on a limited basis and through very special arrangements is a natural and straightforward result of parliamentary-PR forms of democracy.

PR and Economic Policy Making

The question of which form of democracy is most conducive to economic development is more difficult to answer. We simply do not have enough cases of durable Third World democracies representing the different systems (not to mention the lack of reliable economic data) to make an unequivocal evaluation. However, the conventional wisdom that economic development requires the unified and decisive leadership of a strong president or a Westminster-style dominant cabinet is highly suspect. First of all, if an inclusive executive that must do more bargaining and conciliation were less effective at economic policy making than a dominant and exclusive executive, then presumably an authoritarian government free of legislative interference or internal dissent would be optimal. This reasoning—a frequent excuse for the overthrow of democratic governments in the Third World in the 1960s and 1970s—has now been thoroughly discredited. To be sure, we do have a few examples of economic miracles wrought by authoritarian regimes, such as those in South Korea or Taiwan, but these are more than counterbalanced by the sorry economic records of just about all the nondemocratic governments in Africa, Latin America, and Eastern Europe.

Second, many British scholars, notably the eminent political scientist S.E. Finer, have come to the conclusion that economic development requires not so much a *strong* hand as a *steady* one. Reflecting on the poor economic performance of post-World War II Britain, they have argued that each of the governing parties indeed provided reasonably strong leadership in economic policy making but that alternations in governments were too "absolute and abrupt," occurring "between two sharply polarized parties each eager to repeal a large amount of its predecessor's legislation." What is needed, they argue, is "greater stability and continuity" and "greater moderation in policy," which could be provided by a shift to PR and to coalition governments much more likely to be centrist in orientation.[16] This argument would appear to be equally applicable both to developed and developing countries.

Third, the case for strong presidential or Westminster-style governments is most compelling where rapid decision making is essential. This means that in foreign and defense policy parliamentary-PR systems may be at a disadvantage. But in economic policy making speed is not particularly important—quick decisions are not necessarily wise ones.

Why then do we persist in distrusting the economic effectiveness of democratic systems that engage in broad consultation and bargaining aimed at a high degree of consensus? One reason is that multiparty and coalition governments *seem* to be messy, quarrelsome, and inefficient in contrast to the clear authority of strong presidents and strong one-party cabinets. But we should not let ourselves be deceived by these superficial appearances. A closer look at presidential systems reveals that the most successful cases—such as the United States, Costa Rica, and pre-1970 Chile—are at least equally quarrelsome and, in fact, are prone to paralysis and deadlock rather than steady and effective economic policy making. In any case, the argument should not be about governmental aesthetics but about actual performance. The undeniable elegance of the Westminster model is not a valid reason for adopting it.

The widespread skepticism about the economic capability of parliamentary-PR systems stems from confusing governmental strength with effectiveness. In the short run, one-party cabinets or presidents may well be able to formulate economic policy with greater ease and speed. In the long run, however, policies supported by a broad consensus are more likely to be successfully carried out and to remain on course than policies imposed by a "strong" government against the wishes of important interest groups.

To sum up, the parliamentary-PR form of democracy is clearly better than the major alternatives in accommodating ethnic differences, and it has a slight edge in economic policy making as well. The argument that considerations of governmental effectiveness mandate the rejection of parliamentary-PR democracy for developing countries is simply not tenable. Constitution makers in new democracies would do themselves and their countries a great disservice by ignoring this attractive democratic model.

NOTES

I gratefully acknowledge the assistance and advice of Robert W. Jackman, G. Bingham Powell, Jr., Harold L. Wilensky, and Kaare Strom, the research assistance of Markus Crepaz, and the financial support of the Committee on Research of the Academic Senate of the University of California at San Diego.

1. Donald L. Horowitz, "Comparing Democratic Systems," Seymour Martin Lipset, "The Centrality of Political Culture," and Juan J. Linz, "The Virtues of Parliamentarism," *Journal of Democracy* 1 (Fall 1990): 73-91. A third set of important decisions concerns institutional arrangements that are related to the difference between federal and unitary forms of government: the degree of government centralization, unicameralism or bicameralism, rules for constitutional amendment, and judicial review. Empirical analysis shows that these factors tend to be related; federal countries are more likely to be decentralized, to have significant bicameralism, and to have "rigid" constitutions that are difficult to amend and protected by judicial review.

2. For a fuller discussion of the differences between majoritarian and consensus government, see Arend Lijphart, *Democracies: Patterns of Majoritarian and Consensus Government in Twenty-One Countries* (New Haven: Yale University Press, 1984).

3. Giovanni Sartori, "Political Development and Political Engineering," in *Public Policy*, vol. 17, eds. John D. Montgomery and Alfred O. Hirschman (Cambridge: Harvard University Press, 1968), 273.

4. The first scholar to emphasize the close connection between culture and these constitutional arrangements was G. Bingham Powell, Jr. in his *Contemporary Democracies: Participation, Stability, and Violence* (Cambridge: Harvard University Press, 1982), 67. In my previous writings, I have sometimes classified Finland as a presidential or semipresidential system, but I now agree with Powell (pp. 56-57) that, although the directly elected Finnish president has special authority in foreign policy, Finland operates like a parliamentary system in most other respects. Among the exceptions, Ireland is a doubtful case; I regard its system of the single transferable vote as mainly a PR method, but other authors have classified it as a plurality system. And I include Australia in the parliamentary-plurality group, because its alternative-vote system, while not identical with plurality, operates in a similar fashion.

5. Stein Rokkan, *Citizens, Elections, Parties: Approaches to the Comparative Study of the Processes of Development* (Oslo: Universitetsforlaget, 1970), 157.

6. Douglas V. Verney, *The Analysis of Political Systems* (London: Routledge and Kegan Paul, 1959), 18-23, 42-43.

7. Powell, op. cit., esp. 12-29 and 111-74.

8. Juan J. Linz, "The Perils of Presidentialism," *Journal of Democracy* 1 (Winter 1990): 51-69.

9. Scott Mainwaring, "Presidentialism in Latin America," *Latin American Research Review* 25 (1990): 167-70.

10. Wilensky's ratings are based on a five-point scale (from 4 to 0) "for each of three policy clusters: existence and length of maternity and parental leave, paid and unpaid; availability and accessibility of public daycare programs and government effort to expand daycare; and flexibility of retirement systems. They measure government action to assure care of children and maximize choices in balancing work and family demands for everyone." See Harold L. Wilensky, "Common Problems, Divergent Policies: An 18-Nation Study of Family Policy," *Public Affairs Report* 31 (May 1990): 2.

11. Because of missing data, Austria is not included in the parliamentary-PR average.

12. Robert A. Dahl, *Polyarchy: Participation and Opposition* (New Haven: Yale University Press, 1971), 231-45.

13. This multiple-correlation analysis shows that societal division, as measured by the degree of organizational exclusiveness of ethnic and religious groups, explains 33 percent of the variance in riots and 25 percent of the variance in political deaths. The additional explanation by type of democracy is only 2 percent for riots (with plurality countries slightly more orderly) and 13 percent for deaths (with the PR countries slightly more peaceful).

14. Comparable unemployment data for Austria, Denmark, and New Zealand are not available, and these countries are therefore not included in the unemployment figures in Table 2.

15. Horowitz, op. cit., 76-77.

16. S.E. Finer, "Adversary Politics and Electoral Reform," in *Adversary Politics and Electoral Reform*, ed. S.E. Finer (London: Anthony Wigram, 1975), 30-31.

14. THE PROBLEM WITH PR

Guy Lardeyret

***Guy Lardeyret** is president of the Paris-based Fondation pour la Démocratie, a nongovernmental organization that is currently providing advice and support to heads of state, government officials, or party leaders in about 20 countries in Asia, Africa, the Middle East, Eastern Europe, and South America.*

Arend Lijphart's article on "Constitutional Choices for New Democracies" [*Journal of Democracy* 2 (Winter 1991): 72-84] attempts to provide scientific evidence for the superiority of proportional representation (PR) to the system of plurality elections. The author presents a comparative analysis designed to show that regimes based on plurality elections do not measure up to parliamentary-PR regimes in terms of "democratic performance."

Lijphart considers the effects of electoral systems on eight variables, which we will consider successively. The first correlation suggests that PR favors the representation of "minorities" and pressure groups. As clearly shown by the statistics, women legislators are more numerous in Nordic countries, which also tend to spend more money on family policies. Although tradition plays a role, the phenomenon is made possible by PR: candidate slates are chosen by party leaders, who are more easily influenced by strong women's movements.

The relationship between PR and voter participation is not as clear. If it were calculated on the European basis (as a proportion of registered voters), U.S. voter turnout would be similar to that of Western Europe. Moreover, Lijphart's figures would look quite different if he had not made some questionable decisions in categorizing countries. France, for instance, might be counted as a presidential-plurality democracy alongside the United States. Germany (whose mixed electoral system has majoritarian effects) belongs among the parliamentary-plurality regimes, while Spain and Portugal (which Lijphart ignores) should be included among the third group, the parliamentary-PR democracies.

Lijphart's next set of figures indicates that northern European countries have a more equal distribution of income, which is not surprising. If there is a link between the electoral system and the greater degree of economic equality in these countries, it may not have much to do with democracy. When conservatives win elections in such countries as Sweden, Denmark, Norway, and Finland, they must form coalitions with other parties, which makes it hard for them to pursue their democratically mandated program of reducing the welfare state.

Lijphart's use of Robert Dahl's system for rating "democratic quality" raises the question of what criteria best measure democratic performance. If the index includes variables such as turnout (as measured in the U.S.), the number of parties, and the strength of interest groups, it introduces a strong bias in favor of PR with this sample of countries.

Finally, the correlations with inflation, economic growth, and unemployment (underestimated in Nordic countries because of highly protected jobs) are difficult to exploit. These indicators are much more powerfully influenced by many other important factors.

Consequences of Electoral Systems

Lijphart accepts from the beginning a fundamental hypothesis—namely, that the electoral system largely determines the party system and through it the structure of the government. Thus, countries where PR is the rule end up with multipartism and coalition governments, while plurality elections favor the two-party system and single-party governments. But as Lijphart notes, opinions diverge on how the party system affects the exercise of democratic governance. It is precisely on this point that it would have been fruitful for Lijphart to test the hypothesis against empirical data.

Such an analysis would have clearly shown that bipartism favors governmental stability and decision-making capacity as well as periodic alternations in power. Multipartism, on the other hand, is positively correlated with ephemeral governments, periods when the chief executive office goes unfilled, repeated elections, and long tenures in office for fixed groups of key politicians. The more parties a country has, moreover, the greater is the incidence of these phenomena.

When the government rests on a homogeneous majority, it remains in power for the duration of its mandated term (stability); can apply its program (efficiency); and is likely, should it falter, to lose power to a strong and united opposition (alternation). By contrast, the coalition governments so common in PR systems often cannot survive serious disagreement over particular measures (instability); need inordinate amounts of time to build new coalitions (executive vacancy); and when they fall, call new elections that generally return the same people (nonalternation).

The contention that PR favors the representation of "minorities" is true, in a sense: PR gives any well-organized pressure group—be it a union, a religion, an ethnic group, a profession, or an ideological faction—a chance to win seats. A party that polarizes one important issue of common interest like environmental protection will attract votes. Dividing the electorate in this way tends to exacerbate the conflicts in a society. For example, the introduction of PR in local and European elections in France during the 1980s made possible the growing prominence of Jean-Marie Le Pen's National Front (FN), a far-right party that condemns immigration. The Front's rise has in turn sparked the formation of a number of left-wing "antiracist" groups that are no less intolerant than the FN itself. This unhealthy situation can be attributed largely to PR.

It can also be shown that PR is dangerous for countries faced with ethnic or cultural divisions. In Belgium, for instance, linguistic parties sprang up after PR was introduced early in this century. Belgian politics became little more than a feud between the Flemings and the French-speaking Walloons. Without the monarchy to cement its national unity, Belgium could have fallen apart.

The risks of coalition governments should also be recalled. Such governments are often reluctant to make unpopular decisions because of the resistance of some coalition partner. The Palestinian problem in Israel will probably never be solved unless Israel's electoral law is changed or extraordinary foreign pressure is exerted.

Proportional representation tends to give small parties disproportionate power because such parties control the "swing" seats needed to make up a majority coalition. Germany's Free Democratic Party, for instance, has been able to participate in all governments since World War II. Sometimes coalitions can be political absurdities: in Greece recently, the right forged an alliance with the communists in order to keep the socialists out of the government. The political annals of the Scandinavian countries offer numerous examples of cases where the only party to have made significant gains in a given election was unable to find partners and had to remain in opposition.

Even more problematic is PR's tendency to give extremist parties a chance to participate in government. Such a party may eliminate its coalition partners by an internal coup, as Mussolini's Fascists did in Italy in the 1920s. Without PR, the Communists and the Nazis would probably not have been able to storm onto the German political scene as they did in the 1930s.

An election is not a poll aimed at giving the most accurate representation of all the various opinions or interests at play in a given society. Were that the case—there being no fixed limit to the possible divisions in a society—the most democratic assembly would be one where each member represented a sharply defined interest or particular ideological nuance. Such an assembly would present an absurd caricature of democratic government.

An electoral system is intended to give citizens the power to decide who shall rule and according to what policy. It should produce an efficient government, supported by the bulk of the citizens. Plurality elections force the parties to coalesce before the balloting occurs. They must synthesize the divergent interests and opinions of as many voters as possible, offer the electors a coherent program for governing, and prove their ability to gather a majority. Parties in plurality systems tend to be moderate because most votes are to be gained among the undecided voters of the center.

Proportional representation places the responsibility of choosing both the personnel and the policy of the new government on party leaders, deliberating out of public view and after all the votes have been cast. What distinguishes one system from the other thus has less to do with "consensus" than with differences in their methods of forging political compromises. The method of plurality elections is more democratic as well as more efficient, because the decisions are taken by the citizens themselves. The choice is clear, and the contract is limited in time.

Rediscovering the Westminster Model

Once a homogeneous majority exists in parliament, there is no need, strictly speaking, for the direct election of a separate chief executive. The head of the majority party in parliament can do the job, and this avoids the risk of conflict between the two sources of democratic legitimacy. The parliamentary majority provides competent ministers who remain in touch with the legislature. The executive has the initiative in proposing legislation; the legislators' main role is to improve bills through amendments, and not to obstruct policies that have received the support of the electorate.

We thus rediscover the Westminster model, which has been working smoothly for the past 300 years in England while France has changed regimes 20 times in two centuries and is still experimenting with various possible combinations of electoral systems with parliamentary and presidential regimes. France's greatest single institutional advance came in 1958, when the faltering parliamentary-PR Fourth Republic gave way to the presidential-de-facto-plurality Fifth Republic under Charles de Gaulle. Yet serious conflicts of competence emerged between the president and the prime minister during the "cohabitation" period of 1986-88, when for the first time in the history of the Fifth Republic, a president from one party (Socialist François Mitterand) was teamed with a premier from another (Gaullist Jacques Chirac). This situation, which could soon recur, creates pressure for a move toward the parliamentary-plurality model.

There is now massive evidence that, among the four possible combinations of institutions (presidential or parliamentary) and electoral systems (PR or plurality), the order of rank according to standards of both efficiency and democracy is the following: the Westminster model, presidential-plurality, parliamentary-PR, and presidential-PR. Among the PR systems, the worst is pure PR (Italy, Israel), and the least bad is PR with majoritarian devices (Germany, Greece).

It is almost impossible to get rid of PR, because doing so requires asking independent parties to cooperate in their own liquidation. The coalition of threatened parties will almost always be strong enough to thwart electoral reform, which must then await a major national crisis. The shift from presidentialism to parliamentarism is fairly easy in semi-presidential regimes. Portugal has recently made this move, and Finland has done practically the same thing, which may soon be confirmed by a constitutional change (not that one is indispensable: parties can agree not to nominate their leaders as presidential candidates).

This helps to explain the institutional problems which, as Lijphart acknowledges, can be observed in Latin America. Electoral divisions in parliament tend to reinforce the power of the president. Political competition then focuses on the presidency to a degree that can encourage military coups. One way to avoid that risk is the establishment of a presidential party that entrenches itself in both the state apparatus and many sectors of society. The classic case is Paraguay, where President Alfredo Stroessner stayed in office for 35 years at the head of his Colorado Party machine. To prohibit the reelection of the president simply shifts the power to the ruling party, as Mexicans have learned under the longstanding rule of the PRI.

Building a Democracy

Although the electoral system is a major determinant of a political regime—albeit one curiously omitted in most constitutions—it would be a mistake for new democracies to assume that good democratic performance can be ensured by choosing the right electoral system, or that democracy can be simply defined as a political system where the rulers are freely elected (although that is certainly a necessary condition). Although Boris Yeltsin was freely elected president of the Russian Republic, the RSFSR is still not a democracy.

To become a democracy, a regime must meet two fundamental conditions. Because sovereignty resides with the citizens, who delegate power only to solve problems of common concern, a democracy must above all respect the distinction between the private and public spheres.[1] The transition to democracy in most of the countries of Eastern Europe will depend primarily on their capacity to disengage the state from economic and social life. It is much more difficult to restore the springs of individual initiative, which have been destroyed by years of stifling bureaucracy and irresponsibility, than to ratify a formal constitution. On the other hand, countries such as Korea, Taiwan, or Singapore, where an authoritarian regime has allowed the growth of an effervescent private and economic life, can easily become democratic as soon as free and fair elections are organized.

The second great principle to follow in building a democracy is to diffuse power by dividing control over the public sphere among various levels and centers of authority. The rule here is that decisions should be taken at the level closest to the citizen. Switzerland presents a splendid example of this principle in action. Decentralization can also be spread by competence, with decisions delegated to people concerned with the subject. To set the executive and legislative branches directly against one another, whether at the local or the national level, is more likely to cause inefficiency than political equilibrium. When a country contains populations from widely differing cultures, each intent upon its autonomy, federalism (usually involving a second legislative chamber) is the best institutional solution. A good constitution will find ways to establish these prerequisites of democracy, along with an independent judiciary to guarantee the rule of law.

Ethnic divisions present especially thorny difficulties in Africa. Despite the existence of interesting local democratic traditions in many parts of the continent, national elections there tend to degenerate into ethnic contests over legislative seats and public offices. The best way to counteract these propensities is to oblige members of each group to run against one another on (transethnic) political and ideological grounds in single-member districts. The worst way is to adopt PR, which tends to reproduce ethnic cleavages in the legislature.

In this regard, the unique case of South Africa becomes especially intriguing. The "white tribe" has installed a political regime that basically respects the first two conditions of democracy. As the country moves toward fuller democracy, it remains to be seen whether South Africa's new citizens will array themselves along cleavages of ideology or ethnicity. South Africa's prospects will be grim if it cannot build big and moderate multiethnic parties. There can be no question that a system of plurality elections offers the best conditions for the growth of such parties.

Lijphart's article proves at least that political scientists still have a long way to go even to reach a consensus, much less to discover the definitive truth—if it exists—on this fundamental issue.

NOTES

1. For a thorough analysis of the concept of democracy, see Jean Baechler, *Démocraties* (Paris: Calmann-Levy, 1985). An English translation is forthcoming from New York University Press.

15.
PR AND DEMOCRATIC STATECRAFT

Quentin L. Quade

***Quentin L. Quade** is Raynor Professor of Political Science and Director of the Blum Center at Marquette University in Milwaukee, Wisconsin, where he has also served as dean of the graduate school. His writings include over 60 essays in journals such as the* Review of Politics, Freedom at Issue, First Things, Thought, *and* Parliamentary Affairs.

In "Constitutional Choices for New Democracies," Arend Lijphart sets out to describe and evaluate some of the primary institutional alternatives available to new democracies. Lijphart knows that the choice of electoral system is especially important, since it will likely determine whether many or few parties will compete, and whether coalition or single-party governments will result. He also knows that once chosen, the electoral system will be hard to change. Lijphart favors proportional representation (PR), welcomes proliferated parties, and esteems coalitions. I have publicly defended the opposite view. I urge plurality voting in single-member districts, hope and expect that this will encourage a two-party system, and applaud the single-party government that would result.[1]

How is it that two democrats with similar starting points like Lijphart and myself could come up with such starkly contrasting practical advice for newly emerging democracies? As in real estate, the key is to inspect the premises. Even a brief and selective inspection, as this one must be, will show why our recommendations differ so sharply, and why I think Lijphart's position rests on questionable, even utopian, foundations.

Advocates of proportional representation typically describe it as more "fair" and more "just." Lijphart's article says PR produces "consensus" politics, promotes "conciliation and compromise," and is more "representative" than plurality voting. In fact, each of these good words applied to PR begs a question and calls for a rarely given philosophical argument to establish a meaning for "fair," "just," "representative," and so on. No such arguments are presented or even summarized by Lijphart. The only thing certain about PR is that it will tend to re-create society's divisions and locate them in the legislature. That is its purpose, logic, and result.[2]

Whether a system that encourages party proliferation is any of the good things its proponents call it—fairer, more just, more representative—depends on a theory of statecraft and democratic form. What is the purpose of the state? Does the adoption of democracy eliminate or even lessen the traditional requirements of state action? In particular, does democratic statecraft have a diminished responsibility to synthesize society's parts, unify and defend its people, or identify and pursue the common good—meaning those values that no particular part of society will ever seek as its own but on which all particular parts depend? Or does democratic politics exist to do all the things states exist for, but to do them in a new way, a responsible and accountable way? If it does, then the first test of fairness, justice, and representation that democratic politics must pass will be the test of excellence in state action. The second and no less important test will be that of accountability. But for Lijphart and his fellow PR advocates, the first question appears to be: how well are society's natural divisions re-created and relocated in the legislature? Where he equates the number of women in legislatures with representation of women's interests, for example, Lijphart uses the term "representation" as identical to re-creation. In his uncritical implicit reliance on the "picture theory" of legislative representation, Lijphart writes as if Edmund Burke had never lived.

To prove that PR's tendency to re-create divisions and proliferate parties is indeed a good thing, an extended argument is required. It must explain how a political system will be "fair" if it succumbs to the centrifugal pull of interests, how it can advance the general welfare if it "represents" only minute and particular aspects of society, and how a government cobbled together out of postelection splinters by a secretive process of interparty bartering can be considered responsible and accountable. Only by doing this can PR advocates escape the charge of question-begging.

Easy Cases and Unfounded Speculations

I have suggested that PR advocates generally, and Lijphart in particular, tend to make their work easy by eliding from PR's tendency to re-create societal divisions to an unexamined designation of such re-creation as good. Another labor-saving approach, greatly evident in Lijphart's article, is to build the argument for PR on easy cases developed in unusually auspicious circumstances.

It is axiomatic that the difficulty of the tests a political system faces will be commensurate with the severity of the prepolitical conditions it must confront. I refer to such obvious variables as economic health or sickness, ethnic tension or harmony, religious cleavages or unity, geopolitical peril or security. It is also obvious that a relatively weak political structure may work under "fair-weather" prepolitical conditions, while a stronger system may founder if it must endure unusually foul prepolitical weather. Thus, if one could know for sure that nation X would never confront any but the most peaceful circumstances, the strength of its political structure would be of little concern. Such an idyllic environment would leave ample room for error; even if the government were prone to stumble, the natural buoyancy of society would save the state from falling.

"...the Weimar Republic, where coalition was endemic and weakness perpetual, might be the best of all test cases for PR."

Much of my difference with Lijphart derives from his inclination to test PR in too-easy cases. Most of his "successful" examples of PR are drawn from very small societies. Some, like the Scandinavian countries, are nearly homogeneous, with low levels of racial, ethnic, or religious turbulence. Nor have they experienced any severe economic stress during the period of Lijphart's observations. Moreover, all the positive examples from the era he studies have lived under the umbrella of American military protection, an artificial and temporary condition that has spared them most of the stresses of balance-of-power machinations. Many also were beneficiaries of the Marshall Plan, which spurred an era of unprecedented economic recovery and growth in Western Europe.

Lijphart's list of examples contains mostly fair-weather cases; the favorable conditions they enjoyed bear scant resemblance to the arduous circumstances that now confront struggling new democracies. Nor does his list include any of the obvious and dramatic cases in which PR clearly contributed to governmental weakness and systemic collapse. Pre-Mussolini Italy, with its splintered parties and political gridlock, would be a worthy example. France's Fourth Republic (1945-1958), chronically crippled and finally made suicidal by its inability to deal with colonial and domestic problems, would be another. Finally, the Weimar Republic, where coalition was endemic and weakness perpetual, might be the best of all test cases for PR. F.A. Hermens definitively established PR's direct contribution to the regime's inability to develop moderate strength and to rid itself of its extremist elements.[3] As Herman Finer once observed, PR's version of "justice"—lodging social splinters in the legislature—kept both Nazism and Communism alive so that together they could murder the Weimar Republic.[4] "Conciliation and compromise" were conspicuous by their absence.

It seems strange to me that a list of PR examples contains only the beneficiaries of sunny prepolitical conditions. It seems stranger still that it makes no reference to illustrations of PR's most calamitous effects.

In addition to its unwarranted ascription of "good" words to PR and its reliance on easy cases, Lijphart's effort suffers from a third difficulty. To put the case broadly, Lijphart presumes to know things that the evidence simply does not indicate. He imagines, for instance, that Italy's relative economic success over the last few decades, Germany's evident success during the same period, and Britain's relative weakness can all be appreciably attributed to the shape of the central political institutions in each country. If that were true, then one could infer that splintered parties and weak, unstable coalitions (as in Italy) are as good as or better than majority-forming parties that produce strong single-party governments (as in Britain).

Though Lijphart says that the "empirical evidence" suggests all this, it actually suggests nothing of the sort. Instead, the empirical evidence should remind us of the numerous and sometimes mysterious variables that one must take into account when considering such complex social and economic realities. As previously noted, all we know *for certain* about electoral systems is that PR tends to proliferate parties, while plurality voting encourages two-party arrangements. All we know *for certain* about coalitions is that they are subject to stress and dissolution more than a single-party majority would be (witness Italy in the spring of 1991 as it deposed its forty-ninth postwar government); and that to govern they must form postelection groupings outside of public view (no member of Italy's electorate voted for its fiftieth government). Abstract logic—plus experience with cases like Weimar Germany and the Fourth French Republic—suggests that coalitions will be a less secure basis for governance than would be a single-party majority. Such majorities are clearly able to act, even while constantly debating and maneuvering against an opposition striving to become the next government.

But what of Italy's economic good fortune, Germany's robustness, Britain's pale comparison? One could attribute these conditions to their respective political institutions only by arguing *post hoc, ergo propter hoc*. Such an argument simply ignores the array of other variables that any objective analysis should bring to mind. I have mentioned already the artificiality of the foreign-affairs responsibilities that have confronted Italy and Germany in the age of the Marshall Plan and the NATO alliance, as well as the jump-start that the former gave to their economies. I would also note that policies which encourage economic growth can be adopted by weak governments, while strong governments are not assured of making all the right decisions. It is not unreasonable to suggest, for example, that Germany's economic strength since the Marshall Plan derives in great part from the horrible economic lessons learned during the PR-induced paralysis of the Weimar period. Certainly the deep-seated German fear of inflation is derived from those experiences. It would be a mistake to attribute Germany's cautious monetary policy to the country's contemporary system of modified PR when in fact this penchant for caution is a negative lesson from Germany's ruinous pre-Hitler PR experience.

By the same token, attempts to attribute Britain's relatively pallid economic record to its majority-forming system are entirely unconvincing. Britain has performed poorly by comparison to some other countries—a weak showing that is traceable in part to poor decisions and not just difficult circumstances. But wise decisions are not guaranteed by *any* political system, and the impact of unpromising circumstances should not be underestimated. Britain, after all, went into World War II in substantial decline, and emerged from it greatly weakened. It did not receive the same massive help from the Marshall Plan that others did. It had to endure the rapid dissolution of a massive overseas empire that was tightly interwoven with the fabric of its economy. Decolonization has required not merely economic adaptation, but a seismic social-psychological adjustment as well. On top of all this is the extraordinarily thorny prepolitical problem posed by the Irish question.

The point of this litany is this: while Britain's economic performance in the postwar era can hardly be called a triumph of the Westminster model, neither can it be explained simply as one of that model's failures. The array of influences on those countries that have done better, the degree to which an economy operates independently of day-to-day political influence, and the large number of debilitating conditions Britain has confronted all make it simply unrealistic to cite the British political system as the main debilitator of the British economy. It is wise, as a rule, never to speculate when you can ascertain. Among this rule's many corollaries is this one: never fail to speculate when you cannot ascertain, but never imagine you have ascertained when in fact you are only speculating. The causal relationships that Lijphart claims his "empirical evidence" has established turn out, upon closer inspection, to be purely speculative.

The Virtues of Plurality Systems

Lijphart's dedication to PR rests on his assumption that we can get all of PR's alleged virtues (re-creationist representation, all voices heard, consensus, compromise, etc.) without any of its alleged vices (invitation to extremism, governmental weakness and instability, political unrealism, unaccountability to the electorate, etc.). But both analysis and history strongly suggest that you cannot buy it that way. Even if fair-weather conditions make PR tolerable over some period of time, it is unlikely that modern mass nation-states will forever or even for long have such happy circumstances before them. The natural centrifugal stresses and strains in human existence that call the state into being argue for majority-based systems to ensure its capacity for action. And if popular control is to be genuine, the people need to be able to see who is doing what and what each side has to offer, and to make serious judgments between them.

Plurality voting encourages the competing parties to adopt a majority-forming attitude. The parties incline to be moderate, to seek conciliation, to round off their rough edges—in short, to do *before* the election, in the public view, the very tasks that Lijphart applauds PR systems for doing *after* the election. Majorities formed in plurality systems are more likely to be strong enough to sustain effective government without becoming unresponsive and rigid, for majorities thus formed are innately fickle, always falling apart, always needing rebuilding.

Moreover, well-chosen policies, including respect for subsidiarity, can foster vibrant local governments and civil societies, thus encouraging the very multiplicity for which PR strives without incurring the deleterious effects of governmental weakness and unaccountability. In contrast to Lijphart, I maintain that PR's true virtues (accommodation of differences, a hundred flowers blooming, etc.) can be had without any of its debilitating vices under a majority-forming plurality system. That being the case, why run the well-known risks of PR? Emerging democracies, facing very difficult prepolitical circumstances, need the best political structures they can get. The best combine great capacity for action with clear accountability and thus provide power-made-responsible. This happy combination is most likely to occur in majority-forming electoral systems operating within parliamentary structures. Of course, even the best arrangements cannot guarantee success in this imperfect world, any more than inferior systems make wise policy impossible. But the best systems will ensure both that the paralysis of government itself does not become the chief problem before the nation, and that it will be the voters who truly elect and depose governments.

NOTES

1. Compare my essay "Democracies-to-Be: Getting It Right the First Time," in *Freedom at Issue* 113 (March-April 1990), 4-8.

2. Since societal divisions are potentially innumerable, one sometimes finds PR advocates like Lijphart introducing distinctions between "extreme" and "moderate" forms of PR. In the latter, PR's natural tendencies are frustrated by devices that give government a better chance to form and function—a repudiation, however unacknowledged, of the logic of PR.

3. F.A. Hermens, *Democracy or Anarchy? A Study of Proportional Representation* (Notre Dame, Indiana: University of Notre Dame Press, 1941).

4. Herman Finer, *Governments of Greater European Powers* (New York: Henry Holt, 1956), 623.

16. DOUBLE-CHECKING THE EVIDENCE

Arend Lijphart

***Arend Lijphart**, professor of political science at the University of California at San Diego, is the coeditor of* Electoral Laws and Their Political Consequences *(1986) and the author of numerous other books. His article "Constitutional Choices for New Democracies" appeared in the Winter 1991 issue of the* Journal of Democracy.

In my article "Constitutional Choices for New Democracies," I presented systematic empirical evidence concerning the relative performance of various types of democratic systems in an effort to transcend the usual vague and untestable claims and counterclaims that surround this topic. I compared four parliamentary-plurality democracies (the United Kingdom, Canada, Australia, and New Zealand) with nine parliamentary-proportional representation (PR) democracies (Germany, Italy, Austria, the Netherlands, Belgium, and four Nordic countries—Sweden, Denmark, Norway, Finland) with regard to their performance records on minority representation and protection, democratic quality, the maintenance of public order and peace, and the management of the economy. I found that, where differences between the two groups of democracies appeared, the parliamentary-PR systems showed the better performance. There were sizable differences with regard to minority representation (as measured by the representation of women in national parliaments), the protection of minority interests (measured by innovative family policy), democratic quality (measured by voter turnout), and control of unemployment; smaller differences on income inequality and control of inflation; and little or no difference with regard to the maintenance of public order (as measured by riots and deaths from political violence) and economic growth. Since, according to the conventional—but also rather old-fashioned—wisdom, PR may be superior to plurality as far as minority representation is concerned but leads to less effective decision making, even my finding of minor or no differences on some of the performance indicators must be counted in favor of the parliamentary-PR type.

Guy Lardeyret and Quentin L. Quade, both eloquent exponents of this conventional wisdom, raise a series of objections to my analysis and conclusions—very welcome challenges because they present an opportunity to double-check the validity of my evidence. Lardeyret and Quade argue that 1) the differences in governmental performance may be explained by other factors than the type of democracy, and hence that they do not prove any parliamentary-PR superiority; 2) that, when other important effects of the different types of democracy are considered, plurality systems are superior; 3) that some of my findings are the result of incorrect measurement; and 4) that my findings are biased by my choice and classification of the countries included in the analysis. I shall demonstrate, however, that whenever their objections can be tested against the facts, they turn out to be invalid.

Alternative Explanations

I agree with Lardeyret's and Quade's argument that economic success is not solely determined by government policy; I said as much in my original article. There are obviously many external and fortuitous factors that influence a country's economic performance. Neither do I disagree with Quade's argument that several special circumstances have had a negative effect on Britain. On the other hand, some of the PR countries suffered similar setbacks: the Netherlands and Belgium also lost sizable colonial empires, the "seismic social-psychological" shock of decolonization suffered by Britain was no greater than the shock of defeat and division suffered by Germany, and ethnic strife has plagued Belgium as well as the Celtic periphery of the United Kingdom. But my comparison was not just between Britain and one or more PR countries; I compared the four parliamentary-plurality democracies as a group with the group of nine parliamentary-PR countries. I assumed that when the economic performance of groups of democracies is examined over a long period of time, and when all of the countries studied have similar levels of economic development, external and fortuitous influences tend to even out. In the absence of any plausible suggestion that, as a group, the parliamentary-PR countries enjoyed unusual economic advantages from the 1960s through the 1980s—and neither Lardeyret nor Quade offers any such suggestion—my assumption and hence my findings concerning differences in economic performance remain valid.

Lardeyret and Quade do mention a few things that might provide a basis for alternative explanations: the special characteristics of the Nordic countries, the advantage of having a constitutional monarchy, the difference between moderate and extreme PR, and the advantage of U.S. military protection. All of these can be tested empirically. Lardeyret claims that unemployment in the Nordic countries is underestimated because of "highly protected jobs" and that income inequality is relatively modest because of unusual handicaps that conservative parties must contend with in these countries. Whether these factors change my findings can be checked easily by excluding the Nordic countries and comparing the non-Nordic parliamentary-PR countries with the parliamentary-plurality countries. Average unemployment in the Nordic countries was indeed lower than in the non-Nordic countries—2.7 percent compared with 5.7 percent—but the latter percentage is still slightly better than the 6.1 percent for the parliamentary-plurality countries. As far as income inequality is concerned, there is virtually no difference between the Nordic and non-Nordic parliamentary-PR countries—39.0 and 38.9 percent respectively—both of which score lower than the 42.9 percent in the parliamentary-plurality democracies.

When we compare monarchies with republics, the first point to be made is that, if a constitutional monarchy is an advantage, all of the parliamentary-plurality countries enjoy this advantage, whereas only about half of the parliamentary-PR democracies do. Second, when we compare the monarchical countries (Belgium, the Netherlands, Sweden, Norway, and Denmark) with the republican PR countries (Germany, Italy, Austria, and Finland), their growth rates are virtually identical and their inflation rates exactly the same. Only their unemployment rates differ somewhat: the monarchies have a 4.0 percent average unemployment rate compared with 4.9 percent in the nonmonarchical countries; again, the latter percentage is still better than the 6.1-percent average of the parliamentary-plurality countries. On all of the indicators of minority representation and protection and of democratic quality, there are slight differences between the monarchical and non-monarchical groups, but both still clearly outperform the parliamentary-plurality countries.

Is PR's Achilles' heel revealed when we focus on the countries that have extreme PR (Italy, the Netherlands, Denmark, and Finland) and contrast these with the more moderate PR systems (Germany, Sweden, Norway, Belgium, and Austria)? The empirical evidence disproves this. The inflation and unemployment rates in the extreme PR group are indeed higher (7.4 and 5.5 versus 5.4 and 3.6 percent) but still at least a bit lower than the 7.5 and 6.1 percent in the parliamentary-plurality systems; their growth rates are virtually identical. On the four indicators of representation and democratic quality, the differences are slight, and both groups of PR countries remain way ahead of the parliamentary-plurality countries. My own firm preference remains for moderate PR, but the dangers of extreme PR must not be exaggerated.

As Quade correctly states, the parliamentary-PR countries have had the advantage of living under "the umbrella of American military protection"—but so have all four of the parliamentary-plurality countries. In fact, the only slight exceptions are in the PR group: Sweden's neutral but strongly armed posture entailed heavy military expenditures, and Finland lived in precarious dependence on Soviet restraint. On the whole, however, American military protection benefited all 13 parliamentary democracies more or less equally, and therefore cannot explain any differences in their performance records.

Alternative Standards and Classifications

Partly in addition to and partly instead of the measures that I used to evaluate the performance of different types of democracy, Lardeyret and Quade state that democracies should be judged in terms of factors like accountability, government stability, decision-making capacity, and the ability to avoid "repeated elections." There are several problems with these suggestions. First of all, while accountability is certainly an important aspect of democratic government, it cannot be measured objectively. Second, it is not at all clear that coalition governments are less responsible and accountable than one-party governments. Quade's description of coalition cabinets as governments "cobbled together out of postelection splinters by a secretive process of interparty bartering" may apply to a few exceptional cases like Israel (which combines extreme PR with an evenly split and polarized electorate), but for most PR countries it is a grossly overdrawn caricature. In fact, once they are formed, coalition cabinets tend to be a good deal *less* secretive and more open than one-party cabinets.

Third, government stability can be measured in terms of average cabinet duration. On the basis of previously collected figures, my calculation shows that the average cabinet life in the parliamentary-plurality countries is about twice that in the parliamentary-PR systems.[1] Longer cabinet duration, Lardeyret assumes, means greater decision-making strength because of greater continuity in government personnel. But when coalition cabinets change they usually do not change as much as the radically alternating cabinets in the parliamentary-plurality countries. Lardeyret admits this when he complains about the "long tenures in office for fixed groups of key politicians" in the PR countries. Fourth, if Lardeyret is right about the superior decision-making capacity of parliamentary-plurality governments, the only convincing proof is that their decisions result in more effective policies. This brings us back to the evaluation of government performance in terms of successful macroeconomic policy making and the successful maintenance of public order. As we have already seen, this hard evidence does not show any parliamentary-plurality superiority.

Lardeyret's complaint about unnecessarily frequent elections in the parliamentary-PR systems suggests an additional useful measure of democratic performance—and one that, happily, can be measured and tested easily. In the 29-year period from 1960 to 1988—the same period for which two of the three OECD economic indicators were collected—the parliamentary-plurality countries conducted an average of

10.0 national legislative elections, compared with an average of 8.8 in the parliamentary-PR countries.[2] The frequency of elections is actually *smaller* in the PR systems, contrary to Lardeyret's assertion, although the difference is slight. However, Lardeyret's hypothesis is clearly disproved by this simple test.

Lardeyret and Quade have only a few disagreements with my measurements. One question that Lardeyret does raise is the measurement of voter turnout: the U.S. voter-turnout figure would be considerably higher if counted as a proportion of registered voters. He is quite right on this point, but all of my turnout figures are percentages of eligible voters—which means that all countries are treated equally. Moreover, if turnout figures are used as a measure of democratic quality, the low figure for the United States accurately reflects not only an unusually high degree of political apathy but also the fact that voting is deliberately discouraged by the government by means of onerous registration procedures.

Quade questions my equation of "the number of women in legislatures with representation of women's interests." But I did not equate the two at all: I used a separate measure (the innovativeness and expansiveness of family policy, which is of special concern to women) to test whether women's interests were actually better taken care of in the PR countries—and I found that this was indeed the case.

Finally, Lardeyret questions my use of Robert Dahl's ratings of democratic quality because of their alleged pro-PR bias. I already admitted a slight bias of this kind in my original article, but I decided to use the Dahl ratings anyway since they are the most careful overall ratings that are available. However, since they are obviously less objective than my other indicators, I shall not insist on their being used as evidence.

Quade criticizes my favorable judgment of the parliamentary-PR combination by pointing out some examples in which PR did not work well, especially the two cases that are often regarded as spectacular failures of democracy: the Weimar Republic and the French Fourth Republic. Nobody can disagree with the assessment that the Weimar Republic was a failure, but it is less clear that PR was the decisive factor or that plurality would have been able to save Weimar democracy. Moreover, Weimar was a semi-presidential rather than a parliamentary system. In France, the Fourth Republic indeed did not work well, but a reasonable argument can be made that relatively small reforms within the parliamentary-PR framework might have cured the problems and that the radical shift to semi-presidentialism and away from PR was not absolutely necessary. And examples of PR failures can be matched by examples of the failure of plurality systems, such as the failed democracies of West Africa. Sir Arthur Lewis, who served as an economic advisor to these governments, became convinced that "the surest way to kill the idea of democracy" in these divided societies "is to adopt the Anglo-American electoral system of first-past-the-post [plurality]."[3]

Lardeyret does not question my focus on stable contemporary democracies, but argues instead that some of these countries should have been classified differently. Although France is neither fully presidential nor fully plurality, I accept his suggestion that it is close enough on both counts to be classified alongside the United States. I agree that Spain and Portugal belong in the parliamentary-PR category, but comparable data are lacking since the two countries were not yet democratic during the full period covered by the empirical evidence. I disagree that Germany lacks PR and should be classified as a plurality system; it is almost entirely PR in terms of how Bundestag seats are allocated to the parties, though its 5-percent threshold makes it a moderate PR system.

But let us concede Germany to the plurality category; my analysis still stands. Lardeyret's counter-hypothesis is that in "the order of rank according to standards of both efficiency and democracy," the two plurality systems (parliamentary and presidential) are ahead of the parliamentary-PR systems. This can be tested by comparing the seven plurality systems (the parliamentary-plurality countries plus the United States, France, and, arguably, Germany) with eight PR systems (all of the parliamentary-PR systems except Germany). Thus reclassified, the PR countries still have the better record with regard to control of unemployment (4.6 percent versus 5.5 percent average unemployment) and do not differ much with regard to growth (3.5 versus 3.4 percent) and inflation (6.6 versus 6.5 percent). On the indicators of minority representation and protection and of democratic quality, the PR countries are still far ahead of the plurality systems: 17.5 versus 4.5 percent women in parliament; a score of 8.0 versus 4.4 on family policy; 84.5 versus 73.5 percent on voter turnout; and 38.9 versus 41.9 percent of total income earned by the top 20 percent of households. The evidence clearly disproves Lardeyret's counter-hypothesis.

Choices and Changes

The demonstrable advantages of parliamentarism and PR appear to be appreciated by the citizens and politicians of democratic countries. In many, if not most, presidential countries, there is widespread dissatisfaction with the operation of presidentialism and sizable support for a shift to a parliamentary form of government; the contrary sentiment can be found in hardly any parliamentary democracy. Similarly, there is great unhappiness about how plurality elections work and strong sentiment for a shift to PR in most democracies that use plurality, but few calls for plurality in PR countries. One important reason for this pattern is that the divisive, winner-take-all nature of plurality and presidentialism is widely understood. From the turn of the century on, democracies with ethnic or other deep cleavages have repeatedly turned to PR in order to accommodate such differences. Lardeyret's recommendation of plurality elections for South Africa and other deeply divided countries is therefore particularly dangerous.

Another important reason for PR's popularity is the feeling that disproportional election results are inherently unfair and undemocratic. None of postwar Britain's governing parties was put in power by a majority of the voters; all of these parties gained power in spite of the fact that most of the voters voted against them. Lardeyret's and Quade's opinion that electoral disproportionality is unimportant is simply not shared by most democrats. As a recent editorial in the London *Economist* puts it, "since the perception of fairness is the acid test for a democracy—the very basis of its legitimacy—the unfairness argument overrules all others."[4]

Fundamental constitutional changes are difficult to effect and therefore rare, but the prevailing pattern of democratic sentiment makes shifts from plurality to PR more likely than the other way around. The reason for this is not, as Lardeyret suggests, that "it is almost impossible to get rid of PR, because doing so requires asking independent parties to cooperate in their own liquidation." On the contrary, this is the main reason why the big parties that benefit from the plurality rule will try to keep it. In PR systems, the large parties usually have enough votes to shift to a system that would greatly benefit them, especially because, as Lardeyret correctly observes, the electoral system is "curiously omitted in most [written] constitutions." That they rarely try to do so cannot be explained in terms of narrow partisan self-interest; the feeling that scrapping PR is undemocratic and dangerous plays a major role. Both the empirical evidence and the weight of opinion in existing democracies make a strong case for the proposition that PR and parliamentarism are also the wisest options for new democracies.

NOTES

1. Arend Lijphart, *Democracies: Patterns of Majoritarian and Consensus Government in Twenty-One Countries* (New Haven: Yale University Press, 1984), 83. A cabinet is defined as the same cabinet if its party composition does not change; on the basis of this definition and for the 1945-80 period, average cabinet life in the four parliamentary-plurality countries was 88 months and in the parliamentary-PR countries, 44 months.

2. The dates of parliamentary elections for the 13 countries can be found in the respective country chapters of Thomas T. Mackie and Richard Rose, *The International Almanac of Electoral History*, 3rd ed. (London: Macmillan, 1991).

3. W. Arthur Lewis, *Politics in West Africa* (London: Allen and Unwin, 1965), 71.

4. *The Economist*, 11 May 1991, 13.

17. THE PRIMACY OF THE PARTICULAR

Ken Gladdish

Ken Gladdish *is senior research fellow and former head of the Department of Politics at the University of Reading in England. He has written extensively on the Netherlands, and also on Portugal, and more generally on representation, ethnicity, and the etiology of political science.*

A little more than three generations ago, the eminent British political scientist Sir Henry Maine discussed what he referred to as "that extreme form of popular government which is called democracy." He wrote not as an opponent of the form but as an inquirer into its success, which seemed to him "to have arisen rather from skillfully applying the curb to popular impulses than from giving them the rein."[1] This view, which today may appear unfashionably paternalistic, can be redeemed by stressing the word "impulses." Few contemporary governments would regard it as either sensible or necessary to respond to each and every fluctuation of public opinion in between the settled contests that now determine and legitimate periods of rule by competing sets of politicians. But the question of how these contests should be staged, in terms of the method for translating votes into legislative seats, still leaves much room for argument.

That it is a topical argument is as evident in long-established democratic polities like France and Britain as in the emerging democracies of East and Central Europe, or indeed in the moves toward multiparty politics that have recently occurred in many states which date their independence to the post-1945 collapse of European colonialism.

In the recent debate in the *Journal of Democracy* among Arend Lijphart, Guy Lardeyret, and Quentin L. Quade that followed Lijphart's original article, two opposing positions were presented.[2] Lijphart advocated strict proportionality in the allocation of popular representation. His two critics catalogued the perils of such close attention to the unmediated arithmetic of party support and endorsed plurality elections.

The arguments of the protagonists, however, implied an uncomfortable absolutism, for all rested on the presupposition that a particular electoral system can be advanced as universally superior to all alternatives. This notion had already been challenged in an earlier essay in the *Journal of Democracy* by Larry Diamond. Writing on "Three Paradoxes of Democracy," Diamond had drawn attention to the problem of "representativeness versus governability" and contended that "each country must find its own way of resolving this universal tension."[3]

My purpose is to expand upon that sage contention, which I shall seek to do in three ways: first, by questioning the starkness with which the alternatives were earlier presented; second, by resisting the amputation of electoral systems from the whole body politic; and third, by considering some examples that may suggest greater subtlety in value judgments than attachment to general prescriptions easily allows.

A Range of Formulas

In the first place, the choice does not lie *tout court* between plurality and proportional representation (PR). There is a range of formulas that is so elaborate as to make each set of national arrangements virtually *sui generis*.[4] When, for example, we consider systems that are not based upon mere plurality (and note that plurality systems differ in important ways), we confront provisions as distinct as the additional-member system in Germany, the alternative vote in Australia, and the single transferable vote in Ireland.[5] Furthermore, even where proportionality is embraced as a goal, actual practices extend from Portugal's regional system, with its large variations in the size of constituencies, to the nationwide PR system found in the Netherlands. There is therefore a real danger of setting up a debate that is grossly reductionist in its essential terms. But that is only part of the problem. Lijphart can certainly be commended for his broad-brush search for objective measurements of the various outcomes of different systems. This is a vastly different undertaking, however, from endeavoring to decide which of the two highly generalized alternatives is the ultimate answer.

This is very clearly brought out by the efforts of each of the three debaters to press his case. Two difficulties here seem insuperable. The first—and this is something that the interlocutors themselves largely concede—is the impossibility of separating out the influence of electoral systems from all the other forces that can affect a polity over time. The second is that electoral systems cannot simply be pulled out of a drawer in the way that one might choose a cooking recipe. Each national case is highly circumstantial and reflects both history in all its manifestations and, more specifically, the consequences of particular patterns of political mobilization.

In the Netherlands, on which Lijphart is a widely recognized expert, nationwide PR came about for a number of reasons. Prominent among these was the perceived failure of a plurality system to deliver coherent results, given the fragmented nature of Dutch political competition by the second decade of the present century. This is not of course to argue that the eventual choice was wholly determined by this circumstance, for debate continues in the Netherlands today about the efficacy and desirability of nationwide PR. But it does suggest that the notion of a circumstance-free choice is at odds with reality.

Furthermore, even if it could be convincingly demonstrated (which on the evidence of the debate so far seems unlikely) that PR systems consistently outperform plurality systems, or vice versa, it would still be naive to insist that the apparently more enlightened method should be universally adopted.

Of course, one can explore, as an exercise in comparative politics, the extent to which electoral systems seem to play a significant role in the performance of different polities. If the general findings were persuasive, they would then become an instructive reference for politicians and others who must decide the exact "rules" of the electoral "game" in their various countries. But this merely reemphasizes the point that each polity is distinct, and must therefore work out its own formula.

In Britain today, there is renewed debate about the wisdom of retaining a plurality system based upon single-member constituencies. Many ingredients are discernible in the cases for and against, but the dominant concern is whether "simple" plurality still provides for a reasonably frequent alternation of parties in government. If this particular anxiety, the result of four successive Conservative victories, had not arisen, the debate would almost certainly not be so high on the agenda. The current concern therefore reflects a highly circumstantial feature peculiar to a particular run of recent electoral outcomes. What is most significant is that there is no consensus on what might replace the traditional plurality system, given that each of the alternative prospects would have important consequences for the complexion of both representation and government.[6] It may be that, in the eyes of God, there is a "perfect" electoral system for Britain. But we do not know what it is, and even if we did, there may be costs that significant groups would be unprepared to pay to secure it.

The latter point, concerning costs, must be taken into account when considering why polities do or do not adopt particular arrangements. For there is a fundamental dichotomy that runs through all discussions about how popular votes should be related to the distribution of seats in a legislature: in systems based on popular sovereignty, the people need to be both represented and governed. In each and every democracy, some appropriate relationship between these two needs must be established; it seems obvious that the solutions chosen will vary considerably from country to country.

Nevertheless, one general statement can be confidently made about the prime difference between plurality systems and PR systems: the former tend to limit significant representation in the assembly to two parties, thus facilitating single-party majority government, while the latter, subject to whatever thresholds might be imposed, provide for the legislative representation of all measurable contenders. To put it most simply, plurality systems reduce the prospect of legislative fragmentation; proportional systems increase it.

The Netherlands, France, and Germany

Having questioned the grounds on which the debate has so far proceeded, I shall now attempt to demonstrate the importance of particular cases rather than the persuasive force of general propositions. Let us begin with the previously mentioned example of the Netherlands. Even as it was adopting universal suffrage, Holland replaced its constituency system by a formula of nationwide PR. The main circumstance prompting this change was the sheer geometry of political mobilization, which meant that contests in single-member seats had become unmanageable.[7] By 1914, five significant political groupings were competing on an increasingly national basis, and ad hoc alliances formed to produce majorities in individual constituencies were unable to solve the problem of coherent representation. It seemed inevitable therefore that some other method of staging the national electoral competition would have to be adopted.

The solution of nationwide PR was a resort to the arithmetic of overall party strengths at the cost of a direct linkage between voters and representatives. That this has been no light cost is evidenced by the continuing Dutch debate, which surfaced dramatically in the latter half of the 1960s, about the need to address the problem of linkage. Under nationwide PR, Dutch MPs have no constituents and Dutch voters have no local representatives in the legislature. As several commentators have explained, this has serious consequences for the conduct of national politics.[8]

A further cost is that the meticulous registration of party strengths, with no minimum threshold, results in a multiparty legislature from which governments have to be forged, often with considerable delay and with no reference back to voters. It so happens that, for a number of reasons, this seems not to cause undue damage to governmental continuity.[9] But the reasons are highly specific to Dutch political practice and—dare one use the term?—culture. In other polities it is likely that such prolonged cabinet formations, and the sometimes painful delivery of unexpected governments via the midwifery of party leaders acting in the wake of elections, could cause considerable dislocation and disaffection.

If we turn to the much discussed case of contemporary France, other matters come into view. Although the precise classification of successive French electoral systems has become an academic cottage industry, it is clear enough that under the Fifth Republic single-bloc legislative majorities were sought by the device of second ballots in single-member constituencies.[10] What is more open to conjecture is exactly what ensued from the adoption of PR with department-wide districts for the 1986 elections to the National Assembly. John Frears contends that this move "generated a storm from political elites, indifference from the public, and a commitment from the new government to get rid of it again."[11] In the same vein, Roy Pierce and Thomas Rochon hold that it "was widely interpreted as a move to avert electoral disaster by the Socialist party, by preventing the two main rightist parties from together winning a large majority of the seats in the Assembly."[12]

The Right did, in the event, secure a legislative majority. The Socialists were not destroyed, though they lost a quarter of their seats. What has attracted most comment, however, is that Jean-Marie Le Pen's National Front was able to secure as many seats as the Communists. Whereas, according to Frears, "If the two-round system had been maintained, the National Front would have won virtually no parliamentary seats though winning the same number of votes."[13]

Here we confront a frequent objection to PR that applies even to mild specimens like Mitterand's provision for departmental lists. Lardeyret regards the success of the National Front, and the emergence of extreme opponents to it, as "an unhealthy situation [that] can be attributed largely to PR." But surely the real question is another one: Socialist motivations apart, what would have been the best electoral formula for dealing with not only the threat of extremism, but all the other circumstances of French politics in the mid-1980s?

As already noted, all electoral systems have costs—a fact that was not exactly highlighted by the earlier contributors. The French situation may appear somewhat peculiar to an outsider in that powerholders seem able to shuffle electoral systems at will (Greece would be a similar instance). While such maneuverings might conceivably be regarded as commendable attempts to respond to the fluctuations of political mobilization, there is ample evidence that less pure instincts are at work in both countries.

Clearly, profound issues arise when the consequences of any given electoral system are confronted. A provision that has attracted much enthusiasm on the part of electoral reformers in plurality systems is the German additional-member formula, which the Federal Republic adopted at the time of its formation in 1949. This recipe provides both for constituency representatives chosen in plurality elections and for representation in terms of national party strengths. It includes a threshold applying to both constituency and national party support, so that a party has to achieve at least 5 percent of the total number of votes cast in order to secure seats in the Bundestag. This level of support, but often little more, has been recurrently achieved by the Free Democratic Party (FDP), which accordingly occupies a pivotal position between the much larger forces of the Christian Democratic Union (CDU) and of the Social Democratic Party (SPD). As Gordon Smith explains, "The strategic position in the party system occupied by the Free Democratic Party . . . gives the party a weight quite out of proportion to its parliamentary representation."[14] From this pivotal position, the FDP has been able to exert a powerful influence on the formation and operation of governments. Indeed, it has been able to change the whole complexion of government without benefit of elections, as when the FDP abandoned its coalition with the SPD in 1982 and ushered the CDU into office.

Disproportionate leverage wielded by small but strategically positioned "fulcrum" parties like the FDP is not an inherent feature of PR systems. It is generally lacking in the Scandinavian countries, for instance. Where such parties do exist, moreover, their power derives more from the particular geometry of mobilization patterns (which produce political situations where majorities cannot be formed without the inclusion of smaller parties) than from PR as such. But plurality systems, given their tendency to marginalize third parties, do make the rise of fulcrum parties less likely, which is one reason for the resistance to PR in Britain.

The New Systems of Central Europe

If we turn from established West European systems to the admittedly still larval systems of Central Europe, we find an interesting variety of cases. In the Czech and Slovak Federative Republic, postcommunist elections were held in June 1990 for both the bicameral Federal Assembly and the respective Czech and Slovak National Councils. A party-list system was adopted in all three cases, but there was concern about two issues.[15] One was a fear of the sort of fragmentation that beset interwar legislatures; the other was an anxiety about overweening party machines, another feature of earlier practice. Several devices were therefore adopted to impede these possibilities. They included, though the detail is complex, what amounted to a 5-percent threshold for the federal parliament and the Czech assembly and a provision for preferential voting within party lists.

Hyperfragmentation was indeed avoided, though this could be largely ascribed to Civic Forum's success in gaining widespread support as a transitional political movement closely identified with the Velvet Revolution. The Forum gained some two-thirds of the seats in each house of the Federal Assembly as well as in the Czech National Council.

Despite the prognostications of pollsters and commentators, the results of the second Federal Assembly elections, held in June 1992, also reflected a consolidation of the leading Czech and Slovak formations (Civic Democracy and the Movement for a Democratic Slovakia, respectively).[16] Yet this very same consolidation has served to promote the impending split of the 74-year-old federation into a Czech republic and a separate Slovakia. Hindsight thus reveals that the bogeyman was less party fragmentation than national fission, though it would hardly be plausible to argue that a system designed to produce less consolidation in each of the two parts of the federation would have offered a more constructive approach.

The case of Poland, though alarming, is a more straightforward example of the problems of electoral mechanics. There the October 1991 elections for the Sejm resulted in the emergence of 29 parliamentary parties, the largest of which obtained less that 13 percent of the total vote and less than 14 percent of the available seats.[17] Turnout was a mere 42 percent. The elections were held on the basis of proportional representation, without a threshold, in 37 districts with between 7 and 17 seats each. A further 15 percent of the total seats (69 out of 460) were allocated nationally with a 5-percent threshold and a requirement of support in at least five districts.[18] It took almost two months of intensive interparty negotiation before a government could be assembled, and there has subsequently been a succession of governmental changes.

The Czech and Polish experiences exemplify the uncertainties of the early phases of transition from an effectively one-party to a competitive system. But each transition has its own problems and peculiarities, and electoral mechanisms remain merely one facet of the prism of political competition. In Hungary, the pace of the political transition away from the one-party system fell somewhere between the long march led by Solidarity in Poland and the abrupt Velvet Revolution in Prague. Over three years elapsed between the beginning of intense debate, negotiation, and organizing work in mid-1987 and the first multiparty parliamentary elections in April 1990, as Hungarians dismantled communism and put together a new constitution.

Roundtable talks in the fall of 1989 hammered out the electoral system for the first free elections in postcommunist Hungary. A Hungarian political analyst has characterized the outcome as follows:

> The historical parties (Smallholders, Social Democrats, Christian Democrats) favored proportional representation with county-based party lists, which was used in 1945 and 1947. However, the general mood in the country, especially among the MPs in the parliament, made it impossible to abolish the existing local constituency representation. Since there were no huge popular movements behind the new political parties, their legitimacy was limited. The local notables and the citizens did not want to let the whole nomination process be controlled by party bureaucracies. The long debate and the general mood made it impossible to introduce any election system based on a single principle. Therefore

> the electoral system became a combination of different principles and techniques. The 386 seats of the unicameral Hungarian parliament were divided into three categories: 176 were to be elected in single-member constituencies, 152 from regional party lists, and 58 from national party lists.[19]

In single-member constituencies, a second ballot was required where no candidate received an absolute majority in the first round. On the second ballot, a plurality would suffice for election. The regional party-list seats and the national seats were subject to a 4-percent threshold. The whole formula was intended to help prevent party proliferation. That it had its costs is indisputable: turnout was unimpressive, and hardly any constituency seats were filled on the first ballot. Given the complexity of the electoral provisions, it would be hard to determine how proportional the results actually were in terms of the ratio of seats to initial party votes. Nevertheless, they did deliver a parliament with only six parties, which enabled a majority coalition to be formed by an alliance of the largest single party and two ancillaries.

Merits and Defects

My examples so far have tended to suggest that various forms of PR produce outcomes that are less than optimal from the standpoint of stable, coherent, and effective government. None of this, however, should be taken as pointing to the absurdly simple-minded conclusion that PR is always the wrong choice. For not only can PR work well in certain national contexts (such as Norway, Sweden, and the Netherlands), but plurality systems (as in Britain) can display grave defects of their own.

Britain, like the United States, is a land of single-member legislative districts and first-past-the-post elections. To win, a candidate need not secure an overall majority of votes in the constituency. That will, of course, be the case if only two candidates compete; in practice, however, three or more contenders seek election in most British constituencies. Candidates may therefore be elected with just over a third of the votes cast where there are three contenders, or just over a quarter where there are four, and so on.

Two serious problems arise under the British system. The first, and the one most commonly cited by critics, is the lack of provision for proportionality between total national party votes and party parliamentary seats. It is invariably the smallest of the three significant national parties, the Liberal Democrats (formerly the Liberals), which is the most heavily penalized. In the April 1992 parliamentary elections, which were fairly typical, the Liberal Democrats gained 17.8 percent of the total national vote, but having obtained a plurality in only 20 constituencies, they secured a mere 3 percent of the seats in the House of Commons. Since the system is not designed to deliver proportionality, exact equivalents of national votes and seats are rare for the two larger parties as well.[20] On the other hand, the system does usually manage to produce single-party majority governments. Of all the elections held in Britain since 1945, only one (the February 1974 balloting that returned Harold Wilson to Number 10 Downing Street at the head of a Labour-Liberal coalition) has failed to return one party with an overall legislative majority.

The less frequently voiced criticism of the British system stresses the apathy it seems to breed among the vast majority of voters, who may reasonably feel that it matters little whether or not they vote. In April 1992, only 52 of 651 parliamentary seats changed hands across parties. In perhaps a further 50 seats there may have been a possibility of an upset. In more than five hundred seats, therefore, no change was remotely likely; this is the case in every election. In a fully proportional system, all votes would go toward the distribution of legislative seats. Even though there might not be dramatic overall changes from election to election, such a set-up would do much more than the current one does to justify the act of voting.

From a standpoint that is concerned purely with translating votes into representation, a proportional system may appear, at least in principle, to deliver the democratic goods. If parties are the sole vehicle of popular representation, and if government is based, as it is in all genuinely parliamentary systems, upon relative party strengths in the legislature, there may seem little to justify any system that narrows the range of electoral choices. In practice, however, there are formidable arguments, both general and specific, against proportionality.

The most general argument emphasizes the threat that proportionality can pose to governmental coherence. The process of forming a majority government after proportionality has delivered a highly fragmented legislature is subject to several types of difficulties. The first occurs when long periods of interparty haggling follow parliamentary elections. In the Netherlands, as we saw, prolonged delays in the formation of cabinets have become a normal and not very troublesome feature of national politics. A more worrisome example of delay in cabinet formation would be the recent experience in Belgium, where five months elapsed between the parliamentary election of November 1991 and the creation of a new government. Such severe paralysis cannot be attributed simply to PR, of course, nor does it mean that a plurality system would necessarily be better for Belgium. But it is a troubling instance of a political hiatus arising from fragmentation.

A second kind of difficulty arises when odd coalitions form out of sheer expediency, as with the combination between the Portuguese Socialist Party and its most right-wing opponent, the Social Democratic Center Party, in 1977-78. What is interesting in the Portuguese case is that the very same electoral system (party lists in varied-size districts) that produced this egregious example also delivered single-party majority governments after elections in both 1987 and 1991.[21]

A third type of problem emerges when it proves impossible to form a majority government at all, and a minority administration results. The Scandinavian countries—notably Denmark, which has had only three majority governments since 1945—offer many instances of this dubious phenomenon. Poland today is another case in point.

A further problem of coalition formation in fragmented legislatures is that of accountability to voters when coalitions form only after the elections are over. There is much comment about this on record in the Dutch case.[22] The argument here has two barrels. The first is that voters in such circumstances cannot know the full consequences of their choice of party. This can to some extent be countered by the contention that in all systems voters cannot calculate the precise outcome of casting their vote. The second charge—that such "unsignaled" coalitions lack a democratic mandate—is more difficult to refute because it strikes near the heart of the notion of popular sovereignty. To combine two or more parties, each of which represents an *exclusive* choice by individual voters, where there has been no prior pact known to the electorate, does seem to raise serious questions about governmental legitimacy.

It so happens that the Dutch case also exemplifies the problem, already cited in respect to Germany, of the enormous leverage available to parties that command the center. The major confessional parties in the Netherlands, amalgamated since 1975 under the banner of the Christian Democratic Appeal, have for most of this century largely determined the complexion of each and every coalition cabinet. Until the 1960s, this reflected their regularly demonstrated ability to amass about half of both the votes cast and the seats contested, making them the country's principal political grouping. Yet even their relative decline to around one-third of the national vote has not robbed them of this decisive leverage, and so they continue to preside from the center.

The Test of Practicality

Another question for debate is that of the linkage—or the lack thereof—between voter and representative. The basic structure of parliamentary representation in Britain was established long before the development of either national mass-based parties or universal suffrage. Although it has been modified in recent times, the system's essential characteristic remains that of locality representation. This ostensibly means that each citizen, however he or she may have voted (or not voted), has a representative in the legislature to whom grievances can be directly addressed. This follows from the assumption that each MP serves on behalf of all the interests and concerns within his or her constituency. Given the current primacy of national party strategies, that assumption may now be dubious, but it endures within the minds of citizens and legislators alike. Indeed, in a recent survey of the attitudes of British MPs toward electoral reform, the majority of respondents placed this aspect of the representational system at the top of their list of that system's virtues.[23]

"If an electoral system operates so as to exclude expressions of antidemocratic sentiment, does that not also mean shutting out the lesser voices of democratic sentiment?"

The concrete benefits of locality representation may be variously evaluated, but it is undeniable that where proportionality leaves locality representation out of account, then relations between the citizen and the legislature are affected. This is one reason why so-called mixed systems, like the German additional-member system, have attracted the interest of reformers in a pluralist system like Britain's.

The final item in the critic's arsenal of charges against proportionality is its potential for giving scope to fringe parties (as already noted above with regard to France). The literature on this topic is vast indeed, ranging through the emergence of fascism in the interwar period to the threats posed by the extreme left and right (and now by fundamentalism) in the post-1945 era. The literature can only grow, for the debate is perennially open-ended. If an electoral system operates so as to exclude expressions of antidemocratic sentiment, does that not also mean shutting out the lesser voices of democratic sentiment? Can the problem not be tackled by other means, such as the German Basic Law's proscription of antidemocratic parties? Whatever judgment an impartial referee might reach on this vexed question, it remains a comfort to those who live under long-established plurality systems that the likelihood of an antidemocratic movement gaining significant legislative influence in their countries is small indeed.

Any sensible tribunal weighing the relative merits and demerits of proportionality (in its many possible forms) and plurality (also capable of variations) would refuse to rule on purely or even largely theoretical grounds. The best test is one of practicality and aptness relative to national circumstance. The most relevant of these—the one that must be given the most weight in the evaluation of alternative electoral mechanisms—is the existing pattern of political mobilization. No reformer, however convinced of the elegance of a particular scheme or provision, could sanely try to graft it onto a polity whose dynamics would make the reform unworkable, damaging, absurd, disruptive, or catastrophic. It is surely one of the tasks of political scientists to analyze the effects of different electoral provisions, but it cannot be in their province to recommend recipes *in vacuo*.

The problems of orchestrating free, fair, and open competition for political power can be especially great in relatively new, resource-strapped states. In such circumstances, one would have to be bold beyond measure to offer general prescriptions for representation. Yet one may still nurse a hope that the debate which this journal has so usefully promoted will be of heuristic value to decision makers in societies where representative government is a new item on the agenda.

NOTES

1. Sir Henry Maine, *Popular Government* (London: John Murray, 1885), vii, xi.

2. See Arend Lijphart, "Constitutional Choices for New Democracies," *Journal of Democracy* 2 (Winter 1991): 72-84; and Guy Lardeyret, "The Problem with PR," Quentin L. Quade, "PR and Democratic Statecraft," and Arend Lijphart, "Double-Checking the Evidence," *Journal of Democracy* 2 (Summer 1991): 30-48.

3. Larry Diamond, "Three Paradoxes of Democracy," *Journal of Democracy* 1 (Summer 1990): 54.

4. An official of the British Electoral Reform Society claimed recently that he knew of three hundred different formulas.

5. All three systems are constituency-based. The additional-member system distributes additional seats in proportion to the national configuration of party support. The alternative vote is a preference system that enables voters to rank candidates in their order of preference and then redistributes the second (or subsequent) preferences of those who voted for the weakest contenders so that a majority is achieved. The single transferable vote operates similarly to the alternative vote, but in multimember constituencies.

6. Current serious proposals include all three systems cited above. There is little discernible support for party-list approaches on either a regional or national basis.

7. See H. Daalder, "Extreme Proportional Representation: The Dutch Experience" in S. E. Finer, ed., *Adversary Politics and Electoral Reform* (London: Anthony Wigram, 1975), and K.R. Gladdish, "The Netherlands" in Vernon Bogdanor, ed., *Representatives of the People? Parliamentarians and Constituents in Western Democracies* (Aldershot, England: Gower, 1985).

8. See K.R. Gladdish, *Governing from the Centre: Politics and Policy-Making in the Netherlands* (London: C. Hurst, 1991), ch. 6.

9. See K.R. Gladdish, "Governing the Dutch," *Acta Politica* 25 (October 1990): 389-402.

10. See Alistair Cole and Peter Campbell, *French Electoral Systems and Elections Since 1789* (Aldershot, England: Gower, 1989).

11. Howard Penniman, ed., *France at the Polls, 1981 and 1986* (Durham, N.C.: Duke University Press, 1988), 211.

12. Ibid., 181.

13. Ibid., 214.

14. Gordon Smith, William Paterson, and Peter Merkl, eds., *Developments in West German Politics* (London: Macmillan, 1989), 71.

15. See Judy Batt, "After Czechoslovakia's Velvet Poll," *World Today* 46 (August-September 1990): 141-43.

16. *The Economist*, 13 June 1992.

17. David Warszawski, "The Elections: Don't Let's Be Shocked," *East European Reporter*, January-February 1992, 19-21.

18. Krzysztof Jasiewicz, "From Solidarity to Fragmentation," *Journal of Democracy* 3 (April 1992): 55-69. Jasiewicz has grave doubts whether juggling with the electoral system would have avoided hyperfragmentation, though from his consideration of alternatives it does seem that it might have been significantly reduced.

19. A. Körösényi, "The Hungarian Parliamentary Elections 1990" in A. Bozóki, A. Körösényi, and G. Schopflin, eds., *Post-Communist Transition: Emerging Pluralism in Hungary* (London: Pinter, 1992).

20. In the case of the April 1992 election, John Curtice has called attention to a surprising quirk in the mathematics: "For the first time ever the system wholly failed to deliver a bonus in seats to the winner. Instead, so far as the Conservatives and Labour are concerned, it acted in a purely proportional way." *Guardian*, 13 April 1992. Clearly what happened—ostensibly for the first time—could have happened on any previous occasion. This prompts the reflection that proportionality is not excluded in a plurality system. It is merely made highly uncertain.

21. A former member of the Portuguese parliament recently delivered the following verdict on the electoral system: "The four main political parties . . . dispute elections according to rules that reduce the individual deputies more to the role of party officials than of representatives of the electorate." She then warned: "Indeed, the functioning of the proportional system in Portugal should be a true object lesson for those naif Britons who believe its introduction might improve British institutions." Patricia Lança, "The Land of Mild Customs," *Salisbury Review*, June 1992, 29.

22. See K.R. Gladdish, "Two-Party versus Multi-Party: The Netherlands and Britain," *Acta Politica* 7 (July 1972): 342-61, and *Parliamentary Affairs* 26 (Autumn 1973): 454-70.

23. K.R. Gladdish, A.T.W. Liddell, and P.J. Giddings, "MPs' Perceptions of the British Electoral System" (University of Reading Politics Group Research Paper No. 1, 1984).

18.
NEW INSTITUTIONS IN THE OLD EAST BLOC

Jan Zielonka

***Jan Zielonka** was born and educated in Poland. An associate professor of political science at Leiden University in the Netherlands, he is currently on leave at the European University Institute in Florence, Italy. His English-language publications include* Political Ideas in Contemporary Poland *(1989) and* Security in Central Europe *(1992).*

Setting the new rules of political bargaining is the essence of democratic consolidation. This especially involves defining the functions and procedures of democracy's three institutional pillars: the executive, the legislature, and the judiciary. Unless these institutions enjoy stability, coherence, and autonomy, democracy cannot work. In the postcommunist countries, however, the entire institutional framework is now in flux, causing chaos, friction, and inefficiency. State institutions are assuming new roles and prerogatives under conditions of intense political struggle, rapid social change, and enormous legal confusion. The core rules of institutional bargaining are constantly being rearticulated and renegotiated. Institutions find it hard to acquire the public support and professional skills (to say nothing of internal coherence and adaptability) that they need to cope with the complex challenges that they face. At the same time, they often clash agonizingly among themselves over prestige, authority, and procedures. The problem has been especially acute in Russia, where institutional rivalries led to the all-out violence of October 1993 and threatened to undo democracy. But protracted and more or less intense conflict concerning the division of powers among the executive, the legislature, and the judiciary is a prominent theme of political life throughout the postcommunist world.

This does not mean that no democratic progress is taking place. Despite the many problems discussed below, democratic consolidation is occurring, and existing institutions are performing their basic functions. Parliaments in each country issue hundreds of laws per year that undo the communist past and lay down foundations for a new democratic regime. The executive branches run economies in a largely new fashion, and they still manage, for better or worse, to administer their countries and to guarantee law and order. The judiciary, released from communist control and operating within a new legal framework, is making remarkable progress in creating a system based on the rule of law. Yet this progress may prove unsustainable if ongoing constitutional conflicts are not settled. In some cases, such as those of Russia and Ukraine, the intensity of the institutional power struggle points more to chaos and the possible recrudescence of dictatorship than to any early democratic consolidation.

Generally speaking, the more complex the laws that determine the competencies of major institutions, the more heated and destructive is the institutional power struggle. The problem of Eastern Europe so far has not been that this or that country has chosen a presidential or parliamentary model, but that there has been no fixed model in place at all. If the East European experience is to provide any answers with wider application, democrats should give up endless debate about optimal constitutional solutions, and focus instead on the speedy adoption of new constitutions. This is, of course, a rather risky way to proceed, which is why I recommend an interim rather than a lasting character for new constitutions, and favor concentrating on regulating the machinery of government rather than securing paper guarantees for individual rights. It also seems clear that emerging political pacts and compromises give the new constitutions a more solid basis than predemocratic legal arrangements will. Checks and balances should appear not only in constitutional drafts, but in the actual process of constitution making itself.

The Roots of Institutional Chaos

There is ample evidence that East European reformers have long realized the damaging effects of prolonged institutional instability. Why, then, the obsessive institutional power struggles in these countries? First and most obviously, because the old system has crumbled and the creation of a new one raises difficult questions about the number, structure, and prerogatives of institutional actors. Second, because institutions—unlike society, the economy, or the culture—are susceptible to "political engineering" by the young democratic elites, and are therefore their prime target. Third, because in the absence of strong parties and loyal constituencies, state institutions represent the only sure political prize. Assuming control of a particular institution and extending its formal powers becomes a new form of political contention in consolidating democracies.

The historical context is also worth considering. Although under communism the party in fact ran everything, most communist constitutions made parliament the highest state organ, superior to the executive and the judiciary. As communism waned, some countries created presidential offices with the aim of securing power for figures such as Poland's General Wojciech Jaruzelski or the Soviet Union's Mikhail Gorbachev. In formal terms, however, the superior position of parliament remained intact. Romania was the only exception: after 1974 the presidential office of Nicolae Ceauşescu enjoyed almost unlimited power to rule by decree.

During the 1989-90 democratic breakthrough, political rather than legal considerations predominated, and no broad vision of legal order emerged. The rise of prodemocracy forces has been incremental in most countries, and thus any quick and overall solution to the unclear division of power has proved difficult, if not impossible, to reach. In Poland, for instance, democrats initially took control of the parliament, but not of the presidency. For some time, four crucial ministerial posts in the Solidarity-led government remained in communist hands. In Moscow, prodemocracy forces asserted their power first on the level of the Russian Republic; the Soviet government remained in the hands of more conservative forces. Within the Russian Republic, democrats rallied mainly around President Boris Yeltsin, while neocommunists remained strong in parliament. In Czechoslovakia, the change of regime was smooth and all-encompassing, but institutional reform was held back by growing tensions between Czechs and Slovaks. Only Romania and Bulgaria managed to strike a new institutional balance quickly, by passing new constitutions as early as 1991. In both countries, the changeover from communism to something more democratic was abrupt rather than incremental. Curiously, however, constitutional change in both countries was orchestrated by the reformed communists, who controlled all major state institutions at the time.

It is worth recalling that for years East European democrats advocated the weakening of the communist-dominated state. After their sudden accession to power, this rhetoric would come back to haunt them. At any rate, the challenge of guaranteeing key human and civil rights initially received more attention than the problem of crafting state institutions. The new elites' understandable reluctance to concentrate much power in existing institutions further delayed the crafting of new power structures.

The reasons for the current institutional chaos are thus complex, and no easy solutions are available. Yet democratic consolidation can hardly proceed any further without dramatic improvements in the institutional field. After all, how can the rule of law be achieved if the functions and procedures of major institutions are unclear? A confusing institutional structure lacking a clear division of powers not only makes it difficult for the government to act effectively, but breeds conflict and stifles the growth of governmental legitimacy.

Establishing a clear separation of powers in the former Eastern bloc meant first of all wiping out the various legal and extralegal prerogatives of each country's communist party. After all, it was the party, and not any particular state institution, that had the real power. When the party collapsed, however, these institutions became central: it was crucial to bring their formal powers into line with the standards of modern democracy. The most spectacular changes took place in the judiciary, which has everywhere been proclaimed independent and augmented by constitutional courts empowered to uphold the basic law through rulings that are for the most part binding on both the legislature and the executive.

The Separation of Powers

Legislators proved more reluctant to curb their own powers vis-à-vis the powers of the executive branch. The formal powers of parliament remain very strong, if not supreme, in every East European country save one. Only Russia has a presidential (or even superpresidential) system. Other countries have opted for either pure parliamentarism (Albania, Belarus, the Czech Republic, Estonia, Hungary, Latvia, and Slovakia) or else parliamentarism with a directly elected president (Bulgaria, Lithuania, Poland, Romania, Slovenia, and Ukraine). In parliamentary systems, of course, the legislative majority has sovereign authority over both cabinet composition and lawmaking.

Poland is a good example of a parliamentary system with a relatively strong president, meaning one who is directly elected by popular vote, who can veto legislation, and who can dissolve parliament if no agreement on a budget can be reached. In addition, Poland's president nominates the prime minister and in the event of parliamentary deadlock can create a "presidential" government. Yet Poland's parliament still has the upper hand, for it can override a presidential veto by a two-thirds vote of the lower house (the Sejm), can name its own prime minister against the president's wishes, and can stymie the creation of a "presidential government" by withholding its formal endorsement.

Since December 1993, the case of Russia has come to look quite different. Under the new Russian Constitution, the president not only controls the government, but also has extensive legislative powers. The president nominates the prime minister for approval by parliament's lower house (known as the State Duma). If the Duma rejects the president's nominee three times, the president is then free to appoint his nominee as prime minister anyway, dissolve the Duma, and call new elections. The president can name individual ministers without parliament's approval, and although parliament has the right to make federal laws, the president can issue edicts and directives that are binding so long as they do not violate those laws. He also has a veto that can be overridden only by a two-thirds vote of both houses of parliament.

Thus the separation of powers principle is hardly observed in Russia: the president possesses extensive legislative *and* executive powers. Nor can one talk about a fair system of checks and balances: the president can veto legislation and dissolve parliament, while parliament's power of impeachment is very difficult to bring to bear. (Impeachable offenses are limited to treason and high crimes. To file the charge, a two-thirds vote is required in the Duma, while actual removal requires a two-thirds vote in the upper house.)

The separation of powers is a murky subject in other countries as well, especially those that are still working with old and oft-amended constitutions left over from the communist era. Powers are frequently vaguely defined, inviting quarrels between the branches. In Ukraine, for instance, as was also the case in pre-1994 Russia, both the president and parliament can unilaterally dismiss cabinet ministers. Moreover, the parliament and the executive have overlapping competencies in such areas as national security and foreign policy.

Although most countries display a similar pattern of legislative-executive relations—a strong parliament and more or less weak president—they got there in many different ways. In Hungary, the outgoing communists tried to establish a strong presidency, but democrats refused to sign a 1989 roundtable agreement that would have allowed direct presidential elections and thus, it was feared, favor the ex-communist Imre Pozsgay. In Poland, on the other hand, the 1989 roundtable agreement between the communist government and the democratic opposition allowed General Jaruzelski to keep his rather extensive prerogatives; these were later transferred to the new democratic president, Lech Wałęsa. In Bulgaria, the weakened communists initially favored a strong presidency, but changed their minds after their unexpected victory in the parliamentary elections of 1990.

Strong parliamentary powers and a weak presidency emerged in Ukraine, Belarus, and initially in Russia as a result of policies that Mikhail Gorbachev adopted during the twilight of the USSR. Gorbachev's successive constitutional amendments in the years 1988 to 1990 were aimed at weakening the Communist party's monopoly on power and at making the superior position of the parliament real rather than fictitious. Democrats (including Andrei Sakharov) strongly supported these efforts. After the Soviet Union collapsed, the superior position of parliaments in the successor states remained largely intact. In Romania, when the Constitutional Assembly decided the division of powers, President Ion Iliescu used his majority support in that body to secure a relatively strong presidency similar to Poland's. These examples show that the powers of major institutions were not crafted according to any legal blueprint; instead, they resulted from complex political bargaining conducted against different historical backgrounds and ever changing political landscapes.

The Three Branches

Although the Eastern bloc's new parliaments possessed extensive formal powers as compared to other institutions, they were poorly prepared in terms of membership, organization, and procedure to perform their numerous functions. First of all, democratically elected MPs were by and large inexperienced in parliamentary affairs. For instance, the Hungarian parliament elected in 1990 had 95.6 percent new members. On the other hand, parliaments with higher percentages of veteran MPs (as in Russia, Romania, or Belarus) suffered from a legitimacy gap, since MPs with predemocratic parliamentary experience were usually associated with the communist regime. Poland's parliament of 1989-91 suffered from both inexperience *and* a lack of legitimacy: over 90 percent of its members were new, and more than half of these had communist ties.

Of course, second or third multiparty elections provided a greater degree of continuity, but the percentage of "fresh," and thus unprofessional, MPs stayed relatively high in most countries. The political base of new MPs was also somewhat vague, with many candidates recruited by movements and parties that disappeared during the subsequent parliamentary term, with predictably disorienting results.

All this could not but influence the quality of parliamentary work. Parliamentary debates were more reminiscent of a Persian bazaar than a forum for responsible deliberation. Interventions from the floor were full of demagogic monologues with little regard for the agreed-on agenda. Voting discipline within party caucuses was rarely observed. Internal rules and procedures were often questioned, if not ignored altogether. There were even brawls between parliamentarians from opposing factions.

Of course, the maturity of MPs' work varied from country to country, and often improved over time. The Russian Supreme Soviet manifested a particularly low level of parliamentary culture, but had no patent on misbehavior. Excesses apart, the daily work of parliaments was hardly a model of effectiveness, even under more or less stable conditions. Overwork, inexperience, political uncertainty, and drastic shortages of technical and support staff all conspired to impede the progress of legislative business. The complex bicameral or even tricameral structures of some parliaments obstructed decisionmaking even further.

Public perception of parliaments was obviously influenced by the numerous weaknesses of their work, which live television broadcasting of parliamentary proceedings often exposed all too well. Freely elected legislatures, which are supposed to be symbols of democracy in action, became symbols of factionalism, grandstanding, procedural inefficiency, and misguided representation. This sorry image persists in spite of some remarkable successes in lawmaking and repeated elections; the threat that it poses to democratic consolidation is obvious.

The weak performance of parliaments has served to highlight the crucial role that executives play in consolidating postcommunist democracies. Unfortunately, however, they seem to be suffering from many of the very same problems that legislatures face.

The legitimacy-versus-professionalism dilemma, for instance, confronts the executive no less than the legislative branch. In many countries, officials from disparate backgrounds (they might be described as "inexperienced dissidents" and "experienced former communists") are locked in uneasy coexistence, with predictably negative effects on administrative efficiency. Specific "professional" traditions in various state sectors, entrenched professional lobbies, and new ministerial elites who use civil service posts as political spoils have hampered change and damaged the competence and continuity of the executive branch.

The volatile partisan and personal rivalries that are common in the region's politics have also affected the work of the executive. In coalition governments, individual ministers tend to show more loyalty to their own political party than to the cabinet as such. Moreover, cabinet posts may often go to incompetents from vital but restive parties in the governing coalition. As for personal rivalries, the tension between Russia's President Boris Yeltsin, and then-Vice-President Aleksandr Rutskoi, which came to a head in the explosion of October 1993, is only the most famous of many such cases throughout the region. Often these were fueled by the unclear and overlapping competencies of various branches of the executive. All the abovementioned factors have undermined the effectiveness of the executive. The question is: would shifting more power from the legislature to the executive improve the situation?

Despite the predilection of some East European parliaments for no-confidence votes and interventions in executive affairs, many of the problems of the region's executive branches are of their own making. There is little reason to think that giving them more powers would help matters. In some countries, such as Slovakia and Belarus, parliaments have behaved as cabinets wanted, and yet one is hardly impressed by the results. Moreover, most executive authorities have not fully or effectively used all the powers they currently possess vis-à-vis parliament. Finally, in countries such as Russia and Ukraine, parliaments granted the executive temporary powers to rule the economy by decree, with decidedly mixed results. Ukrainian premier Leonid Kutchma promised many reforms when he received extraordinary powers in November 1992, but hardly any of his promises had been implemented by the end of his "free hand" tenure in May 1993.

In short, the poor performance of executives has been caused not so much by their weak powers as by the unclear division of powers, the ongoing political conflicts, and a general lack of experience on the part of new ministerial elites. Parliaments at times made life difficult for the executive branch, but the sources of weak executive performance lie largely outside legislative halls.

> ***"Across the postcommunist East, judiciaries seem to be performing much better than either parliaments or executives."***

Across the postcommunist East, judiciaries seem to be performing much better than either parliaments or executives. This is especially true as far as constitutional courts are concerned. They are almost utterly new to the region, are at odds with the traditional East European conception of judicial functions, and must deal with very sensitive political and legal questions. Yet in the view of most outside observers, they are doing their job very well.

The basic purpose of these courts is to ensure compliance with the constitutionally mandated governmental structure, and to determine the constitutionality of proposed or enacted laws. Some courts have also been given jurisdiction over human rights cases, as in Russia and Hungary, or have received the authority to supervise parliamentary and presidential elections, as in Romania and Bulgaria. Their decisions are binding in most countries, and a wide range of public institutions (and sometimes private citizens) can submit issues for consideration.

The range of issues tackled by the courts so far reflects the broad area of their competence. The courts have issued rulings on such fundamental questions as the banning of the communist party in Russia; the right to exist of the Turkish-based Movement of Rights and Freedoms in Bulgaria (since 1992 one of the three parliamentary parties); the lustration law in the former Czechoslovakia; and the property-restitution question in Hungary.

Even more remarkable is the overall high level of compliance with such rulings. Only in Russia have the court rulings not always been observed, as was the case with Tatarstan's insistence on holding its 1992 independence referendum despite the court's ruling that the referendum was unconstitutional. In the aftermath of the October 1993 troubles in Moscow, President Yeltsin temporarily suspended the court's activities, not least because most judges had taken parliament's side in the constitutional showdown.

Why have parliaments and executives agreed to delegate so much authority to small groups of jurists selected for a fixed period of time? Briefly, because these courts represent for the new political elites a guarantee that their constitutional rights will still be protected even if they find themselves on the losing side of political conflicts. Although certainly not free of serious problems, constitutional courts have helped to settle important political and legal battles; imposed a certain balance upon legislative-executive relations; and clarified the rules of political bargaining that flow from what are often confusing new constitutions.

Unfortunately, the regular court system has not earned an equally positive evaluation. The legitimacy-versus-professionalism dilemma is felt from top to bottom in judiciaries throughout the region. Some countries orchestrated virtual purges of judicial personnel, even though qualified candidates with a "clean" past were obviously in critically short supply. With increasing civil and criminal caseloads and a proliferation of imprecise and contradictory new laws, one could hardly expect the regular courts to improve their work dramatically. Thus although the judiciary seems to be the most stable and reliable branch of government in the region, the persistant weakness of the regular court systems hampers the ongoing consolidation of democracy.

The Choice of Electoral Systems

Students of democratic consolidation emphasize two crucial choices facing the architects of new democracies: 1) the choice between plurality elections and proportional representation (PR), and 2) the choice between parliamentary and presidential forms of government.[1] The crucial questions are as follows: Will these choices decide whether postcommunist democracy lives or dies? What are the best methods for improving the efficiency and legitimacy of its main institutional pillars? Are these methods available given the current state of affairs in the region? What priorities should democratic crafters set for themselves as they strive to curb the postcommunist institutional chaos?

The choice of electoral system is considered important because it helps to shape a country's party system, and by extension its institutional framework: the composition of the parliament, the form of the executive, the contours of executive-legislative relations, and so on. Yet, as we shall see, what Eastern Europe's democratic crafters faced was a choice not between plurality elections and PR, but rather between "strong" and "weak" versions of the latter. Moreover, the correlation between choice of electoral system adopted and degree of institutional stability has proved unclear, as has that between the former and the overall progress of democracy. Countries with strong (if not extreme) PR have not necessarily fared worse than those with moderate PR. Clearly, factors other than electoral systems have had large impacts on democracy's progress in the region.

Many things influenced the initial decisions about electoral systems in the young democracies of Eastern Europe: interwar traditions, the insecurity of the new elites, and so on. Yet with the sole exception of

Ukraine, every one of the countries concerned opted for some version of PR, although they differed as to how and to what degree they achieved proportionality.[2] There is little chance that British-style plurality elections will gain support in the region, for such a shift would threaten the prospects of most of the parties that currently hold parliamentary seats. They benefit from the current system, so why should they change it? Thus few politicians in Eastern Europe are likely to follow the advice of those who prescribe plurality voting as a remedy for institutional instability.

The choice of PR rather than plurality elections did not prevent the emergence of clear winners in the region. In the 1992 elections in Albania, for instance, the Albanian Democratic Party captured almost two-thirds of all the seats. In the 1992 Lithuanian parliamentary elections, the Lithuanian Democratic Party won 73 of the 141 seats in the Seimas. In both these cases, however, the proportionality of the system was severely constrained. Indeed, Albania's electoral system is the least proportional in the region: 100 seats are elected in single-member districts, with only 40 seats allocated to provide proportionality nationwide. Yet one can argue that the Albanian Democratic Party would also have captured most of the parliamentary seats under strong PR, for serious competition from other parties during the March 1992 elections was practically nonexistent.

These cases aside, however, Eastern Europe does seem to confirm Giovanni Sartori's observation about the manipulative propensities of all but pure PR systems. Extreme PR can produce a highly fragmented parliament and a multiparty executive.[3] For instance, Poland's 1991 electoral system, with its low electoral threshold and large electoral districts, produced no fewer than 29 different parties in the Polish Sejm; none received more than 13 percent of the vote. In other countries with moderate PR—meaning small electoral districts and a 4-percent or 5-percent threshold—the parliament was less fragmented and the executive consisted of no more than two or three coalition parties (e.g., Hungary in 1990 or the Czech Republic in 1992). When Poland adopted thresholds of 5 percent for single parties and 8 percent for coalitions in 1993, only six parties or coalitions of parties managed to win seats in the new parliament.

Yet moderate PR did not necessarily breed more institutional stability than strong PR. The 1991 Bulgarian elections, based on moderate PR, left three parties with seats in parliament, yet the degree of decision-making paralysis within Bulgaria's parliament was as high as in the Polish parliament with its 29 parties. In late 1992, for instance, the Bulgarians needed two full months to form a new cabinet. Moreover, the Bulgarian moderate-PR system left unrepresented a fourth of the voters—all those who cast ballots for parties that did not reach the threshold.

Poland's extreme PR did indeed produce a rapid succession of cabinets: from November 1991 to September 1993, Poland had four premiers and three governing coalitions. Protracted parliamentary infighting and prolonged executive vacancies were the rule, spelling grave institutional uncertainty. Yet fears that the adoption of strong PR would damage Polish democracy and set back economic reform were not confirmed: at the end of the parliamentary term in the summer of 1993, Poland was the economic success story of the region. The 1993 elections, carried out under more moderate PR than in 1991, have produced a coalition government comprised of two (not six) parties. But the new electoral system also facilitated the return to power of former communists, and left almost 35 percent of voters with no representation in parliament.

This is not to glorify extreme PR, but to show that this system may not be so bad as some critics suggest. Movement from extreme to moderate PR may be in order to prevent excessive parliamentary fragmentation and its associated problems. Yet moderating PR is hardly a cure-all for shaky institutions, and it may exact a price in the form of reduced representativeness and damaged legitimacy. In the worst instance, unrepresented voters (and possibly also nonvoters) might come to feel so frustrated that they start down the road of nondemocratic politics.

Presidents versus Parliaments

While fundamental electoral change is unlikely in the region, the same cannot be said concerning relations between the executive and the legislature. The current predominance of the legislative branch will prove unsustainable in many cases; powerful political forces now afoot favor strong presidencies. Will a shift from parliamentary to presidential systems help or hurt the consolidation of democracy?

Students of democratic transition have divergent views on this question, and their comparative observations apply to postcommunist countries only with certain qualifications. On the one hand, strong, well-disciplined political parties—a usual and rather basic pillar of workable parliamentarism—hardly exist there. On the other hand, a presidential system has only just emerged in Russia, and one can only speculate about its possible virtues and weaknesses there.

Some of the typical arguments for presidentialism or parliamentarism do not seem to be holding up very well in the region so far. For example, advocates of parliamentarism argue that presidents have weaker democratic credentials than parliaments (some presidents gain office with a smaller proportion of the popular vote than many prime ministers who head minority cabinets, while other presidents tend to rely on plebiscitarian rather than democratic legitimacy). Yet it remains true that until very recently countries particularly affected by institutional conflict—namely Russia and Ukraine—had presidents that were chosen through fully democratic elections and parliaments that were not. The region's presidents have indeed shown a plebiscitarian penchant for calling national referenda, but this is more a sign of impotence vis-à-vis parliaments than an indication of dictatorial tendencies. Consider, for instance, President Václav Havel's unsuccessful 1992 effort to call a referendum on the future of the Czech and Slovak Federative Republic (CSFR) or President Boris Yeltsin's successful 1993 effort to hold a referendum on the merit of his reforms and the need for new elections. The Russian referendum produced good results for Yeltsin, but the Congress of People's Deputies chose to view it as no more than a glorified opinion poll. Yeltsin's subsequent "coup" of September 1993—in which he first suspended and then terminated all the functions of parliament—says more about his desperation than his plebiscitarian predilections.

Presidents, it has been said, often find it difficult to be both effective chief executives and combative party politicians. Presidentialism tends to foster a two-party or a two-bloc system, and it usually produces cabinets composed solely of members of the governing party. Again, postcommunist developments so far do not confirm these general observations. Most if not all presidents in the region are not yet linked to any single political party. In Bulgaria, Romania, and Lithuania, presidents are even legally obliged to abandon party membership before assuming their functions. President Lech Wałęsa of Poland and President Zhelu Zhelev of Bulgaria indeed made efforts to create a sort of "presidential party," but this has not led to the creation of a two-party system or to a cabinet dominated by "all the president's men." In fact, a joke told by Poles suggests that not the president's partisanship, but rather his nonpartisanship constitutes a problem: "President Wałęsa sides with the governing coalition three days per week; another three days he sides with the opposition; on the seventh day—Sunday—he rests."

Under such circumstances, one cannot claim that presidentialism in the former Soviet bloc implies the "winner-take-all" syndrome that has proved so damaging in some Latin American countries. In fact, almost all presidents in the region have found it necessary to engage in troublesome give-and-take negotiations with both government and opposition parties in parliament.

Postcommunist politics has often resembled a zero-sum game, but parliaments are as responsible for this as presidents. Some presidents indeed tried to obtain new powers or invoke emergency authority, but parliamentary cabinets were doing the same. Presidential elections elicited as much citizen participation as parliamentary races, and did nothing to elevate political extremists to power. Yeltsin's assault on the Russian parliament is the most disturbing development in the region. But even there one can argue that this confrontation and its terrible climax were in a way provoked by the reckless behavior of a faction within the parliament itself.

This may sound like a presentation of the case for presidentialism, but it is not. The institution of the presidency has created a syndrome of "dual legitimacy" that time and again has produced political deadlock. The mutual independence of presidents and parliaments has tended to fuel rivalries detrimental to both institutions. Presidents have done much to frustrate the development of healthy party systems in the region, and have also failed to provide the most applauded benefit of presidentialism: strong and effective government. Presidential policies have been remarkably indecisive, chaotic, and confusing. Consider President Yeltsin's zig-zag policy on such crucial issues as the shape of the constitution, the nature of the Russian federation, or the pace and scale of marketization; or President Leonid Kravchuk's everchanging stance on nuclear weapons, Ukraine's membership in the Commonwealth of Independent States, or monetary reform.

The Need for Clear Rules

What then is the best institutional solution for the new postcommunist democracies? The answer is twofold: adopt clear rules of the institutional game, and respect the separation of powers principle. The problem is not that a presidential or parliamentary model has been chosen, but that there is no fixed model in place. So far, both countries with presidencies and those without them have compiled mixed records. Yet it is evident that the more confusing the legal distribution of competencies, the more heated and destructive will be the ensuing institutional struggle. It is no accident that Russia has experienced the most damaging institutional conflict: both parliament and the president had overlapping competencies, resulting in parallel decision making and governmental paralysis. For most of 1993, the two institutions annulled each other's decisions whenever possible. On 20 July 1993, for example, the Congress of People's Deputies passed several resolutions cancelling President Yeltsin's edicts aimed at speeding up privatization. On July 28, Yeltsin signed an edict guaranteeing "additional measures to protect Russian citizens' right to participate in privatization." On August 6, parliament voted to block it. Four days later, the president issued yet another edict making officials at all levels of government personally responsible for meeting privatization targets. Under such circumstances, one can hardly talk about any effective form of government. (Unfortunately, the new Russian Constitution also lacks clear procedures for resolving conflicts between parliamentary laws and presidential edicts.)

Institutional confusion in Ukraine and the problems resulting from that confusion have been nearly as grave as in Russia. A three-cornered power struggle pitting the president, the premier, and the parliament against one another made proper decision making of any kind almost impossible. By the summer of 1993, Ukraine found itself on the brink of economic catastrophe and in worrisome international isolation.

Romania and Bulgaria, too, developed alarmingly confrontational political cultures, and yet the institutional struggles that they experienced were much less intense. Credit for this is due primarily to their respective constitutions (each passed in 1991), which clarified the roles of major institutional actors. Poland also managed to quell institutional instability with the adoption of an interim constitution in the autumn of 1992.

There is evidence, then, for the proposition that constitutions, if intelligently crafted and adopted in timely fashion, can be effective in channeling and constraining the struggle for power among various institutions, and in increasing the predictability of their behavior. But how to adopt new constitutions amid the heat of political battle when no proposed draft can be free of the charge of taint? If powerholders exercise self-restraint, the adoption of a new constitution is less than urgent; if they do not, how can paper barriers constrain them? What sort of rules should guide the preparation and adoption of new constitutions? Can old and illegitimate communist constitutions offer legitimate guidance for new democratic constitutions? And how can new constitutions endure when circumstances continue to change rapidly? Can divided and inexperienced elites produce anything more than an incomplete, ineffective, and ephemeral document? These questions may well discourage even the most committed constitutional reformers. Nevertheless, there are several reasons for hope.

First, new constitutions need not be comprehensive; indeed, at the beginning they can be merely interim. This might create some complications at a later stage, but it can greatly facilitate the initial process of constitution-making. What is required at the early democratic stage is a constitution that deals mainly with the machinery of government rather than the rights of individual citizens. The codification and protection of human rights is of course important, especially after several decades of communist oppression—which is why democratic constitutionalists in the region have devoted most of their time to finding ways of preventing new forms of tyranny. Yet as Stephen Holmes has rightly argued:

> The Tocquevillean fixation on the tyranny of the majority is not necessarily helpful in the process of democratization. The most difficult problem facing the countries of Eastern Europe today is the creation of a government that can pursue effective reforms while retaining public confidence and remaining democratically accountable. . . . Negative constitutionalism is very likely to produce a new autocracy in the not-so-long run.[4]

Besides, as the experience of Poland and the Czech Republic indicates, rights can be dealt with in a separate bill or charter of rights and freedoms.

An interim (as opposed to a permanent) constitution facilitates changes required by rapidly shifting circumstances, and eases the way for compromise on specific constitutional arrangements. After all, for the parties involved in an institutional conflict, even the most uncomfortable arrangements are easier to swallow if they are not made irreversible. Of course, constitutions should be more durable than ordinary laws, as they are supposed to be the "chains with which men bind themselves in their sane moments that they may not die by a suicidal hand in the day of their frenzy."[5] But the degree to which constitutional changes are made difficult may differ from case to case, and it is wise to consider more flexible rules for amending a constitution at the early democratic stage. In Slovakia, for instance, three-fifths of parliament can amend the 1993 Constitution, making it one of the most easily alterable in the world. In Russia, on the other hand, amending the new Constitution is practically impossible, which may have disastrous consequences if the office of president is taken over by an extremist such as Vladimir Zhirinovsky.

"...for the parties involved in an institutional conflict, even the most uncomfortable arrangements are easier to swallow if they are not made irreversible."

Another argument holds that new constitutions in Eastern Europe should be created on the basis of postcommunist political compromises rather than on the basis of predemocratic legal arrangements. In other words, constitution making is not "the hour of the lawyers," as Ralf Dahrendorf suggests, but the hour of politicians prepared to make deals with one another.[6] In most countries in the region, there emerged a strong and curious tendency to mold the new constitution in strict conformity to the old communist constitution: a true irony considering that the latter had never been taken seriously. If such a method of proceeding reflected the results of "roundtable agreements" between the communist elites and the representatives of the opposition, the procedure could work (as it did in Bulgaria). But in the CSFR, Slovak nationalists used the old communist Constitution to prevent any workable constitutional arrangement in 1991-92, thus contributing to the collapse of the federation. The Slovak National Council, formally created by constitutional amendment in 1968 but never even convened before the Velvet Revolution of 1989, was able to block constitutional changes that had majority backing in both houses of the Federal Assembly.

Resistance to abandoning old communist procedures for constitutional change was also a major obstacle to the adoption of new constitutions in the countries that needed them the most: Russia, Belarus, and Ukraine. Russia's now-defunct Congress of People's Deputies was particularly stubborn in sticking to the old Brezhnev-era Constitution, even though it was amended (often with questionable legality) more than 300 times in recent years. In such a situation, one could not but agree with Yeltsin advisor Sergei Shahkrai's statement that "all pathways for adopting a new constitution lie beyond the limits of current legality [in Russia]."[7] President Yeltsin's "constitutional coup" of September 1993 was thus a logical if not a necessary step.

Seeking a Constitutional Compromise

What can lay the basis for a workable constitutional compromise? Successful transitions to democracy in other regions indicate three helpful steps. First, political actors must realize that the ongoing institutional power struggle is suicidal for all of them and that almost any sort of constitutional settlement beats total anarchy. Of course, this is easier said than done, but democracy in such countries as Belarus, Russia, or Ukraine can hardly be consolidated without an equivalent of the Spanish Pacts of Moncloa, the 1977 multiparty agreements that outlined the constitutional framework for post-Franco democracy. In the Russian case, this may well require broad consensus if a new and more balanced constitution is to be passed in the future.

Second, major political actors would have to build the separation of powers and appropriate checks and balances into their constitutional proposals. An insistence on untrammeled institutional predominance for either the parliament or the president will put compromise out of reach. The rival constitutional solutions pushed by President Boris Yeltsin and Supreme Soviet Chairman Ruslan Khasbulatov in Russia had no clear separation of powers or effective checks and balances, and thus precluded any workable compromise from the very start. The former's early 1993 constitutional proposal envisaged an unprecedented increase in presidential powers at the same time that it deprived the lower house of parliament of any control over ministerial appointments and dismissals. Khasbulatov, on the other hand, called for the establishment of a new kind of "soviet" rule in Russia, with executive structures completely subordinated to local soviets, and local soviets subordinated in turn to the Presidium of the Supreme Soviet in Moscow. The constitutional draft proposed in Belarus in the spring of 1993 also envisaged the dominance of the president over the parliament and judiciary, thus inviting a version of the constitutional crisis that wracked Russia later that year.

Checks and balances are needed not only in the new constitution itself, but also in the process that produces it. Ideally, the writing and adoption of the constitution should be the task of a special constituent assembly. As Jon Elster observes:

> A main task of a constituent assembly is to strike the proper balance of power between the legislative and the executive branches of government. To assign that task to an assembly that also serves as a legislative body would be to ask it to act as judge in its own case.[8]

The Bulgarian case confirms that an ordinary parliament acting as a constituent assembly tends to grant itself too much power. Only in Belarus did the parliament propose a significant extension of executive powers at its own expense, but one should keep in mind that about seven of every ten Belorusian MPs also work in executive organs. In Russia, on the other hand, the elimination of parliament after the violence of 3-4 October 1993 allowed President Yeltsin to grant himself extensive powers in the constitutional draft that he proposed in the aftermath of the crisis, and which was endorsed by referendum two months later.

Of course, constitutions are not elixirs for all institutional problems; good laws can never substitute for good politics. Nor should one assume that any new constitution will do: a partisan and unbalanced constitution may only further destabilize the political scene. Nor is it realistic to expect that new constitutions, even if adopted smoothly, can remain in place for many years. The speed with which Bulgaria and Romania adopted new constitutions, for instance, may imply that these will be acceptable only in the short term. Yet despite all that, one can hardly envision the ongoing institutional power struggles being curbed without the adoption of new constitutions that specify the roles of various institutions, establish clear rules of institutional bargaining, and set up a workable balance of political power.

Moreover, a troublesome and halting constitution-making process does not imply a bad outcome. A journey marked by fits and starts may still end at the desired destination. Finally and most importantly, the experience of the postcommunist countries during these first years of democratic consolidation has clearly shown that new constitutions generally have a stabilizing effect, while the lack of them has more often than not been a source of instability. Thus the new Russian Constitution, imperfect as it may be, is an asset to Russia's very fragile democracy.

Institutional power struggles form a major obstacle to democratic consolidation, one that will not just disappear by itself over time. On the eve of the democratic transformation, Ralf Dahrendorf voiced the hope that creating new institutional frameworks in constitutional form would be the least time-consuming stage of democratization, taking about six months rather than six years (economic transformation) or six decades (creating a mature civil society).[9] Yet for most countries in the region, restructuring the existing institutions has proved to be a formidable and drawn-out task; in some countries, it has even led to virtual chaos. What can be done to improve the situation? Should democratic crafters focus on actual constitutional choices or on the processes by which they are made? Our conclusion is that the constitution-making process is the more important, and this largely regardless of the concrete constitutional choices made. Arguments for or against a presidential or parliamentary system are inconclusive, while the need for some kind of stable democratic constitutional order is urgent.

NOTES

1. See especially Arend Lijphart, "Constitutional Choices for New Democracies," *Journal of Democracy* 2 (Winter 1991): 72. (Reprinted in Larry Diamond and Marc F. Plattner, eds., *The Global Resurgence of Democracy* [Baltimore and London: Johns Hopkins University Press, 1993], 146).

2. As in the case of West Germany, East European electoral laws manifest hybrids of representational and majoritarian patterns. For a detailed analysis of East European electoral systems, see James McGregor, "How Electoral Laws Shape Eastern Europe's Parliaments," *RFE/RL Research Report*, 22 January 1993, 11-18; or Krzysztof Jasiewicz, "Structures of Representation," in Stephen White, Judy Batt, and Paul G. Lewis, eds., *Developments in East European Politics* (London: Macmillan, 1993), 140-46.

3. See Giovanni Sartori, "The Influence of Electoral Systems: Faulty Laws or Faulty Method?" in Bernard Grofman and Arend Lijphart, eds., *Electoral Laws and Their Political Consequences* (New York: Agathon Press, 1986), 54-55.

4. Stephen Holmes, "Back to the Drawing Board," *East European Constitutional Review* 2 (Winter 1993): 23-24.

5. John Potter Stockton, quoted in J.E. Finn, *Constitutions in Crisis* (Oxford: Oxford University Press, 1991), 5. See also Stephen Holmes, "Precommitment and the Paradox of Democracy," in Jon Elster and Rune Slagstad, eds., *Constitutionalism and Democracy* (Cambridge: Cambridge University Press, 1988), 195-240.

6. Ralf Dahrendorf, *Reflections on the Revolution in Europe* (London: Chatto and Windus, 1990), 79.

7. Sergei Shakhrai quoted in *East European Constitutional Review* 2 (Spring 1993): 22.

8. Jon Elster, "Constitution-Making in Eastern Europe: Rebuilding the Boat in the Open Sea" *Public Administration* 71 (Spring-Summer 1993): 26.

9. Dahrendorf, op. cit., 93.

III.
Civil Society and Democracy

19. TOWARD DEMOCRATIC CONSOLIDATION

Larry Diamond

***Larry Diamond** is coeditor of the* Journal of Democracy, *codirector of the International Forum for Democratic Studies, and a senior research fellow at the Hoover Institution. Among his recent edited works on democracy are* Political Culture and Democracy in Developing Countries *(1993) and (with Marc F. Plattner)* Nationalism, Ethnic Conflict, and Democracy *(forthcoming, 1994).*

In this third wave of global democratization, no phenomenon has more vividly captured the imagination of democratic scholars, observers, and activists alike than "civil society." What could be more moving than the stories of brave bands of students, writers, artists, pastors, teachers, laborers, and mothers challenging the duplicity, corruption, and brutal domination of authoritarian states? Could any sight be more awe-inspiring to democrats than the one they saw in Manila in 1986, when hundreds of thousands of organized and peaceful citizens surged into the streets to reclaim their stolen election and force Ferdinand Marcos out through nonviolent "people power"?

In fact, however, the overthrow of authoritarian regimes through popularly based and massively mobilized democratic opposition has not been the norm. Most democratic transitions have been protracted and negotiated (if not largely controlled from above by the exiting authoritarians). Yet even in such negotiated and controlled transitions, the stimulus for democratization, and particularly the pressure to complete the process, have typically come from the "resurrection of civil society," the restructuring of public space, and the mobilization of all manner of independent groups and grassroots movements.[1]

If the renewed interest in civil society can trace its theoretical origins to Alexis de Tocqueville, it seems emotionally and spiritually indebted to Jean-Jacques Rousseau for its romanticization of "the people" as a force for collective good, rising up to assert the democratic will against a narrow and evil autocracy. Such images of popular mobilization suffuse contemporary thinking about democratic change throughout Asia, Latin America, Eastern Europe, and Africa—and not without reason.

In South Korea, Taiwan, Chile, Poland, China, Czechoslovakia, South Africa, Nigeria, and Benin (to give only a partial list), extensive mobilization of civil society was a crucial source of pressure for democratic change. Citizens pressed their challenge to autocracy not merely as individuals, but as members of student movements, churches, professional associations, women's groups, trade unions, human rights organizations, producer groups, the press, civic associations, and the like.

It is now clear that to comprehend democratic change around the world, one must study civil society. Yet such study often provides a one-dimensional and dangerously misleading view. Understanding civil society's role in the construction of democracy requires more complex conceptualization and nuanced theory. The simplistic antinomy between state and civil society, locked in a zero-sum struggle, will not do. We need to specify more precisely what civil society is and is not, and to identify its wide variations in form and character. We need to comprehend not only the multiple ways it can serve democracy, but also the tensions and contradictions it generates and may encompass. We need to think about the features of civil society that are most likely to serve the development and consolidation of democracy. And, not least, we need to form a more realistic picture of the limits of civil society's potential contributions to democracy, and thus of the relative emphasis that democrats should place on building civil society among the various challenges of democratic consolidation.

What Civil Society Is and Is Not

Civil society is conceived here as the *realm of organized social life that is voluntary, self-generating, (largely) self-supporting, autonomous from the state, and bound by a legal order or set of shared rules.* It is distinct from "society" in general in that it involves citizens *acting collectively in a public sphere* to express their interests, passions, and ideas, exchange information, achieve mutual goals, make demands on the state, and hold state officials accountable. Civil society is an intermediary entity, standing between the private sphere and the state. Thus it excludes individual and family life, inward-looking group activity (e.g., for recreation, entertainment, or spirituality), the profit-making enterprise of individual business firms, and political efforts to take control of the state. Actors in civil society need the protection of an institutionalized legal order to guard their autonomy and freedom of action. Thus civil society not only restricts state power but legitimates state authority when that authority is based on the rule of law. When the state itself is lawless and contemptuous of individual and group autonomy, civil society may still exist (albeit in tentative or battered form) if its constituent elements operate by some set of shared rules (which, for example, eschew violence and respect pluralism). This is the irreducible condition of its "civil" dimension.[2]

Civil society encompasses a vast array of organizations, formal and informal. These include groups that are: 1) *economic* (productive and commercial associations and networks); 2) *cultural* (religious, ethnic, communal, and other institutions and associations that defend collective rights, values, faiths, beliefs, and symbols); 3) *informational and educational* (devoted to the production and dissemination—whether for profit or not—of public knowledge, ideas, news, and information); 4) *interest-based* (designed to advance or defend the common functional or material interests of their members, whether workers, veterans, pensioners, professionals, or the like); 5) *developmental* (organizations that combine individual resources to improve the infrastructure, institutions, and quality of life of the community); 6) *issue-oriented* (movements for environmental protection, women's rights, land reform, or consumer protection); and 7) *civic* (seeking in nonpartisan fashion to improve the political system and make it more democratic through human rights monitoring, voter education and mobilization, poll-watching, anticorruption efforts, and so on).

In addition, civil society encompasses "the ideological marketplace" and the flow of information and ideas. This includes not only independent mass media but also institutions belonging to the broader field of autonomous cultural and intellectual activity—universities, think tanks, publishing houses, theaters, film production companies, and artistic networks.

From the above, it should be clear that civil society is not some mere residual category, synonymous with "society" or with everything that is not the state or the formal political system. Beyond being voluntary, self-generating, autonomous, and rule-abiding, the organizations of civil society are distinct from other social groups in several respects. First, as emphasized above, civil society is concerned with *public* rather than private ends. Second, civil society *relates to the state* in some way but does not aim to win formal power or office in the state. Rather, civil society organizations seek from the state concessions, benefits, policy changes, relief, redress, or accountability. Civic organizations and social movements that try to change the nature of the state may still qualify as parts of civil society, if their efforts stem from concern for the public good and not from a desire to capture state power for the group per se. Thus peaceful movements for democratic transition typically spring from civil society.

A third distinguishing mark is that civil society encompasses *pluralism* and diversity. To the extent that an organization—such as a religious fundamentalist, ethnic chauvinist, revolutionary, or millenarian movement—seeks to monopolize a functional or political space in society, claiming that it represents the only legitimate path, it contradicts the pluralistic and market-oriented nature of civil society. Related to this is a fourth distinction, *partialness*, signifying that no group in civil society seeks to represent the whole of a person's or a community's interests. Rather, different groups represent different interests.

Civil society is distinct and autonomous not only from the state and society at large but also from a fourth arena of social action, *political society* (meaning, in essence, the party system). Organizations and networks in civil society may form alliances with parties, but if they become captured by parties, or hegemonic within them, they thereby move their primary locus of activity to political society and lose much of their ability to perform certain unique mediating and democracy-building functions. I want now to examine these functions more closely.

The Democratic Functions of Civil Society

The first and most basic democratic function of civil society is to provide "the basis for the limitation of state power, hence for the control of the state by society, and hence for democratic political institutions as the most effective means of exercising that control."[3] This function has two dimensions: to monitor and restrain the exercise of power by democratic states, and to democratize authoritarian states. Mobilizing civil society is a major means of exposing the abuses and undermining the legitimacy of undemocratic regimes. This is the function, performed so dramatically in so many democratic transitions over the past two decades, that has catapulted civil society to the forefront of thinking about democracy. Yet this thinking revives the eighteenth-century idea of civil society as *in opposition* to the state and, as I will show, has its dangers if taken too far.[4]

Civil society is also a vital instrument for containing the power of democratic governments, checking their potential abuses and violations of the law, and subjecting them to public scrutiny. Indeed, a vibrant civil society is probably more essential for consolidating and maintaining democracy than for initiating it. Few developments are more destructive to the legitimacy of new democracies than blatant and pervasive political corruption, particularly during periods of painful economic restructuring when many groups and individuals are asked to sustain great hardships. New democracies, following long periods of arbitrary and statist rule, lack the legal and bureaucratic means to contain corruption at the outset. Without a free, robust, and inquisitive press and civic groups to press for institutional reform, corruption is likely to flourish.

Second, a rich associational life supplements the role of political parties in stimulating political participation, increasing the political efficacy and skill of democratic citizens, and promoting an appreciation of the obligations as well as the rights of democratic citizenship. For too many Americans (barely half of whom vote in presidential elections), this now seems merely a quaint homily. A century and a half ago, however, the voluntary participation of citizens in all manner of associations outside the state struck Tocqueville as a pillar of democratic culture and economic vitality in the young United States. Voluntary "associations may therefore be considered as large free schools, where all the members of the community go to learn the general theory of association," he wrote.[5]

"The democratization of local government goes hand in hand with the development of civil society."

Civil society can also be a crucial arena for the development of other democratic attributes, such as tolerance, moderation, a willingness to compromise, and a respect for opposing viewpoints. These values and norms become most stable when they emerge through experience, and organizational participation in civil society provides important practice in political advocacy and contestation. In addition, many civic organizations (such as Conciencia, a network of women's organizations that began in Argentina and has since spread to 14 other Latin American countries) are working directly in the schools and among groups of adult citizens to develop these elements of democratic culture through interactive programs that demonstrate the dynamics of reaching consensus in a group, the possibility for respectful debate between competing viewpoints, and the means by which people can cooperate to solve the problems of their own communities.[6]

A fourth way in which civil society may serve democracy is by creating channels other than political parties for the articulation, aggregation, and representation of interests. This function is particularly important for providing traditionally excluded groups—such as women and racial or ethnic minorities—access to power that has been denied them in the "upper institutional echelons" of formal politics. Even where (as in South America) women have played, through various movements and organizations, prominent roles in mobilizing against authoritarian rule, democratic politics and governance after the transition have typically reverted to previous exclusionary patterns. In Eastern Europe, there are many signs of deterioration in the political and social status of women after the transition. Only with sustained, organized pressure from below, in civil society, can political and social equality be advanced, and the quality, responsiveness, and legitimacy of democracy thus be deepened.[7]

Civil society provides an especially strong foundation for democracy when it generates opportunities for participation and influence at all levels of governance, not least the local level. For it is at the local level that the historically marginalized are most likely to be able to affect public policy and to develop a sense of efficacy as well as actual political skills. The democratization of local government thus goes hand in hand with the development of civil society as an important condition for the deepening of democracy and the "transition from clientelism to citizenship" in Latin America, as well as elsewhere in the developing and postcommunist worlds.[8]

Fifth, a richly pluralistic civil society, particularly in a relatively developed economy, will tend to generate a wide range of interests that may cross-cut, and so mitigate, the principal polarities of political conflict. As new class-based organizations and issue-oriented movements arise, they draw together new constituencies that cut across longstanding regional, religious, ethnic, or partisan cleavages. In toppling communist (and other) dictatorships and mobilizing for democracy, these new formations may generate a modern type of citizenship that transcends historic divisions and contains the resurgence of narrow nationalist impulses. To the extent that individuals have multiple interests and join a wide variety of organizations to pursue and advance those interests, they will be more likely to associate with different types of people who have divergent political interests and opinions. These attitudinal cross-pressures will tend to soften the militancy of their own views, generate a more expansive and sophisticated political outlook, and so encourage tolerance for differences and a greater readiness to compromise.

A sixth function of a democratic civil society is recruiting and training new political leaders. In a few cases, this is a deliberate purpose of civic organizations. The Evelio B. Javier Foundation in the Philippines, for instance, offers training programs on a nonpartisan basis to local and state elected officials and candidates, emphasizing not only technical and administrative skills but normative standards of public accountability and transparency.[9] More often, recruitment and training are merely a long-term byproduct of the successful functioning of civil society organizations as their leaders and activists gain skills and self-confidence that qualify them well for service in government and party politics. They learn how to organize and motivate people, debate issues, raise and account for funds, craft budgets, publicize programs, administer staffs, canvass for support, negotiate agreements, and build coalitions. At the same time, their work on behalf of their constituency, or of what they see to be the public interest, and their articulation of clear and compelling policy alternatives, may gain for them a wider political following. Interest groups, social movements, and community efforts of various kinds may therefore train, toughen, and thrust into public notice a richer (and more representative) array of potential new political leaders than might otherwise be recruited by political parties. Because of the traditional dominance by men of the corridors of power, civil society is a particularly important base for the training and recruitment of women (and members of other marginalized groups) into positions of formal political power. Where the recruitment of new political leaders within the established political parties has become narrow or stagnant, this function of civil society may play a crucial role in revitalizing democracy and renewing its legitimacy.

Seventh, many civic organizations have explicit democracy-building purposes that go beyond leadership training. Nonpartisan election-monitoring efforts have been critical in deterring fraud, enhancing voter confidence, affirming the legitimacy of the result, or in some cases (as in the Philippines in 1986 and Panama in 1989) demonstrating an opposition victory despite government fraud. This function is particularly crucial in founding elections like those which initiated democracy in Chile, Nicaragua, Bulgaria, Zambia, and South Africa. Democracy institutes and think tanks are working in a number of countries to reform the electoral system, democratize political parties, decentralize and open up government, strengthen the legislature, and enhance governmental accountability. And even after the transition, human rights organizations continue to play a vital role in the pursuit of judicial and legal reform, improved prison conditions, and greater institutionalized respect for individual liberties and minority rights.

Eighth, a vigorous civil society widely disseminates information, thus aiding citizens in the collective pursuit and defense of their interests and values. While civil society groups may sometimes prevail temporarily by dint of raw numbers (e.g., in strikes and demonstrations), they generally cannot be effective in contesting government policies or defending their interests unless they are well-informed. This is strikingly true in debates over military and national security policy, where civilians in developing countries have generally been woefully lacking in even the most elementary knowledge. A free press is only one vehicle for providing the public with a wealth of news and alternative perspectives. Independent organizations may also give citizens hard-won information about government activities that does not depend on what government *says* it is doing. This is a vital technique of human rights organizations: by contradicting the official story, they make it more difficult to cover up repression and abuses of power.

The spread of new information and ideas is essential to the achievement of economic reform in a democracy, and this is a ninth function that civil society can play. While economic stabilization policies typically must be implemented quickly, forcefully, and unilaterally by elected executives in crisis situations, more structural economic reforms—privatization, trade and financial liberalization—appear to be more sustainable and far-reaching (or in many postcommunist countries, only feasible) when they are pursued through the democratic process.

Successful economic reform requires the support of political coalitions in society and the legislature. Such coalitions are not spontaneous; they must be fashioned. Here the problem is not so much the scale, autonomy, and resources of civil society as it is their distribution across interests. Old, established interests that stand to lose from reform tend to be organized into formations like state-sector trade unions and networks that tie the managers of state enterprises or owners of favored industries to ruling party bosses. These are precisely the interests that stand to lose from economic reforms that close down inefficient industries, reduce state intervention, and open the economy to greater domestic and international competition. The newer and more diffuse interests that stand to gain from reform—for example, farmers, small-scale entrepreneurs, and consumers—tend to be weakly organized and poorly informed about how new policies will ultimately affect them. In Asia, Latin America, and Eastern Europe, new actors in civil society—such as economic-policy think tanks, chambers of commerce, and economically literate journalists, commentators, and television producers—are beginning to overcome the barriers to information and organization, mobilizing support for (and neutralizing resistance to) reform policies.

Finally, there is a tenth function of civil society—to which I have already referred—that derives from the success of the above nine. "Freedom of association," Tocqueville mused, may, "after having agitated society for some time, . . . strengthen the state in the end."[10] By enhancing the accountability, responsiveness, inclusiveness, effectiveness, and hence legitimacy of the political system, a vigorous civil society gives citizens respect for the state and positive engagement with it. In the end, this improves the ability of the state to govern, and to command voluntary obedience from its citizens. In addition, a rich associational life can do more than just multiply demands on the state; it may also multiply the capacities of groups to improve their own welfare, independently of the state. Effective grassroots development efforts may thus help to relieve the burden of expectations fixed on the state, and so lower the stakes of politics, especially at the national level.

Features of a Democratic Civil Society

Not all civil societies and civil society organizations have the same potential to perform the democracy-building functions cited above. Their ability to do so depends on several features of their internal structure and character.

One concerns the goals and methods of groups in civil society. The chances to develop stable democracy improve significantly if civil society does not contain maximalist, uncompromising interest groups or groups with antidemocratic goals and methods. To the extent that a group seeks to conquer the state or other competitors, or rejects the rule of law and the authority of the democratic state, it is not a component of civil society at all, but it may nevertheless do much damage to democratic aspirations. Powerful, militant interest groups pull parties toward populist and extreme political promises, polarizing the party system, and are more likely to bring down state repression that may have a broad and indiscriminate character, weakening or radicalizing the more democratic elements of civil society.

A second important feature of civil society is its level of organizational institutionalization. As with political parties, institutionalized interest groups contribute to the stability, predictability, and governability of a democratic regime. Where interests are organized in a structured, stable manner, bargaining and the growth of cooperative networks are facilitated. Social forces do not face the continual cost of setting up new structures. And if the organization expects to continue to operate in the society over a sustained period of time, its leaders will have more reason to be accountable and responsive to their constituency, and may take a longer-range view of the group's interests and policy goals, rather than seeking to maximize short-term benefits in an uncompromising manner.

Third, the internally democratic character of civil society itself affects the degree to which it can socialize participants into democratic—or undemocratic—forms of behavior. If the groups and organizations that make up civil society are to function as "large free schools" for democracy, they must function democratically in their internal processes of decision-making and leadership selection. Constitutionalism, representation, transparency, accountability, and rotation of elected leaders within autonomous associations will greatly enhance the ability of these associations to inculcate such democratic values and practices in their members.

Fourth, the more pluralistic civil society can become without fragmenting, the more democracy will benefit. Some degree of pluralism is necessary by definition for civil society. Pluralism helps groups in civil society survive, and encourages them to learn to cooperate and negotiate with one another. Pluralism within a given sector, like labor or human rights, has a number of additional beneficial effects. For one, it makes that sector less vulnerable (though at the possible cost of weakening its bargaining power); the loss or repression of one organization does not mean the end of all organized representation. Competition can also help to ensure accountability and representativeness by giving members the ability to bolt to other organizations if their own does not perform.

Finally, civil society serves democracy best when it is dense, affording individuals opportunities to participate in multiple associations and informal networks at multiple levels of society. The more associations there are in civil society, the more likely it is that they will develop specialized agendas and purposes that do not seek to swallow the lives of their members in one all-encompassing organizational framework. Multiple memberships also tend to reflect and reinforce cross-cutting patterns of cleavage.

Some Important Caveats

To the above list of democratic functions of civil society we must add some important caveats. To begin with, associations and mass media can perform their democracy-building roles only if they have at least some autonomy from the state in their financing, operations, and legal standing. To be sure, there are markedly different ways of organizing the representation of interests in a democracy. Pluralist systems encompass "multiple, voluntary, competitive, nonhierarchically ordered and self-determined . . . [interest associations] which are not specially licensed, recognized, subsidized, created or otherwise controlled . . . by the state." Corporatist systems, by contrast, have "singular, noncompetitive, hierarchically ordered, sectorally compartmentalized, interest associations exercising representational monopolies and accepting (de jure or de facto) governmentally imposed limitations on the type of leaders they elect and on the scope and intensity of demands they routinely make upon the state."[11] A number of northern European countries have operated a corporatist system of interest representation while functioning successfully as democracies (at times even better, economically and politically, than their pluralist counterparts). Although corporatist arrangements are eroding in many established democracies, important differences remain in the degree to which interest groups are competitive, pluralistic, compartmentalized, hierarchically ordered, and so on.

While corporatist-style pacts or contracts between the state and peak interest associations may make for stable macroeconomic management, corporatist arrangements pose a serious threat to democracy in transitional or newly emerging constitutional regimes. The risk appears greatest in countries with a history of authoritarian *state corporatism*—such as Mexico, Egypt, and Indonesia—where the state has created, organized, licensed, funded, subordinated, and controlled "interest" groups (and also most of the mass media that it does not officially own and control), with a view to cooptation, repression, and domination rather than ordered bargaining. By contrast, the transition to a democratic form of corporatism "seems to depend very much on a liberal-pluralist past," which most developing and postcommunist states lack.[12] A low level of economic development or the absence of a fully functioning market economy increases the danger that corporatism will stifle civil society even under a formally democratic framework, because there are fewer autonomous resources and organized interests in society.

By coopting, preempting, or constraining the most serious sources of potential challenge to its domination (and thus minimizing the amount of actual repression that has to be employed), a state-corporatist regime may purchase a longer lease on authoritarian life. Such regimes, however, eventually come under pressure from social, economic, and demographic forces. Successful socioeconomic development, as in Mexico and Indonesia, produces a profusion of authentic civil society groups that demand political freedom under law. Alternatively, social and economic decay, along with massive political corruption, weakens the hold of the authoritarian corporatist state, undermines the legitimacy of its sponsored associations, and may give rise to revolutionary movements like the Islamic fundamentalist fronts in Egypt and Algeria, which promise popular redemption through a new form of state hegemony.

Societal autonomy can go too far, however, even for the purposes of democracy. The need for *limits* on autonomy is a second caveat; paired with the first, it creates a major tension in democratic development. A hyperactive, confrontational, and relentlessly rent-seeking civil society can overwhelm a weak, penetrated state with the diversity and magnitude of its demands, leaving little in the way of a truly "public" sector concerned with the overall welfare of society. The state itself must have sufficient autonomy, legitimacy, capacity, and support to mediate among the various interest groups and balance their claims. This is a particularly pressing dilemma for new democracies seeking to implement much-needed economic reforms in the face of stiff opposition from trade unions, pensioners, and the state-protected bourgeoisie, which is why countervailing forces in civil society must be educated and mobilized, as I have argued above.

In many new democracies there is a deeper problem, stemming from the origins of civil society in profoundly angry, risky, and even anomic protest against a decadent, abusive state. This problem is what the Cameroonian economist Célestin Monga calls the "civic deficit":

> Thirty years of authoritarian rule have forged a concept of indiscipline as a method of popular resistance. In order to survive and resist laws and rules judged to be antiquated, people have had to resort to the treasury of their imagination. Given that life is one long fight against the state, the collective imagination has gradually conspired to craftily defy everything which symbolizes public authority.[13]

In many respects, a similar broad cynicism, indiscipline, and alienation from state authority—indeed from politics altogether—was bred by decades of communist rule in Eastern Europe and the former Soviet Union, though it led to somewhat different (and in Poland, much more broadly organized) forms of dissidence and resistance. Some countries, like Poland, Hungary, the Czech lands, and the Baltic states, had previous civic traditions that could be recovered. These countries have generally made the most progress (though still quite partial) toward reconstructing state authority on a democratic foundation while beginning to constitute a modern, liberal-pluralist civil society. Those states where civic traditions were weakest and predatory rule greatest—Romania, Russia, the post-Soviet republics of Central Asia, and most of sub-Saharan Africa—face a far more difficult time, with civil societies still fragmented and emergent market economies still heavily outside the framework of law.

This civic deficit points to a third major caveat with respect to the positive value of civil society for democracy. Civil society must be autonomous from the state, but not alienated from it. It must be watchful but respectful of state authority. The image of a noble, vigilant, organized civil society checking at every turn the predations of a self-serving state, preserving a pure detachment from its corrupting embrace, is highly romanticized and of little use in the construction of a viable democracy.

A fourth caveat concerns the role of politics. Interest groups cannot substitute for coherent political parties with broad and relatively enduring bases of popular support. For interest groups cannot aggregate interests as broadly across social groups and political issues as political parties can. Nor can they provide the discipline necessary to form and maintain governments and pass legislation. In this respect (and not only this one), one may question the thesis that a strong civil society is strictly complementary to the political and state structures of democracy. To the extent that interest groups dominate, enervate, or crowd out political parties as conveyors and aggregators of interests, they can present a problem for democratic consolidation. To Barrington Moore's famous thesis, "No bourgeois, no democracy," we can add a corollary: "No coherent party system, no stable democracy." And in an age when the electronic media, increased mobility, and the profusion and fragmentation of discrete interests are all undermining the organizational bases for strong parties and party systems, this is something that democrats everywhere need to worry about.[14]

Democratic Consolidation

In fact, a stronger and broader generalization appears warranted: the single most important and urgent factor in the consolidation of democracy is not civil society but political institutionalization. *Consolidation* is the process by which democracy becomes so broadly and profoundly legitimate among its citizens that it is very unlikely to break down. It involves behavioral and institutional changes that normalize democratic politics and narrow its uncertainty. This normalization requires the expansion of citizen access, development of democratic citizenship and culture, broadening of leadership recruitment and training, and other functions that civil society performs. But most of all, and most urgently, it requires political institutionalization.

Despite their impressive capacity to survive years (in some cases, a decade or more) of social strife and economic instability and decline, many new democracies in Latin America, Eastern Europe, Asia, and Africa will probably break down in the medium to long run unless they can reduce their often appalling levels of poverty, inequality, and social injustice and, through market-oriented reforms, lay the basis for sustainable growth. For these and other policy challenges, not only strong parties but effective state institutions are vital. They do not guarantee wise and effective policies, but they at least ensure that government will be able to make and implement policies of some kind, rather than simply flailing about, impotent or deadlocked.

Robust political institutions are needed to accomplish economic reform under democratic conditions. Strong, well-structured executives, buttressed by experts at least somewhat insulated from the day-to-day pressures of politics, make possible the implementation of painful and disruptive reform measures. Settled and aggregative (as opposed to volatile and fragmented) party systems—in which one or two broadly based, centrist parties consistently obtain electoral majorities or near-majorities—are better positioned to resist narrow class and sectoral interests and to maintain the continuity of economic reforms across successive administrations. Effective legislatures may sometimes obstruct reforms, but if they are composed of strong, coherent parties with centrist tendencies, in the end they will do more to reconcile democracy and economic reform by providing a political base of support and some means for absorbing and mediating protests in society. Finally, autonomous, professional, and well-staffed judicial systems are indispensable for securing the rule of law.

These caveats are sobering, but they do not nullify my principal thesis. Civil society can, and typically must, play a significant role in building and consolidating democracy. Its role is not decisive or even the most important, at least initially. However, the more active, pluralistic, resourceful, institutionalized, and democratic is civil society, and the more effectively it balances the tensions in its relations with the state—between autonomy and cooperation, vigilance and loyalty, skepticism and trust, assertiveness and civility—the more likely it is that democracy will emerge and endure.

NOTES

This essay has evolved from a two-year research project on "Economy, Society, and Democracy" supported by the Agency for International Development, and from lectures and conference papers presented at the Kennedy School of Government, the Gorée Institute in Senegal, the Human Sciences Research Council in South Africa, and the Institute for a Democratic Alternative, also in South Africa. I am grateful to all those who made comments at these gatherings, as well as to Kathleen Bruhn for research assistance on an earlier draft.

1. Guillermo O'Donnell and Philippe C. Schmitter, *Transitions from Authoritarian Rule:*

Tentative Conclusions about Uncertain Democracies (Baltimore: Johns Hopkins University Press, 1986), ch. 5.

2. This conceptual formulation draws from a number of sources but has been especially influenced by Naomi Chazan. See in particular Chazan, "Africa's Democratic Challenge: Strengthening Civil Society and the State," *World Policy Journal* 9 (Spring 1992): 279-308. See also Edward Shils, "The Virtue of Civil Society," *Government and Opposition* 26 (Winter 1991): 9-10, 15-16; Peter Lewis, "Political Transition and the Dilemma of Civil Society in Africa," *Journal of International Affairs* 27 (Summer 1992): 31-54; Marcia A. Weigle and Jim Butterfield, "Civil Society in Reforming Communist Regimes: The Logic of Emergence," *Comparative Politics* 25 (October 1992): 3-4; and Philippe C. Schmitter, "Some Propositions about Civil Society and the Consolidation of Democracy" (Paper presented at a conference on "Reconfiguring State and Society," University of California, Berkeley, 22-23 April 1993).

3. Samuel P. Huntington, "Will More Countries Become Democratic?" *Political Science Quarterly* 99 (Summer 1984): 204. See also Seymour Martin Lipset, *Political Man* (Baltimore: Johns Hopkins University Press, 1981), 52.

4. Bronislaw Geremek, "Civil Society Then and Now," *Journal of Democracy* 3 (April 1992): 3-12.

5. Alexis de Tocqueville, *Democracy in America*, 2 vols. (New York: Vintage Books, 1945 [orig. publ. 1840]), 2:124.

6. María Rosa de Martini and Sofía de Pinedo, "Women and Civic Life in Argentina," *Journal of Democracy* 3 (July 1992): 138-46; and María Rosa de Martini, "Civic Participation in the Argentine Democratic Process," in Larry Diamond, ed., *The Democratic Revolution: Struggles for Freedom and Pluralism in the Developing World* (New York: Freedom House, 1992), 29-52.

7. Georgina Waylen, "Women and Democratization: Conceptualizing Gender Relations in Transition Politics," *World Politics* 46 (April 1994): 327-54. Although Waylen is correct that O'Donnell and Schmitter speak to the dangers of excessive popular mobilization during the transition, her criticism of the democracy literature as a whole for trivializing the role of civil society is unfairly overgeneralized and certainly inapplicable to work on Africa. Moreover, accepting her challenge to treat civil society as a centrally important phenomenon in democratization does not require one to accept her insistence on *defining* democracy to include economic and social rights as well as political ones.

8. Jonathan Fox, "Latin America's Emerging Local Politics," *Journal of Democracy* 5 (April 1994): 114.

9. Dette Pascual, "Organizing People Power in the Philippines," *Journal of Democracy* 1 (Winter 1990): 102-9.

10. Tocqueville, *Democracy in America*, 2:126.

11. Philippe C. Schmitter, "Still the Century of Corporatism?" in Wolfgang Streeck and Schmitter, eds., *Private Interest Government: Beyond Market and State* (Beverly Hills: Sage Publications, 1984), 96, 99-100.

12. Ibid., 126. See 102-8 for the important distinction between societal (democratic) and state corporatism.

13. Célestin Monga, "Civil Society and Democratization in Francophone Africa" (Paper delivered at Harvard University, 1994). This paper will appear in the same author's forthcoming French-language work, *Anthropologie de la colère: Société et démocratie en Afrique Noire* (Paris: L'Harmattan, 1994).

14. Juan J. Linz, "Change and Continuity in the Nature of Contemporary Democracies," in Gary Marks and Larry Diamond, eds., *Reexamining Democracy: Essays in Honor of Seymour Martin Lipset* (Newbury Park, Calif.: Sage Publications, 1992), 184-90.

20. CIVIL SOCIETY THEN AND NOW

Bronislaw Geremek

***Bronislaw Geremek**, a medieval historian who was a key advisor to Lech Wałęsa from the earliest days of Solidarity, spent over a year in prison during the period of martial law. In 1989 he was elected to parliament and became leader of Solidarity's parliamentary caucus. He currently is Chairman of the Foreign Affairs Committee in the Polish Parliament and parliamentary leader of the Union of Freedom. This article is a revised version of his keynote address at a conference on "The Idea of a Civil Society" held 21–23 November 1991 at the National Humanities Center in Research Triangle Park, North Carolina.*

It is an old epistemological truth that an entomologist can write about ants without having been one. In presuming to speak on the topic of civil society, I face a completely different problem, for I wonder whether my own experience of having been an "ant," as it were, hinders reflection upon the lives of ants and thus bars me from properly executing the "entomologist's" role. Not being sure of an answer to that question, I can only declare at the outset that the following reflections come from an observer who is anything but indifferent.

The concept of civil society appeared fairly late in the annals of Central and East European resistance to communism. Its advent resulted from the realization that the state had fallen completely into the hands of the communist oligarchy, and from the conviction that society nonetheless retained the power to organize itself independently as long as it eschewed anything overtly "political" and stuck to "nonpolitical politics." The main form of resistance was the phenomenon of dissidence, which usually was of an isolated, marginal, and even self-consciously hopeless character. Yet however quixotic "dissidentism" may have seemed, it did constitute a form of public involvement that defied the communist system. Dissidents engaged in their own peculiar type of mental resistance, which typically began with a refusal to participate in falsehood, grew into a desire to bear loud witness to one's own views and conscience, and then finally drove one to political action. The scope for such action long remained extremely narrow, for communism's all-pervasive power was carefully calculated to leave as little room as possible for any kind of independent civic action.

The concept of civil society, understood as a program of resistance to communism, first appeared in Poland during the late 1970s and early 1980s, primarily in conjunction with the Solidarity movement. At long last there had appeared in the communist world an independent mass movement to contradict the ruling system. Organized as a labor union, Solidarity could boast not only ten million urban members—both workers and intellectuals—but also the support of the peasants, who made up in anticommunist intensity what they lacked in organization. Even Poland's three-million-member Communist Party could not be said to be fully outside of this movement, for one-third of its members also belonged to Solidarity—and by no means simply as fomenters of internal division. When Solidarity spoke, therefore, it could do so in the name of "We, the People."

Confronting this enormous popular movement was the power apparatus of the regime: the military, the police, and the political administration (including the Communist Party bureaucracy and the *nomenklatura*). Yet these had no legitimacy; they remained outside of societal control, but they also lacked any societal support. We in Solidarity hoped to surround this unwanted creature with something like a cocoon, gradually isolating and then marginalizing the party-state apparatus.

The naivete of this conviction was obvious, but its power could not be ignored. The simple old ethical injunction "Do not lie" had, after all, enormous political significance in widening resistance to the communist system. Moreover, the cost of such nonviolent resistance was low, while its consequences were far-reaching indeed. Even the crudest totalitarian system requires a certain amount of societal acquiescence. Such systems thrive on political passivity, but they also need a certain amount of participation, even in fictional forms such as voting in fake elections designed to foster the appearance of democratic legitimacy. Moral resistance, though seemingly hopeless against systems that are based on political and military force, functions like a grain of sand in the cogwheels of a vast but vulnerable machine. The idea of a civil society—even one that avoids overtly political activities in favor of education, the exchange of information and opinion, or the protection of the basic interests of particular groups—has enormous antitotalitarian potential.

The History of an Idea

The concept of civil society *in opposition* to the state has its roots in the eighteenth century. An important place in the thought of the

Enlightenment was occupied by the conviction that society exists prior to ruling authority, and that while ruling authority is founded on a contract, society rests on man's natural freedoms. This understanding of civil society as a community of free and equal citizens—as manifested, for example, in the French Declaration of the Rights of Man and Citizen in 1789—proved of immense value in struggles against despotism. Although major emphasis was placed on individual human rights, a significant role was reserved for public opinion, understood as expressing the "collective will," whose formation then becomes the goal of political activity. In this early tradition, civil society with its various guilds, associations, and parties stood opposed not so much to the state per se as to absolute monarchy. Republicanism and constitutional monarchy came to the fore as the preferred regimes for guaranteeing those natural or contractual rights on the basis of which a civil society could become a state.

Beginning in the mid-nineteenth century, Karl Marx and other socialist thinkers offered their own gloss on the relationship between society and the state. Seeing the state as an instrument of class rule and a servant of capitalism, they took as a goal the state's eventual abolition and the formation of a stateless society. In practice, however, socialism has never brought about the weakening of the state, but on the contrary has strengthened it and enormously extended its control over economic and social life. The Jacobin model of a powerful centralized state heavily influenced both the socialist parties of the nineteenth century and the communist movement of the twentieth. In communist countries, the "withering away" of the state lingered on as a rhetorical trope, but was never a serious practical possibility. The Italian Marxist Antonio Gramsci, in his prison notebooks, envisioned a "regulated" society that he thought could function smoothly without the institution of the state or any other wielder of force. In this manner, he hoped, the state might become marginal, with political life centering on a kind of positional warfare over hegemony in civil society rather than power in the state.

In both the liberal and the socialist visions of civil society, the organizing principle is some notion of human rights—and by no means only those that concern the political sphere. Social and economic rights also had their place in these visions. In keeping with this approach, there appeared trade unions, sports associations, and various types of local brotherhoods. While hopeful visions of the future fired the social imagination of the nineteenth century, the twentieth would in fact witness a dramatic deepening of the void between state and society. The state, at least in Europe, would become an omnipresent Leviathan bent on shrinking the autonomy of individual areas of life and asserting its control over even the most intimate spheres of private existence. Out of this overweening twentieth-century European state, the totalitarian systems of our time would be born.

One useful way of thinking about totalitarianism is to see it as a particularly brutal attempt to settle the conflict between the state and society by utterly subordinating the latter to the former. Totalitarian authority not only undertakes the extreme centralization of the state, but also strips citizens of their rights and conquers or destroys all those autonomous structures that normally give shape to social life. Fascism at least left a significant part of the economic sphere outside of its monopoly of power; communism lacked even that minimal restraint. In both types of totalitarian systems, the liquidation of civil society was thought necessary to guarantee the state's continued monopoly of power.

A different notion of how to resolve the state-society tension also arose around the turn of the last century. Adherents of this vision hoped for the overthrow of the state, seen as an apparatus of force, through the organization of societal resistance "from the bottom up." Organizational tasks once accomplished only with raw power and the threat of force would be solved through voluntary cooperation, thus simultaneously supplanting the state and depriving it of its very reason for being. This vision of future development would come to be known as anarchism.

Anarchism, of course, was destined to be marginalized during the twentieth century, though it has still, in one form or another, managed to haunt modern politics right up to our own day. Sometimes the anarchist impulse shows up in would-be utopias of communal life or countercultural youth movements—examples of which flowered briefly in both Europe and North America during the late 1960s—and occasionally it appears in the dismal and dangerous guise of terrorism.

Beside these anomic or violent methods for overcoming the contradiction between state and society there stands a third option that clearly respects the distinction between the one and the other. Contemporary public life evinces a troubling drift toward the politicization of all aspects of human existence; the result is an increasingly pervasive societal disgust with politics and politicians in general. In this situation, the vision of a society organizing itself becomes a guide for activities meant to hold the line against creeping overpoliticization.

Confronting Communism

Throughout all of recent history, the concept of civil society seems to have been endowed with a life of its own. It has gone through various fluctuations, certainly, but has remained continually with us, at least in thought or political imagination. It has taken on its greatest power, however, during times of direct confrontation with the communist system.

The euphoria that came from overthrowing communism and returning to the community of democratic nations furnished most of the emotional "start-up capital" for the transition period that began, for us Poles, with the elections of June 1989. Our jumping-off point was that very singular situation in which an entire people looks around and suddenly realizes that it can take charge of its own destiny by building a sense of solidarity based on commonly held convictions. This passage from individual and small-group dissidence to independent mass organizations such as the Solidarity trade union, the Solidarity farmers' union, and the Independent Students' Union was understood, not only by learned observers but by the participants themselves, to be the first flowering of a new, postcommunist civil society. The magnificent phrase "We, the People" kept popping up in underground literature and opposition rhetoric. In the Roundtable talks of 1989, one side went under the name "party-governmental," while the other side was called—and called itself—"societal." The Catholic Church, in its role as an arbitrator and moderator of the negotiations, continually employed this usage. This meant that politics had prevailed over geometry, squaring the "roundtable" to give it two opposing sides. The longstanding contradiction between Poland's communist state and its noncommunist society had at last found expression in the language of politics.

It took a decade—from Solidarity's birth in the Gdansk shipyards in August 1980, through the years of martial law and repression, to the elections of 1989—for our civil society to assert itself fully. In most of the other communist countries of Central Europe—thanks in part, perhaps, to the Polish example—the peaceful triumph of civil society seemed to occur with a stunning suddenness.

Still more remarkable was the series of events that took place in Russia during the memorable summer of 1991. The August putsch looked like a sure winner; its success seemed not only probable but simply unavoidable. Let us remember that Boris Yeltsin's call for a general strike and mass resistance at first aroused no echo. The brave crowds that took to the streets in defense of democracy in those grim early hours after the coup plotters struck appeared merely to be displaying that strain of doomed gallantry which has so often manifested itself in the history of Russia, a country where one drinks toasts to "the success of our hopeless cause."

Then everything began to change; the hopeless cause succeeded. The events of last August showed that even veteran Soviet *apparatchiki* were no longer immune to the contagion of democracy and rights—that force could lose. The "strength of the weak"—of solidarity among ordinary people—made itself felt. The events of those days and nights brought people together, freed them from fear, and added hope to determination. Careful analysts have noted that only a small part of society took part in these events. In the eye of the hurricane itself, in Moscow, hardly one-hundredth part of the people was involved. Yet those days were decisive for the whole society, for as they wore on, the awareness of a new arrangement of power was taking hold. A mass movement of resistance against unjust force was emerging, bringing with it a sense both of power and of brotherhood. That special moment still resonates, and plays a role in the politics of Russia similar to that played in Poland by memories of Solidarity at its peak of cohesiveness and moral clarity. In Poland, however, the myth of brotherhood rediscovered also went hand in hand with independent social organizations in the spheres of culture, education, information, and the professions.

I have already mentioned that the euphoria and exhilaration of the beginning provided the initial "capital" needed to meet the exigencies of Poland's democratic transition. This capital was useful during the painful period of "shock therapy" that was needed to free the economy from the crippling embrace of central planning and state ownership and to usher in free enterprise and markets. The patience and hope springing from this initial moment of joy made possible a kind of psychic amortization of the reductions in real wages and social services that shock therapy brought.

The Postcommunist Letdown

Now, however, the reality of everyday life is gaining the upper hand on the impulse of enthusiasm. Memory's influence is inevitably waning; hopes and fears about the future overshadow the glow of past achievements. After two years of reform, in Poland as in postcommunist countries generally, frustration and dejection are on the rise, and patience and hope are in short supply. Growing xenophobia and national separatism, searches for scapegoats, and animosity toward Jews, Gypsies, and other minorities are all tokens of this postcommunist letdown. There are those who say that the appearance of virulent nationalism amidst the ruins of communism in Central Europe is unavoidable. Once again, Bosnia and Herzegovina are on the front pages of the world press; once again, Sarajevo has an ominous ring. The hope that the disintegration of communism will be accompanied by rising chances for peace and order in the old communist lands is thus weakened, if not altogether dashed.

Along with the nationalist threat, we are witnessing the return of other dangers that once seemed to belong to already-closed chapters of European history. Even in the former East Germany, where the costs of economic transition are being defrayed by massive aid from Western Germany, horrifying examples of social pathology are springing up. The pain of economic reform has also affected the recent elections in Poland, where demagoguery and populism have evoked a significant, though certainly far from overwhelming, response in society.

Between an ever more prosperous and unified Western Europe and the poor, unstable postcommunist East, a civilizational gulf is widening. The nations of the European Community are in no position, however, to wall themselves off and to look down with detachment at the postcommunist turmoil that is troubling the eastern half of their continent. The destiny of Europe as a whole is intimately bound up with the East's still unresolved transition from communism to freedom. It is as if the festival lights have suddenly gone dim, and in the place of enthusiasm and rejoicing have appeared fear and perhaps even regret for the lost stability of the Cold War world.

Looking back from our present vantage point—after communism, but after the rise and fall of postcommunist euphoria as well—we veterans of that independent social movement and moral crusade called Solidarity have cause to wonder whether our hope of creating a civil society was only an illusion. I do not believe that it was. Under the oppressive conditions of the communist system, the very *idea* of a civil society had real liberating power. It helped make possible—thanks to the adamantine independence of the Catholic Church and to Solidarity—areas of genuinely independent action. Moreover, these zones of independence were, by the standards of other peoples living under communism, undoubtedly enormous. Yet there is another sense in which our hopes have been exposed as illusory, for we believed that the civil society we were forming in the midst of our struggle against communism would prove a strong buttress upon which a future democratic order could lean after the collapse of authoritarian power.

The destruction of communism and the recovery of freedom are necessary but not sufficient conditions for the birth of democracy. Democracies are built only over time, through the forming and functioning of democratic institutions; through peaceful competition among political parties; through the existence of independent means of mass communication; through successive free elections and changes of governments; and finally, through the growth of a democratic political culture. The process is one of gradual maturation, both of democracy itself and of people in the ways of democracy.

After the elections of 1989, I was among those who tried to preserve the unity of Solidarity in public life. Poland's postcommunist party system was raw and inchoate then, as it still remains at the time of this writing. New parties were springing up like mushrooms after a rainfall—in 1991 there were close to 300 of them—and the call for political pluralism was being answered with a vengeance. Yet like the citizens of most other postcommunist countries, many Poles viewed the whole phenomenon of political parties with profound unease. The idea of civil society naturally suggested an effort to maintain the national unity and civic spirit of Solidarity, so Solidarity activists created both a national civic foundation and a nationwide network of Citizens' Committees from the village level on up. We called the democratically elected parliamentary bloc representing Solidarity the Civic Caucus. We repeatedly invoked the words "civic" and "citizen" with the conviction that they were in keeping with the notion of civil society.

In retrospect, it is apparent to me that we were trying to change hard realities with mere words. The unity of honest and altruistic people in solidarity with one another was supposed to overshadow social atomization, conflicting interests, and group and individual egotism. The magic of the word "citizen," in Poland or in Czechoslovakia, came from the widespread sense that it referred less to one's subordination to the state and its laws than to one's membership in an authentic community, a community whose essence was summed up in the term "civil society."

Our search for this kind of community may be regarded as naive or even irrational, but there is no denying that it was a highly effective force against totalitarianism. The problem is that when the common enemy of totalitarianism disappears, the reason for being of such a community begins to evaporate. It is then that a fundamental choice emerges: an open society or nationalism.

A Return to Public Life

Nationalism—to the meaning of this word in Anglo-Saxon political discourse and tradition it would be appropriate to add here a negative connotation—does meet, in a certain way, the need of community. Nationalism gives a community a clear contour by appealing to ethnic ties. It treats national history not as something that provides a choice of traditions but as a kind of tribal biography, and those outside the magic circle, whether they reside within or beyond the country's borders, are viewed as enemies. Finally, nationalism exploits memories of how national feelings were stifled by the communist regime, and how they helped to cement the resistance against communism.

It is significantly more difficult to meet the need for unity—a need that is especially visible in all of the postcommunist countries during these difficult times—in the context of an open society. Democracy is not, after all, the constitutive substance of the community but the play of competing interests. It is based not on emotions but on the rationality of lawfulness, stability, and control. Freedom easily awakens passions and fascinations, but it results in democracy, if at all, only with great difficulty. I am convinced that established no less than fledgling democracies must concern themselves with developing mechanisms to engage citizens in the common enterprise of public life.

Jürgen Habermas has spoken about the self-organized spheres of public life based on solidarity and communication. He referred to them by the well-known phenomenological term *Lebenswelt* (life-world). Habermas was talking, of course, about civil society, though not in the specific (or exotic) context of resistance against communism, or of the postcommunist "transition" period. Politics in the established democracies is becoming dominated by professional expertise and large, impersonal structures or parties. The Russian word *apparatchik*, meaning a functionary with powers that do not result from elections and who is not responsible to a designated constituency, describes a type that did not disappear completely with the collapse of communism. The *apparatchik* also exists (albeit in far less malign forms) in contemporary Western democracies, and is even becoming stronger as the technology of power grows ever more complicated. As the political role of the *apparatchik* waxes, that of the citizen must wane accordingly.

In the American political system one can detect—at least from the point of view of a European observer—the functioning on a wide scale of a civil society, though the term itself is not very popular. The enormous scope of social, philanthropic, educational, cultural, and trade or professional activities takes place beyond the influence or control of federal or state administration. Foundations, associations, and self-help and neighborhood groups take on certain public obligations, making their independence from the state the basis for their existence. The fundamental question remains, however, as to what degree this directly bears upon public life or politics. American political parties, after all, fulfill the function of association only to a limited extent; first and foremost, they are structures that serve the electoral process.

In European countries the extent of autonomous societal activity varies, as does the degree of state interference in the life of the individual. The relation between the private and public spheres varies as well. It can be said, however, though with some risk of oversimplification, that a real danger is presented by the fall in interest in politics, by retreatism from public life.

There is no greater threat to democracy than indifference and passivity on the part of citizens. A monarchy or a despotism can get by with mere subjects; democratic republics cannot survive without citizens. Political parties in Western Europe are in a state of crisis. Politics is focusing increasingly on the personalities of candidates rather than on parties and their programs. Aversion to the ubiquitousness of the state and growing citizen alienation from politics have restored urgency to the question of civil society and its role in democratic civilization.

Let me return, in closing, to what I know best—the experience of Poland. It is interesting to compare how Solidarity was perceived by U.S. and West European public opinion. In America, Solidarity aroused enthusiasm and gained wide support as the only mass anticommunist movement and independent trade union behind the Iron Curtain. Europe was fascinated primarily by the spontaneous organizational power, the authenticity of involvement, and the peculiar climate of brotherhood that characterized Solidarity. One might even say that European opinion was transfixed by the vision of a civil society that Solidarity embodied during its heroic period of 1980-81.

In light of the dangers that have appeared on the horizon for Poland in particular and for Central and Eastern Europe in general, we must ask whether the idea of a civil society—however effective it was in helping to bring down communism—will turn out to be useless in the building of democracy.

I do not think that it will. Rather, the concept of civil society will retain its validity, both as an instrument of analysis and as a program of pragmatic action. Its internal content has changed, however. The civil society of 1980 was the projection into the future of a vision that rested upon an awesome emotional unity. The civil society of more than ten years later cannot and should not base itself on emotions, but on the building of carefully nurtured institutions; on the practical realization of ethical values; and on the involvement of the greatest possible numbers of people in public life. The main task now is constructing democratic mechanisms of stability, such as constitutional checks and balances; civic education in the spirit of respect for law; and the encouragement of citizen activism. Civil society does not act in opposition to the democratic state, but cooperates with it. It no longer has to be a kind of "parallel polis," but now can simply be part of the polis.

Political operatives and politicians perceive public life in terms of the technology of power and immediate results. Statesmen and philosophers want to make political strife and competition for power subject to moral principles and long-range visions. The truth, as usual, lies in the middle: what is needed is a technology of power that is not foreign either to the "ethics of conviction" or the "ethics of responsibility." In the end, a robust civil society offers the best prospects for overcoming the divergence of state and society and bringing citizens into active engagement with public life. Only under such conditions can democracy be made secure.

21. POSTCOMMUNISM AND THE PROBLEM OF TRUST

Richard Rose

Richard Rose *is professor and director of the Centre for the Study of Public Policy at the University of Strathclyde in Glasgow, Scotland, and a fellow of the British Academy. For three decades he has been conducting research on comparative public policy in democratic societies. Since 1991, in collaboration with the Paul Lazarsfeld Society in Vienna, he has been conducting surveys to monitor mass response to transformation in 15 postcommunist countries of Central and Eastern Europe and the former Soviet Union.*

Trust is a necessary condition for both civil society and democracy. The people, after all, do not rule directly, but must place their faith in representative institutions that bear responsibility for aggregating the interests and preferences of millions of individuals. Some representatives, such as elected members of parliament or congress, are officials of the state. Others, such as trade unions, business associations, churches, and universities, belong to civil society and are relatively independent of the state. Political parties are uniquely important to the functioning of democracy, furnishing two-way channels of communication between the mass of individuals and the institutions of government.

Distrust is a pervasive legacy of communist rule. Since the communist party insisted that it alone knew best how society ought to be ruled, there was no point in individuals' expressing their views through elections or through institutions organized independently of the party-state. Communist logic underwrote the totalitarian organization of society, in which all institutions were expected to participate in the collective task of building socialism. While communist societies boasted many institutions—trade unions, writers' guilds, and the like—that paralleled those found in Western societies, these bodies were merely puppets of the party-state. Individuals were compelled to join communist organizations and to make a public show of loyalty to the party and its aims. The result of this pervasive intrusion into every corner of society was massive popular distrust of institutions that repressed rather than expressed people's real views.

Substantial majorities of citizens in postcommunist regimes want democracy, but find that their societies lack a key ingredient: trustworthy institutions capable of mediating between individuals and the state. Distrust of party politics is endemic among people for whom "the party" meant exploitative *apparatchiki* and the pseudoscientific propositions of Marxism-Leninism. The systematic suppression of independent institutions over a period of nearly half a century has made it difficult for new organizations to take root. This presents an obstacle not only to the privatization of economic enterprises, but also to the popular acceptance of representative institutions, including political parties.

This is not to say that democracy necessarily requires a high level of trust in government. One need only recall the numerous instances of scandal and corruption in the world's best-established democracies to believe that suspicion of the state and its officials can be warranted. Public opinion polls in the United States and Western Europe recurringly find a significant degree of distrust in institutions of government. Yet because these societies are so well supplied with institutions competing for people's trust, the vast majority of citizens can find *some* institutions in which to place their confidence, just as they may distrust others. Relatively few individuals in the West are wholly alienated in the sense of believing themselves represented by no organization whatsoever.[1]

The persistence of distrust in postcommunist societies has done nothing to prevent people from enjoying their newfound freedom from the state, but it has stunted the growth of democracy. The new regimes of Eastern Europe are democratic in the sense that free, competitive, and regular elections are now held, but voting fails to produce representative government, for the winners do not represent established institutions. In general, the citizens of postcommunist Eastern Europe do *not* trust the parties that they vote for. The legacy of distrust is so great that, if forced to choose, a majority of East Europeans would prefer weak and ineffective government to strong government.

A Legacy of Distrust

Democracy is the process by which citizens select their governors from among competing elites. These elites, in turn, generally derive their standing from prominence in large, formal organizations that are part of civil society. Individuals may win votes purely through personal appeal, but the institutional means for holding such persons accountable are weak. Democracy, therefore, requires regular competition between organized groups, each of which seeks to convince individuals that it represents their interests and deserves their trust.

Individuals may be the starting point in the construction of a civil society, but they are not the only element. Individuals do not live in isolation. The family is the simplest and most trusted form of association. By forming friendships beyond the family, individuals voluntarily extend their network of trusted associates. Even when citizens are dissatisfied with the state of governance and of the economy, most remain satisfied with their family and friends. Acquaintances from work or leisure pursuits further extend an individual's primary group network. Within this network, an individual can decide whom to trust on the basis of extensive firsthand observation, and can in turn establish a reputation for trustworthiness.

Modern societies are much more complex than primary groups, and require a host of formal organizations to act collectively on behalf of individuals and sometimes even in the interest of society as a whole (as in the issuance of currency, the punishment of lawbreakers, or the determination of war and peace). The institutions of civil society—whether designed to make a profit or not—may be privately controlled, state-licensed or certified (as is the case with hospitals or liquor stores), partially or wholly state-funded (as is the case with defense contractors), or even state-owned (as is the case with many universities).

The organizations of civil society do not diminish democracy but complete it, creating what Robert Dahl has called the "social separation of powers."[2] They act as checks upon the emergence of too strong a state. Government cannot control wages and prices, for example, as long as corporations are free to act in the interests of their shareholders and unions are free to act in the interests of their members. Nor can government control thought, as long as universities safeguard academic freedom and the press remains independent. These institutions can also help to generate new ideas and demands for government policies.

Trustworthy organizations are especially important for the orderly transition from authoritarianism to democracy. This transition requires negotiations between the leaders of the departing regime and the leaders of the opposition, who expect to become the governors under democracy. Such negotiations can occur only if the undemocratic regime is not totalitarian, showing limited toleration toward opposition groups. An agreement regarding the transition, however, will be effective only if the bargaining elites represent real forces in political society and are trusted by those whom they claim to represent. Without this trust, and without genuine representation, the bargaining process will collapse. The period of transition from authoritarianism to democracy gives the people the opportunity to repudiate self-proclaimed leaders who arouse its mistrust.

In communist regimes, the party-state always comes first. In Vladimir Shlapentokh's words, "A Soviet-type society has a very weak civil society. Such Soviet organizations as the party, the trade unions, the

Young Communists' League and others could be regarded as pertaining to civil society, but in fact they are parts of the state apparatus."[3] The doctrine of the inquisitor in Arthur Koestler's *Darkness at Noon*—"There is no salvation outside the party"—could also be taken to mean, "There is no social organization outside the party."

"Soviet politics was horizontal politics, a constant struggle among different elites, institutions, and interests for bigger shares of the power, wealth, and prestige to be had from the state."

When Soviet troops and communist cadres entered Eastern Europe in the final stages of the Second World War, one of their first goals was to eliminate any and all organizations that might compete for authority with the communist apparatus. Politicians were exiled, imprisoned, or shot. Political parties and trade unions were dissolved or turned into communist satellite organizations. Professors who did not follow the party line found themselves dismissed. Private enterprises and business associations fell under the control of the party-state. The press, publishing houses, and broadcast outlets became mouthpieces propagating the party line. Churches were constricted through the closure of seminaries, the persecution or subversion of clergy and lay believers, and the like.

The Stalinist war on civil society was brief, for once the last institutions had been dissolved or stripped of their independence, there was virtually nothing left for the communists to fight. Willingly or not, individuals were recruited into communist organizations in early youth, and remained within the ambit of such groups all their lives. Politically aware individuals who managed to avoid membership in official organizations found themselves isolated and unable to mobilize strong opposition to the regime. The masses were kept in line through such devices as tight government control of scarce consumer goods. The *nomenklatura* system that determined people's fortunes in most walks of life made it clear to anyone with even a modicum of ambition that there was "no promotion outside the party."

The suppression of civil institutions is reflected in dissident poet Nadezhda Mandelstam's epigram: "In Russia everything always happens at the top." Soviet politics was horizontal politics, a constant struggle among different elites, institutions, and interests for bigger shares of the power, wealth, and prestige to be had from the state. The military-industrial complex is one example of such an interest. The military services, however, did not represent foot soldiers or ordinary seamen, nor did tank manufacturers seek to protect the interests of their workers. Instead, the generals, admirals, and factory managers lobbied on behalf of their own priorities—bigger budgets, larger forces, new weapons, spare parts, more machine tools, and so on. Experts on Soviet politics have argued at great length over the extent to which the existence of such competing interests made the Soviet Union a pluralistic society. There is general agreement that such competition as did exist was "bounded pluralism," contained within limits set by the party-state. These limits determined which groups could organize, and thus kept conflicts from spilling outside the party-state apparatus.

The pathologies and irrationalities of the communist system spawned an "underground" or "unofficial" network of social relations, as leaders of major institutions regularly violated formal party precepts in order to get things done. Rules could be violated in order to meet the targets set by the planners of the command economy, or evaded for the sake of self-interest. Of course, every political system has back channels or informal procedures routinely employed to take care of otherwise difficult tasks. The communist system was distinctive, however, in pressing its claims to societal control so far that these channels could never be officially acknowledged.

Communist rule transformed public opinion into private opinion. Individuals held different views about government, politics, and Moscow's domination, but there were no institutional means to aggregate or express such ideas. Official opinion was the only opinion that could be circulated through the media. The party-state did not ask the people what they wanted, but rather claimed to know what they were supposed to want. Independent expression of opinion was dangerous because it was potentially subversive.

Individuals prudently confined their thoughts to their own private circles of relatives and close friends. In this way, face-to-face primary groups became a substitute for civil society rather than an integral part of it. People devised strategies for communicating ideas without stating them directly. Czechs like to tell the story of a countryman who went up to a Russian soldier in Prague after the 1968 invasion and complained: "Two Swiss soldiers have stolen my Russian watch!" When the soldier replied: "Do you think I'm stupid? You mean two Russian soldiers have stolen your Swiss watch," the Czech gleefully exclaimed: "You said it! You said it! I didn't!"

Dissidents organized clandestine gatherings to exchange views and information. Samizdat publications circulated ideas to a larger audience, but one that was necessarily confined to those in trusted and small unofficial networks. Almost everyone else, meanwhile, got their information from officially approved media. Dissidents could seek to enlist support from the West, but their need to do so only highlighted the limits placed on political action within their own societies. While almost everyone who lived under communist rule held negative views of the regime, very few ever dared to express them publicly. The party-state thus kept a secure lid on the possibility of effective dissent. As

Thomas Remington notes, "There must be institutional bases for impersonal organization and leadership. Family and friendship can go only so far in organizing oppositional activity."[4]

Deconstructing the Monolith

The first step in fostering civil society in postcommunist countries is cutting the state down to size by reducing its control over society. In less than five years since the fall of communism, much has been done to "deconstruct" the monolithic institutions of the former party-state. Censorship no longer restricts what can be said in public, and state security forces no longer terrorize people who wish to speak their minds. The bookstalls that have sprouted on the streets and in the subway stations of East European capitals testify to a booming marketplace of ideas. Even though what is printed is often commercial, banal, or sensationalist, it is evidence of a thriving culture of free expression.

The elaborate system of visas and armed border guards that prevented movement of individuals and ideas across the Iron Curtain has been dismantled. All that remains of the Berlin Wall are the memorials to those who were killed there while trying to flee to freedom. Czechs who want to visit Germany or Austria are no longer confronted with automatic weapons at road checkpoints and high barbed-wire fences strung across Bohemia's woods and fields. Now the only barrier to travel is money.

Dismantling the institutions of a command economy is another important step toward creating favorable conditions for the growth of civil society. This means, among other things, freeing trade unions from subservience to the party-state and encouraging private enterprise. In time, the process can become self-sustaining, with greater economic liberty producing rising standards of living that in turn make it possible for individuals to form local and national organizations that might further their interests and views. Economic privatization is a complex and time-consuming but absolutely vital step in the development of a flourishing civil society.

Now that competitive elections are becoming routine events in Eastern Europe and the former Soviet Union, there is a standing incentive for anyone with political aspirations to join or even create a political party. Election outcomes have thus far shown that no one party represents even half of the spectrum of public opinion, let alone the whole spectrum. The use of proportional representation usually prevents any party from gaining more than a third of the parliamentary seats; in some postcommunist countries, up to a dozen parties have gained parliamentary representation.

Free elections have produced too many parties with too little effective political organization. Groups that a few years ago maintained their cohesion while meeting clandestinely to avoid repression now use their new freedom to quarrel in public. The split in Poland's Solidarity, a bulwark of opposition to the communist regime throughout the 1980s, is an especially dramatic example. In Russia, party organization is now so weak that independents were the biggest winners in single-member districts in last December's parliamentary elections.

Every postcommunist capital boasts as a monument to freedom an empty plinth on which a statue of Marx, Lenin, Stalin, or some other communist hero once stood. Those statues have been consigned, quite literally, to the scrap heap of history. But do people really feel free? The very fact that we can now conduct opinion surveys that ask people to articulate publicly what were formerly secret thoughts is one significant sign of freedom.

Russia offers an excellent test of the extent to which "destatization" has actually made people feel free. When Russians are asked to compare their freedoms before *perestroika* with the liberties that they enjoy today, the answer is clear. For the six measures listed in Table 1, an average of 57 percent say that they feel freer to say and do what they like now than they did under the communist regime. More than half also report that they are now free *not* to take an interest in politics, a step that was risky under the old regime, when the party-state pressured everyone to make a public show of supporting official policy. Overall, only one in ten Russians claims to feel less free in the wake of communism's demise.

The average Russian reports an increase of freedom in four of the six areas covered in the questions in Table 1. One-sixth say that they feel freer on all six counts, and only 12 percent say that they do not feel

Table 1 — Russians' Evaluation of Level of Freedom Today
(New Regime Compared to Old Regime)

MEASURE	MORE	SAME	LESS
Decide whether or not to believe in God	71%	29%	2%
Say whatever you think	65	27	8
Join any organization	63	28	9
Decide whether or not to take an interest in politics	57	39	4
Live without fear of unlawful arrest	51	42	6
Travel and live wherever you want in Russia	36	32	32

Source: Richard Rose, I. Boeva, and V. Shironin, *How Russians Are Coping with Transition: New Russia Barometer II* (University of Strathclyde Studies in Public Policy No. 216, Glasgow, 1993), questions 146-51. Nationwide representative sample survey conducted by means of face-to-face interviews with 1,975 respondents, 26 June-22 July 1993.

freer in any way. The low rating that respondents gave to freedom to travel is more likely a result of the growing expense and unreliability of state transport services than a sign of any new state-imposed restrictions.

The sense of freedom from state oppression is felt throughout the postcommunist societies of Central and Eastern Europe. People may be dissatisfied with their current living standards or fearful of losing their jobs, but they have not forgotten the great gains made in freedom from fear and censorship. East Germans offer a splendid example of people making sensible distinctions between freedom and economic security. When asked to compare conditions in the former communist state with life in the German Federal Republic, 73 percent rate East Germany as better at providing social security. But when asked to compare the two systems in terms of permitting people to speak freely, 69 percent rate the Federal Republic as superior.[5]

The good news is that East Europeans show little fear of a return to rule by a party-state. Nor would this be possible, for it took the power vacuum created by the Second World War, the might of Stalin's occupying Red Army, the ruthlessness and ideological discipline of a Marxist-Leninist party, and the material resources of the old Soviet Union to impose monolithic communist regimes. Such force no longer exists.

Privatization Without Civilization

The deflation of the party-state's ideological claim to be the sole rightful organizer of society has legitimized private life. Unofficial activities that were potentially subversive in a communist regime, such as forming a group to read the Bible or discuss modern art, are now publicly acceptable. But the emergence of such free associations does not mean that the process of building a fully functioning civil society is complete. In the West, political parties, large business and financial concerns, trade unions, and media organs usually take decades to create; most major universities are at least a century old, and many are far older.

Observers should be wary of concluding that, merely because people feel free to join this or that group, they necessarily trust all or most of the organizations around them. When Russians were asked whether they trusted or distrusted key institutions of civil society, the average respondent expressed distrust of seven out of ten (see Table 2). A similar level of distrust was expressed by people in the Czech Republic, Slovakia, Hungary, and Poland. In all these countries, levels of public trust in institutions are significantly lower than the levels that researchers typically find in both Western Europe and the United States.[6]

Political parties lead the list of institutions that Russians distrust. This

Table 2 — Russians' Trust in Institutions

INSTITUTION	TRUST	DISTRUST
Political parties	7%	93%
Supreme Soviet	20	80
Local government	21	79
Trade unions	24	76
Police	27	73
President (Yeltsin)	33	67
Television	36	64
State security sevice (old KGB)	38	62
Courts	40	60
Army	62	38

Source: Same as for Table 1, questions 144, 152-60.

may explain their readiness to vote for independents with good local reputations but no ties to nationwide movements, or to support a "flash" party like Vladimir Zhirinovsky's ultranationalist Liberal Democratic Party, which appeals to people's emotions rather than to organized interests. Even though people may vote for a certain party, this does not mean that they trust it or feel much allegiance to it. The ten-nation New Democracies Barometer finds that only a third of East Europeans feel any stable sense of identification with a political party.[7] People are more likely to respond negatively to party labels, finding it easier to identify one or more parties that they distrust and for which they would never vote.

In the summer of 1993, the Supreme Soviet ranked second on the list of institutions that ordinary Russians distrusted. Evidently President Yeltsin shared this view; he himself closed the Parliament in September and then shelled its building, the White House, in early October. But Yeltsin himself does not inspire confidence; two-thirds of the Russians polled said that they viewed him with distrust. Further questioning showed that two-fifths trusted neither the president nor the Supreme Soviet and preferred a state of gridlock, in which each could exercise veto power over the other.

By wide margins, Russians also distrust their local government, which is responsible for overseeing social-welfare programs and administering such basic services as education and garbage collection. Incompetent delivery of such services is likely to arouse resentment among citizens. This reaction will be compounded if the officials responsible for such services have a reputation for corruption. Corruption was widespread under the communist command economy, when artificial ceilings on prices created shortages, and bribes were an effective way to obtain consumer goods that could not normally be found in the state-run stores. In addition, bribes were sometimes used to ensure access to nominally free state services such as health care, housing repairs, and a good education for one's children.

In the former "workers' paradises," trade unions are highly distrusted as well. Unions under communism had a dual role: they were supposed to promote the interests of their members and the fulfillment of the party-state's economic plan. In Russia, the balance was tipped in favor of the latter; workers' groups served, in effect, as tame company unions of state-run enterprises. Socialist ideology itself declared the impossibility of any fundamental conflict between the interests of workers as employees and their interests as citizens of a socialist state. By contrast, in free societies such as Britain or Sweden, labor unions can and do challenge government, even when it is in the hands of a social democratic party.

Television is more trusted than any conventional institution of political representation. This is perhaps not all that surprising, since the collapse of communism left the media dramatically freer to report frankly and comment freely on national affairs. But the growth of "adversarial" institutions is only one element of an emerging civil society. Newspapers like the *Washington Post* are an integral part of a free society, but the United States government cannot be driven solely by stories that highlight its failures and shortcomings. A political system also needs institutions that can be trusted to make government work honestly and effectively.

The least distrusted institutions in Russian society are those concerned with the maintenance of order—namely, the army, the criminal courts, and the state security service (formerly the KGB). Only the army enjoys the trust of a majority of Russians. Trust in such institutional bulwarks of order is also common in established democracies, but it does not exist in a context of widespread distrust of other institutions of civil society. Moreover, in Russia, institutions of order were not established to maintain the rule of law. Their task, rather, was to enforce the communist doctrine of "socialist legality," another name for the unchallenged rule of the party-state.

The development of the market in Russia is minting millionaires, but it is not fostering trust in those who make money. People do "trust" businessmen in a certain ironic sense: they are expected to be intelligent and enterprising, but also dishonest and ready to take whatever advantage of people. The new wealth accumulated by businessmen is not seen as the result of their providing better or cheaper goods in the marketplace. Instead, the great majority of Russians believe that businessmen become wealthy by exploiting foreign and domestic connections.[8]

About half of all Russians do not trust any significant cluster of institutions. This distrust is a major obstacle to the emergence of a civil society in which representative institutions can link the interests of individuals and families with the actions of government. Most Russians continue to see their country as divided between "us" (the individual and his family and friends) and "them" (distrusted institutions of authority). Among those who show some trust, most place their confidence in the institutions that enforce order. Only a sixth of the population indicate general trust in representative institutions. The level of trust is not quite so low in other postcommunist societies, but the overall pattern is similar.

Living with Distrust

If East Europeans do not trust the governments that they have elected, why should foreign emissaries? In the old days, trust was irrelevant: communist regimes had ample coercive power, and ruled through fear and inertia. Today, however, East Europeans are free to ignore leaders whom they distrust, thus making government ineffective. Even if public opinion polls should show a majority favoring a policy such as giving priority to fighting inflation rather than unemployment, a government that has only tenuous ties to its electorate would not necessarily feel confident about adopting such a policy.

Western policy makers repeatedly seek—and, even worse, declare that they have found at the head of East European states—reliable leaders who can show their country the way to democracy, free markets, and international cooperation. "Gorbymania" was an example of this. "Yeltsophiles" are not as numerous today as 12 months ago, yet it is a matter of record that the Clinton administration decided to "back Boris" without ever bothering to ascertain whether the Russian people backed him as well. President Clinton's January 1994 whistle-stop tour of the former Soviet Union seemed to underscore the Administration's hopes that a little handshaking with elites in Minsk and Kiev might deliver Belarus and Ukraine too.

The International Monetary Fund (IMF) has acted as if the Russian government can and should be held to the same standards as a stable Third World dictatorship, receiving aid in return for the fulfillment of commitments to stabilize its currency. Yet last December's elections, which handed Russia's economic reformers an ignominious defeat, show that no Russian president can be expected to deliver a quick political fix. The visit of IMF head Michel Camdessus to Moscow in March 1994 to secure agreement on conditions for an IMF loan could hardly have been more badly timed. Camdessus showed up when the Moscow grapevine was humming with stories of a plot to overthrow Yeltsin. What reliable agreement can be struck with a president who is distrusted by most of his country's citizens and elected legislators, and who has in turn good reasons for distrusting the officialdom of his own government?

Trust in institutions cannot be decreed into existence. Trustworthy institutions are the fruit of a long and positive history of cooperation and accommodation. Civil society has evolved over generations in America and Britain. Hitler's Third Reich was fortunately too short-lived to uproot fully the German civil institutions that subsequently became bases of democracy in the Federal Republic. Italy shows that democracy can coexist for decades with substantial civic distrust, but the upheavals of the March 1994 elections demonstrated that in a free society, those who persist in corruption risk repudiation.

Western institutions that are charged with aiding the countries of the post-Soviet East would do well to trust the same organizations that the people there trust. This means that the West will probably need to shift more of its attention to small-scale institutions that resemble face-to-face primary groups or extended friendship networks. Examples might include links between scientists in the "invisible college" of researchers, or between importers and exporters who depend upon one another for their mutual prosperity.

Trust must be earned. The construction of trustworthy institutions is more likely to happen from the bottom up than from the top down. East Europeans know those whom they trust, and trust those whom they know. Their customary practice is to make inquiries among friends or friends-of-friends in order to find out whether strangers can be trusted. A bottom-up strategy for developing trustworthy institutions would put less emphasis on the activities of the central government, since the great majority of Russians and East Europeans live not in the metropolis but in medium-sized cities, small towns, or the countryside, and see the central state as a remote and suspect entity.

A new enterprise employing a handful of workers can help its employees to realize that their future lies with the market, and not with the state and its subsidies. A social services center established by local initiative is less vulnerable to corruption and more likely to be responsive to actual needs than one planned and administered from the capital city, for local people do not have money to waste, and they know what their neighbors can be trusted to do.

Small-scale initiatives may not be popular with leaders looking for "big" agreements that will make news and be hailed as "breakthroughs" in the media, but these more modest advances may prove more durable over the long haul. Creating a civil society is like cultivating a garden. It is not a project to be achieved overnight by planting institutions in alien soil, by grafting institutions from abroad, or by drawing up a host of paper organizations that are no more real than plastic plants. It is a process that can be brought to fruition only by the patient cultivation of institutions in soil that communism for generations sowed with distrust.

NOTES

This essay is part of a study of social welfare and individual enterprise in postcommunist societies supported by grant Y 309-25-3047 from the British Economic and Social Research Council. The Russian survey results presented here were financed by a grant from the British Foreign Office Know How Fund. I am solely responsible for interpretation of the data.

1. See, for example, the results of a Harris poll reported by Laurence Parisot in "Attitudes about the Media: A Five-Country Comparison," *Public Opinion* 10 (1988), 18; and, more generally, S.M. Lipset and William Schneider, *The Confidence Gap* (New York: Free Press, 1983).

2. Robert A. Dahl, *A Preface to Democratic Theory* (Chicago: University of Chicago Press, 1956), 83.

3. Vladimir Shlapentokh, *Public and Private Life of the Soviet People* (New York: Oxford University Press, 1989), 9.

4. Thomas Remington, "Regime Transitions in Communist Systems: The Soviet Case," *Soviet Economy* 6 (1990), 175.

5. See Richard Rose, Wolfgang Zapf, Wolfgang Seifert, and Edward Page, *Germans in Comparative Perspective* (University of Strathclyde Studies in Public Policy No. 218, Glasgow, 1993), questions 48, 49.

6. Cf. Fritz Plasser and Peter Ulram, "Zum Stand der Democratisierung in Ost-Mitteleuropa," in Plasser and Ulram, eds., *Transformation oder Stagnation?* (Vienna, Austria: Signum, 1993), 56.

7. See Richard Rose and Christian Haerpfer, *Adapting to Transformation in Eastern Europe: New Democracies Barometer II* (University of Strathclyde Studies in Public Policy No. 212, Glasgow, 1993), Appendix, Table 32.

8. See Richard Rose, I. Boeva, and V. Shironin, *How Russians Are Coping with Transition: New Russia Barometer II* (University of Strathclyde Studies in Public Policy No. 216, Glasgow, 1993), questions 1-8.

22. RUSSIA'S FOURTH TRANSITION

M. Steven Fish

***M. Steven Fish** is assistant professor of political science at the University of California at Berkeley. He has previously taught at the University of Pennsylvania and has carried out extensive research in Russia. He is the author of* Democracy from Scratch: Opposition and Regime in the New Russian Revolution *(1995).*

During the decade that has passed since Mikhail Gorbachev rose to the pinnacle of the Soviet empire, Russia has experienced momentous changes and dramatic twists of history. Unfortunately, the emergence of a robust civil society cannot be numbered among these developments. Civil society—defined here as the realm of autonomous, voluntary associations that pursue limited ends in the public sphere[1]—remains inchoate and underdeveloped. Why is civil society in Russia so weak? With the old regime in ruins, does the strength of civil society even matter for the consolidation of democracy? Can a vigorous civil society possibly evolve in Russia? If not, what alternatives remain?

Russia during the Gorbachev era never produced a well-developed civil society of the type found in the West or in many developing countries. It nevertheless witnessed the rise of myriad organizations growing out of social movements, most of which focused their energies on bringing down the communist regime and ushering in some form of democracy. Some of these organizations, including the umbrella group known as Democratic Russia (DemRossiya), referred to themselves as movements; others, including many of DemRossiya's member associations, called themselves political parties. Some groups, such as Memorial, sought to prepare the way for democratization by exposing the crimes of the regime and reviving the nation's historical memory. Few if any of these groups, however, managed to assume genuine intermediary functions—which would have been impossible under Soviet rule anyway. Nonetheless, many of these organizations did develop significant mobilizational and expressive capacities. They roused public opposition and organized demonstrations of popular discontent with the regime. They published extensively and helped to break the state's monopoly on mass communications.

Most of the groups that spearheaded the democratic movement during communism's twilight have not fared well in the post-Soviet setting. Instead of evolving into more coherent and better-organized formations, many have weakened and fragmented, or even disappeared altogether. For example, of the half-dozen parties that made up the core of DemRossiya, only the Democratic Party of Russia gained the backing necessary to run candidates in the parliamentary elections of December 1993, and it barely surpassed the 5-percent threshold for representation in the new parliament. Nor have labor groups like the massive, politically muscular coal miners' organizations of the late Soviet period become well-structured and effective trade unions. Newer organizations have arisen, though many of them, including religious cults, criminal gangs, and associations of Russian chauvinists, cannot be regarded as elements of a civil society.

"The enfeeblement and fragmentation of state institutions in Russia pose formidable barriers to the development of civil society."

The chief causes behind the persistent weakness of Russia's civil society are the decay, corruption, and disorganization of state institutions, as well as the broader socioeconomic and political legacies of totalitarian rule.

The enfeeblement and fragmentation of state institutions in Russia pose formidable barriers to the development of civil society. While the erosion of the state's hegemony under Gorbachev was crucial to the emergence of autonomous political actors, there comes a point at which the withering of state institutions may actually hinder the growth of a strong civil society. The presence of a decrepit state structure—one whose offices can be bought or coopted by private interests—engenders patterns of interest organization that deviate sharply from those associated with a normal civil society. One crucial function of the institutions of a civil society is to advance the interests of their members by applying pressure on the state. The organizations of civil society must enjoy independence from the state in order to function normally, but state institutions also must possess a degree of autonomy if they are to respond to demands in a manner that encourages pluralist competition. In post-Soviet Russia, however, the functions of state agencies are highly nebulous. Constrained neither by laws nor by firmly established norms, the custodians of those agencies employ their offices largely to reap private gain; their services and favors are available to the highest bidder. Such conditions stimulate the growth of criminal syndicates, informal alliances between officials and holders of private wealth, and "mafias," rather than interest groups, political parties, labor unions, and the like. Although the divide between state and society is always somewhat unclear in practice, if it becomes so blurred that the two lose their mutual autonomy, then civil society cannot flourish.

The second major impediment to civil society in Russia is found in the inheritance bequeathed by the old regime. The social and economic aspects of the communist legacy are found in a highly peculiar and weakly differentiated social structure. Scholars who attributed the rise of Gorbachev and the initiation of his reforms to the rise of a "new middle class" in the Brezhnev-era Soviet Union identified little more than a phantom. State control over property and employment, the absence of markets, and the pervasiveness of policies that compressed wage differentials and divorced material compensation from occupational station and economic performance have left post-Soviet Russia with a social structure that differs starkly from that found in the West and in most of the Third World. Socialism to a large extent did what it was supposed to do: eliminate classes. Peaceful struggle between and within classes, waged by organizations based on ideology, sector, occupation, and profession, is, after all, much of what civil society is all about. The Soviet regime not only blocked the emergence of genuine classes; it also undermined many of the other sources of interest and identity on which the institutions of civil society are built. The eclipse of Orthodox Christianity and other confessions over seven decades of repression, for example, has greatly reduced the potential of religion and spiritual commitment as bases for political organization. Consequently, the interests, issues, and divisions around which political and social organizations normally develop are now far more weakly present and much less differentiated in Russia than in most other countries.

The legacy of socialist rule, moreover, has also had effects beyond the socioeconomic realm. The total ban on free association for political, economic, or social ends—the essential defining feature of totalitarianism—meant that the intermediary realm between state and society was driven out of existence. In sociopolitical terms, Soviet Russia consisted on the one hand of a state that monopolized all associational life, and on the other of an ultraprivate realm of networks of individuals bound together by ties of kinship, ethnicity, personal friendship, or informal economic exchange. With the state fractured and disintegrating and the ban on autonomous associations only a memory, the enormous breach between the state and the individual has become a powerful vacuum. Rushing to fill that vacuum are the remnants of the old Soviet order—fragments of the old party-state, as well as outgrowths of private interpersonal networks. The former encompass, for instance, the large alliances of enterprise administrators, such as the Union of Industrialists and Entrepreneurs, along with many firms and syndicates organized by former (and present) officials from the state security agencies. The latter include the countless clan-based and nationality-based "mafias" that have flourished in post-Soviet Russia, as well as their affiliated business organizations.

Neither of these sources of interest organization can furnish a good base for the construction of a genuine civil society. Pieces of the old party-state apparatus are, by reason of their origins, insufficiently autonomous or rooted in societal interests to serve as the building blocks of a civil society. The outgrowths of interpersonal networks are, for the most part, intensely private, even secretive. They serve profoundly particularistic needs and possess an inward-looking ethos. To the extent that they encourage any virtues, these are private rather than public. Such groups are not well-positioned to operate effectively in the *public* sphere; it is here, after all, where individuals enjoy a shared identity as citizens, that civil society puts down its roots and draws its nourishment.[2]

Is Civil Society Necessary?

Perhaps the weakness of civil society in Russia is not of great importance to the country's prospects for democracy. The communist regime has been relegated to history and the early stages of transition have already been traversed. Much of the scholarly literature on democratization depicts civil society's role as crucial primarily in the moments leading to, and perhaps immediately following, "founding elections." Once the tasks of *transition* have been accomplished, the challenges of *consolidation* are thought to be mostly matters of political institutionalization. During this latter phase, the organizations of civil society normally play only a supporting role.

In a country facing the daunting task of shifting from a command economy to capitalism as well as consolidating democracy, the absence of a vigorous civil society might even be seen as an advantage. Economic liberalization requires painful austerity and enormous popular sacrifice; the weakness of intermediary societal institutions might reduce the risk of an "overload" of demands on a fragile and resource-strapped system. It might broaden officials' leeway to pursue reforms in macroeconomic policy and property rights that are essential to capital accumulation and long-term prosperity, but that are certain to encounter strong popular resistance in the short run.[3]

The experiences of postsocialist countries, however, belie such a view. Those countries in which civil society was eclipsed only partially or for a shorter period of time, or which had strong resistance movements during communist rule, are enjoying far smoother transitions to both democracy *and* capitalism than countries that experienced longer and harsher spells of totalitarianism. Both democracy and liberal economics now enjoy firmer footing in Poland, Hungary, the Czech Republic, and the Baltic states than in Romania, Bulgaria, and the core Slavic republics of the former Soviet Union. To be sure, transitions in the former countries, which enjoy much stronger civil societies, have not been without their problems, yet they have made more progress than their counterparts in the latter countries, none of which has developed a strong civil society. Both political institutionalization and the progress of liberal economic reform have been most impressive in those countries where civil society is the most robust. Within the former House of Lenin, it seems, "all good things" do go together. So, it seems, do "all bad things."

Indeed, the experiences of former socialist countries show how inseparable political institutionalization is from the development of civil society. The weakness of the organizations of civil society in present-day Russia means that the question of who speaks for whom remains murky, thus rendering the stable, organized representation of interests highly problematic or even impossible. Under such conditions, even the presence of regular periodic elections and a new Constitution ratified by referendum will not engender a consolidated representative democracy. Democracy will persist, if it does at all, only by default—that is, by virtue of the weakness of authoritarian forces. Lacking a richer and more differentiated civil society, democratic consolidation has little hope in Russia. The best possible outcome will be the persistence of a crisis-prone democracy by default.

Yet as long as Russia avoids harsh authoritarian reversion, there is a chance that civil society and democratic political institutions can develop *simultaneously*. Even if democracy cannot be fully consolidated in the absence of a stronger civil society, the process of democratization may still continue. Civil society may be a requisite, but not necessarily a prerequisite, of consolidation.

Is Civil Society Possible?

Despite the enduring weakness of Russian civil society, a number of recent transformations may portend its growth in richness and vigor. The first of these changes involves the Russian economy. Economic reform in itself hardly creates a civil society, but certain types of reform do open up opportunities for the emergence of stronger and more differentiated societal institutions.

The centerpiece of economic reform during the first two years of the post-Soviet period has been privatization. Macroeconomic stabilization policy has followed an erratic course at best, and has not, contrary to the misguided conventional wisdom that predominates in the West, added up to a program worthy of the name "shock therapy." In fact, the only major economic reform (price liberalization aside) that has been pursued consistently since the end of the Soviet period is privatization. But in terms of its effects on politics and society, privatization is of far greater significance than fiscal, monetary, credit, and exchange-rate reforms put together. Macroeconomic policies can readily be adjusted or even reversed. Privatization cuts much deeper. It determines—perhaps definitively—who gets what. It reshapes wants, needs, and interests.

Privatization has not moved as quickly in Russia as in several of the fastest-reforming East European countries, but it has proceeded more rapidly and extensively than is often recognized by Western observers. As of April 1993, about half of all trade outlets, restaurants, and cafes had already fallen into private hands.[4] By late January 1994, some estimates placed the fraction of the Russian work force employed in the private sector at 40 percent.[5] The speed of privatization has lent the process momentum; it is now moving so fast that its opponents cannot stop it. During the summer of 1993, for instance, the (now-defunct) Supreme Soviet undertook a major initiative against the government's privatization program, adopting measures to deflate the value of privatization vouchers and to undermine the State Property Committee's scheme for accelerating the denationalization of enterprises. The campaign largely failed: the vouchers' value did not suffer a major setback, and the frequency of privatization auctions scarcely slackened.[6] The speed of privatization has been uneven across cities and regions, but in few major areas has privatization been stymied completely. In some cases where local officials have dragged their feet, raiders from other areas have even moved in to grab control of privatization auctions.[7] Privatization in Russia is almost certainly on the threshold of irreversibility. Even a future government hostile to private property and market economics would have to accommodate a large sector outside state control.

How does privatization affect the prospects for civil society? Much depends on how the process distributes wealth. To date, members of the former *nomenklatura*, and especially enterprise directors, have benefited disproportionately. Although most privatized enterprises have been acquired by their "work collectives," enterprise administrators themselves often enjoy ample opportunities for buying out their employees and manipulating the distribution of shares. Still, the ranks of Russia's new property holders are not restricted to custodians of the old regime. Privatization and liberalization in general have released a burst of entrepreneurial energy among less advantaged groups, especially the young, who did not previously enjoy access to power and resources. The privatization of dwellings, moreover, has given many residents ownership rights for a token payment, significantly widening the ranks of small-scale property holders.

Due to the legacy of the Soviet period, the social structure of Russia will continue to differ substantially from what one finds in either the

West or the developing world. Class formation is, in any event, a lengthy process. But the scope and pace of privatization now raise the possibility that a genuine middle class of small property holders will arise in Russia. Privatization has already begun to remold the interests of various social groups—indeed, to shape or reshape the groups themselves. The socioeconomic differentiation that privatization and other economic reforms are inducing has produced a more variegated society, and one whose structural features might be more conducive to the growth of intermediary societal organizations. The emergence and diversification of producers' associations has furnished preliminary evidence of the effect of economic reform on the growth of autonomous organizations. The largest of such groups remain rooted in the old *nomenklatura*. They are more bureaucratic alliances than constituent parts of civil society, and certainly cannot be regarded as "liberal." But the "directors' lobby" has became somewhat less uniformly antireformist and statist since early 1993, as some industrialists and managers have begun to realize what they stand to gain in a market economy. Groups such as Entrepreneurs for a New Russia and the Union of Privatized Enterprises have added the weight of those who advocate radical reform to the tug-of-war over economic transition.[8]

"The scope and pace of privatization now raise the possibility that a genuine middle class of small property holders will arise in Russia."

In addition to influencing interest formation, privatization promises to recast the relationship between the citizen and the state. In the old Soviet system, the workplace served as the main locus of social control. The state's monopoly on employment and control over enterprises, combined with management's ability to grant or deny access to scarce goods and services supplied through the workplace, guaranteed the state's hegemony over the citizen. The system also killed off the professions and professional organizations as autonomous entities and as possible sources of intermediation between the individual and the state.[9] Privatization, along with the fragmentation of the old *nomenklatura* system, has already released some Russians from direct dependence on the beneficence of the state. Political control over employment and occupations has fallen off, opening the way for genuine professions and professional associations to emerge. The spread of property ownership has also created pools of autonomous resources in society—sources that political parties, interest groups, independent trade unions, and church organizations might draw on for material support. In fact, while autonomous organizations are still weak, they are now far better endowed than they were during the Gorbachev period. Before the demise of the Soviet system, independent associations of all types struggled in poverty, relying for material support mainly on collections taken at public demonstrations. Since the demise of the Soviet system, however, even minor political parties have been able to find affluent private sponsors.

Economic transformation does not represent the only source of change creating opportunities for the emergence of a stronger civil society. Greater political freedom has opened numerous spaces for nonstate activity where little or none existed before. In a country where only a half-decade ago the state monopolized public information and couched communication in a mind-numbing, surreal ideological argot, lively free media now play a prominent role in public life. The press in Russia today is highly diverse, and some of it is of high quality. It has helped to relieve the organizational and informational problems posed by the weakness of interest groups, political parties, and other intermediary associations. Although some electronic media are still run by the government, the real extent of the president's control is modest and diminishing. Leading Russian newspapers such as *Segodnya* and *Nezavisimaya gazeta* show no more mercy to liberals than to communists and nationalists, and editors jealously guard their independence.

Elections and electoral reform represent a second aspect of political change that has prompted the growth of intermediary groups. The campaign leading up to the December 1993 parliamentary elections, and the electoral rules under which half the seats in the lower house were filled by party lists, furnished a stimulus to party formation. The undistinguished showing of liberal parties such as Russia's Choice and Yabloko, along with the relatively strong performance of conservatives and nationalists, naturally disappointed many of those who expected the new Federal Assembly to be much more progressive than the old Supreme Soviet. But the results of the elections did not necessarily annul the political advantages brought by the arrival of more highly structured and more clearly differentiated parties. The elections encouraged prominent politicians to take an interest in joining or forming party organizations. Before 1993, few of the most high-profile politicians in Russia took much notice of political parties. Many leaders saw great virtue in remaining "above" politics and political organizations. A government post, in any event, furnished a surer ticket to prominence than leadership of a party. But the elections induced major figures such as Yegor Gaidar, Grigory Yavlinsky, and Sergei Shakhrai—none of whom earlier had shown an interest in work outside government—to launch their own parties and work hard at building them up.[10] The elections did not produce a progressive majority in the lower house of parliament. Nor did they put an end to personalism in Russian political life, as shown by the rise of the outré demagogue, Vladimir Zhirinovsky. But they may have spurred the development of civil society by encouraging some leaders to begin moving away from the political free-lancing that was so much in evidence during the late Gorbachev and immediate post-Soviet periods.[11]

In sum, the Russian polity is not bereft of forces favorable to the development of a stronger and more differentiated civil society. But what if civil society remains weak and underdeveloped? How might this affect Russia's democratic prospects?

Alternatives to Civil Society

There are two alternatives to civil society in Russia, neither of which is consonant with any form of consolidated democracy. The first, *parochialization*, is highly likely if state capacities (meaning particularly central authority) continue to erode. In this scenario, the voluntary sector would grow in strength vis-à-vis the state, but its dominant forms of organization would represent particularistic, inward-looking, or "anomic" tendencies.[12] Society's institutional landscape would be dominated by ethnically, confessionally, and territorially exclusive categories and organizations, rather than by pluralist principles and associations geared to open competition in a mutually recognized public realm. In such a system, political action and struggle would not normally focus on interest-group competition and on efforts to place one's representatives in public office and to "lobby" state officials. Instead, it would center on attempts to colonize all or some parts of the state apparatus or, alternatively, to place one's own group beyond the reach of the law and of state power generally.

The extensive parochialization of Russian society is hardly inconceivable. Indeed, present-day Russia already exhibits some features of parochialization. Fanatical nationalist and religious movements, criminal syndicates, and producers' associations devoted to preserving monopoly power within a given sector or to promoting autarky within a given region are all on the rise. Each of these forms of organization represents parochializing tendencies. None fits within the realm of civil society. Parochialization is not uncommon in other parts of the world. It is currently a dominant trend in many African polities, and is also present in other places where civil society has remained weak and state capacities for administration and law enforcement have severely eroded.

The second alternative is *state corporatism*. Its emergence is probable if civil society stays weak while the state recovers and gets stronger. Interest intermediation would then be managed in large part by official and semiofficial organizations created from above. As in all state corporatist systems, intermediation would include some means for channeling demands from the bottom to the top, but the dominant current would flow the other way.

The full assumption of state power by a coalition of industrialists and their allies, devoted not just to enriching themselves but to restoring a strong state and launching a program for national integration and development, might place the country on the path to some form of state corporatism. Many in Russia now speak admiringly of a modernizing, "progressive" form of authoritarianism: the South Korean, Chinese, Chilean, and Brazilian "models" each have their proponents in Moscow. Under current Russian conditions, implementation of any such model would require an authoritarian regime and the state-led organization of societal interests. To many enterprise administrators and state officials—most of whose careers have revolved around the dual imperative of fulfilling state orders and enforcing labor quiescence—state corporatist arrangements, whatever specific forms they took, might look comfortable and familiar.

State corporatism would be consonant with some form of populist, as well as technocratic-developmental, authoritarianism. Peronism, no less than more "modern" bureaucratic forms of authoritarianism, typically involves extensive state-led structuring of societal interests. A feeble civil society, moreover, creates ample opportunities for the emergence and empowerment of populist elites. Strong independent political parties, trade unions, and interest associations serve as the only reliable prophylactics against destructive populism. The absence of such groups facilitates the emergence of populist demagogues and enhances their opportunities for mobilizing mass support.

Civil Society, Democracy, and Capitalism

The current situation in Russia and other former socialist countries is often conceived of as a dual transition, a simultaneous transformation of political and economic regimes. The political transition is typically seen as a matter of political institutionalization—constructing a new democratic electoral system, guaranteeing basic rights, and so on. The economic transition consists of privatization and a shift from command to market relations. Some analysts of Russia speak of a third transition, one involving territorial issues. This third transition requires not only fixing external boundaries, but also creating a federal system that can secure decentralization without sparking national disintegration. It includes establishing undisputed boundaries between provincial units and a clear division of authority between central and provincial organs of power. This third transition obviously poses a far more serious challenge in a large, multiethnic federation-in-the-making such as Russia than in smaller, more homogeneous countries such as Hungary or Poland.

The progress of civil society in Russia depends partly on what happens in these three transitions. For example, the formation of intermediary organizations hinges on how privatization—the core of the economic transition—distributes property among the population. Political reforms such as the establishment of a new electoral system have already generated more differentiated political parties.

Conversely, the progress of civil society will influence the outcome of these multiple transitions. Consolidated representative democracy will not arise in the presence of an underorganized, politically inarticulate society. Capitalism is possible in the absence of civil society. But without civil society, capitalism will not create a "civil economy."[13] Rather, Russian capitalism will be highly speculative, nonproductive, and parasitic, and it will engender grossly inequitable patterns of accumulation and distribution.

The progress of civil society not only will affect democratization and the transition to capitalism, but may even influence Russia's prospects for maintaining its own territorial integrity. Formidable interest associations, trade unions, political parties, and other intermediary entities organized on a national basis may counterbalance the powerful centrifugal forces created by the decay of central authority, the country's vastness and diversity, and the growth of localist and separatist pressures. Thus given the importance of the development of civil society, a fourth—distinctly *societal*—transition must be added to the already daunting array of transitions that Russia must negotiate.

While the fate of civil society in Russia rests to a large extent on structural factors, simple human agency may also play a significant role. Unfortunately, those actors who are best equipped to forge civil-societal organizations—from the president in Moscow to activists on the local level—have often proven more effective as orators and pamphleteers than as organizers. Xenophobes, nationalist demagogues, religious fanatics, criminal bosses, and other champions of anticivil parochialization have, at least since the downfall of communism, taken problems of organization and mobilization far more seriously. Their fortunes are now on the ascent. Whether or not they continue to rise depends in part on whether the potential builders of civil society learn the lessons of the past several years and recommit themselves to the mundane but vital tasks of organization.

NOTES

1. There are many definitions of civil society. Some writers conceive of it as virtually all nonstate groups and activities. Others offer restrictive conceptions that exclude political parties, associations that are completely "self-regarding" or based on categories such as tribal or ethnic affiliation, illiberal groups, and organizations that lack "participatory" or "democratic" internal norms and structures. My own conception of civil society is moderately restrictive. It excludes fanatical organizations and groups that seek to seize control of the state and rule exclusively. It emphasizes *autonomy*, thereby ruling out groups that are fused with the state. Since it encompasses only *voluntary* associations that operate in the *public* sphere, it excludes purely parochial groups or those based solely on ascriptive categories. It includes political parties (in *competitive*, multiparty systems), trade unions, interest groups, and many other types of voluntary associations, including those that do not necessarily espouse liberal goals or enjoy "democratic" internal governance.

2. See Ken Jowitt, "The Leninist Legacy," in Ivo Banac, ed., *Eastern Europe in Revolution* (Ithaca: Cornell University Press, 1992), 209-15.

3. See Ellen Comisso, "Property Rights, Liberalism, and the Transition from 'Actually Existing' Socialism," *East European Politics and Societies* 5 (Winter 1991): 162-88.

4. "Investment Crisis Stalls, Privatization Picks up Steam," *Commersant* (Moscow), 28 April 1993.

5. "Russian Reform Lingers Near Life," *New York Times*, 30 January 1994.

6. "Vaucher protiv skeptikov" ["The Voucher versus Skeptics"], *Kuranty*, 20 July 1993; "Parlament ostanovil protsess, kotoryi uzhe poshel" ["Parliament Stopped a Process that Already Took Place"], *Megapolis Express*, 28 July 1993; "Share Prices Go Through the Roof" and "Privatization Auctions Now a Daily Occurrence," *Commersant* (Moscow), 16 June 1993.

7. "Ural Voucher Auction: Two Locales, Two Attitudes, Which Will Prevail?" *Commersant* (Moscow), 21 April 1993.

8. Sergei Markov, "Reform of Property Rights: The History, the Players, the Issues," *Conversion: Report on Russia's Defense Industry* (Center for International Security and Arms Control, Stanford University, August 1993).

9. See George Kolankiewicz, "The Reconstruction of Citizenship: Reverse Incorporation in Eastern Europe," in Kazimierz Z. Poznanski, ed., *Constructing Capitalism: The Reemergence of Civil Society and Liberal Economy in the Post-Communist World* (Boulder, Colo.: Westview Press, 1992), 143.

10. On the decline of free-lance political entrepreneurship, see "Perevorot imeni Gaidara" ["A Coup Named for Gaidar"], *Moskovskii Komsomolets*, 10 July 1993; and "Sergei Shakhrai: my stroim svoiu partiiu tak, kak khoteli by postroit' novoe rossiiskoe gosudarstvo" ["Sergei Shakhrai: We're Building Our Party Like We Would Like to Build a New Russian State"], *Izvestiia*, 19 August 1993.

11. See the symposium on Russia's December 1993 election in *Journal of Democracy* 5 (April 1994): 3-4.

12. A useful distinction between civil and parochial groups within the voluntary sector is offered in Naomi Chazan, "Africa's Democratic Challenge," *World Policy Journal* (Spring 1992): 279-308.

13. Richard Rose, "Toward a Civil Economy," *Journal of Democracy* 3 (April 1992): 13-26.

23. PLURALISM IN THE ARAB WORLD

Iliya Harik

***Iliya Harik**, professor of political science at Indiana University, has conducted field research in Egypt, Tunisia, Morocco, and Lebanon. He is the author of* Politics and Change in a Traditional Society *(1968),* The Political Mobilization of Peasants *(1974),* The Political Elites of Lebanon *(1972; in Arabic), and* The Illusive Path to Development: Economic Policies and Reform in Egypt *(forthcoming).*

In seven of the Arab world's twenty states—from Yemen on the Indian Ocean to Morocco on the Atlantic—a process of guarded democratization has been taking place. Ordinary citizens are receiving more opportunities to participate freely in politics, while economic privatization and the encouragement of free enterprise are also gathering steam. In both cases, functions once performed by government agencies are being fully or partially delegated to citizens and corporations, making for a more voluntaristic and self-regulated civil society.

In addition to discussing these liberalizing and democratizing trends in Arab countries, this essay also seeks to assess whether the growth of a flourishing "civil society" is a *prerequisite* for the installation of a democratic government or, alternatively, whether the development of a civil society and a democratic government may be pursued simultaneously.

Democratic governments function poorly, if at all, in the absence of certain explicit and implicit cultural practices and assumptions. A number of attitudes must be first ingrained in the social order, such as a certain degree of individualism, public-spiritedness, respect for and tolerance of others, and acceptance of winning and losing according to "the rules of the game." Indeed, a major reason for the emphasis placed on civil society is the belief that a democratic system of government planted in a hostile and alien culture is not likely to survive, let alone prosper. Can one find in Arab societies attitudes and concepts supportive of democracy?

The first place to look is in the sphere of high culture. Is there a line of thought among the Arabs that can serve as a philosophical bedrock for the establishment of civil society? The Arab political tradition remains to this day tightly intertwined with Islamic doctrines and the historical precedents set by premodern Islamic states, which were typically ruled by authoritarian sultans. Islam itself contains the seeds of individual dignity and group integrity, understood as reflections of the divine spark that all the world's revealed religions confirm and celebrate. In this respect, Islam is similar to the natural rights idea, which also has its deepest roots in convictions about a divine order. Islamic thought is vast and complex; what concerns us here are those strains that may serve as a basis for the growth of civil society among Islamic peoples.

In Islam, one finds the idea of individual integrity juxtaposed with that of integral membership in the community (*al jamaa'a*), a dualism that has served those who preferred a strong civil society as well as those who wanted a strong and authoritarian system of government. Those today who favor civil society—mainly Muslim jurists scandalized by the injustices of autocratic governments—understand *al jamaa'a* in a sense consistent with the idea of civil society. Their major contribution has been to argue that the implementation of Islamic law is the preserve not of government but of Muslim leaders and councils at all levels of society working closely with their communities. We see this position stressed again now by contemporary Muslim writers such as Muhammad 'Abid al-Jaabiri of Morocco and Sheikh Hassan al-Turabi of Sudan. Arab believers in civil society today, however, are not confined to the religious tradition. Many, like the scholars at the Ibn Khaldun Center in Cairo, are secular and approach the subject from a liberal democratic point of view.

The more dominant line of thought—one widely held by Islamic revivalists—is that a Muslim government is an essential pillar of the Islamic religion. Fundamentalists take as their political cornerstone the belief that the main *raison d'être* of government is the implementation of divine law (*shari'a*). While Muslims of this persuasion are not necessarily less committed to a reduced governmental role in society, in general they tend to leave less space for individuals and organizations and put more emphasis on the Islamic character of government. However, moderate advocates of the Islamic state have recently sought to present themselves as sympathetic to the notion of limited government. Certainly, adherence to the rule of law is cherished in Islam no less than in the West. Also favorable to civil society is the Islamic emphasis upon the economic liberty of individuals and associations. Thus rarely do we see an Islamic government opposing privatization from a doctrinal point of view. Iran remains the most divided on this issue, but leans toward the private sector.

With respect to the other main ideological tributary of modern Arab political culture—Arab nationalism—the story is more troubling. During this century, Arab nationalism has shown itself to be less tolerant and has allowed less room for democracy, both in theory and in practice, than Islam. Concerned mainly with vindicating communal identity and winning freedom from colonialism, Arab nationalism has long stressed political unification and uniform national character, allowing very little room for diversity. Ironically, its founders were not Arab governments, but rather Arab intellectuals. Nationalism thus arose first in civil society, and then spilled over into the making of the authoritarian national state.

The Need for Strong Government

The happy coincidence of democratic civil societies and democratic states in the advanced industrial countries makes it possible for advocates to dwell at length on the virtues of civil society, not the least of which is its role in advancing and consolidating democracy. The case is markedly different in Arab and other less developed countries.

The challenge for those who deal with developing societies is to determine what to do when an authoritarian system of government is a reflection of authoritarian relations in society. In the Arab world, authoritarian relations prevail in the family, the religious community, the workplace, and between social classes. Moreover, in many Arab and other less developed countries, the expansion of governmental roles has been directly related to the large empty space left by society. In countries such as Saudi Arabia and the Gulf states, governments (bolstered by oil revenues) have moved in to take primary responsibility for education, health, housing, and industrial development. Governments became entrepreneurs in such areas as banking, industry, and commerce.

Moreover, the culturally conservative (and decidedly nonsocialist) attitudes of officials in those countries seem to reflect the predilections of the people, who even take initiatives to maintain that conservatism in the forefront of national policy. As a result, these conservative regimes, with the possible exception of Saudi Arabia, do not seem to be experiencing the severe tensions common in some other countries in the Arab world, nor are they as frequently featured on lists of the worst violators of human rights.

One should treat with caution the claim that less developed countries tend to have strong societies and weak states. In terms of social policy effectiveness, it is true, almost all less developed countries have weak governments, but when it comes to internal security, these same states are potent and very effective. This is true of Morocco, Egypt, Tunisia, Iraq, and Syria. Moreover, the apparent failure of so many Third World regimes has had much to do with the ambitious targets they set for themselves; we should take care, therefore, to avoid underestimating their actual achievements.

Scholars agree that the aggrandizement of governments in less developed countries has been a response to societal pressures. The extensive role of government in less developed countries may thus be as much a concession to popular demands and expectations as it is a grab for power. In many of these states, citizens are heavily dependent on government. About 40 percent of the population continued to live below the poverty level in the late 1970s in Egypt, even after strenuous official efforts to redress income inequality and introduce a welfare system. The situation is not much better in most other non-oil-rich Middle Eastern countries. In most such countries, the high birthrates and the dislocation of rural dwellers to squalid cities have aggravated an already difficult situation. Most workers live below but not outside the market economy. They are either underproductive or underpaid. In either case, they are needy and must have a patron; typically, it is the government. In Arab countries without oil wealth, the dependency ratio—the number of unemployed in a family to those employed—is as high as six to one. Considering that most of the employed earn barely more than subsistence wages, the clamor for government to play the role of provider is understandable.

The high dependency ratio suggests that civil society may itself be the source of government's augmented role. And an expansive government, we must remember, is a much better candidate to turn authoritarian than a limited one. Whether one looks at socialist-oriented countries with regimes based on mass mobilization (such as Iraq, Syria, Egypt, Tunisia, and Algeria) or formerly poor countries grown rich off petroleum (such as Saudi Arabia, Kuwait, Qatar, Bahrain, Oman, and the United Arab Emirates), society has demanded actively munificent governments. The only difference is that the latter countries have had the wherewithal to manage such extensive responsibilities, while the former have not.

A focus on civil society alone is thus not likely to do much for democratization in Arab societies. A more inclusive approach is far better, because the interdependence between governmental institutions and private, civil associations is quite strong. Moreover, the strengthening of civil society in Arab countries may well depend upon the rise of greater governmental effectiveness. Fortunately, the key to such effectiveness may lie not in expanding government but in reducing its size and scope.

Ambiguities of Democratization

If democracy is the goal, does one start by building civil society as the necessary foundation, or is it better first to confront the issue of political power squarely and deal with governmental institutions straightaway? The writing that Arabs have been producing on civil society is not enlightening in this regard, but then neither is the Western literature on civil society.

To begin with, the claim that a democratic society is essential to a democratic government, a truism in the developed West, may serve in most less developed countries (including all the Arab states except Lebanon) only to hinder the progress of democracy by allowing those who wish to delay the process of democratization to argue that the building of civil society must precede democratic political change. Any effort to make the path to democracy pass first through a strong civil society will mean the indefinite postponement of democracy.

Another problem is that in most Arab countries, traditional solidarities constitute the most common social bonds, whether tribal, ethnic, communal, religious, or kinship-based. Yet Arab intellectuals—the biggest promoters of civil society—generally loathe traditional loyalties and attitudes, and offer a vision with no place for associations based on primordial ties. To these intellectuals, only modern associations with voluntary memberships are acceptable.

Yet civil society, let us recall, is supposed to act as an intermediary between the individual and national leaders, and in doing so is also supposed to serve as a check on the power that those leaders can wield. Should Arab intellectuals succeed in marginalizing traditional associations, they would harm the cause of democratic transformation by knocking out precisely those groups that are best able to mediate between citizens and their government, and that have the ability to restrain the latter's power.

Lebanon, whose democratic tradition is based on the acceptance of communal ties as politically relevant, has long drawn severe criticism from liberal Arab intellectuals who consider communalism backward and blame it for the civil war there. Such attacks are misguided, for Lebanon's communal-based democracy is a mechanism for conflict resolution rather than a cause of communal strife. Other democratizing Arab states have strong and diverse communities; is it prudent to portray democratization as a threat to communal identity and a communal role in the polity? Even aside from such practical considerations, Arab intellectuals have yet to offer any theoretical justification for denying traditional associations a role in the democratization process.

Another point of concern is that private groups, whether corporations or traditional associations, often have predatory tendencies, which introduce ambiguity into the relationship between civil society and democratization. Attempts by individuals or private groups to gain advantage at the expense of the public are a problem in all societies. The special favors that some private companies and businessmen enjoy in Saudi Arabia and Kuwait practically amount to the privatization of government. In Egypt, conversely, the rapid growth of the Islamic Investment Funds and their influence in and out of government circles led a fearful government to destroy them. The government's fears, it may be noted, were not entirely unfounded.

Two other arguments further justify rejection of the thesis that civil society should be treated as a precondition for democracy in the Arab world. First, processes of privatization or political liberalization in many Arab countries have begun as government initiatives. Second, many of the Arab countries' most "modern" associations—business groups, labor unions, professional and intellectual societies—show little or no interest in democratization. It was academics and journalists, after all, who in 1992 publicly urged President Mubarak of Egypt to go slow on democratization, for fear of repeating the Algerian example, in which rapid democratization measures taken by the government brought about an Islamist majority.

This raises the question of just who in Arab society has a vested interest in democracy. Among the "modern" groups listed above, each has its reasons for lacking a vigorous concern with democratization. Moreover, authoritarian governments have in many cases succeeded in making clients of such groups. Businessmen have been reduced in power and functions, made to depend on government commissions, and seduced with favors such as licenses, credit, or subcontracts. In the oil-rich countries of the Gulf, businessmen have done very well off of government largesse and see no reason to rock the boat.

Trade unions, on the other hand, have played a more mixed role. In Egypt, Algeria, and Syria, trade unions became partners in single-party regimes, giving up the right to strike in return for special favors. In Egypt, nonetheless, some unions spurned this old bargain and staged wildcat strikes, while in Tunisia unions proved largely unwilling to surrender their activism and went through a costly struggle with the overbearing regime of President Bourguiba. Without much support from other groups, they made very little headway in democratizing the Tunisian political system, and have shown more caution recently under President Ben Ali, who has shown himself to be no less authoritarian than his predecessor. Trade unions in Morocco, like their Tunisian counterparts, have a distinguished record of fighting for freedom and democracy, but have never had to resist attempts to incorporate them into the regime. In the oil-producing countries, transient and foreign work forces plus official opposition have made labor organizing a forlorn hope.

Intellectuals, the third "modern" group, remain an enigma. While they have a considerable stake in democracy and freedom of expression, their record in most Arab countries has not been impressive. While it is true that some intellectuals have been in the forefront of the human rights organizations that have cropped up across the Arab world since the early 1980s, intellectuals as a class have shown few signs of strong commitment, understanding, or leadership in the struggle for democracy.

The human rights groups, moreover, remain limited in following and influence.

The ambivalence among intellectuals comes partly from ideology and partly from career considerations. Having been major allies of socialist and nationalist regimes, Arab intellectuals have become bitter and cynical in the wake of socialism's failure. Many cling to the belief that socialism is just, while democracy is not. They fear that liberalization will widen the gap between classes, work against the poor, and favor the rich. Most Arab intellectuals, moreover, remain government employees and do not enjoy the luxury of freely expressing (much less acting upon) views that might run contrary to their employer's interests. Although liberalization and privatization may eventually change the conditions facing Arab society's quiescent "modern" groups, and in so doing spur a change in their attitudes and behavior, for the time being one must describe their role in democratization as quite modest.

In regimes in which some political liberalization has taken place, political parties have done the most to seize the opportunity. Yet these parties tend to be undemocratically run; unless checked, most would act in an authoritarian fashion once in power, just as the National Islamic Front (NIF) has done in Sudan and the Islamic Salvation Front, to judge from its pronouncements, was about to do in Algeria. At any rate, political parties are not, strictly speaking, parts of civil society.

A Dependent Relationship

Another reason to reduce the emphasis usually placed on civil society is its dependent relationship with government. In the Arab world, governments have taken the major initiative in the development of civil society. As far back as the 1940s, the Iraqi government tried to create an entrepreneurial class by building industries that could later be turned over to private entrepreneurs. Most of the entrepreneurs in Tunisia today are former government officials who left, with some official encouragement, to start their own businesses. The Egyptian and Tunisian governments have been actively involved since the 1970s in supporting cottage industries and encouraging the formation of small groups and associations. Agrarian reform in Egypt contributed not only to the welfare of poor peasants but to the emergence of new political leaders amongst them. It was also government-induced agrarian reform that created local institutions such as cooperatives and elected municipal councils.

In the oil-rich Gulf countries, government largesse helped to spawn a middle class of businessmen and professionals. Finding the private sector very small, the Saudi government decided both to expand the public sector and to encourage private entrepreneurs through grants, easy loans, subsidies, and commissions.

In the vital area of education, the governments of most Arab states have shouldered responsibility for providing free schooling from the primary grades all the way through university, and have made tremendous progress in the last 30 years. Today, thanks to such governmental efforts, the educated middle class constitutes a major formation in those societies.

"Important as the democratic character of civil society is, it is not a precondition for political democracy."

Although socialist regimes in the 1960s undermined many well-established entrepreneurs in Egypt, Syria, and Iraq (and to a lesser extent in Libya during the 1970s), the expansionist macroeconomic policies generally pursued by other Arab governments during that era proved quite helpful to private entrepreneurs, who found much demand for their services in the public sector.

If there is a single overriding reason why liberalization and democratization measures have been so slow in making progress in most of the Arab world, it is that they were introduced at the pleasure of governments and for reasons of state, and not because of pressure from civil society. Unable to cope with the business, services, and welfare responsibilities that they had undertaken, Arab governments in the 1980s decided that their survival hinged on shifting part of the burden to private groups. At best, such groups showed no more than a very cautious willingness to respond. In the face of government delays and double-talk, entrepreneurs shied away from confrontation or political activism, resorting instead to subterfuge and to uncivic activities such as smuggling and black marketeering.

Democratization must be seen as an objective in its own right that calls for concentration on the structure and behavior of government, whether or not a country has a democratic civil society. One of the major conditions of democratization lies in active communication and cooperation between governments and social groups, especially in developing countries where the formal structures of government are not sufficiently developed or responsive to popular demands. A cooperative relationship between government and such groups, regardless of their character, is likely to contribute to the viability of democracy and a more successful government.

Important as the democratic character of civil society is, it is not a precondition for political democracy. Democratic government is feasible in a society in which the internal decision making of most groups and organizations is not democratic. Independent groups, whatever their internal decision-making structures, contribute to pluralism, to the division of power, and to the control of government. The dichotomy between government and civil society that is posited in many of the standard scholarly accounts of democratization is more apt to be confusing than helpful when it comes to the Arab countries, where the role of government in the democratization process is so prominent.

Having stressed the role of government, it would be useful to consider the exceptional cases of Morocco and Lebanon, where civil society is strong and its strength is reflected in the active relationship with government. Although Morocco's King Hassan II (r. 1961-) has been willing to take steps in the direction of liberalization and democratization, labor unions and political parties have been instrumental in steering the government down that path. In Morocco, freedom of the press and of association has been the rule since independence in 1956, albeit with some interruptions. While the monarchy's autocratic tendencies were as pronounced there as anywhere else, years of pressure from unions, the press, and the parties (by no means all secular or internally democratic) have produced considerable democratic progress.

In Lebanon, another unusual case, civil society is stronger than the government. The former spawned private militias that fought a 17-year civil war while the government sat on the sidelines. Not only did civil society carry on essential activities such as banking, schooling, and publishing during the war, it also added new ones. The most remarkable was the flourishing of the broadcast media, which had been a public monopoly before the war. Warlords and private entrepreneurs alike took advantage of the government's inability to enforce its regulations and started their own radio and television stations, most of which quickly became profitable and soon surpassed the established public radio and television networks by leaps and bounds, connecting the country to important international media sources. Now the government is trying to restrict the programming on these stations, drawing a chorus of opposition from various sources including the Islamist party, Hezbollah. Many Lebanese newspapers and magazines migrated to European cities and published there during the war, but most have returned by now, and the written press remains free and prosperous.

The Lebanese combination of a vibrant civil society and a democratic system of government is quite rare in the Arab world. Yet Lebanese civil society bears many fundamental similarities to other Arab societies. Political parties and corporations are not run democratically, but are dominated by traditions of familial and sectarian loyalty. Indeed, the national parliament does not revolve around party alignments, for parties control no more than a third of the seats. Most members of parliament are independents, whose ties with their local constituencies are strong enough to elect them without the aid of a political party. Although this is by no means a "modern" system of government, it has worked for half a century.

The main reason why Lebanon's non-Western system of democracy works is the pluralism of competing actors. Competition checks authoritarian tendencies. When five or more hierarchically organized and led associations compete in one arena, they check one another just as much as when five democratically run and led agencies do. To regard such a system as nondemocratic simply because it does not correspond to or mimic Western forms of democracy would be both intellectually indefensible and shortsighted.

Recent Progress and Setbacks

Whereas in 1970 Lebanon had the only democratic government in the Arab world, by 1994 seven states—Egypt, Kuwait, Jordan, Yemen, Tunisia, Morocco, and Mauritania—had moved in the direction of democratization. With the exception of Egypt, where halting democratization began in the late 1970s, all have made their moves since 1990. In all these states, a parliament has been more freely elected, either for the first time or with increased powers. In Yemen, however, democratization is currently in a precarious situation with the outbreak of renewed conflict between the northern and southern halves of the country, unified only since 1990.

Sudan and Lebanon are special cases. In the former, the head of state is an army officer; opposition parties are banned, and some of their leaders are imprisoned, under house arrest, or in self-imposed exile. The Sudanese press is muzzled and is limited now solely to government newspapers. (Although the government theoretically permits the establishment of private newspapers, the only one to test this freedom, *The Sudan International*, was suspended and its editor and staff jailed in March 1994.)

Sudan's record on human rights has been under attack from Amnesty International, Middle East Watch, the Arab Organization of Human Rights, the Federation of Arab Lawyers, and the Cairo-based periodical *Civil Society*. The UN General Assembly in December 1992 indicted the Sudanese government for rights abuses. The setback to civil society resulting from the coming to power of the NIF has been grievous. Among other things, the NIF-military regime has succeeded in abolishing the constitution; imposing a state of emergency; arresting people without warrant; setting up special courts to try political opponents; dissolving the elected councils of trade unions and associations in favor of NIF-appointed special committees; purging members of the opposition from the bureaucracy; and replacing about a thousand officers and 57 judges with NIF loyalists. About 40 daily and weekly publications have been closed and more than a thousand journalists dismissed. Summary executions and torture of prisoners have been common. Islamic law has also been imposed on the country and women forced to wear the veil.

Since it took over in June 1989, the NIF-military government has also expanded Khartoum's war against the largely Christian and animist dissidents of the south, whose main demands are local autonomy and exemption from Islamic law. Apologists for Sheikh Hassan al-Turabi, the NIF's leader, claim that he continues to hold democratic views, but it is very difficult to feel assured about al-Turabi and the Sudan at the present time considering the NIF's known penchant for forming militias and intimidating its political opponents. It is possible that extraordinary measures have been resorted to temporarily in order to establish an Islamic order, but it is difficult to imagine an Islamic or any other order imposed by force continuing to survive without force.

Lebanon, as usual, is complicated and exceptional. It has recently emerged from civil war with a new political arrangement that redistributes power among its various communities in a way that more closely reflects demographic facts. In August 1992, parliamentary elections took place for the first time since 1972, and most militias had laid down their arms. The country is now enjoying peace, and reconstruction is proceeding at a feverish pace. Muslim professional women fill numerous important positions in organizations as varied as banks and schools. Another striking fact is that only in Lebanon has a Muslim fundamentalist party, Hezbollah, been allowed to run for parliament. It has won eight seats in parliament, follows a policy of accommodation with other parties and factions in Lebanese domestic politics, and is quite vociferous in its defense of liberties. In Lebanon the private sector of the economy has always been predominant, and the government is now also proposing to privatize the telephone, electrical, and railway systems, as well as other parts of the country's infrastructure.

Nevertheless, enough problems linger to keep Lebanon from being fully democratic or fully at peace. The once-preeminent Maronite community boycotted the parliamentary elections, citing serious objections to the electoral law and to holding elections under the guns of the Syrian army. In some constituencies, voter turnout was 10 percent or less. Some candidates gained office who would have had no chance of winning truly competitive elections. Human rights organizations have expressed serious concerns about isolated incidents of violations, especially of prisoners' rights. Moreover, the government has recently prohibited private radio and television stations from presenting news reports, pending the passing of a new broadcast-regulation law. The written press, long famous as the freest and liveliest in the Arab world, continues to flourish, though not without some government harassment.

Under the pretext of resisting Israeli occupation, Hezbollah is the only group allowed to carry arms, not only in the south but also as far north as Baalbeck. The Syrians continue to maintain an undiminished military presence in the country despite the Taif Agreement, which set a timetable for their withdrawal, and the Syrian government enjoys a transparent hegemony over Lebanese affairs. Moreover, part of southern

Lebanon is still under Israeli occupation. Thus it is small wonder that many Lebanese see their country as falling short of total peace or democracy.

If the case of Lebanon offers grounds for guarded hope, Yemen's story is the stuff of tragedy. In the early 1990s, the Yemenis achieved political unity between the north and south, and then introduced constitutional democracy. Today, civil war is threatening to engulf the country in blood as powerful parties square off over regional issues and disputes concerning the power-sharing arrangements that made unification and free elections possible.

Of all the Arab countries, Morocco and Kuwait have perhaps made the most progress in democratization recently. In 1993, Morocco conducted its freest parliamentary elections since the 1960s and undertook extensive privatization of government-owned corporations and properties. When parliamentary elections were first resumed in the 1970s, the legislature was hardly more than a rubber stamp for the king. The elections of 1993, however, were carried out under a new electoral law and a new constitution that increased the powers of parliament. Eleven political parties and a score of independent candidates participated in an election held under judicial supervision. For the first time, the opposition parties gained a plurality, though not an outright majority. Moreover, two women were elected out of a record number of 33 female candidates.

The king still names the prime minister, but the latter now chooses the cabinet himself. For the first time, parliament can hold votes of no-confidence in the government. Under the new constitution, moreover, a third of the MPs are to be indirectly elected from Morocco's local chambers of commerce, its agricultural and professional syndicates, and its popularly elected municipal councils. In just one other Arab country, Egypt, is such corporate representation recognized. Its importance for invigorating civil society should not be underestimated. Finally, it should be noted that even during the repression of 1965-77, Morocco's political parties and its press enjoyed some freedom.

In Kuwait, the monarchy's defeat at the hands of Saddam Hussein's invading army in 1990, at a time when parliament had been dissolved, damaged royal prestige. Kuwait's experience with elected parliaments goes back to 1962 (the year after its independence), but has not been uninterrupted. In 1992, the opposition asserted itself in newly liberated Kuwait and returned to parliament with increased powers. Although the Constitution still forbids the formation of political parties, seven political "formations" took part in the 1992 voting. In addition to the election of a new parliament, the emir agreed to select six cabinet ministers from among the ranks of MPs, a first in Kuwaiti history. The new parliament has proved to be the most assertive ever, especially in fiscal matters. It has forced the government to compromise on the defense budget and the issue of military preparedness, as well as on the paramount question of how to settle the royal family's bank loans. Kuwait has enjoyed a lively and relatively free press since independence, and free debates also occur regularly in small private gatherings called *diwaaniyas*.

Egypt is perhaps the best-known case of liberalization in the Arab world. Reforms began under the late President Anwar al-Sadat in the mid-1970s, but serious progress was made only in the 1980s under President Hosni Mubarak, who succeeded the assassinated Sadat in 1981. Mubarak has pursued a policy of gradual liberalization and democratization, and has followed the same approach in the area of economic reforms and privatization. Eleven political parties now compete; seven of them were licensed by an administrative-court ruling that overturned the government's attempt to deny them legal status. The press remains mostly state-run; a private opposition press has emerged and gained in confidence, but now faces a clampdown at the hands of a government made nervous by violent Muslim-extremist groups. The courts remain independent and willing to rule against the government.

Still, Egypt's democracy is marred by three major flaws. First there are the state-of-emergency laws, which have been in effect since 1981 despite strong opposition. Second, presidential elections continue to be plebiscitary rather than competitive. No contender has run against the incumbent since Gamal Abdel Nasser and his Free Officers movement abolished the constitutional monarchy in 1953. As in Mexico, the ruling party continues to maintain uninterrupted dominance. Finally, the fight against the Islamic insurgency has resulted in many human rights violations and a retrenchment in the democratization process.

Small Steps Forward

Democracy remains at the embryonic stage in some Arab states, and is nonexistent in most. It has made respectable progress in countries like Morocco, Kuwait, and Lebanon, and more modest gains in Jordan and Tunisia. In Egypt, on the other hand, it is barely holding its own, while it has suffered outright reverses in Algeria, Yemen, and Sudan. Libya and Iraq are still dictatorships; the Arabian peninsula, dominated by authoritarian monarchies, remains politically conservative.

Both practically and theoretically speaking, the best approach to gauging the status of democracy in the Arab states is to disaggregate the concept and then consider which aspects of it are making progress and where. This approach enables us to acknowledge small steps forward and not become too discouraged over the paucity of achievements. Although what has been achieved falls well short of full democratization, it nonetheless deserves recognition, assistance, and consolidation.

This essay has questioned the notion that civil society in the Arab world can perform an essential role in the democratization process. In examining the Arab states, we have discovered that government and civil society mirror each other in certain ways. Civil society reflects the government in its weakness as well as in its authoritarian attributes; it therefore has limited potential as an engine of democratization—a judgment that can only become firmer when one considers the traditional dependence of civil society on government in the Arab world.

In practice, the best way to assist civil society is to encourage the privatization of cultural and social organizations. Governments have already begun to implement enterprise privatization; they should extend the process to include cultural institutions such as schools, newspapers, journals, publishing houses, movie studios, theaters, radio and television stations, and the like. Privatization should also extend to trade unions, cooperatives, and professional syndicates—institutions which in many countries have long been dominated and manipulated by governments. Governments that manage or manipulate these organizations should give them complete freedom. In other cases, autonomy rather than total independence would be more helpful. Sports clubs, for instance, are rarely self-supporting in less developed countries, and can benefit considerably from government subsidies. In short, privatization in the abovementioned areas is essential for improving the quality of democracy and consolidating it in Arab countries.

Too much emphasis on the concept of civil society seems to distract one from focusing on democratization. If the government's authoritarian attitudes are shared by civil society, democrats may well view the latter as part of the problem rather than part of the solution. If, on the other hand, civil society tends to be democratic, it will probably already be supporting democratization. In this case, it is more difficult (though probably less important) to know where and how to intervene.

In the long run, of course, a democratic government needs a democratic political culture, and vice versa. A glimmer of hope resides in the decisions that Arab governments have been making, usually for their own reasons, to reduce their own powers and responsibilities and to introduce democratic measures. With the passage of time, democratic practices may become firmly rooted. Second, as we have seen, governments in Arab states have had more to do with creating and promoting civil society than civil society has had to do with democratizing government. Then, too, many traditional organizations not usually included under the rubric of civil society have a contribution to make in establishing limits on governmental powers in Arab states. Finally, the sheer presence of a multiplicity of organizations (whether "democratic" or not) in the political arena serves to create checks and balances. These groups limit one another's power, and all together they tend to limit the state, thus creating a situation favorable to democracy.

24. BOWLING ALONE: AMERICA'S DECLINING SOCIAL CAPITAL

Robert D. Putnam

***Robert D. Putnam** is Dillon Professor of International Affairs and director of the Center for International Affairs at Harvard University. His most recent books are* Double-Edged Diplomacy: International Bargaining and Domestic Politics *(1993) and* Making Democracy Work: Civic Traditions in Modern Italy *(1993), which is reviewed elsewhere in this issue. He is now completing a study of the revitalization of American democracy.*

Many students of the new democracies that have emerged over the past decade and a half have emphasized the importance of a strong and active civil society to the consolidation of democracy. Especially with regard to the postcommunist countries, scholars and democratic activists alike have lamented the absence or obliteration of traditions of independent civic engagement and a widespread tendency toward passive reliance on the state. To those concerned with the weakness of civil societies in the developing or postcommunist world, the advanced Western democracies and above all the United States have typically been taken as models to be emulated. There is striking evidence, however, that the vibrancy of American civil society has notably declined over the past several decades.

Ever since the publication of Alexis de Tocqueville's *Democracy in America*, the United States has played a central role in systematic studies of the links between democracy and civil society. Although this is in part because trends in American life are often regarded as harbingers of social modernization, it is also because America has traditionally been considered unusually "civic" (a reputation that, as we shall later see, has not been entirely unjustified).

When Tocqueville visited the United States in the 1830s, it was the Americans' propensity for civic association that most impressed him as the key to their unprecedented ability to make democracy work. "Americans of all ages, all stations in life, and all types of disposition," he observed, "are forever forming associations. There are not only commercial and industrial associations in which all take part, but others of a thousand different types—religious, moral, serious, futile, very general and very limited, immensely large and very minute. . . . Nothing, in my view, deserves more attention than the intellectual and moral associations in America."[1]

Recently, American social scientists of a neo-Tocquevillean bent have unearthed a wide range of empirical evidence that the quality of public life and the performance of social institutions (and not only in America) are indeed powerfully influenced by norms and networks of civic engagement. Researchers in such fields as education, urban poverty, unemployment, the control of crime and drug abuse, and even health have discovered that successful outcomes are more likely in civically engaged communities. Similarly, research on the varying economic attainments of different ethnic groups in the United States has demonstrated the importance of social bonds within each group. These results are consistent with research in a wide range of settings that demonstrates the vital importance of social networks for job placement and many other economic outcomes.

Meanwhile, a seemingly unrelated body of research on the sociology of economic development has also focused attention on the role of social networks. Some of this work is situated in the developing countries, and some of it elucidates the peculiarly successful "network capitalism" of East Asia.[2] Even in less exotic Western economies, however, researchers have discovered highly efficient, highly flexible "industrial districts" based on networks of collaboration among workers and small entrepreneurs. Far from being paleoindustrial anachronisms, these dense interpersonal and interorganizational networks undergird ultramodern industries, from the high tech of Silicon Valley to the high fashion of Benetton.

The norms and networks of civic engagement also powerfully affect the performance of representative government. That, at least, was the central conclusion of my own 20-year, quasi-experimental study of subnational governments in different regions of Italy.[3] Although all these regional governments seemed identical on paper, their levels of effectiveness varied dramatically. Systematic inquiry showed that the quality of governance was determined by longstanding traditions of civic engagement (or its absence). Voter turnout, newspaper readership, membership in choral societies and football clubs—these were the hallmarks of a successful region. In fact, historical analysis suggested that these networks of organized reciprocity and civic solidarity, far from being an epiphenomenon of socioeconomic modernization, were a precondition for it.

No doubt the mechanisms through which civic engagement and social connectedness produce such results—better schools, faster economic development, lower crime, and more effective government—are multiple and complex. While these briefly recounted findings require further confirmation and perhaps qualification, the parallels across hundreds of empirical studies in a dozen disparate disciplines and subfields are striking. Social scientists in several fields have recently suggested a common framework for understanding these phenomena, a framework that rests on the concept of *social capital.*[4] By analogy with notions of physical capital and human capital—tools and training that enhance individual productivity—"social capital" refers to features of social organization such as networks, norms, and social trust that facilitate coordination and cooperation for mutual benefit.

For a variety of reasons, life is easier in a community blessed with a substantial stock of social capital. In the first place, networks of civic engagement foster sturdy norms of generalized reciprocity and encourage the emergence of social trust. Such networks facilitate coordination and communication, amplify reputations, and thus allow dilemmas of collective action to be resolved. When economic and political negotiation is embedded in dense networks of social interaction, incentives for opportunism are reduced. At the same time, networks of civic engagement embody past success at collaboration, which can serve as a cultural template for future collaboration. Finally, dense networks of interaction probably broaden the participants' sense of self, developing the "I" into the "we," or (in the language of rational-choice theorists) enhancing the participants' "taste" for collective benefits.

I do not intend here to survey (much less contribute to) the development of the theory of social capital. Instead, I use the central premise of that rapidly growing body of work—that social connections and civic engagement pervasively influence our public life, as well as our private prospects—as the starting point for an empirical survey of trends in social capital in contemporary America. I concentrate here entirely on the American case, although the developments I portray may in some measure characterize many contemporary societies.

Whatever Happened to Civic Engagement?

We begin with familiar evidence on changing patterns of political participation, not least because it is immediately relevant to issues of democracy in the narrow sense. Consider the well-known decline in turnout in national elections over the last three decades. From a relative high point in the early 1960s, voter turnout had by 1990 declined by nearly a quarter; tens of millions of Americans had forsaken their parents' habitual readiness to engage in the simplest act of citizenship. Broadly similar trends also characterize participation in state and local elections.

It is not just the voting booth that has been increasingly deserted by

Americans. A series of identical questions posed by the Roper Organization to national samples ten times each year over the last two decades reveals that since 1973 the number of Americans who report that "in the past year" they have "attended a public meeting on town or school affairs" has fallen by more than a third (from 22 percent in 1973 to 13 percent in 1993). Similar (or even greater) relative declines are evident in responses to questions about attending a political rally or speech, serving on a committee of some local organization, and working for a political party. By almost every measure, Americans' direct engagement in politics and government has fallen steadily and sharply over the last generation, despite the fact that average levels of education—the best individual-level predictor of political participation—have risen sharply throughout this period. Every year over the last decade or two, millions more have withdrawn from the affairs of their communities.

By almost every measure, Americans' direct engagement in politics and government has fallen steadily and sharply over the last generation.

Not coincidentally, Americans have also disengaged psychologically from politics and government over this era. The proportion of Americans who reply that they "trust the government in Washington" only "some of the time" or "almost never" has risen steadily from 30 percent in 1966 to 75 percent in 1992.

These trends are well known, of course, and taken by themselves would seem amenable to a strictly political explanation. Perhaps the long litany of political tragedies and scandals since the 1960s (assassinations, Vietnam, Watergate, Irangate, and so on) has triggered an understandable disgust for politics and government among Americans, and that in turn has motivated their withdrawal. I do not doubt that this common interpretation has some merit, but its limitations become plain when we examine trends in civic engagement of a wider sort.

Our survey of organizational membership among Americans can usefully begin with a glance at the aggregate results of the General Social Survey, a scientifically conducted, national-sample survey that has been repeated 14 times over the last two decades. Church-related groups constitute the most common type of organization joined by Americans; they are especially popular with women. Other types of organizations frequently joined by women include school-service groups (mostly parent-teacher associations), sports groups, professional societies, and literary societies. Among men, sports clubs, labor unions, professional societies, fraternal groups, veterans' groups, and service clubs are all relatively popular.

Religious affiliation is by far the most common associational membership among Americans. Indeed, by many measures America continues to be (even more than in Tocqueville's time) an astonishingly "churched" society. For example, the United States has more houses of worship per capita than any other nation on Earth. Yet religious sentiment in America seems to be becoming somewhat less tied to institutions and more self-defined.

How have these complex crosscurrents played out over the last three or four decades in terms of Americans' engagement with organized religion? The general pattern is clear: The 1960s witnessed a significant drop in reported weekly churchgoing—from roughly 48 percent in the late 1950s to roughly 41 percent in the early 1970s. Since then, it has stagnated or (according to some surveys) declined still further. Meanwhile, data from the General Social Survey show a modest decline in membership in all "church-related groups" over the last 20 years. It would seem, then, that net participation by Americans, both in religious services and in church-related groups, has declined modestly (by perhaps a sixth) since the 1960s.

For many years, labor unions provided one of the most common organizational affiliations among American workers. Yet union membership has been falling for nearly four decades, with the steepest decline occurring between 1975 and 1985. Since the mid-1950s, when union membership peaked, the unionized portion of the nonagricultural work force in America has dropped by more than half, falling from 32.5 percent in 1953 to 15.8 percent in 1992. By now, virtually all of the explosive growth in union membership that was associated with the New Deal has been erased. The solidarity of union halls is now mostly a fading memory of aging men.[5]

The parent-teacher association (PTA) has been an especially important form of civic engagement in twentieth-century America because parental involvement in the educational process represents a particularly productive form of social capital. It is, therefore, dismaying to discover that participation in parent-teacher organizations has dropped drastically over the last generation, from more than 12 million in 1964 to barely 5 million in 1982 before recovering to approximately 7 million now.

Next, we turn to evidence on membership in (and volunteering for) civic and fraternal organizations. These data show some striking patterns. First, membership in traditional women's groups has declined more or less steadily since the mid-1960s. For example, membership in the national Federation of Women's Clubs is down by more than half (59 percent) since 1964, while membership in the League of Women Voters (LWV) is off 42 percent since 1969.[6]

Similar reductions are apparent in the numbers of volunteers for mainline civic organizations, such as the Boy Scouts (off by 26 percent since 1970) and the Red Cross (off by 61 percent since 1970). But what about the possibility that volunteers have simply switched their loyalties to other organizations? Evidence on "regular" (as opposed to occasional or "drop-by") volunteering is available from the Labor Department's Current Population Surveys of 1974 and 1989. These estimates suggest that serious volunteering declined by roughly one-sixth over these 15 years, from 24 percent of adults in 1974 to 20 percent in 1989. The multitudes of Red Cross aides and Boy Scout troop leaders now missing in action have apparently not been offset by equal numbers of new recruits elsewhere.

Fraternal organizations have also witnessed a substantial drop in membership during the 1980s and 1990s. Membership is down significantly in such groups as the Lions (off 12 percent since 1983), the Elks (off 18 percent since 1979), the Shriners (off 27 percent since 1979), the Jaycees (off 44 percent since 1979), and the Masons (down 39 percent since 1959). In sum, after expanding steadily throughout most of this century, many major civic organizations have experienced a sudden, substantial, and nearly simultaneous decline in membership over the last decade or two.

The most whimsical yet discomfiting bit of evidence of social disengagement in contemporary America that I have discovered is this: more Americans are bowling today than ever before, but bowling in organized leagues has plummeted in the last decade or so. Between 1980 and 1993 the total number of bowlers in America increased by 10 percent, while league bowling decreased by 40 percent. (Lest this be thought a wholly trivial example, I should note that nearly 80 million Americans went bowling at least once during 1993, *nearly a third more than voted in the 1994 congressional elections* and roughly the same number as claim to attend church regularly. Even after the 1980s' plunge in league bowling, nearly 3 percent of American adults regularly bowl in leagues.) The rise of solo bowling threatens the livelihood of bowling-lane proprietors because those who bowl as members of leagues consume three times as much beer and pizza as solo bowlers, and the money in bowling is in the beer and pizza, not the balls and shoes. The broader social significance, however, lies in the social interaction and even occasionally civic conversations over beer and pizza that solo bowlers forgo. Whether or not bowling beats balloting in the eyes of most Americans, bowling teams illustrate yet another vanishing form of social capital.

Countertrends

At this point, however, we must confront a serious counterargument. Perhaps the traditional forms of civic organization whose decay we have been tracing have been replaced by vibrant new organizations. For example, national environmental organizations (like the Sierra Club) and feminist groups (like the National Organization for Women) grew rapidly during the 1970s and 1980s and now count hundreds of thousands of dues-paying members. An even more dramatic example is the American Association of Retired Persons (AARP), which grew exponentially from 400,000 card-carrying members in 1960 to 33 million in 1993, becoming (after the Catholic Church) the largest private organization in the world. The national administrators of these organizations are among the most feared lobbyists in Washington, in large part because of their massive mailing lists of presumably loyal members.

These new mass-membership organizations are plainly of great political importance. From the point of view of social connectedness, however, they are sufficiently different from classic "secondary associations" that we need to invent a new label—perhaps "tertiary associations." For the vast majority of their members, the only act of membership consists in writing a check for dues or perhaps occasionally reading a newsletter. Few ever attend any meetings of such organizations, and most are unlikely ever (knowingly) to encounter any other member. The bond between any two members of the Sierra Club is less like the bond between any two members of a gardening club and more like the bond between any two Red Sox fans (or perhaps any two devoted Honda owners): they root for the same team and they share some of the same interests, but they are unaware of each other's existence. Their ties, in short, are to common symbols, common leaders, and perhaps common ideals, but not to one another. The theory of social capital argues that associational membership should, for example, increase social trust, but this prediction is much less straightforward with regard to membership in tertiary associations. From the point of view of social connectedness, the Environmental Defense Fund and a bowling league are just not in the same category.

If the growth of tertiary organizations represents one potential (but probably not real) counterexample to my thesis, a second countertrend is represented by the growing prominence of nonprofit organizations, especially nonprofit service agencies. This so-called third sector includes everything from Oxfam and the Metropolitan Museum of Art to the Ford Foundation and the Mayo Clinic. In other words, although most secondary associations are nonprofits, most nonprofit agencies are not secondary associations. To identify trends in the size of the nonprofit sector with trends in social connectedness would be another fundamental conceptual mistake.[7]

A third potential countertrend is much more relevant to an assessment of social capital and civic engagement. Some able researchers have argued that the last few decades have witnessed a rapid expansion in "support groups" of various sorts. Robert Wuthnow reports that fully 40 percent of all Americans claim to be "currently involved in [a] small group that meets regularly and provides support or caring for those who participate in it."[8] Many of these groups are religiously affiliated, but many others are not. For example, nearly 5 percent of Wuthnow's national sample claim to participate regularly in a "self-help" group, such as Alcoholics Anonymous, and nearly as many say they belong to book-discussion groups and hobby clubs.

The groups described by Wuthnow's respondents unquestionably represent an important form of social capital, and they need to be accounted for in any serious reckoning of trends in social connectedness. On the other hand, they do not typically play the same role as traditional civic associations. As Wuthnow emphasizes,

> Small groups may not be fostering community as effectively as many of their proponents would like. Some small groups merely provide occasions for individuals to focus on themselves in the presence of others. The social contract binding members together asserts only the weakest of obligations. Come if you have time. Talk if you feel like it. Respect everyone's opinion. Never criticize. Leave quietly if you become dissatisfied. . . . We can imagine that [these small groups] really substitute for families, neighborhoods, and broader community attachments that may demand lifelong commitments, when, in fact, they do not.[9]

All three of these potential countertrends—tertiary organizations, nonprofit organizations, and support groups—need somehow to be weighed against the erosion of conventional civic organizations. One way of doing so is to consult the General Social Survey.

Within all educational categories, total associational membership declined significantly between 1967 and 1993. Among the college-educated, the average number of group memberships per person fell from 2.8 to 2.0 (a 26-percent decline); among high-school graduates, the number fell from 1.8 to 1.2 (32 percent); and among those with fewer than 12 years of education, the number fell from 1.4 to 1.1 (25 percent). In other words, at *all* educational (and hence social) levels of American society, and counting *all* sorts of group memberships, *the average number of associational memberships has fallen by about a fourth over the last quarter-century.* Without controls for educational levels, the trend is not nearly so clear, but the central point is this: *more Americans than ever before are in social circumstances that foster associational involvement (higher education, middle age, and so on), but nevertheless aggregate associational membership appears to be stagnant or declining.*

Broken down by type of group, the downward trend is most marked for church-related groups, for labor unions, for fraternal and veterans' organizations, and for school-service groups. Conversely, membership in professional associations has risen over these years, although less than might have been predicted, given sharply rising educational and occupational levels. Essentially the same trends are evident for both men and women in the sample. In short, the available survey evidence confirms our earlier conclusion: American social capital in the form of civic associations has significantly eroded over the last generation.

Good Neighborliness and Social Trust

I noted earlier that most readily available quantitative evidence on trends in social connectedness involves formal settings, such as the voting booth, the union hall, or the PTA. One glaring exception is so widely discussed as to require little comment here: the most fundamental form of social capital is the family, and the massive evidence of the loosening of bonds within the family (both extended and nuclear) is well known. This trend, of course, is quite consistent with—and may help to explain—our theme of social decapitalization.

A second aspect of informal social capital on which we happen to have reasonably reliable time-series data involves neighborliness. In each General Social Survey since 1974 respondents have been asked, "How often do you spend a social evening with a neighbor?" The proportion of Americans who socialize with their neighbors more than once a year has slowly but steadily declined over the last two decades, from 72 percent in 1974 to 61 percent in 1993. (On the other hand, socializing with "friends who do not live in your neighborhood" appears to be on the increase, a trend that may reflect the growth of workplace-based social connections.)

Americans are also less trusting. The proportion of Americans saying that most people can be trusted fell by more than a third between 1960, when 58 percent chose that alternative, and 1993, when only 37 percent did. The same trend is apparent in all educational groups; indeed, because social trust is also correlated with education and because educational levels have risen sharply, the overall decrease in social trust is even more apparent if we control for education.

Our discussion of trends in social connectedness and civic engagement has tacitly assumed that all the forms of social capital that we have discussed are themselves coherently correlated across individuals. This is in fact true. Members of associations are much more likely than nonmembers to participate in politics, to spend time with neighbors, to express social trust, and so on.

The close correlation between social trust and associational membership is true not only across time and across individuals, but also across countries. Evidence from the 1991 World Values Survey demonstrates the following:[10]

1) Across the 35 countries in this survey, social trust and civic engagement are strongly correlated; the greater the density of associational membership in a society, the more trusting its citizens. Trust and engagement are two facets of the same underlying factor—social capital.

2) America still ranks relatively high by cross-national standards on both these dimensions of social capital. Even in the 1990s, after several decades' erosion, Americans are more trusting and more engaged than people in most other countries of the world.

3) The trends of the past quarter-century, however, have apparently moved the United States significantly lower in the international rankings of social capital. The recent deterioration in American social capital has been sufficiently great that (if no other country changed its position in the meantime) another quarter-century of change at the same rate would bring the United States, roughly speaking, to the midpoint among all these countries, roughly equivalent to South Korea, Belgium, or Estonia today. Two generations' decline at the same rate would leave the United States at the level of today's Chile, Portugal, and Slovenia.

Why Is U.S. Social Capital Eroding?

As we have seen, something has happened in America in the last two or three decades to diminish civic engagement and social connectedness. What could that "something" be? Here are several possible explanations, along with some initial evidence on each.

The movement of women into the labor force. Over these same two or three decades, many millions of American women have moved out of the home into paid employment. This is the primary, though not the sole, reason why the weekly working hours of the average American have increased significantly during these years. It seems highly plausible that this social revolution should have reduced the time and energy available for building social capital. For certain organizations, such as the PTA, the League of Women Voters, the Federation of Women's Clubs, and the Red Cross, this is almost certainly an important part of the story. The sharpest decline in women's civic participation seems to have come in the 1970s; membership in such "women's" organizations as these has been virtually halved since the late 1960s. By contrast, most of the decline in participation in men's organizations occurred about ten years later; the total decline to date has been approximately 25 percent for the typical organization. On the other hand, the survey data imply that the aggregate declines for men are virtually as great as those for women. It is logically possible, of course, that the male declines might represent the knock-on effect of women's liberation, as dishwashing crowded out the lodge, but time-budget studies suggest that most husbands of working wives have assumed only a minor part of the housework. In short, something besides the women's revolution seems to lie behind the erosion of social capital.

Mobility: The "re-potting" hypothesis. Numerous studies of organizational involvement have shown that residential stability and such related phenomena as homeownership are clearly associated with greater civic engagement. Mobility, like frequent re-potting of plants, tends to disrupt root systems, and it takes time for an uprooted individual to put down new roots. It seems plausible that the automobile, suburbanization, and the movement to the Sun Belt have reduced the social rootedness of the average American, but one fundamental difficulty with this hypothesis is apparent: the best evidence shows that residential stability and homeownership in America have risen modestly since 1965, and are surely higher now than during the 1950s, when civic engagement and social connectedness by our measures was definitely higher.

Other demographic transformations. A range of additional changes have transformed the American family since the 1960s—fewer marriages, more divorces, fewer children, lower real wages, and so on. Each of these changes might account for some of the slackening of civic engagement, since married, middle-class parents are generally more socially involved than other people. Moreover, the changes in scale that have swept over the American economy in these years—illustrated by the replacement of the corner grocery by the supermarket and now perhaps of the supermarket by electronic shopping at home, or the replacement of community-based enterprises by outposts of distant multinational firms—may perhaps have undermined the material and even physical basis for civic engagement.

The technological transformation of leisure. There is reason to believe that deep-seated technological trends are radically "privatizing" or "individualizing" our use of leisure time and thus disrupting many opportunities for social-capital formation. The most obvious and probably the most powerful instrument of this revolution is television. Time-budget studies in the 1960s showed that the growth in time spent watching television dwarfed all other changes in the way Americans passed their days and nights. Television has made our communities (or, rather, what we experience as our communities) wider and shallower. In the language of economics, electronic technology enables individual tastes to be satisfied more fully, but at the cost of the positive social externalities associated with more primitive forms of entertainment. The same logic applies to the replacement of vaudeville by the movies and now of movies by the VCR. The new "virtual reality" helmets that we will soon don to be entertained in total isolation are merely the latest extension of this trend. Is technology thus driving a wedge between our individual interests and our collective interests? It is a question that seems worth exploring more systematically.

What Is to Be Done?

The last refuge of a social-scientific scoundrel is to call for more research. Nevertheless, I cannot forbear from suggesting some further lines of inquiry.

• We must sort out the dimensions of social capital, which clearly is not a unidimensional concept, despite language (even in this essay) that implies the contrary. What types of organizations and networks most effectively embody—or generate—social capital, in the sense of mutual reciprocity, the resolution of dilemmas of collective action, and the broadening of social identities? In this essay I have emphasized the density of associational life. In earlier work I stressed the structure of networks, arguing that "horizontal" ties represented more productive social capital than vertical ties.[11]

We need to explore creatively how public policy impinges on social-capital formation. In some well-known instances, public policy has destroyed highly effective social networks and norms.

•Another set of important issues involves macrosociological crosscurrents that might intersect with the trends described here. What will be the impact, for example, of electronic networks on social capital? My hunch is that meeting in an electronic forum is not the equivalent of meeting in a bowling alley—or even in a saloon—but hard empirical research is needed. What about the development of social capital in the workplace? Is it growing in counterpoint to the decline of civic engagement, reflecting some social analogue of the first law of thermodynamics—social capital is neither created nor destroyed, merely redistributed? Or do the trends described in this essay represent a deadweight loss?

• A rounded assessment of changes in American social capital over the last quarter-century needs to count the costs as well as the benefits of community engagement. We must not romanticize small-town, middle-class civic life in the America of the 1950s. In addition to the deleterious trends emphasized in this essay, recent decades have witnessed a substantial decline in intolerance and probably also in overt discrimination, and those beneficent trends may be related in complex ways to the erosion of traditional social capital. Moreover, a balanced accounting of the social-capital books would need to reconcile the insights of this approach with the undoubted insights offered by Mancur Olson and others who stress that closely knit social, economic, and political organizations are prone to inefficient cartelization and to what political economists term "rent seeking" and ordinary men and women call corruption.[12]

• Finally, and perhaps most urgently, we need to explore creatively how public policy impinges on (or might impinge on) social-capital formation. In some well-known instances, public policy has destroyed highly effective social networks and norms. American slum-clearance policy of the 1950s and 1960s, for example, renovated physical capital, but at a very high cost to existing social capital. The consolidation of country post offices and small school districts has promised administrative and financial efficiencies, but full-cost accounting for the effects of these policies on social capital might produce a more negative verdict. On the other hand, such past initiatives as the county agricultural-agent system, community colleges, and tax deductions for charitable contributions illustrate that government can encourage social-capital formation. Even a recent proposal in San Luis Obispo, California, to require that all new houses have front porches illustrates the power of government to influence where and how networks are formed.

The concept of "civil society" has played a central role in the recent global debate about the preconditions for democracy and democratization. In the newer democracies this phrase has properly focused attention on the need to foster a vibrant civic life in soils traditionally inhospitable to self-government. In the established democracies, ironically, growing numbers of citizens are questioning the effectiveness of their public institutions at the very moment when liberal democracy has swept the battlefield, both ideologically and geopolitically. In America, at least, there is reason to suspect that this democratic disarray may be linked to a broad and continuing erosion of civic engagement that began a quarter-century ago. High on our scholarly agenda should be the question of whether a comparable erosion of social capital may be under way in other advanced democracies, perhaps in different institutional and behavioral guises. High on America's agenda should be the question of how to reverse these adverse trends in social connectedness, thus restoring civic engagement and civic trust.

NOTES

1. Alexis de Tocqueville, *Democracy in America*, ed. J.P. Maier, trans. George Lawrence (Garden City, N.Y.: Anchor Books, 1969), 513-17.

2. On social networks and economic growth in the developing world, see Milton J. Esman and Norman Uphoff, *Local Organizations: Intermediaries in Rural Development* (Ithaca: Cornell University Press, 1984), esp. 15-42 and 99-180; and Albert O. Hirschman, *Getting Ahead Collectively: Grassroots Experiences in Latin America* (Elmsford, N.Y.: Pergamon Press, 1984), esp. 42-77. On East Asia, see Gustav Papanek, "The New Asian Capitalism: An Economic Portrait," in Peter L. Berger and Hsin-Huang Michael Hsiao, eds., *In Search of an East Asian Development Model* (New Brunswick, N.J.: Transaction, 1987), 27-80; Peter B. Evans, "The State as Problem and Solution: Predation, Embedded Autonomy and Structural Change," in Stephan Haggard and Robert R. Kaufman, eds., *The Politics of Economic Adjustment* (Princeton: Princeton University Press, 1992), 139-81; and Gary G. Hamilton, William Zeile, and Wan-Jin Kim, "Network Structure of East Asian Economies," in Stewart R. Clegg and S. Gordon Redding, eds., *Capitalism in Contrasting Cultures* (Hawthorne, N.Y.: De Gruyter, 1990), 105-29. See also Gary G. Hamilton and Nicole Woolsey Biggart, "Market, Culture, and Authority: A Comparative Analysis of Management and Organization in the Far East," *American Journal of Sociology* (Supplement) 94 (1988): S52-S94; and Susan Greenhalgh, "Families and Networks in Taiwan's Economic Development," in Edwin Winckler and Susan Greenhalgh, eds., *Contending Approaches to the Political Economy of Taiwan* (Armonk, N.Y.: M.E. Sharpe, 1987), 224-45.

3. Robert D. Putnam, *Making Democracy Work: Civic Traditions in Modern Italy* (Princeton: Princeton University Press, 1993).

4. James S. Coleman deserves primary credit for developing the "social capital" theoretical framework. See his "Social Capital in the Creation of Human Capital," *American Journal of Sociology* (Supplement) 94 (1988): S95-S120, as well as his *The Foundations of Social Theory* (Cambridge: Harvard University Press, 1990), 300-21. See also Mark Granovetter, "Economic Action and Social Structure: The Problem of Embeddedness," *American Journal of Sociology* 91 (1985): 481-510; Glenn C. Loury, "Why Should We Care About Group Inequality?" *Social Philosophy and Policy* 5 (1987): 249-71; and Robert D. Putnam, "The Prosperous Community: Social Capital and Public Life," *American Prospect* 13 (1993): 35-42. To my knowledge, the first scholar to use the term "social capital" in its current sense was Jane Jacobs, in *The Death and Life of Great American Cities* (New York: Random House, 1961), 138.

5. Any simplistically political interpretation of the collapse of American unionism would need to confront the fact that the steepest decline began more than six years before the Reagan administration's attack on PATCO. Data from the General Social Survey show a roughly 40-percent decline in reported union membership between 1975 and 1991.

6. Data for the LWV are available over a longer time span and show an interesting pattern: a sharp slump during the Depression, a strong and sustained rise after World War II that more than tripled membership between 1945 and 1969, and then the post-1969 decline, which has already erased virtually all the postwar gains and continues still. This same historical pattern applies to those men's fraternal organizations for which comparable data are available—steady increases for the first seven decades of the century, interrupted only by the Great Depression, followed by a collapse in the 1970s and 1980s that has already wiped out most of the postwar expansion and continues apace.

7. Cf. Lester M. Salamon, "The Rise of the Nonprofit Sector," *Foreign Affairs* 73 (July-August 1994): 109-22. See also Salamon, "Partners in Public Service: The Scope and Theory of Government-Nonprofit Relations," in Walter W. Powell, ed., *The Nonprofit Sector: A Research Handbook* (New Haven: Yale University Press, 1987), 99-117. Salamon's empirical evidence does not sustain his broad claims about a global "associational revolution" comparable in significance to the rise of the nation-state several centuries ago.

8. Robert Wuthnow, *Sharing the Journey: Support Groups and America's New Quest for Community* (New York: The Free Press, 1994), 45.

9. Ibid., 3-6.

10. I am grateful to Ronald Inglehart, who directs this unique cross-national project, for sharing these highly useful data with me. See his "The Impact of Culture on Economic Development: Theory, Hypotheses, and Some Empirical Tests" (unpublished manuscript, University of Michigan, 1994).

11. See my *Making Democracy Work*, esp. ch. 6.

12. See Mancur Olson, *The Rise and Decline of Nations: Economic Growth, Stagflation, and Social Rigidities* (New Haven: Yale University Press, 1982), 2.

IV.
The Global Democratic Prospect

25. THE TIDE UNDERNEATH THE "THIRD WAVE"

Henry S. Rowen

Henry S. Rowen *is Edward B. Rust Professor at the Graduate School of Business, Stanford University, and senior fellow at the Hoover Institution. He has been president of the RAND Corporation, chairman of the National Intelligence Council, and assistant secretary of defense for international security affairs.* *He wishes to thank Bruce Donald and George Wilson for their help in preparing this article.*

The collapse of the socialist model, the increase in the number of democracies throughout the world, and the growing influence of East Asia have made the relative prospects of various political-economic systems a matter of high current interest.

Several political analysts, Samuel P. Huntington prominent among them, have observed that democracy has advanced in waves since the early nineteenth century, with each wave giving way to partial reversals followed by new gains.[1] By Huntington's count, the net number of democracies went from zero before 1828 to 59 in 1990. The current wave—the third by his reckoning—began in the mid-1970s and has seen the number of democracies increase by about 30. Most of the increase, moreover, has taken place amid the ranks of non-Western countries. It is the thesis of this article that trends in both income and education bode well for the future of liberal democracy throughout the world, although there will certainly be setbacks in some countries and there may be periods of overall retreat. These setbacks, however, will be more than offset by a slowly rising tide of democracy.

The word "democracy" has different meanings in different contexts, as the burgeoning debate about "Asian" versus "Western" models of democracy attests. To measure the plight of the liberal, Western model, Freedom House annually assesses the actual status of political and civil rights in every nation of the globe. Political rights include free and fair elections, the opportunity to organize a real opposition with a realistic chance of coming to power, and so on. Civil ones include equal treatment under law, plus the freedoms of the press, discussion, assembly, and the like.[2]

This system of measurement is not without its difficulties, of course. One is the problem of aggregation: with so many separate vectors under both the political and civil categories, how they are weighted and combined can produce different overall assessments. Another snag is the relative neglect in this metric of the rights needed for the creation of wealth, including the protection of property, and of the increased personal liberties that directly flow from wealth. A third problem is raised by proponents of "Asian" democracy, who point to what they see as the ills flowing from extreme individualism in the West and praise the virtues of Asia's more "communal" ways. Taking all these difficulties into account, I would still maintain that the Freedom House rating system serves as a good yardstick for what it is meant to measure—namely, Western, liberal democracy.

Income and Democracy

Since 1960, when Seymour Martin Lipset published his pathbreaking study *Political Man*, it has been well known that the higher a nation's income, the more likely its politics are to be democratic.[3] What Lipset confirmed empirically, others had long intuited. As Lipset reminds us: "From Aristotle down to the present, men have argued that only in a wealthy society in which relatively few citizens lived at the level of real poverty could there be a situation in which the mass of the population intelligently participate in politics and develop the self-restraint necessary to avoid succumbing to the appeals of irresponsible demagogues."[4]

In a modern setting, one might add that making economic activities largely independent of political control places salutary limits on the power of government, although a competent state is still needed to set and enforce the rules that protect and facilitate productive activity. A people that enjoys even modest levels of property, prosperity, and education is unlikely to become servile. Indeed, the more means people acquire, the more likely they are to want a say in making the rules under which they live; the upshot is a wider domain of political freedom.

Zhao Ziyang, the former head of the Chinese Communist Party who lost his job after the 1989 Tiananmen Square uprising, reportedly put it this way in a secret speech to the Party leadership in June 1989:

> I used to think that so long as we did well in reforming the economy and people's living standards went up, then the people would be satisfied and society would be stable. But as I later discovered, this is not the way things are. After living standards and cultural levels have been raised, the people's sense of democracy and sense of political participation will grow

stronger. If the building of democracy and a legal system fails to keep up, then society will not be stable.[5]

Supporting this view is a cross-national survey, done for this essay, of the relationship between income and freedom in 1990. According to the combined Freedom House rating system for civil liberties and political rights, only Singapore, out of the 28 countries then with per-capita GDPs over $8,000 per year, was rated less than wholly free. All the West European and European-rooted countries are free and almost all are rich. Some nonrich countries are also free, or largely so, Bangladesh, India, Costa Rica, Uruguay, and Botswana among them. Most important, a regression of freedom versus income (1990 data) for 175 countries is significant at the 0.1-percent level. (See the Technical Note on pages 63-64 below for details on the regressions.)

Recently there have been several inquiries into the sources of this correlation: specifically, does democracy cause wealth, or vice versa, or is there a common cause of both?

The fact that several (initially) authoritarian governments in East Asia and Latin America have recently seen their countries' economies do well has suggested to some that such politics are needed to overcome resistance to growth-favorable policies and to ward off growth-damaging ones. Yet things are not that simple. Lawrence Sirowy and Alex Inkeles, surveying the literature on this subject (and noting its serious shortcomings), could find no well-established tie. Adam Przeworski and Fernando Limongi, summing up their own survey, conclude that "we do not know whether democracy fosters or hinders economic growth." John Helliwell found that a country's degree of democracy in 1960 yields no significant net influence on later economic growth (although this result might mask a negative direct effect of democracy on growth combined with a positive indirect one of established democracy on schooling and investment). In contrast, Mancur Olson argues that democracies do a better job over the long run in protecting property rights, an observation that is consistent with the long-sustained economic lead of the stable democracies.[6]

Because several nations, including South Korea, Taiwan, Chile, and Mexico, have become politically more pluralistic as they have become wealthier, the second possibility—that higher incomes promote democracy—has attracted attention. This position, that of Aristotle and Zhao Ziyang, receives support from the literature. For example, starting with 1960 income levels, Helliwell finds the effects of higher earlier incomes on democracy in the 1970s and 1980s to be significantly positive, while Przeworski and Limongi observe that "the *prima facie* evidence in support of this hypothesis is overwhelming: all developed countries constitute stable democracies while stable democracies in the less developed countries remain exceptional."

As to the third possibility—a common cause for both wealth and democracy—the joint evolution over many centuries of the institutions of capitalism and of liberal politics in Northern Europe strongly suggests an intimate relationship. Whatever the original connections in Europe, a regression analysis of 1990 incomes versus democracy that excludes Northwestern Europe and countries of British settlement leaves the wealth-freedom correlation highly significant (at the 0.5-percent level). The correlation is still significant (at the 1-percent level) when all other former British colonies are also eliminated on the grounds that Britain did a good job of transferring democratic norms and institutions to many of its colonies.

Of particular interest are the outliers, the countries that are markedly more—or less—democratic than their incomes suggest that they "should" be.

These results support the interpretation that the wealth-democracy nexus is more than just a Western phenomenon, but leaves open the possibility that some other unexplained influences account for the presence of this nexus among non-Western nations. In order to eliminate factors that are common to subgroups of countries, one can examine the income-freedom nexus within each subgroup. Lipset did this by dividing his sample of nations into European/English-speaking and Latin American subgroups and making comparisons within each of them. The importance of taking a finer-grained look becomes all the more apparent when one considers that 49 of the 72 states rated "free" in 1990 by Freedom House were either European or former British colonies. There were a few European states that were only "partly free," but they had just recently been liberated from Soviet thrall. There were several countries with a heritage of British rule that were less than "free"; most were in Africa, including Zambia and Nigeria. (A possible explanation is that British colonial rule in those places did not last long enough to have the deep effects that it did in North America, the West Indies, and elsewhere.)

Of particular interest are the outliers, the countries that are markedly more—or less—democratic than their incomes suggest that they "should" be. Examples on the more democratic side are Bangladesh, India, Costa Rica, and Greece. Some of these have a British colonial past, some may not be stably democratic, and some warrant a closer look. Those on the less democratic side relative to income levels (aside from those enriched by oil) include Singapore and Syria.

In his recent, much-discussed essay arguing that future conflicts will be between "civilizations," Samuel Huntington identified eight of them: Western, Latin American, Slavic-Orthodox, Islamic, Hindu, Confucian, Japanese, and possibly African.[7] The results from income-versus-freedom analyses within each of these groups are striking: the correlation holds within six of the seven that contain enough countries to support a statistical analysis (the Hindu set was the one that had to be excluded). The exception is Islam (with a negative correlation at the 20-percent level). If the eight small, oil-rich, and distinctly nondemocratic Islamic countries are excluded from the sample, there is *no* significant correlation. Among the Arab nations there is a negative correlation between wealth and freedom (at the 10-percent level), but with the oil-rich Arab states again excluded there is no significant correlation. In contrast, non-Arab Islamic nations without much oil correspond to the nearly universal high-income-equals-high-freedom norm (at the 10-percent level).

The Islamic countries that have significant democratic attributes are non-Arab and might be regarded as being less Islamic culturally than the Arab core because of Westernizing influences (Turkey); large non-Islamic populations (Malaysia); or an indigenous culture that survived Islamization (Indonesia). As for the Arabs, they are the direct heirs of the central Islamic tradition, in which there is no distinction between religious and secular authority (the caliph has both kinds). In many Islamic countries secular authority has been established without a religious component, but this goes very much against the grain of these societies and may partly explain why Arab states are usually nondemocratic. In any case, the Arab record of constitutionalism and representative government is one of failure.

The finding that income and democracy are correlated (with varying degrees of significance) within every civilization but one in which a test is possible should help put to rest the notion that Western democracy is culture-bound. A question remains about its applicability to Arab countries, however.

Education and Democracy

Many commentators, from Lord Bryce and John Dewey to Lipset, Gabriel Almond, and Sidney Verba, have seen education as the basic requirement of democracy. Alex Inkeles and David H. Smith, in their investigation of the correlates of modernity in six countries (Argentina, Chile, Bangladesh, India, Israel, and Nigeria) found that education was the single most important variable in creating "modern man," whom they describe as "an informed participant citizen [with] a marked sense of personal efficacy."[8]

There are two ways in which education can influence democracy: one is directly, through the effect that an educated citizenry can have on political processes and institutions. The other is indirectly, through education's contribution to higher incomes. That education is one of the major sources of economic growth has been an important finding of modern growth economics. Costas Azariadis and Allan Drazen found

Table 1—Average Years of Schooling (For Ages 25+)

	1960	1985
West	6.5	8.7
Latin America	3.0	4.9
Orthodox	5.0	7.6
Sub-Saharan Africa	1.3	2.8
Confucian	4.3	7.1
Buddhist	2.6	4.2
Islamic	1.1	3.1

that no country grew rapidly in the postwar era without a highly literate labor force. Also, Robert Barro found that the level of primary and secondary enrollment in 1960 was significant in explaining later economic growth in a large sample of developing countries.[9]

There is yet another link between education and income: investment in education is income-elastic. Thus anything that increases income—whether it be education, advances in technology, physical investment, or exploitation of natural resources—will foster more education and, in turn, more democracy.

The content of education presumably also matters. Thus Germany, which had become an advanced industrial country by the end of the nineteenth century and had a clearly democratic government after its defeat in World War I, fell prey to Nazi demagoguery and totalitarianism. One of the things that made Nazism's rise possible was the authoritarian value system commonly conveyed by German schooling. Japanese education after the 1868 Meiji Restoration had a similar character. Today, the values expressed in Islamic schools, especially those of a strongly fundamentalist cast, might harm later prospects for democracy in Islamic countries.

The general level of education in a society is usually best measured by the average number of years of schooling across the entire population. Thus measured, educational levels are steadily rising worldwide, although not at the same rate everywhere. Between 1960 and 1985, the average amount of schooling for people over 25 years of age increased by nearly 2 years. Table 1 shows average schooling-attainment figures for seven "civilizations" in 1960 and 1985. A 174-nation regression analysis (using freedom as the dependent variable) on numbers of years of schooling in the population over 25 years of age in 1990 shows that each added year of schooling improves the freedom rating by 6.6 percentage points.[10]

For all nations, educational attainment by itself seems to have a modestly higher correlation with democracy than does income alone.

Although education is a major contributor to income and the correlation between the two variables is high, at 75 percent it is less than perfect. For example, the average over-25 Soviet citizen in 1990 had more schooling (9 years) than the average Italian (7.3), but Soviet per-capita income was about one-half of Italy's while the USSR's freedom level was abysmal. Because it is a highly predictable variable, more so than income, education may serve the purpose of forecasting better than income.

Just as the economic outliers are of interest, so also are the educational ones (i.e., those countries that have markedly more or less freedom than their levels of education would predict). Extreme outliers on the "not free" side relative to their educational levels in 1990 were Cuba, North Korea, Kuwait, and Albania. There was (and is) a resulting tension within these countries, one that pulls them toward greater freedom. A similar tension that existed earlier in the Soviet Union and much of Central Europe has since been released. Outliers on the poorly educated but "free" side were several small countries, some of them new: the Solomon Islands, Gambia (before its recent coup), Botswana, Papua New Guinea, and Namibia. The tension works the opposite way for them: continuing low levels of education might render their hold on freedom tenuous.

The question of causation also arises in the relationship between education and freedom, although it seems to have attracted less attention than the link between income and freedom. One method of proceeding, which parallels Helliwell's examination of income, is to take levels of education for each nation over various years and use these to predict freedom levels. The results show that each additional year of education adds an average of 4.8 points to the freedom rating—significantly less than the all-nation 1990 cross-national relationship. This is probably a better point-in-time measure of causation than the cross-national one.

Again, paralleling Helliwell, one can examine the initial effects of freedom on educational growth. The finding is that higher levels of earlier freedom significantly increase later education (by 0.01 years per initial freedom point).

In contrast with the generally high correlation of income and freedom within most of Huntington's "civilizations," the relationship between education and freedom within these same respective sets of countries yields mostly insignificant results (the main exception to this is the "Confucian" group). This is puzzling given the strong positive correlations that hold between education and income and between education and freedom when we consider the set of *all* nations, and doubly puzzling when we consider the strong correlation between income and freedom within civilizations. This question needs further study.

A simultaneous-regression analysis of education and income on freedom shows the contribution of each to be independently significant (education at the 0.1-percent level, income at the 20-percent level), although, of course, less than each independently.

Projecting the Future

Projected increases in educational and income levels promise to have large political consequences, the most important among these being the spread and consolidation of democratic forms of government. The growing trend toward increased school enrollments, together with the large differences in years of schooling between young and old workers today, will add about three years to average years of schooling in the work forces of the developing nations by 2020, bringing this measure of their human capital to an average of about seven years. This change is highly predictable. If one knows the current average schooling level in a population and has current enrollment data for various ages or grades, one can forecast quite well the average educational level of a population several decades from now. Table 2 shows the schooling-attainment level for 1990 and the projected level for 2020 in the 16 most populous developing countries; the increase for this set, within which three-fourths of the developing world's people live, is 2.69 years. If we assume that the past relationship between education and democracy will hold in the future, this change enables us to predict future freedom levels.

As noted above, a rule of thumb is that an additional year of schooling in a population improves the freedom rating of a country an average of 6.6 percentage points. The projected three years' average

Table 2—Projected Changes in Educational Attainment
(For Ages 25+ in 16 Large Countries, 1990-2020)*

COUNTRY	1990	2020	CHANGE
China	4.8	7.0	2.2
India	2.4	6.8	4.4
Indonesia	3.9	6.4	2.5
Brazil	3.9	7.5	3.6
USSR	9.0	10.1	1.1
Nigeria	1.2	3.9	2.7
Pakistan	1.9	3.2	1.3
Bangladesh	2.0	3.6	1.6
Mexico	4.7	7.8	3.1
Vietnam	4.6	6.7	2.1
South Korea	8.8	11.1	2.3
Philippines	7.4	8.7	1.3
Turkey	3.5	7.1	3.6
Thailand	3.8	7.6	3.8
Iran	3.9	7.3	3.4
Egypt	2.8	6.9	4.1

AVERAGE CHANGE: 2.69

*Data from United Nations Development Programme.

increase in the educational level of the developing countries will, if the future is like the past, increase their freedom ratings by 20 points. Although this is an average tendency and many countries will deviate from it (with some backsliding likely), it might move, say, Croatia, Guatemala, and Malaysia (with below-average freedom ratings in 1990) to the level of Panama, Thailand, and Mexico (then about average); the latter to the level of Argentina, South Korea, and Lithuania (better than average); and so on.

Applying the average increase in educational levels for all developing countries (using the 1990 regression between education and freedom) allows us to predict that the number of "free" countries should increase from 61 in 1990 to 74 in 2020, and the number "partly free" from 56 to 77, while the number "not free" should shrink from 58 to 24. Using the other method described above, which relates freedom to earlier levels of education together with changes in education, the number of "free" countries should increase a bit less, from 61 to 66, and the number "partly free" should increase from 56 to 75, while the number "not free" should shrink a bit less, from 58 to 34.

The cross-section regression results reported above, along with Helliwell's longitudinal results, also enable us to make a projection of freedom based on income—provided that we have some basis for projecting incomes. Assuming a 3-percent average annual per-capita growth rate, and assuming that additions to income keep adding to freedom as much as in the past, the number of "free" countries should go from 61 in 1990 to 75 in 2020, while the number "not free" should shrink from 58 to 43.[11] If one believes that growth will be slower, say at the past average rate for the developing countries of 2 percent annually per capita, then this political evolution should occur more slowly.

In addition to the separate effects that income and education are likely to have on future freedoms, there are combined effects to be considered. Assuming a 3-percent annual growth in per-capita incomes and an increase in average educational levels of 3 years, the number of "free" countries should increase from 61 in 1990 to 75 in 2020, the number of "partly free" should go from 56 to 75, and the number of "not free" should plummet by more than half from 58 to 25.

That these different methods yield broadly similar results is to be expected, given the close connection that exists between education and income. All methods point to a substantial increase in the number of "free" and "partly free" countries, and a significant decline in the number of "not free" ones.

In fact, if the above regressions and projections are methodologically and analytically sound, and accurately anticipate the percentage growth of free countries in the world, then the number of free countries in 2020 figures to be significantly greater than the 74 or 75 projected above—which is roughly the number of free countries in the world *today*. As a result of the cataclysmic political events that led to the breakup of the Soviet Union, Yugoslavia, and Czechoslovakia in 1990-93, there were significantly more countries *and* more *free* counties in the world in 1993 as compared to 1990. The number of countries in this region increased from 8 to 27. The average freedom rating of these countries declined by 3 percentage points (from 54 to 51, on the converted Freedom House scale). The number of countries rated "free" went from 3 to 7, those "partly free" from 3 to 14, and the number "not free" from 2 to 6. All those rated "not free" in 1993 were in Central Asia and the Caucasus plus the former Yugoslavia.

Thus as a result of the post-1990 breakup of the Soviet empire, in 2020 there will be more countries, but the overall projected distribution of freedom reported above should be little changed. It seems reasonable to assume that the Central European states, if they are able to maintain their independence, will be predominantly free because most are so today (Serb-dominated Yugoslavia being the outstanding exception), and education and income trends should make them more stable democracies. As for the countries of the former Soviet Union, only Estonia and Lithuania were rated "free" in 1993, but educational and income trends should move the 13 others gradually up the freedom scale. Russia's political character, however, will make a large difference to the region because of its power and because of domestic pressures to re-create something like the empire. So although Russia will be subject to the same liberalizing forces as other nations and its high educational level is a favorable factor, antidemocratic forces might come to dominate it—and therefore other lands in the "near abroad." To repeat, these are statistical relationships and do not enable one to say with confidence what will happen in any given nation.

A Rising Tide

There are other caveats that one must mention in making a projection so far into the future: past patterns of relations may change; some "civilizations" might not take to Western-style democracy as their incomes rise (as is suggested by the analysis of the Arab countries); and the "third wave" might, as the first two did, retreat and not soon be overtaken by a "fourth wave." But overall it seems appropriate to regard democracy as rising on a deep "tide"; the "waves" are surface phenomena that run sometimes with, sometimes against, the underlying trend. Given continued educational and economic growth and the absence of some now unknown hostile force, freedoms will grow.

One might infer from this analysis that the best way to promote democracy is to foster economic development and education. This position was at the heart of the recent debate in the United States over extending most-favored-nation trade status to China. In that instance, what might be called the "development-will-help-democracy" position prevailed; this analysis supports that position. Yet to infer that the rich democracies should do nothing directly to support democratic institutions in other lands would be to draw too narrow a conclusion. In order for democratic institutions to become rooted they must first be adopted; people need experience with them. As the successive advances and retreats of democracy show, countries sometimes have to try and try again in order to gain robust democracy. Italy, Germany, Spain, and Japan are stable democracies whose respective paths to this condition were hardly smooth. There are always some people in nations with authoritarian regimes eager to bring about democratic political change; help from outside in the form of information or moral and political support can sometimes make an important difference.

Finally, one aspect of the debate about Western versus Asian democracy has to do with end positions or equilibrium conditions. This analysis simply shows that Asian nations, along with many others, are heading the Western way and projects that this process will continue at least for several decades.[12] It does not enable us to say with confidence what will be their long-term destiny, much less what the future character of Western democracy will be on its own home grounds.

NOTES

1. Samuel P. Huntington, *The Third Wave: Democratization in the Late Twentieth Century* (Norman: University of Oklahoma Press, 1991).

2. The Freedom House metric runs from 1 to 7 (with the lowest number being most democratic) for each of the political and civil rights. In the data presented below, these two measures, which are highly correlated, have been added and converted to a scale of 0 to 100.

3. Seymour Martin Lipset, *Political Man: The Social Bases of Politics* (rev. ed., Baltimore: Johns Hopkins University Press, 1981). That wealth is not a condition for democracy is evident; Bangladesh is proof of this. There are such other correlates as the well-known one involving Protestant societies and the perhaps less well known one of having been a colony of Great Britain. On the British connection, see Seymour Martin Lipset, Kyoung-Ryung Seong, and John Charles Torres, "A Comparative Analysis of the Social Requisites of Democracy," *International Social Science Journal* 45 (May 1993): 155-76.

4. Lipset, *Political Man*, 31.

5. Patrick E. Tyler, "In the Twilight of Deng, China's Rising Stars Jostle," *New York Times*, 21 August 1994, A3.

6. See Lawrence Sirowy and Alex Inkeles, "The Effects of Democracy on Economic Growth and Inequality: A Review," *Studies in Comparative International Development* 25 (April 1990): 126-57; Adam Przeworski and Fernando Limongi, "Political Regimes and Economic Growth," *Journal of Economic Perspectives* 7 (Summer 1993): 51-70; John F. Helliwell, "Empirical Linkages Between Democracy and Economic Growth" (National Bureau of Economic Research Working Paper No. 4066, May 1992); and Mancur Olson, "Dictatorship, Democracy and Development," *American Political Science Review* 87 (September 1993): 567-77.

7. Samuel P. Huntington, "The Clash of Civilizations," *Foreign Affairs* 72 (Summer 1993): 22-49.

8. Alex Inkeles and David H. Smith, *Becoming Modern* (Cambridge: Harvard University Press, 1974), 290-91.

9. Costas Azariadis and Allan Drazen, "Threshold Externalities in Economic Development," *Quarterly Journal of Economics* 105 (May 1990): 501-27. Robert J. Barro, "Economic Growth in a Cross-Section of Countries," *Quarterly Journal of Economics* 106 (May 1991): 407-44.

10. Education data are from the United Nations Development Programme (UNDP), *Human Development Report* (1993), and Robert J. Barro and Jong-Wha Lee, "International Comparisons of Educational Attainment," *Journal of Monetary Economics* 32 (December 1993): 363-94 (with July 1993 appendix tables). The Barro and Lee data are reported through 1985 whereas the UNDP data used here are reported for 1990. Differences in country coverage and in reported educational attainment for some countries between these two sources do not affect the statistical results reported here.

11. The justification for a 3-percent estimate of future per-capita growth is found in Henry S. Rowen, "World Wealth Expanding: Why a Rich, Democratic and (Perhaps) Peaceful Era Is Ahead," in Ralph Landau, Gavin Wright, and Timothy Taylor, eds., *Growth and Development: The Economics of the Twenty-first Century* (Stanford: Stanford University Press, forthcoming).

12. A similar view on the evolution of East Asian democracy is in James W. Morley, ed., *Driven by Growth: Political Change in the Asia-Pacific Region* (Armonk, N.Y.: M.E. Sharpe, 1993), 309.

TECHNICAL NOTE

Details of Regressions

Income versus Freedom Regressions (1990 data):

• All nations: significant at the 0.1% level. Freedom (0-100 scale) = 33.2037 (t=11.32) + .00338432 x PPP90 (t=8.61) Adj. R2=.296 n=175 countries

• All nations minus Northwest Europe and countries of British settlement: significant at the 0.5% level. Freedom = 35.8947 (t=10.68) + .002104 x PPP90 (t=3.37) Adj. R2=.064 n=153

• All nations minus Northwest Europe, minus countries of European settlement and minus former British colonies: significant at the 0.5% level. Freedom = 30.5193 (t=8.37) + .00215056 x PPP90 (t=2.87) Adj. R2=.062 n=111

Income versus Freedom Within Civilizations (1990):

• Western nations: significant at 0.1% level. Freedom = 84.4235 (t=27.26) + .000835243 x PPP90 (t=4.14) Adj. R2=.402 n=25

• Latin America: almost significant at the 20% level. Freedom = 53.8091 (t=4.60) + .00454812 x PPP90 (t=1.47) Adj. R2=.058 n=20

• Orthodox nations: significant at the 1% level. Freedom = 2.07915 (t=0.14) + .0089026 x PPP90 (t=3.62) Adj. R2=.574 n=10

• Sub-Saharan nations: significant at the 0.1% level. Freedom = 16.1901 (t=3.80) + .00866091 x PPP90 (t=3.69) Adj. R2=.218 n=46

• Confucian nations: significant at the 5% level. (In the regressions, Japan is counted as "Confucian.") Freedom = 4.97036 (t=0.33) + .00450245 x PPP90 (t=3.19) Adj. R2=0.56 n=8

• Buddhist nations: significant at the 0.5% level. Freedom = -9.50294 (t=-1.09) + .021936 x PPP90 (t=5.19) Adj. R2=0.812 n=7

• Islamic nations:

= All: almost *negatively* significant at the 20% level. Freedom = 32.9515 (t=7.68) - .0106484 x PPP90 (t=-1.49) Adj. R2=.029 n=33

= All minus predominantly oil producers: not significant. Freedom = 29.4069 (t=5.45) + .00121905 x PPP90 (t=0.74) Adj. R2= -.014 n=33
= Arab nations: *negatively* significant at the 10% level. Freedom = 33.5052 (t=4.40) - .0016104 x PPP90 (t=-1.81) Adj. R2=0.14 n=15
= Arab nations minus predominantly oil producers: not significant. Freedom = 40.9972 (t=4.09) - .00202379 x PPP (t=-0.95) Adj. R2=-.015 n=8
= Non-Arab nations: not significant. Freedom = 29.3616 (t=5.35) - .00102802 x PPP90 (t= -0.71) Adj. R2=-0.2 n=26
= Non-Arab nations minus an oil producer (Brunei): significant at the 10% level. Freedom = 22.4495 (t=3.40) + .00457364 x PPP (t=1.86) Adj. R2=.093 n=25

Education versus Freedom (1990):
• All nations: significant at below the 0.1% level. Freedom (0-100 scale) = 18.989 (t=5.35) + 6.60288 x EdYrs (t=10.71) Adj. R2=.378 n=174

Income and Education versus Freedom (1990):
• All nations: significant at 0.1% level. Freedom (0-100 scale) = 19.95 (t=5.57)***** + 5.40 x EdYrs (t=5.64)***** + 0.00093 x PPP (t=1.63)* Adj. R2=.402 n=174

Education over Time versus Freedom (1973-1992)
• AR1 Adj. Pooled Time Series Cross-Section
• All nations: significant at 0.1% level. Freedom (0-100 scale) = 28.42 (t=8.92)***** + 4.84 x EdYrs (t=8.60)***** Adj. R2=.128 n=788

Education and Changes in Education versus Freedom (1970-1990)
• All nations: significant at 0.1% level. Freedom (0-100 scale) = 20.18 (t=4.29)***** + 7.90 x 1970 EdYrs (t=8.69)***** + 4.48 x Change in EdYrs, 1970-1990 (t-2.58)** Adj. R2=.467 n=110

Educational Growth and Freedom (1970-1990)
Education Increase (1970-1990) = 0.99 (t=4.11)***** + 0.012 x 1973 Freedom (t=2.71)*** + 0.05 x 1970 EdYrs (t-0.89) (ns) Adj. R2=.107 n=106

Significance of difference from zero: *=20%, **=5%, ***=1%, ****=0.5%, *****=0.1%

26.
THE PRIMACY OF CULTURE

Francis Fukuyama

***Francis Fukuyama** is a resident consultant at the RAND Corporation in Washington, D.C. A former deputy director of the Policy Planning Staff of the U.S. State Department, he is the author of* The End of History and the Last Man (1992). *His most recent book* Trust: The Social Virtues and the Creation of Prosperity *was published in 1995.*

What are likely to be liberal democracy's principal ideological and political competitors in the years to come? I believe that the most serious one is in the process of emerging in Asia. I also believe, however, that what happens on the level of ideology will depend on developments at the levels of civil society and culture. A short methodological digression will help explain why this is so.

There are four levels on which the consolidation of democracy must occur, and each requires a corresponding level of analysis.

Level 1: Ideology. This is the level of *normative beliefs* about the rightness or wrongness of democratic institutions and their supporting market structures. Democratic societies obviously cannot survive for long if people do not believe democracy to be a legitimate form of government; on the other hand, a widespread belief in the legitimacy of democracy can coexist with an inability to create or consolidate democratic institutions. Level 1 is the sphere of rational self-consciousness, in which changes in perceptions of legitimacy can occur virtually overnight. Such a change, favorable to democracy and markets, has occurred around the world in the last 15 years.

Level 2: Institutions. This sphere includes constitutions, legal systems, party systems, market structures, and the like. Institutions change less quickly than ideas about legitimacy, but they can be manipulated by public policy. This is the level at which most of the recent political struggle has taken place, as new democracies, aided by older ones, have sought to privatize state enterprises, write new constitutions, consolidate parties, and so on. Most neoclassical economics operates at this level of analysis, as did a great deal of political science up through the end of the Second World War.

Level 3: Civil society. This is the realm of spontaneously created social structures separate from the state that underlie democratic political institutions. These structures take shape even more slowly than political institutions. They are less manipulable by public policy, and indeed often bear an inverse relationship to state power, growing stronger as the state recedes and vice versa. Until recently, civil society was a relatively neglected subject of analysis: in the West, it was often taken for granted as an inevitable concomitant of modernization, while in the East it was denounced by Marxists as fraudulent. Civil society became fashionable again after the fall of communism, because it was recognized that post-totalitarian societies were characterized by a particular deficit of social structures that were a necessary precondition of stable democratic political institutions.[1] Over the past couple of decades, a great deal of interesting work in political science has been done on this level of analysis, resulting in a rich taxonomy and language for describing contemporary civil societies as they relate to democratic institutions.

Level 4: Culture. This deepest level includes phenomena such as family structure, religion, moral values, ethnic consciousness, "civic-ness," and particularistic historical traditions. Just as democratic institutions rest on a healthy civil society, civil society in turn has precursors and preconditions at the level of culture. Culture can be defined as a-rational, ethical habit passed on through tradition; although it is malleable and can be affected by developments in the three upper levels, it tends to change the most slowly of all. Analytically, this is the sphere of sociology and anthropology. In the field of political science, studies excavating the level of culture and exploring its influence on civil society have been much less common than studies of civil society.

In many respects, what Samuel P. Huntington has called the "third wave" of democratic transitions was driven by level 1—that is, by the level of ideology. For one reason or another, perceptions of legitimacy began to change rapidly and dramatically in the late 1970s and 1980s, leading to, among other things, the coming to power of free-market finance ministers in Latin America, the birth of prodemocracy movements in the former communist world, and a general demoralization of authoritarians on both the right and the left. This change in ideology precipitated a massive change on level 2, that of institutions, and spawned many debates over appropriate strategies—for example, gradualism versus shock therapy, or "economic reform first" versus "democracy first." Although the process of institutional consolidation is far from complete, a great deal of progress has been made on this level in all the regions that experienced ideological revolutions in the 1980s.

Change on level 3, that of civil society, has been much slower in coming. And here the pace of change clearly depends to a great degree on the characteristics of level 4, that of culture. Civil society has sprung back to life relatively quickly in Poland, Hungary, the Czech Republic, and the Baltic states, where there were vigorous alternative elites ready to push aside the old communist ones. Economic decline in these countries has bottomed out with the emergence of a healthy private sector, and political life has been slowly moving toward identifiable West European patterns. Civil society's birth pangs have been much sharper in Belarus, Ukraine, and Russia, which remained heavily dependent on old communist elites to staff their new (and sometimes not so new) institutions. These differences can be traced to the cultural level; explicating the specific mechanisms of interaction between levels 3 and 4 will be a central task for future students of democratization.

It is safe to say that the recession of the "third wave" that has been evident in many parts of the world in the past four or five years has been due to the varying rates of change among the four levels. The almost instantaneous change in normative beliefs generated great expectations that could not be met, owing to the greater degree of recalcitrance encountered at successively deeper levels. In some countries, this recalcitrance caused movement toward democracy to stop dead in its tracks, even before institutions had a chance to be created. In others, the gap between expectations and reality threatened the genuine progress that had been achieved in the consolidation of institutions because it began to affect the normative beliefs that had kicked off the democratic revolution in the first place.

The chief difficulties that liberal democracy will face in the future are likely to be encountered at level 3 and especially at level 4. Today there is not a great deal of disagreement at levels 1 and 2: it is difficult to identify plausible ideological competitors, and there are few alternative institutional arrangements that elicit any enthusiasm. Arguments at these levels occur at the margins, dealing with such matters as whether the welfare state should be expanded somewhat or contracted, the merits of presidentialism versus parliamentarism, and so on. Indeed, I would go so far as to argue that social engineering on the level of institutions has hit a massive brick wall: experiences of the past century have taught most democracies that ambitious rearrangements of institutions often cause more unanticipated problems than they solve. By contrast, the real difficulties affecting the quality of life in modern democracies have to do with social and cultural pathologies that seem safely beyond the reach of institutional solutions, and hence of public policy. The chief issue is quickly becoming one of culture.

Competitors to Democracy

Of the readily apparent systemic competitors to liberal democracy, only one is rapidly gaining strength and seems able to challenge democracy on its home turf. That sole serious contender is a form of paternalistic Asian authoritarianism. The other possibilities that suggest themselves are 1) extreme nationalism or fascism, 2) Islam, and 3) a revived neo-Bolshevism. Each of these has problems as a worldwide ideological movement; most notably, all three have shown a limited ability to adapt to the requirements of modern natural science, and hence are constrained from becoming integrated into the increasingly technological global economy.

In recent years, ethnic conflicts have revealed a sizeable hole in traditional liberal political theory.

Take the case of fascism. In recent years, ethnic conflicts and immigrant movements around the world have revealed a sizeable hole in traditional liberal political theory: by treating citizens only as individuals, the liberal state ignores the group-oriented character of real-world populations that, for better or worse, find great satisfaction in ascriptive collective identities. It is not clear, however, that this is an insuperable problem for liberal states. Most have found it possible to accommodate a moderate degree of group-oriented pluralism within institutions based on the principle of individual rights. By contrast, more extreme nationalist states like Serbia that violate fundamental liberal principles of tolerance have not fared well. Because populations are not homogeneous, their emphasis on ethnic purity leads them to conflict, war, and destruction of the economic basis of modern power. It is thus not surprising that Serbia has failed to become a model society for anyone in Europe, East or West, apart from a few discontented fringe groups in countries like Russia, Moldova, and Hungary. Although ethnic conflict is a severe threat to democracy in the short run, there are a number of reasons for thinking that it will be a transitional phenomenon. Similarly, while the Islamic fundamentalist wave has not yet receded among marginalized populations in the Middle East, no fundamentalist state has proved that it can master the process of industrialization. Even those lucky enough to have inherited natural-resource wealth have not dealt effectively with the social problems that helped bring them to power; discontent in Iran today remains extremely high. This only reinforces Islamic fundamentalism's lack of appeal for anyone not culturally Islamic to begin with.

Least serious of all as an ideological competitor to liberal democracy is a renewed form of communism. It is true that former communists have been returned to power in Lithuania, Poland, Hungary, and eastern Germany, while in some sense never having left power in other parts of the former communist world. But these groups have not sought to do more than slightly reduce the speed of the transition to capitalism and push for a broader safety net. Polling data indicate that their support comes mainly from pensioners, members of the former communist elite, and others with a stake in the old system. Needless to say, the neo-Bolshevik economic agenda does not hold out the prospect of long-term economic renewal.

That fascism, Islam, and neo-Bolshevism lack good prospects as global ideologies does not mean that they will not continue to expand within their own regional spheres. There they will do considerable damage to the quality of life of local populations, while delaying or in some cases making impossible the consolidation of workable democratic political systems. But they are unlikely to gain either the appeal or the power to reach much farther afield.

This leaves some form of Asian paternalistic authoritarianism as the most serious new competitor to liberal democracy. Obviously, Asian authoritarianism is a "regional" phenomenon no less than fascism or Islam. No one in North America or Europe is seriously thinking of adopting Confucianism as a national ideology. But the Asian experience has forced people in the West to confront weaknesses in their own societies in a way that none of the other three ideological alternatives has. Only Asians have been able to master the modern technological world and create capitalist societies competitive with those of the West—indeed, some would argue, superior in many ways. This alone is enough to suggest that Asia's relative share of global power will increase steadily. But Asia also poses an ideological challenge.

Most conventional definitions of the Asian alternative betray the bias of modern Western political philosophy toward defining sociopolitical systems in exclusively institutional terms. Hence it is common to say that Asian "soft" authoritarianism combines relatively free markets with relatively strong political authority favoring group consensus over individual rights. This analysis is correct as far as it goes, but it misses an essential characteristic of Asian societies. In traditional Asian cultures, political authority has not rested so much on the correct engineering of institutions as on broad moral education that guarantees the coherence of fundamental social structures. (In this respect, the orientation of Confucianism resembles that of Western classical political philosophy.) That is, while modern Western political thought tries to construct a just social order from the top down, emphasizing levels 1 and 2, traditional Asian cultures start from levels 4 and 3 and work upward. Hence Confucianism socializes individuals to subordinate their individualism to the family—the fundamental building block of a Sinitic society. Larger political structures are supersets of these lower-level elements: the lineage is a family of families, while the entire Chinese imperial system is the family of the Chinese people as a whole, with the emperor's authority modeled on that of the father.

Because Asian societies begin at level 4 and work upward, the kind of political structures they produce, or are compatible with, is somewhat indeterminate. For this reason, it has been possible in the twentieth century for modernizing Asian societies to separate what the Confucian scholar Tu Wei-ming calls "political Confucianism" from the Confucianism of "everyday life."[2] Traditional political Confucianism, which mandated the imperial system with its elaborate hierarchy of mandarins and gentleman-scholars, could be jettisoned relatively easily and replaced with a variety of political-institutional forms without causing the society to lose its essential coherence. Hence it is not correct to identify the Asian alternative with a particular set of institutional arrangements, such as the presence of a parliament or the absence of guarantees of certain individual rights. The essence of the Asian alternative is a society built not around individual rights, but around a deeply engrained moral code that is the basis for strong social structures and community life. Such a society can exist in a democracy like Japan, or in a semiauthoritarian state like Singapore. Although certain institutions would obviously be incompatible with this kind of social order (communism, for example), it is the social structures and their cultural coherence rather than the institutions that define it.

Civil Society in Asia and in America

If we understand the Asian alternative in this noninstitutional fashion, we see that it has some interesting implications for the future of democracy around the world. In the first place, it is not clear that Confucianism and other elements of traditional Asian culture constitute significant barriers to the advance of liberal democracy in Asia. That it does constitute such a barrier is argued by Asians like Singapore's former prime minister Lee Kwan Yew and by Westerners like Samuel P. Huntington. On Lee's part, this represents a deliberate, self-serving distortion of Confucianism, which he identifies with the political order that he found it convenient to establish in Singapore at the particular moment when he was in power. Other Asian societies, such as Taiwan and Korea, have been moving toward a very recognizable form of Western democracy in the past decade without thereby losing their Confucian character. Needless to say, Japan's semi-Confucian culture has proved quite compatible with democratic institutions for two generations. The political upheaval that began with the Liberal Democratic Party's loss of power in July 1993 has inaugurated a process that will eventually make Japan a more American-style democracy than it has been in the past. The kind of aggressively anti-Western and overtly antidemocratic rhetoric that has come from Singaporean and Malaysian officials and intellectuals in recent years is very much related to the personalities of Lee and Malaysian prime minister Datuk Seri Mahathir. With the next generation of leaders, it is much more likely that both societies will move toward the Japanese-Taiwanese-Korean version of democracy than away from it.

The mistake on Huntington's part is more conceptual in nature. He misidentifies the essence of Confucianism as political Confucianism, when in fact the part that has best survived is a doctrine about the family and other lower-level social relationships.[3] There is no theoretical reason why Confucian social structures could not coexist perfectly well with democratic political institutions. Indeed, the case can be made that democratic institutions would be considerably strengthened by them.

On the other hand, the fact that Confucianism is compatible with modern democracy does not mean that democracy will inexorably advance in Asia. The prestige of democratic institutions in the future will depend on Asian perceptions not so much of the effectiveness of Western institutions as of the problems of Western society and culture. That prestige has dimmed considerably over the past couple of decades: not only have modern means of communication made people in Asia much more aware of developments in the United States, but American social problems—the usual litany of pathologies like violent crime, drugs, racial tensions, poverty, single-parent families, and so on—have themselves gotten worse. In other words, while Americans look down their noses at Asians when comparisons are made on levels 1 and 2, Asians increasingly feel that their own societies have certain key advantages over America on levels 3 and 4. Asian critics of the United States such as Lee Kwan Yew assume that levels 1 and 2 are inextricably linked to levels 3 and 4—that is, that liberal, rights-based institutions have a corrosive effect on civil society and culture, and that democracy eventually leads to the breakdown of the social fabric. The fate of liberal democracy in Asia will therefore depend in large measure on the degree to which the United States can deal successfully not with its relatively minor institutional problems, but with its more intractable sociocultural ones.

There is indeed a linkage between levels 1 and 2 on the one hand, and levels 3 and 4 on the other, but it is a good deal more complicated than Lee and others imagine. Liberalism based on individual rights is quite compatible with strong, communitarian social structures and disciplined cultural habits. Indeed, one can argue that the true importance of civil society and culture in a modern democracy lies precisely in their ability to balance or moderate the atomizing individualism that is inherent in traditional liberal doctrine, both political and economic. As Tocqueville, Weber, and many other observers of American society have pointed out, America has never resembled a "sand heap" of atomized individuals, because other factors (such as the sectarian character of American Protestantism) have exerted a powerful countervailing pressure in a more group-oriented direction. It is only during the past 50 years that individualistic currents have come to predominate over the more communitarian ones. It is not an accident that the American system produced this outcome. But its emergence was by no means inevitable, and was not a necessary consequence of "democracy" as such. The United States, as constitutional scholar Mary Ann Glendon points out, has its own unique "language of rights" that is quite distinct from those of European democracies.[4] This American liberal dialect has come to be associated, in the minds of many Asians, with democracy per se.

Thus the struggles that will help determine the fate of liberal democracy will not be over the nature of institutions, about which there is already a great deal of consensus around the world. The real battles will occur at the levels of civil society and culture. These realms have been broadly recognized as crucial for new democracies emerging from an authoritarian past. But as the ongoing "culture wars" in the United States make clear, the health and dynamism of civil society are problematic in long-term and apparently stable democracies as well.

NOTES

1. For a discussion of the complex, contingent origins of civil society, see Ernest Gellner, *Conditions of Liberty: Civil Society and Its Rivals* (London: Hamish Hamilton, 1994).

2. Tu Wei-ming, *Confucian Ethics Today: The Singapore Challenge* (Singapore: Curriculum Development Institute of Singapore, 1984), 90.

3. I will take up this issue at greater length in an article on Confucianism and democracy to be published in the April 1995 issue of the *Journal of Democracy*.

4. Mary Ann Glendon, *Rights Talk: The Impoverishment of Political Discourse* (New York: The Free Press, 1991).

27. MORE LIBERAL, PRELIBERAL, OR POSTLIBERAL?

Philippe C. Schmitter

***Philippe C. Schmitter** is professor of political science at Stanford University. He has previously taught at the University of Chicago and the European University Institute in Florence. Currently, he is working on a book entitled* Essaying Democracy *that deals with the issues faced by countries attempting to consolidate democratic institutions.*

As we approach the end of the twentieth century, democracy's general prospects have never been more favorable; yet it has rarely been more difficult to discern what type or degree of democracy we should expect in the future. It is as if, having swept almost all of their "systemic" opponents from the field, the proponents of democracy have at long last been freed to squabble among themselves over the meaning and application of their preferred political order.

As long as the most recent "wave of democratization" was exerting its powerful effect, actors of all kinds had every incentive to climb on their varied and exotic surfboards for the exciting ride to freedom. Now that the wave has crested and the direction of future regime changes has become much less predictable, the thrill of reaching a common objective has given way to an increased awareness not merely that consolidating democracy is a much more demanding task than replacing autocracy, but also that all the avowedly democratic surfers might not have had the same beach in mind as a destination.

Part of the problem lies in our unfortunate habit of equating "democracy" with "modern, representative, liberal, political democracy as practiced within nation-states." Admittedly, it is awkward to keep all those qualifiers in mind, much less write them out, every time one refers to democracy. But political scientists, if not practicing politicians, should be aware that:

1) the "classical" democracies that anteceded the present ones (and provided many of their symbols and normative justifications) had very different practices of citizenship and accountability;

2) not only do various "direct" forms of democracy persist, but there are also very different types and degrees of "indirection" in contemporary representative democracies;

3) liberalism, either as a conception of political liberty or as a doctrine about economic policy, may have coincided in some countries with the rise of democracy, but has never been immutably or unambiguously linked to its practice—least of all once democracy was extended to include mass publics, popularly elected executives, specialized interest associations, and boisterous social movements;

4) it has been a matter of considerable controversy whether the generically democratic principles of participation, access, accountability, responsiveness, and competition should be confined to "public" or "political" institutions, or extended to cover "private" and "nonpolitical" institutions that have an impact upon the whole of society;

5) finally, it is a historical accident, having little or nothing to do with democracy, that its practices have heretofore been largely confined to states—that is, to a subset of territorial units of very unequal size, level of development, national unity, cultural homogeneity, and so forth.

My hunch is that all these qualifiers—and perhaps others as well—will be questioned in coming decades. Far from being secure in its foundations and practices, democracy will have to face unprecedented challenges. Its future, as I have suggested previously in these pages, will be increasingly "tumultuous, uncertain, and very eventful."[1]

Exploring the Probable Challenges

Most of these challenges will come from within the established liberal democracies (ELDs), not from the fledgling neodemocracies (FNDs). Certainly the latter will have to face a great deal of disenchantment when performance inevitably fails to meet inflated expectations and the tedium of consolidation replaces the heady excitement of the transition. Yet the one thing that has been almost completely absent from the 50 or so cases of attempted democratization since 1974 is experimentation beyond the basic institutions of liberal democracy. The predominant motif everywhere has been the desire for "normal politics"—that is, for copying the most routine practices of ELDs. Eventually, if they do not fail altogether and regress into some form of autocracy, the politicians and citizens of FNDs may come to recognize the intrinsic dilemmas that are plaguing the ELDs and begin to experiment with new arrangements. In the meantime, however, the leaders of FNDs will remain thoroughly preoccupied with resolving the many serious extrinsic dilemmas that are involved in making even routine democratic institutions compatible with the sundry social, cultural, and economic circumstances of their respective countries.

If my hunch is correct, relatively few of the countries that have ridden this wave will fail outright and regress to autocracy, much less to a form of autocracy that can plausibly present itself as an alternative model for economic development and political stability. Most will be "condemned" to remain democratic, even if only a few will enjoy the full benefits of regime consolidation. From the remaining cases—that is, those that adopt some hybrid form of *dictablanda* or *democradura* or the more numerous ones that manage to muddle through as "unconsolidated democracies"—it is unlikely that any major challenges to democracy will emerge.

Instead, the major challenges will come from within the established "modern, representative, liberal, national, political" democracies. Their ability to adjust their well-entrenched rules and practices to accommodate the growing disaffection of their citizenries will determine the prospects for democracy worldwide. In my opinion, the sources of discontent in the ELDs are not merely conjunctural—even if they have been exacerbated recently by declining economic performance and momentary pressures for adjustment to major changes in the interstate system. Nor are they likely to remain confined to one segment of the political spectrum—even if, in the short run, they have had more impact upon parties and movements of the Left. They will focus increasingly on certain basic principles of "real existing" liberal democracy:

1) its exclusive emphasis on individualism;

2) its commitment to voluntarism in the form and content of political participation, as well as in the recruitment of politicians;

3) its reliance on territorial representation and partisan competition to provide the sole legitimate links between citizen and state;

4) its confinement to the bounds of national state institutions as well as its (tacit) complicity with nationalism;

5) its indifference to persistent and systemic inequalities in both the distribution of benefits and the representation of interests.

Every one of these principles is threatened by one or another of the major trends that characterize the contemporary world: globalization of trade and production systems, changes in the role and sources of technological innovation, concentration of ownership, formation of supranational trading blocs and regional organizations, expansion and interpenetration of communications systems, increased vulnerability to business cycles, necessity for industrial restructuring, liberalization of financial institutions, individuation of personal life situations, and last but not least, growing insecurity due to changes in the role of Great Powers and declining capacity for governance by national institutions. Some of these trends are not new, and liberal democracy has managed to survive analogous challenges in the past; nevertheless, the magnitude and multiplicity of these trends are unprecedented, as is the absence of any "systemically plausible" alternative regime that could cope with them.

As Robert Dahl has argued, democracy has already gone through several revolutions in practice, often without its proponents' being fully aware of what was occurring.[2] Ironically, just as the liberal version of democracy (centering around representative institutions, large-scale governance, and massive but fairly passive citizenries) has become so predominant that it need no longer fear subversion by any other regime type, it must face the prospect of yet another revolution—this time under the scrutiny of a much better educated and more critical public.

There would seem to be three basic possible responses to this prospect: 1) a reassertion and extension of liberalism ("a *more liberal* democracy"); 2) a return to older traditions of civic republicanism ("a *preliberal* democracy"); or 3) the invention of novel, even unprecedented, forms of representation and accountability ("a *postliberal* democracy").

A more liberal democracy? So far, the most likely strategy would seem to be the first: we will see more liberalism—and (implicitly) less democracy. Privatization of public enterprises; removal of state regulations; liberalization of financial flows; conversion of political demands into claims based on rights; replacement of collective entitlements by individual contributions; sacralization of property rights; downsizing of public bureaucracies and emoluments; discrediting of "politicians" in favor of "entrepreneurs"; enhancement of the power of "neutral technical" institutions, like central banks, at the expense of "biased political" ones—all these modifications have two features in common: 1) they diminish popular expectations from public choices, and 2) they make it harder to assemble majorities to overcome the resistance of minorities, especially well-entrenched and privileged ones.

The record among ELDs is admittedly mixed, but those that have been most exposed to the "more liberalism" strategy have tended to have proportionally greater declines in voter turnout, in trade union membership, in the prestige of politicians, in citizen interest in public affairs, in the perceived role of legislatures, in the extent and intensity of party identification, and in the stability of electoral preferences. Conversely, they have seen rates of litigation increase, accusations of corruption escalate, and antiparty candidacies proliferate.

Whether this process of "de-democratization" can continue is, of course, the all-important question. Its justification rests almost exclusively on the superior economic performance that is supposed to accrue to a liberalized system of production and distribution—along with the deliberate effort to foster a strong normative rejection of politics as such. Even if the anticipated material bonus were to emerge and persist—itself a dubious proposition—modern polities, as Albert O. Hirschman has suggested, are subject to cyclical shifts in their involvement with private and public objectives.[3] The prevailing cynicism about recourse to collective as opposed to individual choices may not be sustainable, and could even be reversed in the near future.

A preliberal democracy? There has long been an alternative available: a return to "preliberal" democratic practices and institutions. Advocates of "strong democracy" have criticized each of the five basic liberal characteristics outlined above: individualism, voluntarism, electoralism, nationalism, and especially, indifference to persistent inequalities.[4] The essence of the "strong" democrats' alternative prescription is to revive citizenship. They want to see individuals once again acting directly in the public domain, deliberating collectively in the formation of preferences and deciding on a (presumptively) more equal distribution of public goods. Moreover, this quest for a new "civic republicanism" is usually accompanied by a firm rejection of several features that, while not intrinsic to liberal democracy, have evolved from its practice: professionalization of political elites, centralization of state authority, creation of specialized interest associations, commercialization of the electoral process, trivialization of partisan disputes, personalization of candidate appeals, and manipulation of public opinion.

The specific prescriptions of preliberal democrats are much more varied and less consistent than the package of institutional and policy reforms put forth by advocates of "more liberalism," but they do cover a wide range: radical decentralization and dispersion of state authority, greater recourse to popular referenda and recall initiatives, limits on terms of office for elected representatives, public funding of political parties coupled with strict limits on private contributions, provisions for obligatory voting, quotas for deserving minorities, greater efforts at civic education, incentives for participation in popular movements, and even random selection of representatives instead of competitive elections. These have yet to jell into a clearly identifiable and recognizable program—the American label "left liberal" strikes me as ambiguous if not oxymoronic, and "liberal socialist" even more so—but bits and pieces can be found in several recent academic treatises and in the views of various party factions, on the right as well as the left.[5]

In my view, preliberalism suffers from several irremediable defects that undermine the likelihood of its capturing the initiative from the presently dominant "more liberal" response. First, it lacks the sort of dramatic focal point that "national independence" or "republicanism" or "worker enfranchisement" or "freedom of association" gave to earlier liberal democratizers. Second, it is composed more like a laundry list of relatively minor complaints about existing practices than a set of measures that could bring about major changes in future life circumstances and, hence, be "really" worth struggling for. Third, its appeals, especially for decentralization and deconcentration, deliberately ignore (or wish away) the greatly expanded scale of decision making in the modern national state and the corresponding rise in international dependencies—both of which severely limit the extent to which local participation and autonomy could really affect issues that matter to the welfare of individual citizens. Fourth, advocates of preliberal democracy choose to overlook (or dismiss) the indispensable role that professional intermediaries and permanent organizations have come to play in interpreting the greater complexity of modern society and in acting on behalf of their individual members. Fifth, and most important, preliberalism makes demands of individual citizens—especially upon their time and attention—that are unrealistic given the pace of contemporary life and the availability of so many more appealing ways of spending one's (always scarce) leisure.

A postliberal democracy? Thus I am convinced that the future type and degree of democracy will depend more on the development of a postliberal alternative within ELDs than on the accumulated critiques and proposals of preliberal democrats. This alternative will be less contemptuous of what liberal democracy has accomplished, but will seek to adjust liberal democratic practices to the expanded scale of exchanges and communications that the global future holds in store. It should proceed from the following assumptions, none of which would be acceptable to preliberal—whether "strong" or "communitarian"—democrats:

1) that possessive individualism, habits of rational calculation, and a preference for private goods will persist;

2) that "man's capacity for altruism is limited," as David Ricardo observed, and will remain so;

3) that traditionally ascribed identities or communities will continue to erode;

4) that radical shifts in the distribution of wealth or the rights of property cannot be democratically enacted;

5) that citizens place a limited (though positive) value on political participation;

6) that individuals have preferences and are aware of the need for collective action to defend them, but have a restricted capacity to explore their own interest situation and a strong temptation to free-ride on the actions of others;

7) that organized intermediation between individuals and authorities is here to stay, in part because of the preceding two limitations and in part because of the expanded scale of public policy and private exchanges;

8) that political parties, electoral competition, and territorial representation, for all their manifest imperfections, will retain their primary symbolic importance as links between individuals and the larger body politic; and,

9) finally, that citizens are anxious to improve the performance of democracy—*provided* that the proposed reforms do not generate too much uncertainty, do not cost too much, and do not violate any of the above assumptions.

These assumptions indicate the narrowness of the route that is open for improving the quality of citizenship and the rationality of collective choices in ELDs. Postliberals will have to walk a fine ideological line between some very well entrenched practices that powerful groups continue to value and some not very well elaborated promises that less powerful groups have yet to understand. Moreover, postliberal reformers will have to do this by offering policy changes that are dramatic and significant, and that also can be decided upon and implemented according to the existing rules of liberal democracy.

This is not the place to develop in detail the specific content of the postliberal alternative; indeed, no comprehensive version exists as far as I know. Instead, there has been a flourishing of isolated suggestions for reform that might eventually be assembled into a more coherent and appealing package. For example, proposals have emerged for citizens' juries, for interactive polls, for extending voting rights to future generations, for videodemocracy or teledemocracy, for better ways to enlighten citizens in the formation of their preferences, for reciprocal representation between countries, for vouchers whereby individuals could support a system of "secondary citizenship" for interest associations and social movements, and the like. Needless to say, not all of these notions are deliberately "postliberal" in inspiration, and they are not all compatible with one another. However, through the dissemination of these and other ideas, hopefully combined with experimentation on a small scale, it may prove increasingly possible to delineate this putatively postliberal alternative.

One Final Problem

However intellectually appealing any alternative to liberal democracy may be, it has usually been impossible to specify in advance who would support such a significant change and how it might be successfully (and democratically) implemented. Absent the highly unlikely eventuality of revolution, the basis of sustained support required by any substantial reformist effort becomes less and less evident. It is, therefore, almost impossible to overestimate the inertia built into the structure of contemporary ELDs and the attendant difficulty in convincing people to accept new ideas about fundamental political and economic relations. The reforms presently embedded in liberal democracy all required at least the specter, if not the imminent threat, of revolution.

Short of revolution, what might focus enough attention on the malperformance of existing institutions to make citizens and leaders willing to make the risky, costly switch to some other situation? The more than 40 cases of attempted democratization since 1974 prove that, under certain conditions, agents will be collectively willing to make massive changes—even if few of these changes could have been predicted beforehand and the combinations of actors varied a great deal from case to case, as did the modes of transition.[6]

But what makes transition within ELDs especially hard to attain is the curious fact that those who are presently undermining the performance of liberal democracy are not its declared enemies but rather people who think of themselves as its supporters. Oddly, the task of reform would be much easier if extremists of the Right or Left *were* seeking to replace liberal rules and practices with some other form of governance; in reality, however, extremist programs and movements are and probably will remain inconsequential and unconvincing. Where the greatest threats to democracy come from "normal practitioners"—the usual voters, citizens, deputies, interest representatives, and movement activists engaging in their usual behaviors—it will be much more difficult to convince potential agent-citizens of the need for substantial reform. All they experience in their daily lives are what Antonio Gramsci called "morbid symptoms"—a lot of grumbling, dissatisfaction, and suboptimality, but hardly enough to motivate them to invest in substantial change in either a preliberal or a postliberal direction.

NOTES

1. See my essay "Dangers and Dilemmas of Democracy," *Journal of Democracy* 5 (April 1994): 57-74.

2. Robert A. Dahl, *Democracy and Its Critics* (New Haven: Yale University Press, 1989). See also Anthony Downs, "The Evolution of Democracy: How Its Axioms and Institutional Forms Have Been Adapted to Changing Social Forces," *Daedalus* 116 (Summer 1987): 119-48.

3. Albert O. Hirschman, *Shifting Involvements: Private Interests and Public Action* (Princeton: Princeton University Press, 1982).

4. The expression "strong democracy" is from Benjamin Barber, *Strong Democracy: Participatory Politics for a New Age* (Berkeley: University of California Press, 1984), which could be considered the most complete and consistent statement by a contemporary theorist in favor of what I am here calling "preliberal democracy."

5. In addition to the book by Benjamin Barber listed above, see D. Beetham, "Liberal Democracy and the Limits of Democratization," *Political Studies* 40 (1992): 40-53; A. Botwinick, *Skepticism and Political Participation* (Philadelphia: Temple University Press, 1990); J.S. Dryzek, *Discursive Democracy* (Cambridge: Cambridge University Press, 1990); C.G. Gould, *Rethinking Democracy* (Cambridge: Cambridge University Press, 1988); P. Green, *Retrieving Democracy* (London: Methuen, 1985); J.J. Mansbridge, *Beyond Adversary Democracy* (New York: Basic Books, 1980); C. Pateman, *Participation and Democratic Theory* (Cambridge: Cambridge University Press, 1970); and idem, *The Problem of Political Obligation: A Critique of Liberal Theory* (Cambridge: Polity Press, 1985). The godfather of all of these writers is probably C.B. MacPherson. See especially his *Democratic Theory: Essays in Retrieval* (Oxford: Clarendon Press, 1973) and *The Life and Times of Liberal Democracy* (Oxford: Oxford University Press, 1977).

6. Philippe C. Schmitter and Terry Karl, "Modes of Transition in Latin America, Southern and Eastern Europe," *International Social Science Journal* 128 (May 1991): 269-84.

28. DO ECONOMISTS KNOW BEST?

Guillermo O'Donnell

***Guillermo O'Donnell**, an Argentine political scientist, is Helen Kellogg Professor of International Studies and academic director of the Kellogg Institute of International Studies at the University of Notre Dame. His books include* Modernization and Bureaucratic-Authoritarianism *(1973);* Bureaucratic Authoritarianism: Argentina, 1966-1973, in Comparative Perspective *(1988); and, with Philippe C. Schmitter and Laurence Whitehead,* Transitions from Authoritarian Rule *(1986).*

Discussions about the situation of the world's fledgling democracies often seem so inconclusive that they remind me of the old question about whether the glass is half-empty or half-full. Such indecisiveness reflects the great diversity of perspectives that drive the various assessments and determine what they tend to highlight—and also what they tend to ignore.

Almost all observers agree that "political democracy" means, at a minimum, reasonably free and competitive elections that broadly reflect the voters' preferences and permit the winners to occupy most of the leading governmental positions. Some authors would classify as democratic any country that meets these criteria, while others might want to know more, such as whether those who are elected can actually exercise authority, or whether there are key offices which are not subject to elections or to control by elected authorities. Still other observers, even after agreeing that the vote counting was fair, might want to scrutinize the elections for fairness in terms of access to the media or voter-registration procedures. Even a rather narrow definition of political democracy, consequently, may contain room for disagreement about whether this or that country should properly count as a democracy.

Those who advocate more expansive definitions of democracy (definitions that look for the promotion of social justice, for instance) apply even more stringent criteria. Somewhere in the middle are others, like myself, who believe that while it is wiser to exclude considerations of social or economic equity from the definition of democracy, some factors overlooked by narrow definitions should be considered—especially the extent to which citizenship rights and, in general, the rule of law are effective across the population and territory of a given country. On this view, if one finds a rather low percentage of the population enjoying the rights and guarantees established by a formally democratic constitution, then the democratic character of the case is in grave doubt. We need more elaborate typologies of democracies that would allow judgments of degree (or quality) regarding the democratic character of a given regime. The work of formulating such typologies has barely begun.

If the achievement of democracy—even flawed or ambiguous democracy—is a good thing, then so is its perpetuation (or "consolidation") as a stable feature of political life, taken for granted by virtually all relevant political actors. There are many ideas about how best to achieve democratic consolidation. Some focus on political culture, saying in essence that if we want a consolidated democracy (to say nothing of a fuller or better democracy) we must educate as many people as possible to be democrats. This is a cogent point; the catch is that the creation of a comfortable majority of solid democrats is a long-term project, while the hazards that many new democracies face are immediate.

This may be one reason why nowadays institutionalist solutions prevail among those who are anxious to foster democracy. Political institutions can be designed with varying degrees of imitation and originality, and can be created fairly rapidly. Valuable knowledge is available concerning certain institutional combinations that one should avoid.[1] Yet we know little about the relative costs and benefits of adopting this or that ensemble of institutions, and even less about the paths to be trod (and the costs to be paid) in moving from one institutional setting to a new and hopefully better one.[2] Arguments taking the form that if institution X works in country A, then it should also work in country B—the stock-in-trade of one-country-per-week consultants—are today received with healthy skepticism almost everywhere. Serious institutionalists know that institutions, like fine wines, travel well, if at all, only under very special conditions. They also know that institutions are only part of the story in the consolidation of democracy.

The Hegemony of the Economists

Perhaps because there is so little agreement on definitions and so little reliable policy advice to give, part of political science has taken a back seat to economics—or, more precisely, to certain economists. These latter, drawing on ideas more or less loosely derived from academic research in their discipline, and often "leveraged" by jobs in international financial institutions, have been more than willing to tell the governments of new democracies what to do. To be fair, these economists have indeed shown how to diminish inflation and alleviate fiscal and balance-of-payments deficits. What they do not know, and what they disagree about—both among themselves and with economists of other persuasions—is how to use these short-term achievements as a springboard to sustainable growth. (Another theme, equitable growth, has remained outside the scope of what these economists would consider a serious discussion.) Furthermore, the main institutional supporters of these views, especially the World Bank, have begun to pay attention to the negative developmental consequences of their own prescriptions for economic adjustment. In many countries, for instance, reforms mandated by the World Bank have had the effect of gutting much of the state, with predictably deleterious consequences for long-term economic development.

In spite of these shortcomings (which admittedly are more evident today than they were ten years ago), political scientists working on the political aspects of economic adjustment were overshadowed until recently by the expertise that those economists claimed to have. This claim of expertise amounted to an argument that there were demonstrably optimal economic policies for democratizing countries. Some such policies might be effective (if painful) means for controlling inflation or cutting deficits; others, such as trade or financial liberalization, are much more complicated in their extent, timing, sequence, and consequences. In relation to all of them, however, the view that prevailed from the late 1970s to the early 1990s brought politics into the picture only as an obstacle course filled with impediments to the adoption and implementation of "correct" economic policies.

The view that for a given social problem there is one best solution all too easily leads to the assumption that disagreement is *ipso facto* irrational. If those who disagree mount significant protests, they become "obstacles." In keeping with the mood of the 1980s, much of the economics and political-economy literature to which I have alluded cast the state and trade unions in just such a role. The best response, the thinking went, was to "insulate" policy makers from politics so that they could apply their universalistic rationality without regard to the "particularistic" claims of various obstacle groups.[3]

If this rhetoric seems redolent of authoritarianism, that is no accident. Both old-fashioned authoritarians and newfangled technocrats base themselves on the premise that those who occupy high office know better than the rest of society, and therefore have not only the right but the duty to impose that superior knowledge. No wonder, then, that political scientists of sincerely democratic views sounded uneasy when, following the logic of the "single-best-policy" school, they recommended the "insulation" of economic policy makers from politics. At this point democratization tends to slip out of focus: in the present tense it is seen as a political minefield full of threats to economic rationality; in the future tense, it is seen as a hoped-for consequence of the prescribed economic policies (in the bad old days, this latter view would have come under attack as a blatant example of "economicism"). The upshot typically has been the neglect of topics that are properly political, such as questions regarding the political effects of "correct" economic policies on the legitimacy of democracy and the prestige of democratic institutions and politicians.

In the past few years, some preliminary but significant truths have become clear. It is true, for instance, that important economic successes, such as reductions in inflation rates and fiscal and external-accounts deficits, can be rather rapidly achieved. These achievements are necessary but not sufficient conditions for the resumption of sustainable economic growth. Sufficient conditions are hard to specify: contemporary economics is not particularly strong on theories of growth, and views on this matter are both indecisive and hotly contested.[4] Also, it is unclear how long it may take for some steps commonly accepted as conducive to growth (such as increasing the educational qualifications of the populace) to produce results.

Moreover, in spite of increasing attention to issues of social equity, there are few ideas about how to help the more deprived sectors (which in many new democracies include an appallingly large share of the population) in ways that not only are effective but also do not reinforce their social exclusion. Even less is known about how to help the deprived without antagonizing better-organized and politically crucial layers of society that, objectively and subjectively, are often not much better off than the former.[5]

Survey data and first-hand impressions alike suggest that in most new democracies a majority of citizens dislike the authoritarian past more than the present (however flawed), and enjoy having the freedoms of expression, association, and the like that were previously denied. This mood, less enamored of democracy than fearful of authoritarianism, is probably the most valuable asset that democratic leaders have. But this mood coexists, almost everywhere, with very unflattering assessments of democratic politicians, parties, and legislatures. These negative evaluations, fed by politicians' own blunders, do not help at all to advance the cause of democratic consolidation. If things get bad enough, the way may be opened for the rise of "delegative" democracy—a type of regime that can lead only by accident to the strengthening of representative and accountable modes of governing.[6] If societal tensions are very high, and if ambitious leaders believe that they can usurp power without incurring major international costs (typically by redoubling their commitment to mainstream economic policies or by solving worrisome geopolitical issues), then delegative democracy may degenerate into thinly veiled authoritarianism.

The Danger of Slow Death

All of the foregoing I offer by way of a long introduction to the brief answer that I intend to give to the important questions posed by this symposium: I just do not know enough to make the kind of prediction that these questions aim to elicit. Given the many ambiguities surrounding the very definition of democracy, as well as the paucity of scholarship dealing with democratization as a *political* process, it is not even easy to say when a democracy has ceased to exist: consider, for example, recent discussions about whether contemporary Peru is or is not a democracy.

In spite of these limitations, I can proffer a piece of advice. Some time ago I reasoned that there are two ways democracies perish: by a sudden or a slow death.[7] Sudden death occurs by means of civil war, coup d'état, or some other spectacular event that immediately attracts international attention and gives a precise date for democracy's demise. History is not lacking in examples of this kind of death. But a more subtle and safer method for the enemies of democracy is to terminate it slowly. This is accomplished through the gradual erosion of freedoms, guarantees, and processes that are vital to democracy. Here there is no precise date at which democracy can be pronounced defunct (and, consequently, no international media rushing to the country to register the decease). Retrospectively, one can see a period of gradual suffocation when, at each tightening of the noose, democratic actors both at home and abroad lost the chance to fight back because each step, in itself, did not seem sufficiently serious to mobilize them fully. These are periods, usually measured in years, of feeble and decaying democratization.[8] Slow death is insidious: while the violence and repression accompanying it may be as great as in the case of sudden death, a slowly dying democracy may be able to cloak itself in claims of residual domestic and international legitimacy that make it difficult to launch timely and appropriate domestic and international responses. This will be especially true if powerful countries have pragmatic reasons for not wanting to antagonize the suppressors of democracy.

New democracies where the state itself or its territorial boundaries are problematic, or where violent conflict is under way, are particularly prone to sudden death. This is important and worrisome enough. But it should not detract attention from those new democracies which, though free of such dramatic threats, are subject to slow death or else stagnation in a brackish zone where some features of democracy mingle with a strong tincture of surviving or revived authoritarianism. Detecting these risks, describing their evolution, conceptualizing the emerging political entities beyond the not very illuminating assertion that they are "hybrids," and mobilizing timely domestic and international efforts to reverse antidemocratic trends will all be major tasks in the years ahead. For such work, more refined typologies and theories about "really existing" democracies are badly needed.

NOTES

1. See especially the persuasive argument that Scott Mainwaring makes about the negative consequences of a mix of presidentialism, proportional representation, and weak party discipline in "Presidentialism, Multipartism, and Democracy: The Difficult Combination," *Comparative Political Studies* 26 (July 1993): 198-228.

2. Such costs have recently been addressed by Stephan Haggard and Robert R. Kaufman in their criticism of arguments favoring the adoption of parliamentary systems. However preferable parliamentarism may be to presidentialism in principle, they say, there may be prohibitive political costs attached to the transition from the latter system to the former, especially in countries where there is a long presidentialist tradition. See Stephan Haggard and Robert R. Kaufman, "The Challenges of Consolidation," *Journal of Democracy* 5 (October 1994): 5-16.

3. Probably the strongest, but by no means the only, statements of this kind can be found in the chapters that hail the "technopols" in John Williamson, ed., *The Political Economy of Policy Reform* (Washington, D.C.: Institute for International Economics, 1994).

4. See Adam Przeworski, *Democracy and the Market: Political and Economic Reforms in Eastern Europe and Latin America* (Cambridge: Cambridge University Press, 1991) and "The Neoliberal Fallacy," *Journal of Democracy* 3 (July 1992): 45-59.

5. In several of her writings, Joan Nelson has called attention to this problem. See especially her "Poverty, Equity, and the Politics of Adjustment," in Stephan Haggard and Robert R. Kaufman, eds., *The Politics of Economic Adjustment* (Princeton: Princeton University Press, 1992), 221-69.

6. I discuss this theme in "Delegative Democracy," *Journal of Democracy* 5 (January 1994): 55-69.

7. For further elaboration, see my essay "Challenges to Democratization in Brazil: A Threat of a Slow Death," *World Policy Journal* 5 (Spring 1988): 281-300.

8. See especially the illuminating (and worrisome) discussion of regressive patterns in Larry Diamond, "Democracy in Latin America: Degrees, Illusions and Directions for Consolidation," in Tom Farer, ed., *Collectively Defending Democracy* (Baltimore: Johns Hopkins University Press, forthcoming).

29. THE ASIAN SPECTRUM

Muthiah Alagappa

***Muthiah Alagappa**, a native of Malaysia, is a senior fellow at the East-West Center in Honolulu, Hawaii. Previously a visiting professor at the East Asian Institute and the political science department of Columbia University and a senior fellow at the Institute for Strategic and International Studies in Malaysia, he is the editor of* Political Legitimacy in Southeast Asia *(1995).*

Early in the post-World War II era, a majority of countries in East and Southeast Asia had democratic political systems. Over time, however, many of these were supplanted by authoritarian and totalitarian regimes. By the early 1970s, only Japan retained a fully democratic system, with Malaysia and Singapore belonging to the category of semidemocracy. The February 1986 "people power" revolution in the Philippines, however, marked the beginning of a return of democracy to the region. Democratic transitions followed in South Korea, Taiwan, Mongolia, and Thailand, as well as in Bangladesh, Nepal, and Pakistan. These have been interpreted by some Western policy makers and analysts as part of a growing trend toward democratic governance not only in Asia but in the world at large.

According to Samuel P. Huntington, the two variables likely to have the greatest effect on prospects for the spread of democracy are economic development and political leadership.[1] Economically, the countries of East and Southeast Asia are among the most dynamic in the world. Many of them have experienced high-single-digit or double-digit annual growth rates for well over a decade. Even the laggard economies of Vietnam, the Philippines, and Burma are beginning to turn around. Governing elites in nearly all of these countries are committed to economic development and modernization. Provided this rapid economic growth benefits all sectors of society, it should be a positive factor for democratic development in the region.

In a number of countries, however—namely, China, Vietnam, Burma,

Indonesia, Singapore, Malaysia, Brunei, and Laos—the same elites who support economic development reject democracy. In part their rejection of the democratic ideal is a response to the perceived "reactionary imperialism" of the West. In part it is aimed at preserving their own power. Yet it also stems from a conviction that liberal democracy is not well suited to Asian cultures and that it will hinder modernization. Even elites in these countries who are supportive of democracy believe that it must be tailored to reflect national values.

Declining political legitimacy, which Huntington identified as one of the changes that precipitated the "third wave" democratic transitions, is in my view a third key variable influencing regime change.[2] Prospects for democratic development in East and Southeast Asia hinge on the interaction of this factor with the two others described above.

The Challenge of Consolidation

The challenge now facing South Korea, Taiwan, the Philippines, and Thailand is consolidation of their democratic gains. In Taiwan and South Korea, democratic principles are already firmly entrenched and the conditions that foster broad and meaningful political participation are gaining ground. Yet both countries still face significant political and economic problems that will make further democratic development slow and contentious.

Since the lifting of martial law in 1987, Taiwan has traveled rapidly along the democratic path. The 1947 Constitution has been amended in several important respects, free elections have taken place, the Kuomintang (KMT) party and the government are gradually separating from each other, and a competitive party system is emerging. President Lee Teng-hui is committed to further democratization. Contrary to concerns expressed by some Asian leaders that democratic development would impede economic growth, Taiwan's economy has grown by 6 to 8 percent annually since 1987. Moreover, the Taiwanese public strongly supports democratic reform. All of these factors make it unlikely that democratization will undergo a reversal in Taiwan.

Still, a number of complicating factors are likely to slow its progress. Taiwan's future political status gives special cause for concern. There is growing popular dissatisfaction with Taiwan's international isolation, and an increasingly vocal movement for political independence. A democratically elected government might feel compelled to move further in this direction, aggravating tension with the People's Republic of China. In this scenario, the increased salience of security considerations would lead to a greater allocation of resources to defense, possibly triggering a renewed political role for the military.

South Korea, too, has undergone significant democratic development since 1987. Elections have been held at the national and provincial levels, with local elections scheduled for 1995. The 1992 election of the first civilian president, Kim Young Sam, has been interpreted by some observers as marking the definitive end of military rule. As in Taiwan, the forces that fueled the democratic transition are still salient. Industrialization appears likely to continue, the polity has become more complex and differentiated, and civil society has gained strength. Many segments of the population are voicing demands for further economic and political reform.

Yet a number of problems are hindering democratization. Power continues to be concentrated in the executive, money politics and corruption continue to dominate the political process, institutionalization of political parties is yet to be accomplished, and the rule of law has been slow to develop. Serious economic conflicts have emerged, many of them revolving around the equitable distribution of wealth. Moreover, the government is having difficulty managing the transition from a labor-intensive economy to one based on high technology. The changing relationship with North Korea, with its uncertain consequences for democratization, constitutes yet another formidable challenge.

In Thailand and the Philippines, democratic development is less firmly rooted. In Thailand, democratic values have gradually gained ground since 1932, despite periodic reversals. The military leadership's attempt to consolidate its position through the March 1992 elections led to violent political conflict between the military and the new social forces. A democratic government acceded to power in the wake of the September 1992 elections.

Democracy, however, is far from established in Thailand. Political parties are still regional and weak—and sufficiently numerous that the need for coalition governments, vulnerable to crisis and collapse, will likely continue. Owing to rampant vote buying in rural areas, the victors in elections cannot claim to represent the popular will. Moreover, the Thai military remains a formidable political force with which any elected government must contend. So long as the military does not fully accept the principle of civilian control, the democratic system in Thailand will not be the sole repository of power. Finally, many Thais are not fully committed to the democratic ideal. Thus, while over the long term democratic values and procedures will probably continue to gain ground, other factors may be used as a temporary basis of political legitimacy.

In the Philippines, little substantive progress has been made since the restoration of formal democracy in 1986. Although the power and influence of the military and the radical Left have declined, along with the threat these elements pose to a democratic system, the necessary preconditions for broad and meaningful political participation—equality among citizens in access to resources and opportunities, as well as in rights and obligations—appear unlikely to obtain for some time to come. The vast majority of Filipinos continue to live in abject poverty, and there is little prospect for significant improvement in social conditions in the foreseeable future. Most governing elites belong to old political clans, and in recent years there has been a return to pork-barrel and patronage politics. Political parties remain weak; the legal system is inaccessible to most citizens, inefficient, and weakened by widespread bribery and corruption; and violations of civil rights are common.

All this suggests that democracy in the Philippines remains vulnerable to manipulation by a strongman or displacement through a military coup. Given the still fresh memory of abuses during the Marcos era, complete reversal of democracy is unlikely in the immediate future. Nevertheless, moving beyond formal democracy in the Philippines is contingent upon substantial socioeconomic development.

The Weakness of Autocracy

The tide of democracy has so far left many countries in East and Southeast Asia untouched. China, Vietnam, Burma, and Indonesia are among the key countries whose political elites have challenged the universality of the democratic ideal. Yet notwithstanding the negative attitude toward democracy displayed by their current leaders, political liberalization and possibly even a more competitive political system cannot be ruled out in the medium to long term. Two interrelated developments currently give grounds for hope: the declining legitimacy of the present regimes, and the leaders' commitment to economic growth and modernization as a means of recapturing that legitimacy.

The limited political liberalization and economic reform initiated by the Chinese Communist Party (CCP) in 1979 brought substantial benefits for nearly all segments of the Chinese population and shored up the party's legitimacy. But it also eroded the cohesion of the government and undermined the credibility of the Marxist-Leninist system, giving rise to the June 1989 Tiananmen incident. The government's deployment of massive force to suppress the demonstrations reflected its own weakness and further undermined regime legitimacy among the urban population, particularly in Beijing.

Since 1989, China's political leaders have staked their claim to rule even more firmly on strong economic performance. Under these circumstances, any economic downturn may undermine the legitimacy of the regime. Yet the imperative to maintain high growth rates has made controlling inflation difficult, leading to widespread disenchantment, particularly among those already disadvantaged by the current phase of reform. Moreover, rapid economic growth has been accompanied by the development of professional associations and other civil society groups, who may begin to voice demands for political participation. In any case, the CCP leaders themselves realize that economic performance alone cannot serve as a basis of political legitimacy over the medium to long term. Recognizing the current weakness of their ideological credentials, they have sought to tap into nationalism, which has been on the rise in China. Confucianism may also enjoy a revitalization as the leadership seeks a new basis of moral authority. East Asia's successful dominant-party political systems, such as those in Singapore and pre-1987 South Korea and Taiwan, have also attracted the attention of some Chinese leaders and scholars.

Politics in Vietnam has followed a similar course. After reunification in 1975, the socialist policies of the Vietnamese Communist Party (VCP) contributed to an economic crisis in the South. Moreover, poor economic performance in the North, which had been tolerated during the war, led to widespread disenchantment with the regime. Coupled with infighting and corruption within the VCP, these developments undermined the party's legitimacy. To recapture legitimacy, in 1986 the VCP adopted as its goal *doi moi*, or political and economic renovation. This policy has elicited a mixed response. Critics have challenged some crucial aspects of political renovation, while the benefits of improved economic performance have not been shared equally. As in China, while economic reform may shore up the legitimacy of the incumbent leadership, it could also lay the groundwork for challenges to the legitimacy of the system at a more fundamental level. Recognizing this, VCP leaders have tentatively begun to explore alternative models of governance.

In Burma, accumulated resentment against the military-socialist regime of General Ne Win—which, though it never had much legitimacy to begin with, had managed to survive for well over two decades—burst into a countrywide "people power" uprising in 1989. In an effort to silence domestic opposition and gain international legitimacy, the State Law and Order Restoration Council (SLORC) scheduled national elections for May 1990. Despite results that clearly indicated a desire for change, the military has refused to hand over the reigns of power. The SLORC, which is seen as a continuation of the previous military-socialist regime, continues to suffer a fundamental legitimacy crisis, and controls Burma by means of coercion. In an attempt to establish a stronger basis of authority it has begun to liberalize the economy, and it is seeking to provide a formal political role for the military, perhaps along the lines of the Indonesian *dwifungsi* or "dual function" model.

Of the nondemocratic regimes discussed here, the Suharto government in Indonesia currently enjoys the highest degree of legitimacy. It initially staked its claim to rule on the promise of political stability and economic development, which had great appeal to the Indonesian populace in light of the country's continual political upheaval from 1950 to 1965, as well as the sharp deterioration in living standards, especially during the "guided democracy" era (1957-65). In the mid-1980s, however, with political stability assured and Suharto's personal authority subject to increasing criticism, the legitimacy of the regime began to decline. The key principles and goals of the New Order have been challenged by associations of intellectuals, human rights organizations, Islamic organizations, Christian minorities, and some segments of the armed forces. As a result, the government has relied increasingly on economic development as a basis of legitimacy. The country's economic performance since 1965 has been impressive, and by most accounts the benefits of growth have extended to all social classes.

Suharto and his government are still being criticized by those who insist that economic growth has increased inequity and, moreover, that economic performance and stability are not an adequate underpinning of political legitimacy. The demand for democratic government is not yet widespread, however, and the challenges are not likely to spark a political crisis in the near future. On the other hand, the principles and goals undergirding the legitimacy of the present regime will not be enough to support long-term harmony between ruler and ruled. Future governments will have to find a new formula to legitimate themselves.

Alternative Models

Recognition of their declining legitimacy has led political elites in all of the nondemocratic countries of East and Southeast Asia, however grudgingly, to explore alternative models of governance. Given the political, cultural, and socioeconomic context of the region, three such models seem plausible: Islamic theocracy, authoritarian pluralism, and dominant-party democracy. Islam can be considered a competing political ideology only in Indonesia and Malaysia, and even there its appeal is limited to a minority of the Muslim population. In Indonesia, the powerful military opposes the idea of a theocratic state. In Malaysia, the government has sought to coopt Islam by infusing Islamic values into the administration, thereby keeping radical Islam in check.

The authoritarian-pluralist and dominant-party democracy models, though quite distinct, can be viewed as separate stages on a continuum between authoritarianism and democracy. In the authoritarian-pluralist model, the party or other governing group retains a monopoly on political power but is willing to grant a measure of political and cultural freedom at the individual, group, and regional levels. Moreover, some development of civil society is tolerated, particularly in the professional arena. Economic development is governed by market principles. The model holds special appeal for China and Vietnam because it would seem to allow for continued monopolization of political power by the party leadership while facilitating the desired outcomes of social stability and economic growth. Yet, as demonstrated by the experiences of Thailand from 1957 to 1973 and, later, by those of South Korea and Taiwan, the authoritarian-pluralist model contains the seeds of its own destruction. The social changes brought about by economic growth inevitably give rise to political demands that challenge the monopolization of political power by one party or group. Thus the authoritarian-pluralist model is by its very nature a transitional one.

The dominant-party democracy model is an abstraction of the experience of Japan and, to a lesser degree, Malaysia and Singapore. Its chief features are free elections, protection of civil liberties, a dominant party that stays in power over a long period, an interventionist state, a strong central bureaucracy, and management of the political affairs of the country by means of conciliation and consensus-building. Because it is based on the cultural heritage and traditions of East Asia (such as respect for strong authority and emphasis on community interests over individual rights), some see this as a distinct and durable Asian form of democracy. South Korea and, to a lesser extent, Taiwan have sought to emulate the Japanese political system. Owing to abuses of power by the long-reigning Liberal Democratic Party, however, the dominant-party democracy model is currently being challenged in Japan itself. Its future in the region is unclear. In any case, this is presently not an attractive model for China and Vietnam.

In the nondemocratic countries of East and Southeast Asia, sustained economic development, which the governing elite perceive as the mainstay of their legitimacy, will continue to fuel demands for political liberalization and ultimately system transformation. What these changes will be, whether they will be revolutionary or evolutionary, and when they will occur are difficult to predict. It is hard to envisage democratic transitions occurring in the near term in China and Vietnam, where independent political organization has been—and will likely continue to be—hampered by the intolerance of incumbent governments. A new Tiananmen incident would, at best, speed the pace of political change. At worst, it could result in a strengthening of conservative forces and a corresponding diminution of the likelihood of democratic transition.

A more likely scenario is continued gradual political liberalization initiated and controlled by the CCP and the VCP, respectively. In China, significant political change will have to await the demise of patriarch Deng Xiaoping, and its pace will depend on the cohesion, power, and orientation of the new leadership. An important question in both China and Vietnam is whether the "supply" of liberalization will keep pace with demand. If it does, these countries may be able to follow the authoritarian-pluralist model for several decades. If it does not, the process of political change will be marked by tension and conflict.

Prospects for a democratic transition are a bit brighter in Burma and Indonesia. Both countries have previous experience with democracy, and both have political parties in place. The main stumbling block in both cases is the military's refusal to relinquish power. Because the military is a key political force in both countries, any political system that does not take it into account will not be sustainable. One possible scenario is a gradual transition to democracy through power sharing between elected representatives and the military establishment. Yet gradualism requires a strong leader who is also committed to liberalization and eventual democratization. In Indonesia, Suharto has the requisite authority but has not shown signs of moving toward democratization, and he may have missed the opportunity to do so. The Burmese military, though physically in control, is morally bankrupt and fighting for survival, and thus unlikely to take the initiative in democratization. Although history is not always a reliable guide, in the past, political-system transformations in Indonesia and Burma (as well as China and Vietnam) have been abrupt and violent.

While it can be useful to conceptualize political change in terms of broad waves or global trends, each country follows a unique trajectory. System change will be driven mostly by domestic factors—regime legitimacy, elite cohesion, the level and pace of socioeconomic development, the political orientation of the military, income distribution, civil society, and so forth. These conditions must be propitious if international forces are to have a significant impact. In the case of East and Southeast Asia, the current international environment cannot be judged to be prodemocratic. While the United States and other Western nations have made the promotion of democracy an important element of their foreign policies, no Asian government has done so. Even Japan, while remaining firmly committed to democratic government for itself, has shown little enthusiasm for spreading democracy abroad. Moreover, the political influence of the West has declined, and is likely to decline even further if the East and Southeast Asian countries continue to experience rapid economic growth. On the other hand, intraregional influences are likely to be strong. System change in China, for example, is likely to have an impact on Vietnam and North Korea, and developments in Indonesia, Burma, and Thailand will affect one another.

Finally, it is important to remember that Western-style democracy is only one yardstick of political development. If we view Asian countries only through a democratic lens, we run the risk of undervaluing political changes that are quite significant from the perspective of the governed. For example, China today is far from democratic in the Western sense; nevertheless, the China of Deng is vastly different from the China of Mao. Substantial political change has in fact occurred throughout the region over the last decade and a half, though it is often overlooked by observers who focus exclusively on democracy. The democratic paradigm is certainly relevant to Asia, but it is not the whole story.

NOTES

1. Samuel P. Huntington, *The Third Wave: Democratization in the Late Twentieth Century* (Norman: University of Oklahoma Press, 1991), 315-16.

2. Ibid., 45-58.

30.
BETWEEN AFRICA'S EXTREMES

Michael Chege

***Michael Chege** is a visiting scholar at the Center for International Affairs at Harvard University. Formerly a Ford Foundation program officer in eastern and southern Africa and a director of the Institute for International Studies at the University of Nairobi, he has contributed essays on African governance and development to* Foreign Affairs *and other periodicals, as well as to many edited volumes.*

In the brief passages devoted to sub-Saharan Africa in his book on democracy's "third wave," Samuel P. Huntington is largely pessimistic about the prospects of liberal constitutionalism in the region.[1] Yet, despite the well-publicized (and self-inflicted) political calamities that have befallen the continent, developments over the past four years have proved to be more varied than Huntington's remarks would have led one to expect. Since 1990, most of sub-Saharan Africa's 45 states have seen attempts at transition from authoritarianism to democracy. The fate of these efforts runs the gamut from outright disaster to relative success, with stalemate being a frequent outcome (as in Nigeria, Zaire, Togo, Kenya, and Cameroon). The vast range of results was dramatized unforgettably in the spring of 1994, when Nelson Mandela was inaugurated as the first president of a democratic South Africa, an improbable historic event celebrated by democrats the world over, even as ghastly massacres sowed death across Rwanda and began a nightmarish parade of horrors. Those two events represent the two poles of possibility in the face of the same fundamental challenge. For although the political and historical gap that separates South Africa and Rwanda is greater than the 1,500 miles that lie between them, both states were essentially grappling with what has turned out to be the most intractable political problem facing the region: that of crafting representative public institutions on a social foundation of deep-seated ethnic rivalries and economic inequalities.

The key to the outcome in both these cases—and in many others as well—was the quality of political leadership, whether in government or opposition, and its capacity to steer thitherto hostile constituencies toward mutual accommodation. It is becoming increasingly evident that South Africa's fortunate transition was the culmination of drawn-out, behind-the-scenes negotiations between African nationalist leaders who knew the art of driving a hard bargain but also when to compromise, and liberal whites who sought to dismantle the besieged apartheid system for the long-term good of the country. In stark contrast, the Rwandan tragedy came about when the militarily hard-pressed Hutu ethnocracy abjured negotiations and stubbornly sought to preserve its hegemony by means of a Nazi-style "final solution" designed to extirpate the country's Tutsi population as well as Hutu prodemocracy activists.

Broadly speaking, the paths followed by most African nations can be traced to strategies adopted by authoritarian incumbents and the reactions to them displayed by specific citizens and opposition groups. Some incumbents chose to compromise with democratic or potentially democratic challengers, while others opted instead to seek the annihilation or incapacitation of opposition movements. In every case, the new prodemocracy groups and external actors have played critical secondary roles in catalyzing or forestalling positive political change.

It is time to recognize this emerging variability in the process of political and constitutional change in Africa—distinguishing the successes from the cases that have fed the too broadly drawn doomsday scenario broadcast by the world news media—and to identify the actors behind the various outcomes. Above all, if we hope to advance the prospects of democratic governance in Africa, we must begin to deepen our understanding of the political forces at play in each country. For with every passing year, those who study the continent are faced with ever more painful reminders of just how difficult it will be to plant and nurture functioning democratic institutions in the volatile social terrain of sub-Saharan Africa. The optimism that prevailed in 1990 has been steadily tempered by monumental problems of government and civil society, some of which hark back to the very founding of the modern state as we know it.

The Elusiveness of Consensus

The institutionalization of free and popular government requires mutual acceptance of democratic principles, an active middle class, and committed democratic leaders, all working over time in a comparatively orderly and prosperous state. Minimal consensus on the need to preserve the integrity of the state, the inviolability of personal liberties, equality before the law, and dedication to the rule of law is a prerequisite to progress. The euphoria that accompanied the rise of multiparty democracy in Africa from 1990 onward was based on an assumption of viable state structures and a democratic constituency waiting in the wings. All eyes focused—with good reason—on the removal of baleful dictators and their minions. Yet the optimists overestimated the strength of liberalizing forces, while fatally underestimating the capacity of incumbent autocrats to manipulate state institutions and even engineer anarchy in order to preempt democracy.

The handful of textbook cases of political catastrophe in Africa demonstrate the grim reality. Somalia, Liberia, Sudan, Angola, Sierra Leone, and Rwanda have suffered limitless plunder and carnage initiated by besieged dictators. The problems have been aggravated by violent resistance movements that are no more committed to the democratic process, civil liberties, or the rule of law than the harried autocrats whom they seek to replace. The Siad Barre military regime in Somalia (1969-91) wasted the country long before General Mohamed Farah Aydid and his antagonists appeared in Mogadishu. The retreating Rwandan army not only killed innocent citizens but also ravaged farms and factories on its way to Zaire. Similar atrocities have been committed by the rebel National Union for the Total Liberation of Angola (UNITA) in that country and the proliferating armed factions in Liberia. In all these blighted African territories, now awash in light weapons generously supplied by the United States and its Soviet-bloc rivals in the heyday of the Cold War, the implosion of armies and police forces and the absence of a legitimate monopoly on the use of force have led to interminable wars of all against all. In countries of this sort, the first order of business is the establishment of civic order, followed by a gradual laying of the groundwork for functioning institutions of governance. Here democracy as such is not yet on the agenda.

Far beyond this stage are such countries as South Africa, Malawi, Ethiopia, and Uganda, where the overriding aim of political transition has been to consolidate the integrity of the state. The method has been constitutional innovation negotiated among the government, the opposition, and historically entrenched social interests. In South Africa, a new democratic constitution, interparty power-sharing, and reprieve for erstwhile torturers and oppressors were presaged by largely free and fair general elections that avoided the winner-take-all formula that has caused so many problems elsewhere. Malawi recently adopted similar policies despite its first-past-the-post electoral system, and Mozambique was urged by African leaders to do the same after its November 1994 election. In Uganda, the commitment of President Yoweri Kaguta Museveni's government to elections under a nonparty system and the restoration of kingdoms to the Buganda, Toro, and Bunyoro regions are part of an effort to secure broad-based and lasting support for new governance structures. In Addis Ababa, the 1993 decision by the ruling Ethiopian People's Revolutionary Democratic Front (EPRDF) to accede to the secession of Eritrea, as well as to approve a new federalist scheme recognizing ethnic autonomy, provides a salutary lesson that re-creating international and internal boundaries via mutual agreement can be a more positive and humane way of establishing a stable national government than civil war and ethnic cleansing. War-ravaged Sudan and Mauritania, as well as most of the other states in the Sudano-Sahel zone, such as Niger and Mali, might do well to take heed.

Uganda and especially Ethiopia so far have shown themselves less capable than South Africa and Malawi of building a culture of political toleration and respect for individual liberties. Continuing persecution of Amharic and Oromo opponents of the EPRDF in Ethiopia and violence in northern Uganda could jeopardize reform. On the other hand, the peaceful resolution of such problems might enable these countries to join those states that have experienced change through the ballot—Zambia, Benin, São Tomé & Príncipe, the Central African Republic, Niger, Mali, Madagascar, and Lesotho, not to mention such functioning African democracies as Botswana, Namibia, Mauritius, Seychelles, and arguably Senegal.

In his book, Huntington celebrates the triumph of Joseph Schumpeter's definition of democracy—"the institutional arrangement for arriving at political decisions in which individuals acquire power to decide by means of a competitive struggle for the people's vote"—as opposed to classical notions that conceived democracy primarily as benevolent rule based on popular will.[2] The emphasis here is on elections as a basis of authority. Yet if we are correct that Africa's most common political problem is lack of consensus on the fundamental content of democracy and the inviolability of the most basic state institutions, then the continent's democratic activists should first and foremost cultivate a constituency that supports the content and goals of liberal governance and affirms the social benefits of following its rules. The last four years should teach us that many countries have overemphasized multiparty elections as the foundation of democracy, and correspondingly neglected the basic tenets of liberal governance. Africa now harbors a large number of rudderless regimes, drifting between success and catastrophe, with pretensions to electoral legitimacy but no real popular backing to speak of. If badly handled, these vessels could capsize, as experience has already made clear.

Imperfect Elections

Multiparty elections have now been held in 27 of the 45 sub-Saharan states. African dictatorships have so far shown greater dexterity in manipulating these elections than their domestic and external critics had foreseen. Although old-fashioned ballot-stuffing is no longer fashionable, most of the recent elections have taken place under policies, laws, and political conditions that breached the spirit of democratic competition. Multiparty general elections in Kenya, Cameroon, Ghana, Côte d'Ivoire, Guinea-Conakry, Togo, and Gabon, as well as the June 1994 constitutional-assembly elections in Ethiopia, were all deeply flawed. The military toppled Burundi's first democratically elected government by executing the president, Melchior Ndadaye, in October 1993. But perhaps the greatest electoral fiasco of all was the Nigerian military's June 1993 annulment of that country's most honest general election since independence in 1960. In the summer of 1994, the military usurpers put winner Moshood Abiola on trial for treason. The outcome in Nigeria—as in other countries where elections have been disputed—has been continuing paralysis within the government as incumbents and oppositionists conduct a postelectoral battle of wits on a daily basis.

On the assumption that a semi-honest election is better than no election at all, external observers have often grudgingly endorsed such polls as a start, however imperfect, toward democratic rule. This was the verdict on the Kenyan elections by the Commonwealth Secretariat in London, and the position of the French government on Cameroon. Even the softening of the Mobutu government in Zaire in the wake of the Rwandan tragedy by late 1994 was being rewarded with external aid from France and Belgium. Yet in all these cases, autocratic rulers have subsequently tightened the screws of repression and sought to divide and intimidate legitimate opposition movements.

Tragically, some of the new opposition parties have played right into the hands of the autocrats. A two-party system is designed to provide voters with a ready alternative to the government of the day. A multiplicity of small warring parties, however antiauthoritarian they may be, does not constitute a true democratic opposition. Yet in Africa—whether in Ghana, Kenya, Cameroon, Tanzania, Zaire, or Zimbabwe—there has been a marked inability to rally opposition forces behind a unified antiauthoritarian banner.[3] Rather, opposition parties tend to split repeatedly along ethnic and personality lines. Some opposition leaders have even sold out to the government, turning against their erstwhile compatriots. Togo's current prime minister, Edem Kodjo, for example, broke ranks with the victors of the July 1994 legislative elections to join the government of the country's long-lived autocrat, General Gnassingbé Eyadema. In Nigeria, Abiola's vice-presidential running mate Baba Gana Kingibe became foreign minister of General Sani Abacha's military government. In Kenya, nearly a dozen legislators have crossed over to the ruling party, allegedly because they were paid to do so. In fact, in the face of the region's declining economies, a sizeable number of African intellectuals, journalists, and professionals have sold their services to dictators, thus weakening the impetus for both economic and political liberalization. Such amoral, self-seeking behavior has been identified by Jean-François Bayart as a historic flaw of African statesmanship.[4]

Even so, it would be a mistake to overlook what is potentially the strongest hope for democracy in Africa: the politically committed and well-educated members of civic and opposition groups whose belief in the continent's capacity for better government is unshakable. These pioneering democrats—whose numbers, though small, are growing—include members of the Campaign for Democracy and its many allies in Nigeria, prodemocratic lawyers and clergy in Kenya, tough-minded opposition legislators like Ghana's Hawa Yakubu-Ogede and Kenya's Martha Karua, and trade unionists, religious leaders, academics, and independent journalists in Ethiopia, Senegal, Kenya, Mozambique, Zimbabwe, and elsewhere. All of them belie Bayart's portrayal of African leaders as a benighted lot. The social texture and goals of prodemocracy coalitions throughout the continent are similar to those of the movement that broke the back of apartheid in South Africa—a fact that has not been lost on the enemies of the open society elsewhere on the continent.

Civil Society's Potential—and Limits

In preparing themselves for the difficult task of introducing multiparty democracy in Africa, these leaders and organizations must reckon with the strengths and weaknesses of African civil society, which have recently become more visible as a result of the limited political reforms that have already taken place. Careful assessment, by ensuring that the new frameworks of governance are congruent with popular aspirations and realities, will give those structures a better chance at long-term survival.

Against the backdrop of the authoritarianism and depravity of most sub-Saharan governments, the recent rediscovery of a vibrant and largely autonomous civil society has lifted hopes that ordinary citizens could play a larger role in local public decision making, especially as regards development.[5] Though not without merit, some of the "people's empowerment" literature spawned by this perspective echoes the ultimately futile 1960s fascination with rural African socialism; Thomas Callaghy and René Lemarchand have already pointed out this view's potential analytical flaws.[6] With specific reference to the challenge of crafting democracies in Africa, two of the most relevant attributes of African civil society are the salience of ethnic identity and the paucity of the "civic" spirit that Robert Putnam identified as the key to making democracy work in northern Italy.[7]

Most of the elections noted above were characterized by ethnic bloc voting, sometimes without reference to issues. In 1992 in Ghana, for example, Akan-speaking regions voted predominantly against the Jerry

Rawlings government, notwithstanding the increased earnings from cocoa that accrued to them as a result of his economic liberalization policies. Voting patterns in Kenya, Malawi, Zambia, and Guinea-Bissau also reflect ethnic cleavages. Claude Ake has remarked that it is less the persistence of ethnic conflict than malevolent leadership that is the problem.[8] Contrary to received notions about the need to banish ethnicity from African politics, it is indeed possible to reconcile cultural diversity with constitutional democracy. This is clearly shown by the case of Switzerland, as well as the politics of large American cities for most of this century. What are needed are formal and informal structures of power sharing to replace the winner-take-all policies shared by most of the current constitutions and politicians.

Neither is it realistic any longer to discount the role of ordinary African citizens in the political perfidy now tearing the continent apart. Their actions have often disproved the popular polemical tracts published in Africa extolling the virtues of aggrieved but, for the most part, angelic "peasants and workers." Anyone who has closely followed the Rwandan tragedy will attest to the largely voluntary participation of Hutu peasants in the massacres, not to mention their willingness to cover up for one another. In both Kenya and Malawi, at least one-fourth of the electorate voted for the incumbent autocrat merely because he was their ethnic group's favorite son. In Somalia, General Aydid can always count on the support of his Habr Gedir clan, even when he does not represent their best interests. Of course, the strength of a rationalizing civic spirit varies from one African community to the next. In some of them it is quite strong, as shown by voter response to the Abiola campaign outside his Yoruba homeland, and especially in Kano, the home state of his opponent. Yet such differences, and their social roots, are still *terra incognita* for most social scientists, who are fond of generalizing about all of Africa, notwithstanding the continent's roughly two thousand ethnic groups. These distinctions must begin to be recognized, and their policy implications mapped out, for civic virtue is crucial to the long-term survival of liberal democratic institutions.

Meeting the Challenge

The enormous variability in the political landscape of sub-Saharan Africa suggests a corresponding diversity in both the problems of political liberalization in the region and their solutions. Because a majority of the region's countries remain mired in political difficulties, however, the immediate agenda of African democrats and their external allies must consist of establishing the conceptual and institutional foundations for popular government.[9] And here the relevant issues are the same ones addressed by the European and American pioneers of democracy, whose words resonate in the discourse of African democracy today. The real challenge, of course, is adapting those original ideas to local conditions. It is no accident that the transitions to democracy in Namibia, South Africa, and Malawi came in the wake of realistic and lengthy constitution-making processes that took stock of those countries' social complexities.

This is not to say that the elections that have taken place so far in Africa have been in vain. Successful or not, they have helped to expand the horizons of individual liberty to an extent that few could have anticipated in 1990. As the determined bands of crusaders for democracy in the continent speed their march, they would do well to pay as much attention to the local successes that are so inadequately covered by the press as to the all-too-evident catastrophes. The same principle applies to scholarship on contemporary African politics. Prospects for humane and legitimate governance in Africa will depend on the capacity of the emerging liberal leadership to harness fresh and workable ideas to timely policy actions. As long as there are African men and women courageous enough to rise to this challenge, and governments in the region that stand as proof that success is possible, the future of democratic rule in the continent will not be as bleak as the doomsayers insist.

NOTES

1. Samuel P. Huntington, *The Third Wave: Democratization in the Late Twentieth Century* (Norman: University of Oklahoma Press, 1991), 295, 315.

2. Ibid., 6.

3. For an early observation of this weakness, see René Lemarchand, "Africa's Troubled Transitions," *Journal of Democracy* 3 (October 1992): 99.

4. Jean-François Bayart, *The State in Africa: The Politics of the Belly* (London: Longman, 1992).

5. See John W. Harbeson, Donald Rothchild, and Naomi Chazan, eds., *Civil Society and the State in Africa* (Boulder, Colo.: Lynne Rienner Publishers, 1994); and Peter Anyang Nyong'o, ed., *The Popular Struggle for Democracy in Africa* (London: Zed Press, 1987).

6. See Thomas Callaghy, "Civil Society, Democracy, and Economic Change in Africa: A Dissenting Opinion About Resurgent Societies," in Harbeson et al., eds., *Civil Society and the State in Africa*, 231-53; and René Lemarchand, "Uncivil States and Civil Societies: How Illusion Became Reality," *Journal of Modern African Studies* 30 (June 1992): 177-91.

7. Robert D. Putnam, *Making Democracy Work: Civic Traditions in Modern Italy* (Princeton: Princeton University Press, 1993).

8. Claude Ake, "Rethinking African Democracy," *Journal of Democracy* 2 (Winter 1991): 43.

9. Though not addressed in this essay, the positive role that international donors could play in that process is critical. An authoritative evaluation of the impact of external funding for democracy in Africa can be found in Joel D. Barkan, "Can Established Democracies Nurture Democracy Abroad? Lessons from Africa" (paper presented at a Nobel Symposium on "Democracy's Victory and Crisis," Uppsala University, Uppsala, Sweden, August 1994).

31. WHERE EAST MEETS WEST

Marcin Król

***Marcin Król** is professor of the history of ideas at the University of Warsaw and editor of* Res Publica, *an independent intellectual monthly. He has taught at Yale University and the University of Texas, and is a member of the editorial board of the Catholic weekly* Tygodnik Powszechny. *He spent the fall 1994 semester as the E.L. Weigand Distinguished Professor of Democratization at Georgetown's School of Foreign Service.*

About 20 years ago, the great historian of ideas and political thinker John Plamenatz wrote that the most dangerous threat to democracy is not some openly antithetical political system, but rather "sham" democracy.[1] In order to predict whether the "third wave" of democratization will continue to rise or not, we must first acknowledge that many of the world's new democracies are currently situated somewhere between real democracy and sham democracy. There is little doubt that if we restricted ourselves to the survey of institutional forms or democratic facades, we should perceive a still rising wave of democratization. There are countries where institutional democracy will soon arrive (Cuba, North Korea, Vietnam), and there are countries where it has very recently been imposed from above (Russia and some of the Transcaucasian republics of the former USSR). At the substantive level, it is impossible to say at this moment whether the latter countries are moving toward authentic democracy or a debased and counterfeit version of the same.

Even the fate of democratic facades, however, is open to doubt. Why do these strange new countries in the area from East Central Europe to Transcaucasia want to impose democracy on their citizens? Do the citizens of these countries know what they are doing? Are they willing and conscious participants in the democratization process? On the answer to these questions the future of democratization depends.

I strongly suspect that some among the fledgling democracies became democracies because it was expected of them, certainly by public opinion in the West, but most crucially by the United Nations, the World Bank, the International Monetary Fund, the European Union, the Council of Europe, and so on. I do not mean that this was the only reason, or that absent external pressure the new democracies would have become despotisms, but I do mean that such international expectations go a long way toward explaining why leaders like Boris Yeltsin or Lech Wałęsa behave as they do and specifically try to avoid even the slightest suspicion that they might be less than totally devoted to democracy.

The West's possession of such influence abroad carries with it the additional burden of promoting and implementing standards of democracy at home. If the West lowers its own democratic standards, certain political forces inside the new democracies will be encouraged to flout democracy in speech, in deed, or in both. When Jean-Marie Le Pen's National Front in France and the Republicans in Germany seemed to be successful, Polish and Hungarian nationalists immediately drew the lesson that xenophobic nationalism is acceptable in a democracy.

In the sense just outlined, then, the future of democracy in the world—and especially in East Central Europe and the former Soviet Union—depends much more on the state of democracy in the West than it does on developments in the new democracies themselves. The new democracies want to be democratic because in the years leading up to and immediately following 1989, liberal democracy was seen there as the *beau idéal* of political life. If it ceases to be obvious that liberal democracy is a good solution for the major problems of these countries, some of them may turn elsewhere for solutions. I do not fear that there will be a comeback of "real socialism" or even of some milder form of authoritarianism, but I do worry that existing democratic structures will persist without a liberal spirit to animate them. We may end up with collectivist, slightly nationalist, or paternalistic sham democracies.

The somewhat primitive democratic idealism of former dissidents did not survive prolonged contact with the realities of day-to-day politics. When we hear nowadays that President Václav Havel still speaks of an "antipolitical politics," we are less impressed than amused. Public discourse in the new democracies, meanwhile, does not look like a realization of Hannah Arendt's hopes.[2] Venomous invective, accusatory rhetoric, *ad hominem* argumentation, and the like are not unknown in the established democracies, of course, but they do seem to be scarcer and under better social (and perhaps moral) control there than in the newly founded democracies.

Add to this picture the presence—probably unavoidable—of problems regarding the building of party systems, the development of civil society, the spread of political corruption, and the generally chaotic character of the political scene, and one can begin to understand why some of the postcommunist societies try simply to turn away from politics. Even in the established democracies, declining citizen participation has recently become a problem. The lack of participation in the new democracies—where active citizenries are arguably even more vital—may easily lead political leaders to feel that the electorate neither supports nor controls them. Without the mediating institutions of a vibrant civil society, popular influence over politics is going to be limited to election day, and elections in postcommunist Europe all too often revolve around feelings and resentments rather than issues. For exactly these reasons, ex-communists came to power in Lithuania, Poland, and Hungary in 1993-94.

Everything said above reinforces our conclusion that the West is where the fate of democracy will be decided. If we want to solve the "predemocratic" crisis in the new democracies, we have to find at least a partial solution to the "postdemocratic" crisis in the West. The first signs of reflection and debate concerning this crisis can be observed, but it may be that it is already too late. Nor should we forget that there are strong tendencies in the West that aim at a new type of moral isolationism. The perfect intellectual example of these tendencies is in a new book by the American political theorist John Rawls.[3] Rawls wishes no malice and harbors no reactionary views, but simply accepts the notion that the liberal tradition is limited in its effectiveness by specific historical and geographic boundaries. It has been during the last three centuries and in what we now call the West that liberalism has been victorious; according to Rawls, there are no serious intellectual grounds for thinking that liberal ideas will be successful elsewhere. Rawls may well be right: if he is, then further democratization seems very doubtful, and the West will have little choice but to close in on itself in order to fend off challenges from future nonliberal societies. If such an attitude becomes the basis of political (as opposed to merely philosophical) thinking, we should not be surprised to find that the new democracies struggling to emerge from the rubble of the Soviet empire will no longer look to the West as the standard.

From "Negative" to "Positive" Freedom?

But the situation could turn out otherwise. The new democracies could influence democracy in the West for good or ill. Let us look more closely at the possibility of a salutary influence.

When we ask why people in East Central Europe (like others in Africa, Latin America, and Asia) fought for independence and freedom, we can give a relatively simple answer: to obtain what Isaiah Berlin calls "negative freedom," including freedom from persecution, censorship, legal inequality, racial oppression, and so on.[4] They fought for the right to own property, to decide about the future of their children, to be free to travel, write, and speak. This struggle was successful to an astonishing degree, but what now? Now there are problems to be solved that often challenge established liberal democratic theory. Whether and how this theory develops will go a long way toward determining whether such problems are handled democratically. Let us enumerate some examples:

• *Nationalism (or "tribalism," as Michael Walzer aptly calls it).* Criticizing any and all manifestations of national or patriotic feeling—a reaction that is quite understandable from the point of view of the "liberalism of fear," as Judith Shklar has defined the radical liberal position—is nevertheless dangerous because it does not recognize the difference between natural and even necessary national consciousness (particularly in the newborn nation-states) and chauvinist extremism.[5] On the other hand, a positive approach to this question may lead to the elaboration of a well-measured "modern patriotism" that is badly needed in the West as well.

• *The moral background of the free-market economy and of liberal society as such.* The strongly liberal position, which gives democracy priority over philosophy (as Richard Rorty has said), abstains from any value judgments and views with suspicion any type of perfectionism or emphasis on the pursuit of excellence.[6] The example of the new democracies, however, leaves us without any doubt as to the importance of the moral underpinnings of both capitalism and democracy. What is happening now in Russia, Hungary, and Poland proves that democracy and free markets cannot function without a moral orientation. Rawls's "veil of ignorance" is simply not sufficient, which in turn poses a general question concerning the principles of modern liberal thought. Namely, is the liberal idea still dynamic and capable of growth, or has it played itself out and come to a dead end? If the latter is the case, then a few midcourse corrections will not be enough; only a truly epochal rethinking of our values and of the idea of "negative freedom" can suffice. Reflection on the experience of the new democracies might prove very helpful here.

• *Religion and faith as forces working for or against democratization.* In some new democracies (Poland is here a very strong case), religious faith is obviously going to survive the impact of democracy. The widespread opinion that robust religious institutions are natural foes or at least rivals of democracy has strong foundations. If we admit the truth that neither religion nor the liberal democratic state is going to go away and that the American "separationist" solution to the problem of their coexistence is simply not relevant to the situation in most of the new democracies, then we must persevere in seeking some new solution. Otherwise, religion might indeed become a powerful antagonist of modernization and democratization. Any reasonable solution, however, cannot consist simply of trying to limit religious influence. Although theoretically difficult if not impossible, a practical compromise must somehow be reached. Here too, democratic theory will have to learn a new lesson.

My second conclusion, therefore, is that the future of democracy depends on its ability to change, adapt, and learn. The more rigid democratic theory becomes, the less hope we can have. There are firm limits to change, adaptation, and learning, of course: democracy cannot allow itself to become nondemocracy. While this is obvious in principle, it is not always easy to draw dividing lines in practice. Ultimately, there is probably only one way of finding out how much democracy can change, and that is the way of trial and error. Trying requires courage, not only political, but intellectual as well. I understand very well that, after all the tragic experiences of the twentieth century, liberals now think twice about any effort to press the claims of "positive freedom," but such caution may not serve us well in the future.

The Challenge to the West

The "third wave" of democratization is undoubtedly still rising. Nearly every month we have examples of democracy redux (as in Haiti) or democracy stabilizing (as in Brazil). Why, then, are we so troubled about its future? The partial electoral success of ex-communist forces in certain East Central European lands fails to endanger democracy, as does the relative economic fragility of these countries. Neither circumstance is helpful for democracy, of course, but at the same time neither is a source of mortal peril. There are perhaps only two really formidable obstacles that will confront democrats in the years ahead.

The first is external, although it also has a lot to do with liberal democratic principles themselves. We must confront and definitively answer the question of whether liberal democracy possesses universal ambitions and relevance. I cannot imagine a stable continuity of democracy if our answer is that it does not. On the other hand, I cannot imagine the established Western democracies taking on themselves the responsibility of promoting democratic ideas throughout the world and of doing so, if necessary, through the use of force. A good word may sometimes be helpful, but can we really expect that some Muslim or African countries are going to become democratic just because we try to persuade them of the benefits of doing so? We have learned that imposed democracy does not work. Is Samuel P. Huntington's "clash of civilizations" inevitable?[7] If so, how are democrats going to live with such a future?

To ask this is another way of wondering whether liberal democratic theory is prepared to speak about degrees of democracy, which seems to me the only way out of this dilemma. To simplify, I think that we should agree on a minimal threshold of democracy and then accept that different countries belonging to different civilizations with different religions, mores, and traditions will adhere to practices that we would not accept in our own civilization. Such an attitude is often described as multiculturalism, but as Joseph Raz recently wrote, multiculturalism cannot lead to the absolute relativity of values, which means that the "democratic minimum" cannot be subject to local reinterpretation.[8] But who shall define this minimum? It must be the West, however frightened or unprepared it may be to do so at this time.

Democracy cannot be dull. If we democrats become mired in the swamps of pragmatism, we shall lose.

External obstacles can also take the form of enemy regimes—a term we should not shrink from using when appropriate. Enemies of democracy hold power in North Korea, Iraq, China, Cuba, and many other countries. Some of them are prepared to fight against us, with only the military might of democracies preventing an outbreak of war; others simply ignore democracy or have contempt for it and propose other solutions. These enemies of democracy are at the moment either defeated or restrained, but if democracy's luster begins to dim, the alternatives they represent might become more and more attractive. We should remember the lesson of the fellow-travelers of communism in the 1930s, who had grounds for being disenchanted with their own societies, however misguided their attachment to Stalinism.

The second obstacle—one closely connected to the first—consists of the sheer internal inertia of the established democracies. I am well aware that democracy promotes mediocrity and that one cannot maximize everything: equality and creativity, readiness to compromise and absolute authenticity, freedom and order, and so on. But democracy cannot be dull. The first thing that freedom calls to mind for me is excitement. If we democrats become mired in the swamps of pragmatism, we shall lose. I do not intend to invoke the utopia of total participation, of widespread public virtue, or of any Nietzschean will to power. But on the other hand, I cannot bring myself to accept that everything is just a deal and that all the excitement in life must be limited to the private sphere.

To solve this problem we must affirm certain beliefs and attitudes that are now often treated as naive, stupid, or dangerous. I mean here beliefs in the perfectibility of human beings, in the possibility of slow and difficult progress for societies, in the salutary influence of education, and in the spiritual values without which human life is empty. I know it sounds either slightly out of fashion or somehow conservative, but without these beliefs and without continual efforts toward their implementation, the future of democracy is dark indeed. I am persuaded that it is better to die taking reasonable risks for worthy ends than to perish from sheer ennui.

NOTES

1. John Petrov Plamenatz, *Democracy and Illusion: An Examination of Certain Aspects of Modern Democratic Theory* (London: Longman, 1973).

2. Hannah Arendt, *On Revolution* (Westport, Conn.: Greenwood Press, 1963).

3. John Rawls, *Political Liberalism* (New York: Columbia University Press, 1993).

4. Isaiah Berlin, "Two Concepts of Liberty," *Four Essays on Liberty* (Oxford: Oxford University Press, 1968).

5. Michael Walzer, "New Tribalism," *Dissent* 39 (Spring 1992): 164-71; Judith Shklar, "The Liberalism of Fear," in Nancy L. Rosenblum, ed., *Liberalism and the Moral Life* (Cambridge: Harvard University Press, 1989).

6. Richard Rorty, "The Priority of Democracy to Philosophy," in Merrill D. Peterson and Robert C. Vaughn, eds., *The Virginia Statute for Religious Freedom: Its Evolution and Consequences in American History* (Cambridge: Cambridge University Press, 1993).

7. Samuel P. Huntington, "The Clash of Civilizations?" *Foreign Affairs* 72 (Summer 1993): 22-49.

8. Joseph Raz, "Multiculturalism: A Liberal Perspective," *Dissent* 41 (Winter 1994): 67-79.

32.
THE POST-TOTALITARIAN BLUES

Jacques Rupnik

***Jacques Rupnik** is senior fellow and professor at the Fondation Nationale des Sciences Politiques in Paris, and writes extensively on East European politics. His most recent works are* From Sarajevo to Sarajevo *(1992), and* Le déchirement des nations *(1995). This essay, a version of which appeared in the Summer 1994 issue of* L'Autre Europe, *was translated from the French by Deborah M. Brissman.*

The post-totalitarian blues are haunting the countries of the "other Europe." The euphoria that accompanied the fall of communism has given way to disappointment, social anomie, and the emergence of new dangers. The unity of the great mass rallies for democracy has shattered, and wide-ranging economic hardship has overshadowed political gain for most citizens. Instead of civil societies, one sees a splintered landscape teeming with corporatisms and resurgent communal loyalties. Václav Havel paints a somber tableau of postcommunist political life that does not pertain to his country alone:

> Rancor and suspicion between ethnic groups; racism or even signs of fascism; brazen demagoguery; deliberate scheming and lying; political chicanery; wild and shameless squabbling over purely particular interests; naked ambition and lust for power; every kind of fanaticism; new and surprising forms of swindling; Mafia-style machinations; and a general absence of tolerance, mutual understanding, good taste, and a sense of moderation and reflection.[1]

Is this disenchantment part and parcel of any revolution? "Are all revolutions doomed to fail?" as Ralf Dahrendorf asks, hinging as they do on myths of unity, transparency, and innocence.[2] Is it inevitable that a drift toward varieties of nationalism and authoritarianism will follow the first elections?

While it is tempting for historians to compare the revolution of 1989 to others that started in democracy but ended in anarchy and terror, reasoning by analogy is not always the most illuminating method for understanding Eastern Europe's political dynamic, if only because revolutions are not what they used to be. Compared to the modern revolutions that began with the taking of the Bastille or the Winter Palace and continued for years in fire and blood, the negotiated transitions of 1989 were quick, easy, and nonviolent. In fact, 1989 brought to a close the era of revolutions precisely by its rejection of the idea of violence as a midwife for the birth of a new society. The revolutions of 1989 were unique in history because none of them claimed to bear within itself a new societal "project." With no new social utopia, there is little reason to fear the combination of virtue and terror typical of past revolutions. The transitions of 1989 took their bearings quite explicitly from both Western democracy and the precommunist traditions of their own lands. It is in this sense that François Furet speaks of "revolution-restoration," meaning the restoration of national sovereignty, the rule of law, and private property.[3]

The real question, however, is whether a revolution that is negotiated or "velvet" can rightly be called a revolution at all. This is no merely theoretical issue, but one that deeply divides the political landscape of postcommunist Europe. On one side are those who demand a radical break with the institutions and personnel inherited from communism; on the other are those who favor respect for the rule of law, and thus a degree of continuity. The first group emphasizes "restoration"; the second, imitation of Western constitutional models. The paradox is that the partisans of "permanent revolution" generally belong to the conservative (even nationalist) Right, whereas those who support an "evolutionary" approach in the name of law are moderate liberals, who often were former dissidents. In 1980, Poland invented the "self-limiting revolution" in the name of geopolitics and the threat from the East; today, Poland practices it in the name of the rule of law and inducements from the West.

This split over continuity and change is at the heart of a double political game: that of *decommunization* and that of *constitutionalism.*

Justice, Reflection, and Old Scores

We now know that communism dissolves in voting booths. Its sudden collapse, finalized by the holding of free elections, allowed new democratic institutions to develop. But if communism is dead as an ideology and a system of rule, its encumbering legacy continues to haunt the political and social landscape. Since the transition was gentle, the bulk of the old *nomenklatura* remains, attempting at every turn, as Elemer Hankiss puts it, to convert its old politically based privileges into new economic rights. This spectacle has fostered a diffuse but profound sense of injustice and tempted many to follow the radicals in demanding a settling of accounts with officials and the "collaborators" who ran the repressive machinery of the old regime. After a soft transition have come economic and social hardship and a search for those responsible for the crimes of the past and the difficulties of the present.

From the demand for justice it was but a step to a call for a purge, which was explicitly and effectively put into practice in the former East Germany; paid off relatively well in the Czech Republic; failed in Poland and Hungary; currently divides the noncommunist political elites in Bulgaria, Croatia, and Albania; and never made it onto the agenda in Romania, where the old regime's influence has remained strongest.

Supporters of radical decommunization cite a number of arguments. First, they invoke a moral imperative—truth and justice versus the lies and crimes of totalitarianism—that coincides with the need for a clean political break. In a speech to the Sejm in January 1992, then-Polish prime minister Jan Olszewski presented his short-lived government as "the beginning of the end of communism," thereby insinuating that the government of his predecessor Tadeusz Mazowiecki favored continuity. Olszewski contrasted those guilty of "betrayals, crimes, lies, and cruelty" with those having "clear consciences and clean hands." To forgo decommunization, he argued, would confirm the "cynicism of the guilty and discourage everyone else."

In Prague, security considerations were invoked alongside moral and political arguments. Not only was there the danger that highly compromised holdover personnel might be blackmailed; there was also the very questionable wisdom of entrusting the building of democratic institutions to former secret-police collaborators. To those who feared that the "lustration" law would lead to witch-hunts, supporters responded that it was not a penal procedure, but rather a professional ban affecting government posts and the upper ranks of the civil service for a period limited to five years.[4] The turnover of elites is supposed to serve as a guarantee against the return of the old regime. To permit impunity would be to invite that regime to start itself up again.

Moderate liberals reject the logic of "lustration" as the political exploitation of a moral question. To propose to society a few "guilty parties" is an act of political legerdemain that builds up the myth of an innocent society confronting the evil empire. In his speech marking New Year's 1990, Václav Havel stressed the links of complicity and adaptation that allowed the totalitarian system to function. Hence the importance of getting beyond a Manichaean vision, and reflecting upon the past rather than judging it. It is above all important to avoid compromising the élan of a society oriented toward the future out of some desire to settle old scores.

There are other, more pragmatic, considerations that one might add to these. After a negotiated revolution, it would have been awkward to suddenly turn against the very same roundtable partners who allowed the nonviolent transition to occur. While the moral imperative to oust collaborators or the *nomenklatura* is understandable, it could also undermine economic efficiency. Getting rid of the old economic officials, high-level administrators, and judges may be desirable, but who is to replace them? Dissidents? There were not many of them, and while they were surely virtuous, they are not necessarily qualified to manage the economy or modernize the state apparatus. For liberals, however, the most objectionable idea is that decommunization can provide society with a kind of collective catharsis. Communism's legacy in the structures and mentality of the society was decades in the making. The debate about the weight of this legacy thus leads to a pessimistic vision that extends beyond the reach of moral injunctions: the totalitarian experience soils the victim as much as it does the torturer.

Legality and Legitimacy

Continuity or rupture—that is the issue which lies at the heart of the transition's most important dilemma, that of a constitution.[5] Should the transition toward democracy culminate in a democratic constitution, or is a democratic constitution the indispensable prerequisite for a democratic break with the institutions left over from communism?

Expressed another way, the issue concerns the relationship—indeed, the conflict—between legality and legitimacy. Democracy, as we know, needs both. But is it possible to create democratic institutions while respecting a constitution left over from a dictatorship? Conversely, is it possible to create the conditions for democratic pluralism by employing authoritarian methods? On the one hand, liberals, encouraged by Western advice, insist upon respect for the rule of law, and thus on constitutional continuity. Radicals, on the other hand, invoke revolutionary legitimacy and ask how change can be secured while the law remains something inherited from a system designed to control and manipulate society. Which is to be first: change *within* the law or change *of* the law?

The constitution thus lies at the heart of the debate between majoritarian democracy and constitutional democracy—the latter meaning the notion that all power, even the most "legitimate," must bow to the framework and the limits established by the supreme law embodied in a constitution. This classic dilemma, with democracy and participation on one side, and liberalism and law on the other, manifests itself in the postcommunist transition in terms different from those familiar in the democracies of the West. In the latter, to simplify, there are two teams whose players know the rules of the game and accept the intervention of an umpire when the rules have been broken. In the initial phase of the transition in the East, it often seemed as if everyone was running after the ball while changing teams and rules throughout the course of the game. In the West, one can identify the interests behind a proposed law; in the East, one can at best identify an institution or power center. In such a situation, elaborating a new constitution becomes extremely difficult.

András Sajo, an advisor to Hungary's President Arpád Göncz, notes that there is "a constitutional moment" that requires the kind of national unity appropriate to every great turning point in history.[6] If that founding moment is allowed to pass, there remains the procedure of amending the old constitution to allow for the new laws that are needed. Such was the method used in Poland and Hungary.

One must acknowledge that the only countries that succeeded in adopting new constitutions early on (1991), Romania and Bulgaria, are not necessarily the most democratic. The case of Russia seems to confirm this hypothesis. From 1991 to 1993, the Russian constitution was central to the struggle for power. In a slightly surreal struggle the first elected president in the history of Russia decided in early October 1993 to send in the tanks against a parliament dominated by communists claiming to defend—irony of ironies—the constitution and parliamentary sovereignty. By candlelight in September, the Supreme Soviet had designated General Aleksandr Rutskoi head of state. Clad in an Adidas sweatsuit, with a Kalashnikov on his shoulder, the general launched an assault against the Moscow television-broadcast building in a pitiable imitation of the taking of the Winter Palace. For Lenin, socialism was "soviets plus electrification"; democratization Yeltsin-style was the Supreme Soviet without electricity.

Russia must be the only place where the concept of a "democratic putsch" has been seriously broached. To be sure, the Russian conflict was resolved (elections were held after the tanks rolled back to their bases), but at what price? Can a president elicit respect from a legislature by shelling its meeting place? Was not Vladimir Zhirinovsky's electoral victory a high price to pay for the adoption of a made-to-order constitution whose democratic veneer is too thin to hide its authoritarianism (even if it is accepted by the West as a lesser evil)?

If the adoption of a new constitution does not necessarily guarantee a shift to democracy, the experience of Poland and Hungary does seem to suggest that constitutionalism can be a more propitious route to democracy. Poland was preparing a new constitution for the bicentennial of the May 1791 Constitution, but consensus proved unattainable.[7] Poland opted, therefore, for the "little constitution," a phrase used to refer to the gradual but ultimately rather large-scale amending of the old constitution. In Hungary, too, the old constitution was heavily amended. As András Sajo waggishly puts it, all that remains of the original are the words: "The capital of Hungary is Budapest." Constitutionalism, guaranteeing the separation of powers and individual rights, rests on the existence of an arbitrating authority, a constitutional court. This court plays such an important role in Hungary (for example, it rejected the principle of retroactive justice in the matter of the new law covering crimes committed during the suppression of the 1956 rebellion) that some worry that it encroaches on "parliamentary sovereignty." Sajo interprets such coolness toward constitutionalism as a rejection of modernity in societies whose "social and intellectual structures (preserved and even reinforced under communism) are premodern."[8]

Despite fears of a "government of judges" and the risk of confusion and drift in a transition carried out by successive constitutional amendments, the Polish and Hungarian cases suggest two advantages. First, political players see that the construction of democratic institutions is an ongoing process that remains imperfect and incomplete. Second, the political habits of a majoritarian democracy evolve toward respect for the constitution and the legitimacy of its procedures. Governments and parliamentary majorities have time to get used to constitutional limits. Spreading out the making of the constitution in this way creates a *process* of constitutional education, a diffusion of constitutionalism's values among the political elites. In this sense, constitutionalism can become more important than the constitution itself, since it contributes to the transformation of political culture, without which the rule of law can never gain a solid foothold.

The Territorial Framework of Politics

There remains the difficult question of the reciprocal links of legitimacy between the regime and the state. This issue has arisen with particular force in those federations that began to disappear as soon as communism fell. In these cases, the adoption of a constitution became an integral part of building a nation-state. The republics of the former Yugoslavia, for example, solidified their declarations of independence by adopting new constitutions (which often became the focus of controversies, as with the Serb minority in Croatia and the Albanian minority in Macedonia). After two years, the Czechoslovak parliament was unable to adopt a new federal constitution, but the Slovak legislature adopted one for Slovakia in August 1992. On the eve of partition in December 1992, the Czech legislature followed suit. The creation of a new state mandated the adoption of a new constitution.

One of the major problems of the transition to democracy in the postcommunist world is the territorialization of the political. Whether or not the nation-state is the optimal locus of democracy, it remains true that the legitimation of some sort of formally structured state is a precondition for democratic transition. Juan Linz and Alfred Stepan have argued this in the case of Spain, and the former USSR and Yugoslavia confirm it *a contrario*.[9] All of these cases illustrate the crucial importance of electoral sequencing in the transition from dictatorship to democracy. It was vital that the first democratic elections in Spain encompass the entire country, even if this meant that the new constitution would have to include substantial transfers of power to Catalonia and the Basque regions. Likewise, in Yugoslavia at the beginning of 1990, the inability of Prime Minister Ante Marković's federal government to hold free elections over the whole of the territory sounded the death knell for the South Slavic federation. The federal state was delegitimized as soon as the first free elections took place in the republics of Slovenia and Croatia. Power and legitimacy shifted from the federation to the republics, which soon opted for independence to complete their own democratic transitions. The end of communism became entangled with the end of Yugoslavia.

A similar sequence broke up the USSR, leaving the following large question hanging over the future of the Russian transition: How to establish a territorial framework for politics? This is very much a question about the Russian state and its consubstantiality with the empire. The great historian Vasili Kliouchevsky described Russia as "a state that has colonized itself." If that is the case, what is Russia without an empire?[10] For the time being, no one knows. But it seems that Yeltsin and the moderate democrats, under pressure from the military, are already formulating a Russian "Monroe Doctrine" for relations with the "near abroad." The other option, that of Zhirinovsky's extremists, implies a redrawing of Russia's boundaries according to an ethnic definition of the nation. Since 25 million Russians live outside Russia's borders, this would provide all the ingredients for a recurrence of the "Serbian syndrome." This scenario would signal the failure of democratic transition not only for Russia but also for the other new nation-states that have risen from the empire's ashes.

The crisis of the Russian state is all the sharper because the loss of the Soviet empire is coupled with a crisis of authority facing the central government in Moscow in its dealings with the regions. The breakup of Russia will not necessarily follow the breakup of the USSR, but the question of decentralization will be decisive for both the cohesion of the state and the pursuit of a democratic transition. How can these two goals be reconciled? A decentralized (and therefore weak) Russia is, we are told, the precondition of a shift to democracy. Yet would such a Russia be viable?

The crisis of state authority—a palpable reality in most postcommunist countries—is entwined with a necessary redefinition of the state's role. After decades of the omnipresent, omnipotent state, there is a healthy propensity, especially in Central Europe, to diminish the state's influence by limiting the bureaucracy and liberalizing the economy.

How to redefine the role of the state, which is to say the very nature of the social bond? Around two dimensions of security. One is the state's role as protector, a function that is especially pertinent in countries where crime is increasing by 100 percent a year, and where the old institutions of "law and order" lack credibility because of their corrupt relationship with the old regime. This is indeed changing, if a 1993 Polish poll is accurate: it shows that the army and the police rank extremely high in the public trust, far ahead of the church. From this perspective, the turnaround since the days of communism seems to be complete.

The second dimension concerns the state's welfare role. Since the state is no longer taking complete charge of the individual "from cradle to grave," what role should it play in a society where there is more freedom but less economic security? Leaving aside the Czech anomaly (the liberal right's victory in a country that, along with Liechtenstein, has the lowest unemployment rate in Europe), it may be that the most recent Polish elections show the limits to efforts at a "rollback" (even rhetorical) of the welfare state. In order for economic liberalism to take root in Central Europe, it must retain a redistributive function for the state.

The state's disengagement from the socioeconomic sphere is therefore necessary to the ongoing transition, but its limits are already apparent: dismantling an omnipotent bureaucracy does not mean forgoing a competent civil service, for instance. The paradox of many postcommunist countries is that while everyone used to work for the state, the governmental apparatus itself remained relatively modest in size. In France, the Ministry of Finance employs thousands of civil servants; in Ukraine, it has just a few hundred. Ukraine's parliament passes close to 150 important laws every year (compared to about 15 in Western countries), but the government has no means of enforcing them. Breaking up monopolies and establishing a new fiscal system require an efficient civil service. The transition to democracy and markets requires more "government," in the true sense of the word, in order to have less "state."

Presidents or Parliaments?

This redefinition of the state indirectly poses a question about the link between institutional choices and economic transformation. Is a strong executive more apt than a parliamentary system to speed the march toward a market economy while resisting destabilizing effects along the way? This seems to be the dominant idea in Russia (where liberal economists have bet on Yeltsin and a strong executive) but certainly not in Central Europe: the more advanced the economic transition, the more the political center of gravity has moved away from the president (Václav Havel and Lech Wałęsa) and toward the prime minister (Václav Klaus, Hanna Suchocka followed by Waldemar Pawlak).

Experts on democratic transitions like Juan Linz and Alfred Stepan believe that a parliamentary system holds more promise for successful transition than a presidential regime.[11] They note two principal drawbacks of presidentialism. The first is that it is not conducive to the emergence of a multiparty system, since presidentialism promotes a two-party system. This limits considerably the post-totalitarian political field. Second, presidentialism is vulnerable to authoritarian and populist temptations. In contrast, the rise of a Stanisław Tyminski or an Alberto Fujimori would be impossible in a parliamentary system. As for Yeltsin-style presidentialism, there is the considerable danger that the supposed champion of democracy could become a "Bonapartist" if confronted with a recalcitrant parliament. As interesting as may be such theoretical warnings from political scientists, they have not really influenced the political choices of postcommunist Europe.

In the choice between a parliamentary and a presidential regime, Central Europe opted for the first, the Balkans and Russia for the second. Central Europeans' wariness about repeating their history of a strong, centralized executive, along with the evolving balance of political forces, ruled out the presidential option there.

In Hungary, the preelectoral situation in the winter of 1989-90 shifted the new institutions in two important directions. The democratic opposition, thinking it was impossible to avoid the election of the reform communist Imre Pozsgay as president, insisted on the parliamentary character of the new regime and on granting considerable powers to the Constitutional Court as guarantor of personal liberties and human rights. Ironically, it was the candidate of the Alliance of Free Democrats, Arpád Göncz, who was elected president. Despite, or perhaps because of, his very limited powers, he became the most popular politician in Hungary.

In Poland, because of Wałęsa, the first totally free election (held in the autumn of 1990) was not legislative but presidential. Given the influence of Solidarity's leader on the Polish political scene, it would have been difficult to leave him waiting patiently on the sidelines (as his former advisors had hoped) while the people first elected a legislature and then considered General Jaruzelski's replacement. Initially, the rupture that occurred within the core of the Solidarity movement was less a basic disagreement over political orientation than a dispute about power and the rhythm of change. Wałęsa polarized the field by proclaiming his readiness to accelerate political change while slowing economic change. The more important institutional debate became lost in the details of deciding whether to hold presidential elections before legislative ones. When Wałęsa was elected by direct universal suffrage, fears arose in Poland and the West of a drift toward presidentialist authoritarianism. At present, those fears remain exaggerated. True, Wałęsa did try to force an expansion of his powers on the Sejm, but he also knew how to limit himself and accept rebuff from a legislature that hopes to preserve the parliamentary spirit of the "little constitution." Today's fragmented political field and the return of the ex-communists since the autumn of 1993 could play directly into Wałęsa's hands as he seeks to play the "savior" and act as a rampart against the return of the Left in order to remain president.

The Czechoslovak case confirms this Central European ambivalence toward the presidential system. The prewar constitution had been parliamentary, and the communist constitution gave the president merely symbolic duties: real power lay with the general secretary of the communist party. In reality, from the time of the Velvet Revolution in 1989, Václav Havel was clearly the country's major political figure. The former dissident was made president in a late December 1989 vote by the communist parliament. His position was then confirmed in June 1990 by a democratically elected parliament. As during the interwar period under President Tomáš Masaryk, Czechoslovakia had a parliamentary regime on the books, but a semipresidential one in actuality. Since January 1993, however, the situation in the newly established Czech Republic has changed completely.[12] In a system now dominated by Prime Minister Klaus, President Havel is no longer at the hub of power and is more constrained by the constitution.

Whereas Central Europe favors parliamentary constitutions, the Balkans (like Russia) tend more toward presidential regimes: Romania, Bulgaria, and Serbia all held direct presidential elections. Some see this as indicative of a secret nostalgia for the days of the old general secretary—particularly since a goodly number of former general secretaries, from the Serb Milošević to the Ukrainian Kravchuk, have been able to stay in power thanks to universal suffrage. (Their success is also attributable to the extensive fragmentation of the political field and the ability of leftover communist *apparats* to recast themselves as engines of nationalism.)

The use of proportional representation (PR), of course, reinforces political fragmentation. When a totalitarian system crumbles, PR is doubtless bound to enjoy a moment of predilection. The first elections are much like a census: each group needs to identify itself, to stand and be counted, and people expect parliament to reflect society's makeup as closely as possible. The existence of substantial ethnic minorities in most Eastern countries is an additional argument in favor of PR. It would be difficult to integrate politically the Hungarian minorities in Romania and Slovakia or the Turkish minority in Bulgaria without some recourse to the proportionalist principle.

This preference for PR (Hungary excluded), like the preference for presidentialism, occasionally disturbs Western experts who sometimes discern therein the danger of a democracy weakened by political fragmentation and at other times espy the authoritarian temptation. The danger and the temptation do exist, but Western models and standards are not easily transferred to the East. The strict separation of powers in America, the "checks and balances," work because political actors and society at large have internalized a certain juridical and political culture that is understandably absent in lands just emerging from a half-century of communism. British democracy is admired from afar—the Hungarian parliament building in Budapest, built at the close of the last century, is a copy of the Palace of Westminster in London. Yet how can anyone transplant something that rests on a thousand years of tradition and an unwritten constitution? The French Jacobin model, giving the president primary power, seems to inspire certain adepts of power politics, particularly in the Balkans—not necessarily the democrats. The latter tend to prefer the German system, which not only is the closest geographically to the post-Soviet world, but also stands as a successful example of a democracy risen from the ruins of totalitarianism. Its electoral system (PR with a 5 percent nationwide threshold and a corrective dose of majoritarianism), the regional autonomy accorded to the *Länder*, and the important role of the Federal Constitutional Court—all these are elements able to inspire postcommunist constitutionalists.

What Does the Future Hold?

In his book *The Third Wave,* Samuel P. Huntington places the East European democratic breakthrough in a comparative global context.[13] The first wave of democratization, for East Central Europe, began in 1848 and culminated in the aftermath of the First World War. The second wave (post-1945) affected the Axis powers while the other Europe succumbed to totalitarianism. The third wave, ushered in by the Portuguese revolution and the fall of Francoism in Spain in the mid-1970s, was extended by democratic breakthroughs in Latin America and Asia and touched East Central Europe starting in 1989. Looking through a comparative lens, one can examine the factors affecting the emergence and the prospects of the transitions now under way: 1) The international environment: it has been favorable since Gorbachev, but will it remain so? 2) The economic situation: a market-based economy is a necessary but insufficient condition for democracy, which has never prospered amid economic disaster. 3) Social conditions: "No bourgeois, no democracy," as Barrington Moore put it; yet while a renaissance of civil society may take decades, democracy must drop anchor in the here-and-now. 4) Last, the cultural realm: all of the aforementioned democratic institutions have no chance of taking root unless a shared democratic political culture develops, both among the elites and in society at large.

This list of conditions is not exhaustive, but it does distinguish the transition in postcommunist East Central Europe from those of Southern

Europe 20 years ago (with respect to the market and civil society). It also helps us to weigh the risk of reversals. Huntington notes that after each wave of democratization came a reflux. There is surely no danger, however, of the old communist regime reasserting itself. If ex-communists (now converts to "social democracy") are getting votes in Poland or Hungary, it is precisely because they no longer embody the threat of a return to totalitarianism. Other authoritarian and nationalist dangers, however, are certainly present, especially in Russia and the Balkans.

Several future scenarios may be envisioned, region by region: 1) Democracy appears to be on the way to consolidation in Central Europe (Poland, Hungary, Slovenia, and the Czech Republic—Slovakia's case remains doubtful in the wake of Vladimir Mečiar's return to power). 2) In the Balkans and Russia, an incomplete transition is creating hybrid national-populist regimes. Serbia represents the extreme version of a transition from a totalitarian to an authoritarian regime, with a fleeting interlude of democratization and with ethnic nationalism as the dominant new ideology. 3) The Baltic countries come close to the Central European model. Most other ex-Soviet republics are closer to the Balkan model. Bulgaria and Slovakia could go either way.

East Central Europe must construct in very short order what the West took a long time to build. This is an unprecedented experiment, and it is *not* being conducted in laboratory-like isolation (where there is leisure to observe, and to perfect theories about democracy). This is not only because the Iron Curtain has disappeared, leaving the Continent as a whole exposed to the destabilizing consequences that would surely flow from any serious check to the democratic transition in the other Europe, but also because the difficulties and crises of the new democracies are not foreign to us in the West. Shrinking public space, weak political participation, growing mistrust of parties and politicians, and falling confidence in parliamentary institutions are common problems in established democracies. Should we see this as a sign that Central Europe is at the threshold of Western democratic "normality"? Or should we shudder at the parallel, at the profound link between the political crises in the predemocratic societies of the postcommunist East and the postdemocratic societies of the West?

NOTES

1. Václav Havel, *Letní přemítání* (Prague: Odeon, 1991), 95. Published in French as *Méditations d'été* (Paris: Editions Aube, 1992).

2. Ralf Dahrendorf, *Reflections on the Revolution in Europe* (London: Chatto and Windus, 1990).

3. François Furet, *L'énigme de la désagrégation communiste*, (Paris: Fondation Saint-Simon, 1990). See also his *Le passé d'une illusion* (Paris: Calmann-Levy, 1995).

4. Vojtěch Cepl, "Ritual Sacrifices," *East European Constitutional Review* 1 (Spring 1992): 24-25.

5. Andrew Arato, "Dilemmas Arising from the Power to Create Constitutions in Eastern Europe," *Cardozo Law Review* 3-4 (January 1993): 661-90.

6. András Sajo, "The Arrogance of Power," *East European Reporter* 7 (May-June 1992): 46.

7. Marcin Król, "L'autre bicentennaire," *Belvédère* 1 (April-May 1991): 84-90.

8. Sajo, "The Arrogance of Power," 47.

9. Juan Linz and Alfred Stepan, "Political Identity and Electoral Sequence," *Daedalus* 121 (Spring 1992): 123-39.

10. Marie Mendras, ed., *Un état pour la Russie* (Brussels: Complexe, 1992). See also Georges Nivat, "Russie: Le deuil de l'empire," in Jacques Rupnik, ed., *Le déchirement des nations* (Paris: Seuil, 1995), 59-76.

11. Juan J. Linz, "Transitions to Democracy," *Washington Quarterly* 13 (Summer 1990): 153-54.

12. Václav Havel, interview by the author, in *Politique internationale* 58 (Winter 1993): 13.

13. Samuel P. Huntington, *The Third Wave: Democratization in the Late Twentieth Century* (Norman: University of Oklahoma Press, 1993).

INDEX